Self, Consciousness, and Being

Self, Consciousness, and Being
The Transcendent Perspective

Dennis Nicholson

SELF, CONSCIOUSNESS, AND BEING

Copyright © 2025 Dennis Nicholson

ISBN: 978-1-78324-342-6

First Edition

Published in 2025 by Wordzworth
www.wordzworth.com

The author has asserted their moral right
under the Copyright, Designs and Patents Act, 1988,
to be identified as the author of this work.

All Rights reserved. No part of this publication may be reproduced, copied, stored in a retrieval system, or transmitted, in any form or by any means, without the prior written consent of the copyright holder, nor be otherwise circulated in any form of binding or cover other than that in which it is published and without a similar condition being imposed on the subsequent purchaser.

NO AI TRAINING: Without in any way limiting the author's exclusive rights under copyright, any use of this publication to "train" generative artificial intelligence (AI) technologies to generate text is expressly prohibited. The author reserves all rights to license uses of this work for generative AI training and development of machine learning language models.

A CIP catalogue record for this title
is available from the British Library.

Dedicated to Catherine MacLeod Benson, to Keiron, Julie, and Ada, to Catriona, to Nancy, Sheila and Ann, to Uncle Alan and Granny Baxter, and to all the rest of my family, extended family, and friends. With special thanks to Sammy and Margaret, who set the original course.

*We are not going round in circles,
we are moving up. The circle is a spiral...*

– HERMANN HESSE, AUTHOR, 1877-1962

Contents

Part 1 – Everyday Transcendence		**1**
Chapter 1	Introduction and Overview	4
Part 2 – First Design Requirement		**31**
Chapter 2	A Relationship That Varies With our View of it	34
Chapter 3	All Ideas Entail Self-World Perspectives	50
Chapter 4	A Fixed or Wholly-Variable Total Relationship?	66
Chapter 5	Artificial Fixing can Happen as we Develop	75
Chapter 6	Artificial Fixing Probably Happens to Most	96
Chapter 7	A Fixed Self Misdefines us and Should be Avoided	108
Part 3 – Further Design Requirements		**119**
Chapter 8	An Open-Ended, Wholly-Variable Self-view	122
Chapter 9	Fixed Self: Negatives, Positives and Possibilities	135
Chapter 10	Fixed Self: Blocking the Open-Ended Response	154
Chapter 11	A Science-Based Overarching Self-World View?	164
Chapter 12	Empty Consciousness	173
Part 4 – The Transcendent Self-View		**205**
Chapter 13	The Baseline Transcendent Self-View	208
Chapter 14	The First-Pass Transcendent Self-View	241
Chapter 15	A Self-View Hospitable to the Wholly-Variable Approach	258

| Chapter 16 | A Self-View That Improves on the Fixed Self | 264 |
| Chapter 17 | The Best Alternative to Misdefinition | 286 |

Part 5 – Instantiation; Seeing Others; Science — **301**

Chapter 18	Instantiating the Core Perspective	304
Chapter 19	Beyond the Core: Switching	318
Chapter 20	Beyond the Core: Response Repertoire and Choice	326
Chapter 21	Social and Educational Obstacles	332
Chapter 22	The Transcendent Perspective and Science	344

Part 6 – The Hard Problem and Fixed-Self Facets — **357**

Chapter 23	Transcendence and the Brain as a Conscious Experience	360
Chapter 24	The Hard Problem Made Easy	377
Chapter 25	Implications for the Transcendent Perspective	395
Chapter 26	Conscious Experience and the Real Thing	422

Part 7 – Being, Religion and Consciousness — **431**

| Chapter 27 | Creation, Being, Religion, Science, and Consciousness #1 | 433 |
| Chapter 28 | Creation, Being, Religion, Science, and Consciousness #2 | 444 |

Appendices — **453**

| Appendix A | The Transcendent Perspective and Free Will | 454 |
| Appendix B | What if the Self is an Illusion? | 463 |

References — **465**

Index — **485**

Note on the Author — **495**

PART 1

Everyday Transcendence

Outline of the Introduction and Overview

This book offers a response to the question of whether or not there is a best design for the human self. It looks at how we humans should best see and structure the relationship between ourselves and the universe at large – at how we should best see and structure our overall or total self-world perspective or self (and, hence, our overall or total self-world relationship). It makes the case in favour of the transcendent self-view – a perspective on the self that transcends ideas and viewpoints generally, seeing and treating them as subordinate facets of a total self that has empty consciousness, the underlying essence of consciousness itself, as its resting focus and core.

The two key points argued are that this is the one self-view that fully and accurately reflects our true behavioural and experiential nature and that we are not fully developed humans until we adopt it. Other topics covered include **individual differences**, **scientific testability**, **the key role of science** in the perspective, how the perspective helps resolve the **hard problem of consciousness** (and this impacts the perspective), the transcendent human as **a possible baseline in psychology-related sciences**, and **the transcendent view of religious beliefs**. The aim at each stage is to ensure readers can assess for themselves the observational and logical validity of the points argued.

With a view to offering an early grasp of the position defended, **Part 1** consists of a relatively detailed single chapter summarising the salient points made in the book as a whole. This sketches the perspective on the self proposed, something of the case in its favour, and aspects of its impact on other important elements of our world-view. A good grasp of both the **Introduction** and **Overview** sections of this initial chapter (particularly the latter, which also maps out the structure of the work) should help with an understanding of the book as a whole. **Parts 2-7** constitute the remainder of the book. Each of the parts has a preceding summary of the main points argued.

Italics are occasionally used for emphasis, but are also used – throughout the book, but especially in **Chapter 1** – to indicate key terms used in the book. These are usually defined briefly as a first pass, with further clarification added as the work develops. As should become clear, describing the perspective and its various aspects is necessarily a gradual process.

1

Introduction and Overview

Introduction: The Transcendent Self-View

A Generic Human Self-View

The aim of this book is to argue in favour of a particular view of the human self – to identify and defend a self-view that accurately reflects our full behavioural and experiential nature as humans while also allowing us to remain individually unique at a personal level.

The self-view proposed for the role – called here the *transcendent perspective* on the self and the world, or the *transcendent self-view* – is described in detail in Chapters 13 and 14, and the account provided there and thereafter should be regarded as definitive. Something of the flavour of the position will be attempted in this first chapter, however, beginning with the brief initial sketch presented below.

The Transcendent Self-View and Empty Consciousness

The best way to begin to describe the position is to first say a few words about the core of the self-view, an aspect of human experience referred to here as *empty consciousness*.

Empty consciousness is defined in detail in Chapter 12 but,

roughly speaking, means 'consciousness emptied of all other experiential content' (cf., e.g., Metzinger, 2020, p. 1). It is the essence of our every conscious experience, with every way in which individual experiences differ from each other removed – conscious experience without content: empty consciousness. It does not need to be known in the *absence* of other experiential content in order to fulfil its operational role in the self-view envisaged, only as *an identifiable aspect* of our every experiential landscape we can adopt as an important element of our working self-view. If the arguments presented in Parts 2-4 of this work are sound, empty consciousness plays a key role in ensuring that the transcendent self-view accurately reflects our full behavioural and experiential nature as humans.

The Transcendent Self-View: An Initial Sketch

The transcendent self-view as envisaged here is an operational perspective on the self with two interworking elements. One is a core in which empty consciousness is both the *dominant focus* and an experiential container seen as encompassing all imaginable ways of seeing and relating to the world as its subordinate facets or roles; the other is an interactive role-playing element able to deploy all such roles. As a working self, it operates through an ongoing process of switching control back and forth between individual subordinate facets or roles deployed for particular situational purposes and a core or resting state where the self is seen and experienced as encompassing empty consciousness plus every possible facet or role.

In the core or resting state, empty consciousness is the dominant focus; it sits at the core, or heart, or hub of the personal perspective in place and also underpins and contains it. When a subordinate facet or role is deployed, the dominant focus switches from empty consciousness to the heart or hub of the particular way of seeing and relating to the world associated with the subordinate facet or role. This way of seeing and relating to the world then temporarily dominates and determines how the situation a person is in is seen and responded to, relinquishing control back to the core or resting state once the situation changes when empty consciousness again becomes the dominant focus. At that point, all subordinate facets are again seen and treated as limited or partial aspects of the whole self, and the response cycle begins anew.

Facets and Roles in the Transcendent Self-View

Individual subordinate roles within the working self are seen as limited *idea-based subsidiary perspectives* – facets of the total human *self-world perspective* – with the latter being held to entail all of them plus empty consciousness. Each facet is held to be both a perspective on and a determinant of one aspect of the total human *self-world relationship*, with the whole human self-world relationship held to be determined by all of them. More detail on these terms and their interrelationships will emerge as we proceed.

Within the working self, each individual facet is viewed and controlled in a way similar to how an actor views and controls his onstage roles, except that deploying a facet is seen not as play-acting but as enacting a limited (but nonetheless real) facet of the subject's actual self.

Any idea we can have about anything is held to be a possible subordinate facet or role (Chapter 3); even fantastic, nonsensical, and meaningless perspectives on the self, world, or self-world relationship can affect how we act, think, and feel in some situation or another. (Think of a circus clown pretending he sees the world as made of blancmange to make an audience laugh, for example.)

Transcendent and Fixed Overarching Perspectives

The transcendent self-view is proposed here as a preferable alternative to the self-views it is designed to replace – self-views we acquire incidentally as we develop, held to be *fixed* self-views in the terminology employed here. It is preferred primarily because it encompasses every possible way of seeing and relating to the world as a subordinate facet or role – and, hence, every limited idea-based subsidiary perspective entailed in determining the total human self-world relationship and encompassed within the total human self-world perspective. This makes the transcendent self-view a better – and more comprehensive and representative – *overarching* self-view than any fixed self-view, since the various varieties of fixed self encompass only a limited subset of all of the various idea-based subsidiary perspectives humans can acquire through learning or creative thinking.

As defined here, a person's overarching self-world perspective (effectively a self-view; see Chapter 7) is made up of the total repertoire of ways of seeing and relating to the world available as possible responses to situations encountered. Fixed self-views are held to encompass only a limited subset of such subsidiary perspectives; the transcendent perspective is held to encompass all of them (even, it will be argued (Chapter 3), those unknown to the individual and as yet undiscovered by humans generally). The transcendent self-view is preferred because it is an overarching self-world perspective or self that reflects the full human self-world relationship, whereas the various varieties of fixed self reflect only a relatively fixed and limited part of that full relationship. It is preferred because it is argued to be a better – and more comprehensive and representative – overarching self-view or self than the various varieties of fixed self. If the case presented in its favour is sound, it encompasses the full range of perspectives that can have an impact on our behavioural and experiential reactions to any situation we encounter as we move through our lives, whereas a fixed self only encompasses a limited (and relatively fixed) subset.

Two Claims Defended

Two primary claims are defended as regards these overarching self-world perspectives or self-views.

The first claim is that the transcendent perspective on the self is the one self-view that accurately reflects our full behavioural and experiential nature, it being the one self-view that encompasses all of the subsidiary self-world perspectives that help determine how we act, think, and feel in the circumstances we encounter. It should be preferred over the fixed self-views we tend to acquire as we develop – incidentally learned self-views held to misdefine our relationship and skew our behavioural and experiential nature because they are based on limited groups of these subsidiary self-world perspectives rather than on all of them. (A summary of the case made in favour of this view is presented under Parts 2-4 of the Overview section below.)

The second claim is that, since how we see the world and ourselves in it has behavioural and experiential consequences – impacts on how we act, think, and feel (see, e.g., Dweck, 2013, p. xi) – the successful instantiation of this transcendent self-view at a personal level to create the fully developed human is of primary importance. It should be an aim for both the individual and for developmental education efforts.

A Practical Guide to Personal Transcendence

Partly because of this latter point – but also because the perspective must encompass and reference aspects of experience itself rather than just words on a page and labels like 'empty consciousness' to be fully and accurately understood – practical guidance on personal instantiation of the self-view is offered (Chapters 18-20).

Including this in the work may seem to go beyond normal scientific practice, but instantiation is essential both to an understanding of the position presented and to a critical examination of what is claimed for it. Of particular importance in this latter respect is a recognition that the claims made as regards empty consciousness refer to an actual nonverbal experience, not just a meaningful phrase that refers to it – to the actual experience, not just a label.

The Transcendent Self-View: Reasons, Details, Functions

Everyday Transcendence and Empty Consciousness

The focus of the work is thus the why, what, and how of developing beyond the (mostly incidentally acquired) fixed self and its limitations by adopting and instantiating the more widely and accurately scoped transcendent self-view sketched out above – a process and endpoint characterised here as *everyday transcendence*.

The word 'transcendence' is seen as appropriate for reasons we will come to momentarily and is characterised as 'everyday' to highlight two points. The first being that the use of the word transcendence is intended to imply nothing more than 'the act of rising above something to a superior state' (Transcendence – Definition, Meaning & Synonyms, n.d.). No wider connotation is being suggested by the use of this word. The second being that the transcendence entailed equates only to a restructuring of the self-view as described above to make empty consciousness the central focus and core of the self and all idea-based subsidiary perspectives on the human self-world relationship subordinate elements of that central focus and core.

The view taken is that this restructuring can reasonably be claimed to entail *transcending* these idea-based perspectives. Empty consciousness is argued (in Chapter 12) to be the one aspect of human experience that does not entail an idea-based – and hence *relational* – self-world perspective, and to sit outwith or outside of these idea-based relational views it also underpins. On this basis, it is therefore a (uniquely) *nonrelational* central focus and core that both transcends and underpins these subsidiary perspectives and encompasses a wider, more accurate, overarching perspective on the self, one that accurately reflects our full behavioural and experiential nature.

Relational and Nonrelational Aspects of Self

The result of restructuring the self along these lines in this view is a self-view with a nonrelational experience as its core and all possible relational perspectives on its periphery. The question asked is what should a self-view for humans look like and be like, and the answer proposed is one that relegates all of the above-noted subsidiary perspectives on the human self-world relationship to a subordinate role in a transcendent self-view built around empty consciousness. It is a self-view designed to combine the totality of who and what we are or can be when known indirectly in relation to other things (relationally) and the unique empty consciousness view of who and what we are when known directly in relation to only ourselves (nonrelationally). A self-view designed so that it subordinates the former to the latter to create an all-encompassing whole that incorporates both. A whole argued to accurately reflect our full behavioural and experiential nature and to be the self-view we should all adopt and instantiate in order to become fully developed as humans (instantiation being taken to involve *habitually identifying* with the self-view – repeatedly mentally rehearsing it as our preferred self-view until it becomes who we are, operationally speaking).

Moving Beyond the Fixed Self
Misdefinition; Negative Effects; Solving the Hard Problem

Transcendence, as meant here, is then nothing more than the process of becoming a person who develops beyond an incidentally acquired idea-based fixed self, replacing it with this transcendent perspective on the self, and making the change operational. It is the process of rising above or outwith an incidentally acquired fixed self based on a limited number of subsidiary self-world perspectives to a new overarching realisation of self. A process of adopting a transcendent self-view and perspective based on a nonverbal and nonrelational experience that sits outwith and beyond ideas and relational points of view (but underpins – and so encompasses – all of them).

Making this move is seen as the correct thing to do – a change that swaps one of a variety of fixed misdefinitions of self for a correctly defined *wholly-variable* alternative defined equally by every possible idea-based subsidiary self-world perspective (Part 2 of the Overview below has more detail). It is also argued to be a positive move that can free us from a variety of negative behavioural, experiential, perspectival, and social consequences associated with these misdefinitions of self. The ability to rise above these misdefinitions – to move outside of them and become centred in nonrelational empty consciousness – is argued to facilitate avoidance of these negative outcomes caused by adopting a fixed self-view that misdefines us (see Chapters 9 and 15).

A particularly significant example of avoiding one such negative outcome (discussed in Chapters 23-25) appears to resolve what Chalmers (1995, p. 3) has labelled the 'hard problem' of consciousness. Part 6 of the Overview section below gives a summary of the position defended here on this topic.

In essence, the mistaken assumption that the flesh, blood, and brain view of humans is *the* reality of humans – rather than simply a scientifically accurate *perspective* on that reality – seems to lead inevitably to a position in which the problem of explaining consciousness scientifically appears to be uniquely hard. It seems to lead us inevitably to a perspective that suggests that there is an unbridgeable 'explanatory gap' (Levine, 1983) between firing neurons on the one hand and sensations, feelings, and thoughts on the other.

Recognising the error in the assumption, on the other hand, points us towards a position in which there is no explanatory gap and no hard problem of consciousness. It suggests the possibility that we are dealing not with impossibly different realities but with a single reality known from two irreconcilably different perspectives – that the problem is 'epistemic' rather than real (cf. Shand, 2021). It suggests the possibility that our conscious experiences may be ontologically reducible to brain states but have knowledge content that, for purely perspectival reasons, is epistemologically *irreducible* to an outside observer's knowledge of these brain states.

In this view, there is no hard problem, no explanatory gap. The epistemologically irreducible inner perspective is wholly subsumed within the substance of the reality known as a brain state by an external observer. The epistemological irreducibility gives the appearance of an unbridgeable gap if we mistake a way of knowing reality for the reality itself; the ontological reducibility of the irreducible knowledge content means there is no real gap.

Transcendence as Nothing Special

Transcendence: Beyond Mystical Mumbo Jumbo

The word 'transcendence' may have uncomfortable connotations for some readers. However, its use here should not be taken as an indication of what might be called 'mystical mumbo jumbo' ahead. An open-minded reading of the book should show both that the word is appropriate and that there is no better alternative. As we shall see when the question is considered late in the book, it is undoubtedly possible to put a mystical gloss on some aspects of transcendence as described here. However, the primary reason for examining the notion is to explore the role of such mystical perspectives in the developed human self. It is to highlight the need to recognise any such perspectives we do adopt as fictions useful in certain contexts. Aspects of our total potential relationship that have a valid and useful role as long as they are not taken wholly seriously but are recognised at some level as the fictions they are.

The primary thing about transcendence as meant here, however, is not that we can put a mystical slant on it. It is that it is really nothing special – just a sensible endpoint to human development. Nothing more than an everyday kind of transcendence we should arguably all aspire to – a way of seeing and being ourselves that we should all adopt because it is the one self-view that accurately reflects our full behavioural and experiential nature.

A Transcendent View of Everything

It is also (arguably) a way of seeing both the world and the human self-world relationship in transcendent terms, since any given self-view can equally well be expressed and held as either a world-view or a view of the self-world relationship (see Chapter 2). In this view, a transcendent perspective on the self is essentially the same as a transcendent perspective on the world or on the self-world relationship. All three are simply different ways of expressing and instantiating the same perspective – an accurate reflection of our true self-world relationship (and so of how we should see both our self and the world, as well as our self-world relationship).

Transcendence and the Spiritual

Whether or not this is essentially the same transcendence we hear about from writers and thinkers of a more mystical or spiritual bent is a question left for the reader to consider – although arguably there are some grounds for thinking so (see, e.g., Srinivasan, 2020).

That, however, is a side issue. The primary aim in what follows is to explore the question of what self-view we humans should adopt and habitually identify with. It is to argue that the transcendent perspective referred to above should be adopted by us all as the one self-view that accurately reflects our full behavioural and experiential nature, as well as suggesting how this might best be achieved.

What if the Self is an Illusion?

Many psychologists and philosophers argue that our experience of a unified self is an illusion created by the brain (see, e.g., Hood, 2012; Hume, 1888, pp. 251-252). This may appear to suggest that considering and discussing the best design for the human self is not a worthwhile exercise, but that is to misconstrue what is being asserted when the unified self is argued to be an illusion created by the brain. No position is taken on whether or not the self is an illusion in this work. It is, however, assumed that, illusion or not, how we envisage and construct our subjective experience of self nevertheless has a behavioural and experiential impact – and hence that the question of how we should construct it is worth consideration. More detail on the position taken on the question is presented in Appendix B.

Notice, moreover, that discussing the question of the best design for the human self in no way implies an acceptance of the notion that the self is something distinct from our physical bodies that is somehow contained within those bodies. What seems far more likely to be true is that any given one of us is a single entity we experience as a physical body when we know it from an external perspective and as an experience of embodied self when we know it from an internal perspective. In other words, it seems more likely that the self and the body are one entity experienced from different points of view, not two distinct things with one contained within the other. Seen in this light, looking at the question of the best design for the human self is simply asking how we should best see and structure that inner experience of self; it does not imply that it is seen as a distinct and separate entity.

Caveat

Observation and Logic Rather Than Definitive Proof

The claims made for the transcendent perspective in this work are based on, and extrapolated from, a number of reasonable and readily-defensible assumptions identified and examined as the case is developed. In essence, the conclusions reached depend on the author's own personally applied chain of observation and logic rather than anything approaching definitive proof. They only hold true if the observations and assumptions made are accurate, if the logic is sound, and if nothing vital to the chain or the conclusions has been missed under any of these headings. Works referenced in relation to individual elements of the case are offered as supportive rather than evidential in the main. The claims made between these pages regarding the best design for the human self may one day be thought worth testing scientifically; for now, however, the case must rest on shared human experience and logic as outlined in the chapters that follow.

Scientific Testing: Not Impossible but Very Long-Term

More will be required of the position in the longer term, of course. In the last analysis, the only definitive basis for acceptance is an assurance that all of the claims made are able to survive a rigorous and sustained regime of scientific testing. This is not impossible to envisage; the position presented entails behavioural and experiential assertions that can, in theory, be examined and shown to be either supported or refuted by science (as per Popper, 1963). It does, however, entail a range of practical difficulties sufficiently significant to suggest that achieving scientific acceptance can only be a very long-term possibility (see, e.g., Meier, 2023). Accordingly, in the short to medium term at least, readers can only assess the arguments presented and decide on the strengths and weaknesses of the case through a critical examination of the position as presented in what follows.

Overview: Parts 2-7

Parts 2-7 of the book cover the following:

Self-View Design Requirements: 1

Part 2 – Chapters **2** to **7** – draws out the first requirement of a self-view that accurately reflects our full behavioural and experiential nature, suggesting that it must be a wholly-variable rather than a fixed self-view. It argues that a fixed self-view misdefines our overarching or total self-world relationship and makes that misdefinition operationally true by allowing it to determine our operational relationship.

The position defended goes like this:

A Relationship That Varies With our View of it

People are not like planets, trees, boulders, or icicles. Such things behave in a way fixed by their physical nature in particular situations, and science can discover the detail of their behaviour by repeatedly observing the things themselves in the situations in question. People are different. Our behavioural and experiential reaction to particular situations – and our behavioural and experiential relationship to those situations – is not determined solely by our own physical state and that of the situation we are in. How we perceive the situation we are in, our self in that situation, or both – effectively what we know, believe, or assume about our relationship to the situation we are in (about our self-world relationship) – will also have an impact. Our behavioural and experiential relationship to the world depends, to some extent, on how we see it or what we believe it to be.

Any Idea About Anything a Determinant

Any view of the self or the world is effectively a view of the self-world relationship and can influence how we act, think, and feel when used as our preferred way of seeing a situation encountered. Any idea we can have about anything must either be a view of the self or some aspect of the self, a view of the world or some aspect of the world, or a view of the interrelationship between self and world or aspects of self and world. If we divide what we experience into self and world, no other possibility exists. A view of any one of them is effectively a view of the self-world relationship (someone who sees themselves as a hedonist, or the world as a pleasure garden to enjoy, effectively has the same view of their self-world relationship). Any idea we can have about anything must therefore encompass a view of the human self-world relationship that can influence how we act, think, and feel when used as our view of a situation it is used in. We can think of them all as narrowly focused, idea-based, subsidiary perspectives on the human self-world relationship, each one a potential determinant of our behavioural and experiential relationship to the world.

Wholly-Variable Not Fixed

A self-view that accurately reflects our full behavioural and experiential nature must take account of this. It must be a self-view so structured as to ensure that any and every one of these subsidiary self-world perspectives, not just a limited set, is a potential determinant of our behavioural and experiential relationship to the world in any situation we encounter. In the terminology employed here, it must be a self-view where the overarching or total self-world relationship is wholly-variable rather than fixed. It must be a self-view that encompasses every possible idea-based subsidiary self-world perspective (a wholly-variable self-view), not one that encompasses only a limited set (a fixed self-view). A self-view that only encompasses some of the total set of all possible idea-based subsidiary self-world perspectives cannot accurately reflect our full behavioural and experiential nature because it leaves some of the subsidiary perspectives that can determine aspects of that nature out of the mix.

The First Requirement

For a range of reasons, the self-views we acquire incidentally as we develop tend to be of the fixed variety. Aside from anything else, we mostly tend to mentally rehearse ourselves into preferred self-views that actively rule out large sets of idea-based subsidiary self-world perspectives – learning roles that define us as (for example) religious believers, not atheists; left-wingers, not right-wingers; and so on.

Fixing of this kind effectively creates and brings us under the control of a self-view similar to one we might develop through habitually rehearsing an idea of ourselves as a 'liberal', a 'freethinker', or as 'Joe Bloggs, family man'. It misdefines us by creating a self-view based on a limited set of all possible subsidiary perspectives and makes the misdefinition true by allowing that set to determine our operational behavioural and experiential relationship. We become *kinds* of humans with a fixed relationship to the world rather than fully developed humans with a wholly-variable relationship.

The first requirement of a self-view that accurately reflects our full behavioural and experiential nature is that it must avoid such misdefinitions and instantiate a wholly-variable overarching or total self-world relationship based on a correct definition instead.

Self-View Design Requirements: 2-6

Part 3 – Chapters 8 to 12 – draws out five further design requirements of a self-view able to accurately reflect our full behavioural and experiential nature, looking specifically at the requirements of a self-view oriented towards the wholly-variable response discussed above.

The position defended here goes like this:

Open-Ended Requirement

The self-view sought must be one in which every possible subsidiary self-world perspective is both seen and can act as part of the whole self – as one among many equally-weighted potential temporary determinants of our actual relationship in encountered situations. This, in operational terms (see Chapter 8), means an *open-ended* design with two elements. It means a self-view where all such subsidiary self-world perspectives are collectively seen as aspects of the self, descriptively speaking, and one in which there is also no mental block or bias in place to prevent each of them also being *operationally available* in any and every situation encountered.

Every idea we can have about anything – even ideas unknown to us individually or as yet undiscovered by humans generally (which, if discovered through new knowledge acquisition or creative thinking, will also have an impact on our self-world relationship) – must be a possible response. An open-ended design is the only practical way of including both unknown and undiscovered responses and a probably infinite number of known responses. Building a self-view based on learning every one of a possibly infinite number of known ideas that grows every time someone has a new thought is an impractical proposition at best; building one that also encompasses unknown and undiscovered ideas is entirely impossible (by normal means, at least).

Negatives, Positives, Blocks

Fixed selves can have both negative and positive effects on our behavioural and experiential interactions with the world; they can also block the kind of wholly-variable response we are aiming for (Chapters 9 and 10). The self-view sought must be designed to avoid the negative effects, retain the positive effects, incorporate a way of allowing for personally unique self-world interactions, and avoid the fixed-self-type blocks on the wholly-variable response.

No Idea Set – not even a Science-Based Set

The self-view sought cannot be built around any one idea set. Even a wholly complete, wholly accurate, all-encompassing scientific view of how the world is (if such a thing were available at some point) will not do. It would encompass a scientifically accurate view of anything and everything, but it would not encompass all of the various ways in which we can behaviourally and experientially relate to our world – it would not encompass philosophical, religious, political, poetic, humorous, and other ways of interacting with our world.

The self-view sought cannot be based on an idea set. Using any limited set of ideas as the sole basis of how we relate to the world blocks out the range of subsidiary self-world perspectives outwith that limited set, so no approach based on a limited idea set will do. Attempting to build a wholly-variable response based on aiming to add every possible subsidiary self-world perspective to our repertoire is, as was touched on above, impractical in terms of volume and impossible because of unknown and undiscovered perspectives. An idea-based approach cannot support a wholly-variable relationship.

Empty Consciousness

Empty consciousness is the only aspect of our experience that neither is, nor entails, an idea-based self-world perspective (see Chapter 12).

As is argued there, we can only know most elements of our internal and external worlds in terms of their relationships to other elements of these worlds – we can only know them indirectly and relationally (see Chapter 12: '**Indirect and Relational Knowledge is the Norm**'). Knowing itself – and, therefore, empty consciousness – must be known in a more direct way. It must be known directly and nonrelationally as, or in terms of, itself.

Our own acquaintance with our experiential world seems to support this view, but there are also logical grounds for accepting it. To assume it is *not* known in a more direct way is to be led into an infinite regress where the knower and the known must be linked by another (and another and another) way of knowing ad infinitum. Empty consciousness, as defined here (see Chapter 12), is the only aspect of knowing itself that is both directly and nonrelationally known and empty of other relational (idea-based) content. Since it cannot either be or entail a self-world perspective, it cannot be an idea. It is therefore the only possible basis of a self-view that does not give undue weight to some fixed view of our overarching self-world perspective if we habitually rehearse a self-view that has it, rather than an idea set, as its core. Habitually identifying with any idea-based self-view – even a scientifically based one – inevitably blocks out many other idea-based subsidiary self-world perspectives from the total relationship and thereby misdefines us (see Part 2 overview above).

The Transcendent Self-View

Part 4 – Chapters **13** to **17** – builds on the six requirements identified earlier in the book (see Chapters 7 to 12). It expands on the rough outline of the perspective presented earlier in this first chapter and draws out most of the detail of the transcendent perspective on the self defended here, arguing that it meets all of the identified requirements. It also argues two further things. First, that it is the only self-view that can fully reflect our behavioural and experiential nature. Second, that we are not fully developed humans until we each adopt and instantiate it as the basis of our personal self.

The position defended goes like this:

The Transcendent Self-View

A self-view based on empty consciousness offers the basis of the self-view for humans we have been seeking – the transcendent self-view sketched out roughly and briefly earlier in this first chapter and detailed definitively in Chapters 13 and 14 and beyond.

Individuals who adopt this transcendent self-view recognise and treat empty consciousness as the core and dominant mental focus of the self – a nonverbal and nonrelational rest or resting state they see and treat as a control hub for the self they are mentally continually returning to. (Note that there is a significant difference between recognising empty consciousness as the core of the self and treating it as such; see Chapter 12: *'The Momentary Core of our Experiential Landscape'*.) They also recognise and treat any and every possible idea-based subsidiary perspective or relational view of themselves as initially equivalent, equally-weighted, subordinate aspects of that core self sitting within and under empty consciousness and able to be used temporarily and replaced as changing circumstances require. Individual facets – understood to include all possible ways of relating to the world, including even unknown or undiscovered possibilities – are allowed to become temporarily dominant when they are appropriate responses to a situation. They then relinquish that dominant position in favour of empty consciousness when the self returns to its resting state. At that juncture, all facets are again seen and treated as aspects of the whole self, and the cycle begins anew. Each facet is viewed and controlled by the subject in a way similar to how an actor views and controls his onstage roles, except that deploying a facet is seen not as play-acting but as enacting a limited (but nonetheless real) facet of the subject's actual self.

The total self operates in a way designed to support a wholly-variable self-world relationship in the open-ended fashion described in Chapter 8.

Additional Skill Sets

Adopters also develop associated skill sets designed to strengthen their abilities in particular areas.

Aiming to facilitate switching perspective when necessary, they work both to avoid the emotional attachments, habitual preferences, and assumptions of truth that block switching away from individual perspectives in a fixed self and to practise the mental skill of breaking free from any perspective they *have* become emotionally, habitually, or perspectively immersed in.

Aiming to widen the range of subsidiary perspectives available for switching to when a switch is required, they work both to educate themselves in as many new perspectives as they can acquire from both factual and fictional sources and to develop a practised ability for the creative and imaginative thinking needed to uncover new possibilities.

Aiming to ensure that any choice of a replacement perspective in any situation encountered is bias-free, they develop an experienced understanding of the value and limitations of individual perspectives while also becoming practised at avoiding external presentation factors that might cause response selection bias.

Developing these enhanced skill sets strengthens the wholly-variable response described in Chapter 8.

All Requirements Met

The end result is a self-view that meets all of the requirements of the generic self-view for humans being sought. It clearly meets the two interrelated requirements that it not be based on an idea set – even a scientifically based one – but be based on empty consciousness instead. It also, arguably, meets all of the others.

A case can be made (Chapters 13 and 15) for claiming that instantiating the transcendent self-view successfully puts in place a wholly-variable self-view as described in Chapter 8 and that it also avoids the fixed-self blocks on the wholly-variable response noted in Chapter 10. A case can also be made (Chapter 16) for claiming that it retains the positive effects of the fixed self-view, avoids its negative effects, and allows us to remain individually unique in our personal interactions (see Chapter 16: *Personal and Collective Selves*). Finally, a case can be made for claiming that it not only avoids the inherent misdefinitions of fixed self-views, replacing them with an accurate, operational reflection of our true behavioural and experiential relationship, but is the only self-view that can (Chapter 17).

Since empty consciousness is *uniquely* nonrelational, a self-view that has it as its core is the only self-view we can possibly construct that is not dominated by an idea set that blocks out other idea sets. It is open-ended in the sense of allowing even unknown and undiscovered idea-based subsidiary self-world perspectives as possible responses (not only are they actively recognised and not blocked as possible responses, but the adopter has developed a practised ability for the creative and imaginative thinking needed to discover them). It is also, moreover, a self-view that actively and consciously encompasses the unique nonrelational aspect of human experience that is empty consciousness – something we would expect a self-view purported to accurately reflect our full behavioural and experiential nature to do.

The transcendent perspective outlined in detail in Chapters 13 and 14 and clarified further thereafter is the only self-view able to accurately reflect our full behavioural and experiential nature. It is the best design for the human self in the view developed here.

Instantiation; Seeing Others; Science

Part 5 – Chapters 18 to 22 – aims to clarify the transcendent perspective outlined in Part 4 further.

The position defended goes like this:

Full comprehension of the transcendent self-view is only realisable when a person moves beyond mere words on a page, puts the working self-view in place, and experiences it for themselves. This is the first step in clarifying for the individual what the transcendent perspective described in Chapters 13 and 14 truly is. This applies particularly to the nonverbal experience of empty consciousness, which can only function operationally as claimed if the actual experience is implemented as the core of the self and not some verbal description or idea. With this in mind, Chapters 18-20 outline a set of mental exercises designed to assist with personal instantiation.

Beyond this, two additional clarifications are outlined in Part 5.

The first makes the point that the ultimate intention of the transcendental human should be to adopt a transcendent perspective on others as well as instantiating this self-view as a personal self. This means seeing others as we see ourselves – in terms of the inner transcendental perspective on who and what we are in behavioural and experiential terms. Doing otherwise not only gives us an inaccurate view of other adopters of the transcendent self-view, it also blocks our own full adoption of the transcendent perspective.

The second makes the point that there is and must be a strong continuing role for scientific knowledge and a scientific outlook within the transcendent perspective on self and world, despite the requirement to see a scientific view of things as one valid way of relating to the world among many. There is no implication here of a weakening of the role of science in human affairs. Scientific perspectives must be possible responses in situations where an accurate view of the true nature of the world is needed; they should also have an impact on our level of commitment to nonscientific responses in circumstances where these are to be preferred for some reason.

The Hard Problem and Fixed-Self Facets

Part 6 – Chapters 23 to 26 – adds additional clarification. Covering one major perspectival example of avoiding the negative outcomes of fixed selves mentioned earlier in this first chapter, it illustrates the impact of the transcendent perspective in areas beyond the everyday.

Looking at the issue of *fixed-self facets* hidden within everyday assumptions – fixed-self facets being aspects of a partially instantiated transcendent self-view that still behave in a fixed way in particular circumstances – it highlights one such facet that has an impact on the so-called hard problem of consciousness.

It suggests that the presumption that the flesh, blood, and brain view of humans is *the* one reality of who and what we are entails a small but important error – an error that should not occur in a mind where the transcendent perspective has been fully instantiated. Correcting this error leads to the removal of a significant block on the full instantiation of the transcendent perspective and a resolution of the hard problem of consciousness. This, in turn, leads to a further clarification of the transcendent perspective and highlights its possible role as a reference point in the scientific study of human experience and behaviour.

The position defended goes like this:

A Mistaken Assumption That Leads to the Hard Problem

The assumption that the flesh, blood, and brain view of humans is *the* reality of humans – rather than simply a scientifically accurate *perspective* on that reality – has two unhelpful effects. The first is that it blocks the full instantiation of the transcendent perspective by forming a fixed-self facet based on the hidden implication that we are always and only outside observers of humans. The second is that it also seems to lead inevitably to a perspective in which the problem of explaining consciousness scientifically appears to be uniquely hard (as per Chalmers, 1995, p. 3). It seems to lead us inevitably to a perspective that suggests that there is an unbridgeable 'explanatory gap' (Levine, 1983) between firing neurons on the one hand and sensations, feelings, and thoughts on the other – one that makes the problem of explaining consciousness and conscious experience appear unsolvable.

Ontologically Reducible but Epistemologically Irreducible

Recognising the error in the assumption, on the other hand, not only removes the block on the transcendent self-view, it also points us towards a position in which there is no explanatory gap and no hard problem of consciousness. One in which the problem is 'epistemic' rather than real (cf. Shand, 2021) and conscious experiences are brain states experienced from an irreconcilably different perspective (rather than the two appearing to be wholly different realities). It points us towards a position where the nonrelational inner experience of the reality underlying both perspectives is ontologically reducible to the reality itself but – for purely perspectival reasons – epistemologically *irreducible* to the outside observer's relational knowledge of it (it being impossible to express nonrelational knowledge *unchanged* within a relational framework).

In this view, there is no hard problem, no explanatory gap. The inner perspective is wholly subsumed within the reality known as a brain state by an external observer. It essentially *is* that reality experienced directly. The external observer can explain everything about it – including why aspects of it are like whatever they are like (red, blue, sweet, and so on) and why they and it are like anything at all (and not just simple unconscious information with no experiential aspect). The external observer can do this because she knows (or can discover) what these experiences are when the reality that subsumes them is known externally and can explain them in this externally observed guise. (The internal and external perspectives on them being simply different ways of knowing the same aspect of reality.)

A Functional Account Plus

The only thing not encompassed in this functional account is the fact and nature of the inner perspective itself – the fact that it is like what it is like and, indeed, that it is like anything at all. This must be mapped to the functional account of the associated brain state because we cannot fully describe – give a full accounting of – what we are explaining without mapping this additional irreducible knowledge content into our scientific account of the brain state. Failing to do this gives the impression that there is no inner perspective and no irreducible knowledge content; it leaves out a scientifically trivial but nonetheless essential aspect of our *knowledge* of these states from our account. A key characteristic of the physical realities in question is omitted, implying that there is no inner perspective.

Noneliminative Physicalism

Adopting a perspective in line with the transcendent perspective as described in this book leads us to a position in which our inner experiences must be explicitly encompassed in our scientific account and are fully explained by it – a position labelled *noneliminative physicalism* in this work. A position that accords with Dennett's (1988, 1991) claim that conscious experience can be explained in terms of brain functionality but argues against his view that we can simply let qualia disappear once we have accounted for these aspects of our experiences in functional terms. Our inner experiences are not additional, hard-to-explain aspects of reality, but they are scientifically trivial but nonetheless essential aspects of our *knowledge* of reality in this view.

This noneliminative physicalist perspective on the form of a scientific account of conscious experience has implications for the relationship of the transcendent perspective to science (including a possible role as a reference point in disciplines like psychology). It also leads to a further clarification of the transcendent self-view itself and can also be seen as possibly having a peripheral impact on some aspects of the transcendent perspective on religious issues.

Being, Religion, and Consciousness

Part 7 – Chapters **27** to **28** – completes the clarifications section of the book, noting that the transcendent perspective has various implications for religious beliefs and that these implications, in turn, further clarify the transcendent perspective itself.

The position defended goes like this:

Four Impacts on Religion

The transcendent perspective has four impacts on religious beliefs, some arguably positive from a believer's point of view, some less so.

The first of the four is presumably positive: whatever religious beliefs an individual believer holds are seen and treated as having a valid practical role in the overall human relationship to the universe (allowing believers to jointly celebrate a preferred spiritual perspective on being, existence, and life, for example).

The second is at least neutral: the favoured religious view is taken as no more, but also no less, important than scientific perspectives, atheistic perspectives, all other religious viewpoints, philosophical and political viewpoints, and so on, as a way of relating to the world.

The third will surely be seen as positive – and perhaps also as edging the second in the same positive direction. It offers religious believers the possibility of becoming so immersed *temporarily* in their own preferred religious beliefs that they can effectively become like true believers for a while (using an everyday mental skill we all possess already to pull themselves out and back to the core self at need).

Only the last of the four appears truly problematic – especially so for those with a strong belief that an all-powerful deity is responsible for the shape, form, and existence of the universe. The key role of science in the perspective entails a need to regard religious views not as unshakeable beliefs but as useful and meaningful fictions that can reflect a real aspect of the human relationship to the universe.

Useful Fictions

This fourth issue may not be a problem for all religious believers. Some may be able to accept some aspects of their religious perspective on things as fantasies or fictions that contain a kernel of truth – just as a fictional tale (or a parable) can express something true even though it is itself a work of the imagination. Others may be attracted by some form of pantheism with the universe itself as a deity and knowing empty consciousness as knowing this deity in the most direct way possible. Science accepts that the universe exists and would (if the case presented in this book were to be accepted) also presumably accept that empty consciousness does too, so the existence of what a pantheist might regard as a deity and as knowing that deity need not be regarded as fictional.

That said, science finds no need to see the universe as a deity or empty consciousness as a direct way of knowing this 'deity', so those aspects of this imagined pantheistic belief would still have to be seen as useful fictions by those seeing them as personally beneficial. It is possible to put a mystical gloss on some aspects of transcendence as described here, but only if we see the perspectives adopted as useful fictions that have a valid role as one of many ways we can relate to existence, not if we take them as scientifically true.

In conclusion, except for those whose religious beliefs are very hard-line, the transcendent perspective is relatively compatible with a religious outlook, although it does require more flexibility from those espousing religious beliefs than may be palatable for some.

PART 2

First Design Requirement

Part 2: Outline of the Case Presented

The human behavioural and experiential relationship to the world is not fixed. It is partly determined by how the range of views we hold of that relationship – the range of self-world perspectives we hold – interacts with our own physical nature and that of the world **(Chapter 2)**. Any idea we can have about anything entails a view of that relationship – an idea-based and narrowly focused subsidiary self-world perspective – and all are potential determinants of our behavioural and experiential relationship to the world **(Chapter 3)**.

A self-view that fully reflects our behavioural and experiential nature must align with this. It must support a wholly-variable rather than a fixed relationship. It must allow every possible subsidiary perspective, rather than a limited set, to be a *potential* determinant of our total relationship in any situation encountered **(Chapter 4)**.

Various factors, including our own mental habits, can limit our total self-world relationship as we develop, programming our brains and behavioural and experiential responses to make our overarching or total relationship not wholly-variable but fixed **(Chapter 5)**.

Artificial fixing of our overarching relationship probably happens to most, if not all, of us as we develop – not least because the idea of any of us seeking to add every possible idea-based subsidiary perspective to our repertoire is an unlikely and impractical proposition. In fact, as we shall see later, it is impossible to avoid fixing except by adopting the transcendent self-view argued for in this book **(Chapter 6)**.

Artificial fixing of this kind effectively creates and brings us under the control of a self-view similar to one we might develop through habitually identifying with the idea of ourselves as a 'right-winger', a 'freethinker', or as 'Joe Bloggs, family man'. It misdefines us and makes the misdefinition true. We become *kinds* of humans with a fixed relationship to the world rather than fully developed humans with a wholly-variable relationship. The first requirement of a self-view that reflects our full behavioural and experiential nature is that it must avoid such misdefinitions and instantiate a wholly-variable overarching self-world relationship instead **(Chapter 7)**.

2

A Relationship That Varies With our View of it

Variable Responses and Their Causes

How we Differ From the Rocks

The position on the human self developed in this book starts from the premise that people – humans – are not like planets, trees, rolling boulders, or icicles. Such things behave in a way fixed by their physical nature in particular situations, and science can discover the detail of their behaviour by observing the things themselves in the situations in question. The assertion made and defended in this chapter – and the first step towards the case in favour of the transcendent self-view presented in this work – is that we cannot say the same where people are concerned. Our behavioural and experiential relationship, either to particular circumstances or to the world at large, is not determined solely by our own physical state and that of the world but also by our own view or views of that behavioural and experiential relationship.

Points Argued

Four points are argued in this chapter. First, that how a person acts, thinks, and feels in a situation will be partly determined by how they perceive the circumstances they are in – by what they know, believe, or assume about these circumstances. Second, that – to put this more precisely – it will be partly determined by the range of views they hold of the self, the world, or the self-world relationship in respect of that situation. Third, that any view of the self or the world entails a view of the self-world relationship, and that this effectively means that a person's behavioural and experiential relationship to a situation will be partly determined by the range of views of the *self-world relationship* a person holds. Fourth, that the same can be said of a person's overarching behavioural and experiential relationship to the world – the total set of views of the self-world relationship we hold and might apply to any situation (effectively a self-view – see Chapter 7). Our behavioural and experiential relationship, either to particular circumstances or to the world at large, is not determined solely by our own physical state and that of the world but also by our own view or views of that behavioural and experiential relationship.

Our Perceptions Determine how we Act, Think, and Feel

Support From Human Experience

How a person acts, thinks, and feels in a situation will be partly determined by how they perceive the circumstances they are in – by what they know, believe, or assume about these circumstances. Our own experience of being human and knowing other humans tells us this.

Imagine, for example, a person in a room with a time bomb she has no way of stopping. She realises there is a minute left on the clock and immediately runs for the one door she can see. On it, there is an envelope that says, 'Warning: read the note inside before you risk opening this door'. It is in the handwriting of a friend she implicitly trusts, so she believes what it says. Our own experience tells us, does it not, that this person will act, think, and feel differently before and after opening the door and exiting the room depending on what the note inside leads her to believe? If the note says, 'Snipers who want to kill women! Open the door fast and run very quickly to the house on the other side of the street.' and she believes this she will likely act, think, and feel in one way. If it says, 'Snipers out there – but they will not kill women. Open the door carefully, walk out slowly, make sure they know you are female, and you will be fine.' and she believes that she will likely act, think, and feel in a quite different way. Our experience tells us, in other words, that how the person acts, thinks, and feels will be determined not just by their own physical state at the time and that of the situation they are in, but by how they perceive the circumstances they are in. It will be affected by what they know, believe, or assume about those circumstances.

Our own experience of being human and knowing other humans tells us that how a person acts, thinks, and feels in a situation will be partly determined by how they perceive the circumstances they are in – by what they know, believe, or assume about these circumstances.

Empirical Evidence: Dweck and Beyond

The claim also has a significant level of empirical evidence in its favour. As Dweck (2013) points out in her book – a view she supports by referencing a range of research conducted by herself and others (see Dweck, 2013, pp. xi-xii and following chapters) – people's beliefs 'can create different psychological worlds, leading them to think, feel, and act differently in identical situations'.

A particular example of this – taken from Dweck's extensive work on the topic – is illustrated in individuals who have similar levels of cognitive ability but different theories regarding intelligence. Those who see human and, by extension, their own intelligence as something malleable that can be improved through personal effort tend to seek out opportunities to learn and develop and to react to setbacks by working to find ways to overcome them (see, e.g., Dweck, 2013, pp. 20-38). They have what Dweck calls a mastery-oriented perspective on things. Those who see human and, by extension, their own intelligence as something fixed tend to avoid opportunities to learn that might challenge them, to regard setbacks as reflections on their own presumed lack of innate intelligence, and to react in a more floundering fashion as a result. They have what Dweck calls a helpless perspective when encountering setbacks (see, in particular, Chapter 2: Dweck, 2013, pp. 5-14).

These different perspectives were also found to be reflected in the reported thoughts and feelings of the students who held them. Dweck writes that more than a third of the students in the helpless group spontaneously denigrated their intellectual ability in response to failure, whereas none of the students in the mastery-oriented group did so (Dweck, 2013, p. 7). The helpless group also reported negative feelings when encountering difficulties, whereas hardly any of the mastery-oriented group did so.

Dweck also examined the effects of differing beliefs about interpersonal relationships, reporting that individuals whose expectations of romantic relationships are low tend to have less successful, shorter-lived relationships, and more breakups (Dweck, 2013, pp. 64-71). They are more likely to feel rejected by a partner's everyday thoughtlessness and to react in ways that damage the relationship – to become jealous or hostile, for example. Such individuals also tend to be less engaged and less successful in their wider social interactions.

Looking beyond Dweck, it is not hard to find a range of other work reporting further evidence for the claim (that how we act, think, and feel in particular circumstances is influenced by what we know, believe, or assume about these circumstances).

Alquist et al. (2013), for example, found evidence suggesting that believing in free will made subjects less likely to be conformist and that not believing in it made them more likely to be conformist.

Van Roeyan et al. (2020) found evidence that people identified as only pretending to cry by observers were perceived as more manipulative, less reliable, less warm, and less competent than people whose crying was perceived as genuine.

Fein and Spencer (1997) found that the likelihood of stereotyping and taking a prejudiced attitude towards those stereotyped rose when their subjects' self-image was threatened and that derogating those they stereotyped increased their own self-esteem.

Damisch et al. (2010) found evidence that there were performance benefits to having good luck related superstitious thoughts and feelings in areas like sports, cognitive tasks, and physical dexterity.

Wenzel et al. (2017) found a link between higher levels of belief in a just world where people generally get what they deserve and higher levels of dishonesty and speculated that the former is used to justify the latter internally.

Ditto and Lopez (1992) found evidence that information consistent with a preferred conclusion is examined less critically than information inconsistent with a preferred conclusion.

Freeman et al. (2016) found that negative ageing perceptions had a negative impact on depression and anxiety.

Lieberman et al. (2001) found that awareness of mortality can bolster a need to maintain and defend personal world-views, a tendency to display verbal and physical antagonism towards those with alternative world-views, and a less punitive attitude towards those who attacked victims who threatened those alternative world-views.

These studies all support the same basic point. How we see a situation affects how we behaviourally and experientially react to it – how we act, think, and feel in it.

A Widely Accepted View

There is also an abundance of evidence to suggest that the notion (that how we see a situation affects how we act, think, and feel in it) is non-controversial – widely accepted among academics and other professionals with a focus on the topic. It tends to be addressed under a variety of different labels - 'self theories', 'lay theories', 'world-views' and 'mindsets' as well as beliefs as such – but an acceptance of the basic point underlies them all. We need only look at the comments researchers in these areas make in their papers and books to find evidence for this.

Thus, Porot and Mandelbaum (2020, p. 1) point out and document that 'reliance on belief in understanding and predicting behaviour is widespread' (in cognitive science).

Levy et al. (2013, p. 318) note that 'Decades of findings from cognitive, cultural, developmental, and social psychological research... indicate that lay theories are powerful predictors of greater or weaker prejudice, stereotyping, and discrimination towards numerous groups'.

Schroder (2021, p. 1) notes that 'research on mindsets (or implicit theories) – which refer to beliefs about the malleability of self-attributes – reveals that these beliefs predict performance ranging from academic achievement to rebounding from interpersonal stressors'.

Koltko-Rivera (2004, p. 3), who defines worldviews as 'sets of beliefs and assumptions that describe reality', records that 'specialists in various subdisciplines of psychology have indicated that worldview has a central role in' a range of fields. These include developmental psychology, environmental psychology, sport psychology, general counselling and psychotherapy, and multicultural counselling and psychotherapy.

There is, in summary, significant evidence to suggest that the claim made above is not only in line with our own experience as humans but is also both empirically supported and widely accepted. How a person acts, thinks, and feels in a situation will be partly determined by how they perceive the circumstances they are in – by what they know, believe, or assume about these circumstances.

A Range of Self, World, and Self-World Relationship Views

Optional Views of Self, World, and Self-World Relationship

We can clarify the position further by again consulting our own experience of being human and knowing other humans. Based on examples of the kind given below, we can be more specific about the nature of the knowledge, beliefs, and assumptions that help determine how a person acts, thinks, and feels in particular circumstances. We can specify that they are conscious or unconscious views they hold about the world or some situational aspect of it (world-views), about themselves or aspects of themselves (self-views), or about the relationship between themselves and the world, either generally or in the situation in question (self-world relationship views). Obviously, more than one of these three types of viewpoint may have a joint impact in particular cases, but we can ignore this for present purposes.

We can also argue on the same basis that the question of whether or not a person has a range of *options* available as regards views of the self, world, or self-world relationship applicable to the circumstances in question has an impact. We can argue that how people will act, think, and feel in particular circumstances will depend on whether they only have one view that they know, assume, or believe applies in particular circumstances or have two or more sets of such views they see as possibly applicable.

The interrelated set of examples presented below illustrates and supports these claims.

A View of Things Likely to Make us Fearful

Imagine a fisherman who normally fishes close to the shore of his island but one day discovers the fish numbers close to the island are much lower than usual and he is failing to catch as much as he needs to feed and otherwise support himself and his family. Suppose he has been raised to believe without question in the teachings of the local religion, which say, in essence, that God has commanded that his creations should never sail too far from their island and has fashioned their world to punish anyone who disbelieves and disobeys. Suppose these teachings say God has made the world flat with an edge those who sail too far out will fall over to their doom if they disobey. Suppose, in other words, our fisherman believes his relationship to the world is that of a protected believer if he obeys God's rules but is that of a condemned and doomed unbeliever if he disobeys and tries to fish too far out.

We can safely assume that a sailor indoctrinated to see his self-world relationship in these terms will be more likely to act, think, and feel fearfully if faced with the choice of disobeying his God or starving than he would if he held a less threatening view of things. We can readily imagine circumstances in which he will be too afraid to fish further out and will decide to go hunting rabbits instead. We can also imagine that, even if hunger gets the upper hand and he starts to question his beliefs and sails further out to fish anyway, he may feel more scared, think more nervous thoughts, and act more hesitantly than he would if taught to see the world differently. This is especially so if his upbringing has made him so habituated to this view of the relationship between self and world that he is unaware that it is a view and unconsciously assumes it is just the way things are.

We may not be able to say precisely how he will act, think, and feel faced with low fish stocks and starvation, but we can reasonably assume that how he does will be partially determined by his view of his world and his relationship to it. We can reasonably assume that this one, learned, religion-based view of his self-world relationship will have an impact on his reaction to the situation he faces.

We can also reasonably assume that the same fisherman would likely act, think, and feel in a likewise fearful way if he had acquired a similar view of things in other ways. If he had always unconsciously supposed that the world he saw was just obviously flat and must have an edge that ships could crash over to their doom, for example – perhaps since ships that sailed too far out always seemed to disappear, never to return. Or if he had been brought up in a family that taught him to see himself as a dedicated 'shore-hugger', encouraging a self-view and a developed self imbued with an unshakeable belief that some nameless evil awaited those foolish enough to fish too far from shore.

Again, we may not be able to say precisely how he will act, think, and feel in the low fish stocks situation envisaged if he has such a world-view or self-view embedded in his psyche. However, we can reasonably assume that his behaviour and experience in these circumstances – how he acts, thinks, and feels – will be partially determined by whatever version of the flat-world viewpoint he consciously or unconsciously holds.

A View Likely to Have the Opposite Effect

Now suppose instead that the same sailor, in the same circumstances, has acquired a more positive view of things. Perhaps he has had teachers who convinced him (using a ball) that the world was round and had no edge he might plunge over – or has read a particular book and thereby learned to become a person who is a committed devotee of the round-worlder cult. Or perhaps he has simply learned from experience sailing around the world over a period of years to see his self-world relationship as one that raised no concerns about edges that a person could fall over to their doom. Suppose, in other words, that he has acquired a view of the self, the world, or the self-world relationship that does not imply a world he could tumble over the edge of. It is reasonable to assert that he would be less likely to act, think, and feel fearfully if faced with the need to fish further out to sea to avoid starvation than he would if he held a flat-world-based perspective on the self, the world, or the self-world relationship.

A Relationship That Varies With our View of Things

It may again be difficult to say with certainty precisely how our sailor would act, think, and feel in circumstances where he is faced with sailing further out to sea or starving and has one or other of these viewpoints on the self, the world, or the self-world relationship in play. Other factors, such as whether his ship can handle deep sea storms, how much money he has for repairs, and so on, will also have an impact. But it is reasonable to assume that he will be less likely to act, think, and feel fearfully than if he held a flat-world view of things and more likely than not to act, think, and feel differently than he would if he did not hold this round-world view.

It is reasonable to suppose, in other words, that his experiential and behavioural relationship to the world in the low fish stocks situation described will be determined by more than just the circumstances themselves and his own physical state. It is reasonable to suppose that it will also be partially determined by how his consciously or unconsciously held views of himself, the world, or the relationship between the two interact with those circumstances. We can assume, can we not, that his experiential and behavioural relationship to the world in a particular situation will tend to vary according to the view he holds of these things? We can assume that his experiential and behavioural relationship to a situation – how he acts, thinks, and feels in it – will tend to vary according to the view he consciously or unconsciously holds of himself, the world, or the relationship between the two in the situation in question.

A Relationship Determined by Having Optional Views

It is also reasonable to assume that it will tend to vary according to whether he has *optional* views of his self, the world, or his self-world relationship available to him that are applicable in the circumstances he faces.

Suppose our fisherman has two possible ways of seeing and responding to the low fish stocks situation available to him. Suppose he has been taught that the world is flat with an edge to fall over by one teacher and that it is globe-shaped with no edge to fall over by another. Suppose he has two different ways of seeing the failing fish stocks situation available to him and is unsure which is correct and which is not. It is reasonable to assume that his responses in the low fish stocks situation will be determined not just by his own and the world's physical state but also by the fact that he has these two options available and does not know which is true.

He may tend towards the flat-world version while his needs are not extreme but edge towards the round-world version as his hunger and desperation grow. Or he may decide to test out which of the options is his best bet and trick a rival fisherman into fishing further out to discover what happens before trying it himself. Either way, his acting, thinking, and feeling will be influenced not just by one set of self or world or self-world views or another but also by the fact that he has options available and can choose between them. His experiential and behavioural relationship to the world in the circumstances of low fish stocks close to shore will be determined by more than the circumstances themselves and his own physical state. They will also be partially determined by how *the range* of his consciously or unconsciously held views of his self, the world, or the relationship between the two interacts with those circumstances.

Views and Options

On this basis, it is reasonable to conclude that the assertion made earlier in this chapter is true. The human experiential and behavioural relationship to the world in a particular situation is determined by more than just the circumstances of our own physical state and those of the physical world. It is also partially determined by how the range of our consciously or unconsciously held views of our self, the world, or the relationship between the two interacts with those circumstances.

Implied Views of the Self-World Relationship
Any Self or World View is a Self-World Relationship View

For various reasons, it is helpful if we now simplify how we express this position. As will become clear presently (and has been hinted at already above), any conscious or unconscious idea, belief, or viewpoint about the self or about the world implies a conscious or unconscious idea, belief, or view of the self-world relationship.

Recognising this allows us to restate the position in terms of self-world relationships. We can say that the human experiential and behavioural relationship to the world in particular circumstances is determined not just by the situation encountered but also by how the range of our consciously or unconsciously held views of our self-world relationship in that situation interacts with it. We can say that our experiential and behavioural relationship to the world in particular circumstances depends not just on the physical state of ourselves and the world in those circumstances, but also on how we consciously or unconsciously see that relationship.

Imagine someone who believes that Goddess X made the world a 'Shangri La of joy' purely for her followers to take pleasure in. He has a particular notion of the relationship of himself to the world. He sees his relationship to the world as being that of a favoured creation in a world his goddess designed to be one her favoured creations could enjoy as a 'Shangri-la of joy'. We can take it that he will tend to act, think, and feel in the world in a way that is in line with this notion of his self-world relationship.

Now imagine someone who simply sees the world itself as a pleasure playground solely for his enjoyment. We can take it, can we not, that he will tend to act, think, and feel similarly? The view affecting his behaviour is a world-view, but it clearly implies a similar ('Shangri La of joy') view of his self-world relationship.

The same can be said of someone who simply views himself as a hedonist or a pleasure seeker. He has a view of the self, but it is again one that implies a 'Shangri La of joy' view of his self-world relationship.

The flat-world-only fisherman example above illustrates the same thing. Our fisherman will hold a similar view of his self-world relationship regardless of whether he has absorbed a particular religion-based view of that self-world relationship, an unconsciously assumed view that the world is flat with an edge he can fall over, or a view of himself as a shore-hugger.

A Relationship Partly Determined by how we View it

Any view of the self or of the world inevitably implies a particular view of the self-world relationship. Someone who sees himself as a bold adventurer or the world as an exciting and mysterious place will have one view of his self-world relationship. Someone who sees himself as a cautious, risk-averse person or the world as a dangerous place to be approached with great care will have another view of his self-world relationship. Even though the direct focus of the viewpoints he holds is the self or the world rather than the self-world relationship as such, he will still effectively have adopted a view of his self-world relationship.

Our views of the self and the world are essentially views of the self-world relationship. We can therefore say that the human experiential and behavioural relationship to the world in particular circumstances is determined not just by the circumstances themselves but also by how the range of our consciously or unconsciously held views of our self-world relationship interacts with those circumstances. We can say that our behavioural and experiential relationship to the circumstances we encounter is determined in part by how we consciously or unconsciously see that relationship.

Other ways of Expressing Self-World Perspectives

It is, of course, equally and self-evidently true from the examples above that a view of the self-world relationship can also be held or expressed as a view of the self or a view of the world. It is true that we could equally well say that our behavioural and experiential relationship to the circumstances we encounter is determined in part by how we consciously or unconsciously see the self or the world. This is a point we will revisit later: first, when seeing and thinking of our view of our behavioural and experiential relationship as a self-view is helpful, then when seeing and thinking of it as a world-view is.

For the moment, however, it is more helpful to see and think about this question in self-world relationship terms. To stay with the view that the human experiential and behavioural relationship to the world in particular circumstances is determined, not just by the circumstances themselves, but also by how the range of our consciously or unconsciously held views of our self-world relationship interacts with those circumstances. To say that our behavioural and experiential relationship to situations we encounter is partly determined by how we consciously or unconsciously see that relationship and the range of ways in which we see it, even if these can sometimes be expressed as views of the self or the world.

Situational and Overarching Self-World Relationship Views

The Overarching Relationship and the Total Repertoire

Notice, moreover, that our assertion applies not just to one or a few situations but to all situations. This point is important because it means that it also applies to our overarching behavioural and experiential relationship to the world, a relationship defined and determined by every view of our self-world relationship we hold and might apply to any situation (our 'total repertoire' to echo Chapter 1). How we humans act, think, and feel generally in the world at large is determined by more than just our physical state and that of the world as a whole. It is also partly determined by how the range of optional views we consciously or unconsciously hold of our own or the human self-world relationship interacts with the world at large and our own physical state in the various circumstances we encounter.

As we shall see as we proceed, our total range of optional views might be made up in a variety of ways. A single view of certain aspects of the world or self may have been learned and then applied to each individual situation encountered. Or it may be the result of many smaller sets of optional views learned in and associated with instances of particular types of situation or groups of situations. Or it may be made up of a mix of these possibilities.

A person who has learned to see her relationship to the world as that of a 'right- wing libertarian' might act, think, and feel in one set of ways on various issues in a variety of circumstances when faced with reports of extreme poverty and hardship in another country. She might act, think, and feel in quite another set of ways if she has learned to see her relationship to the world as that of a 'left-wing humanitarian' (especially if, as is often the case, the views associated with one perspective tend to block out those associated with the other). She may have learned the different views of her self-world relationship that she applies to particular circumstances in a variety of ways. She may have learned them either in relation to the situations themselves or by learning an overarching view of how a 'right-wing libertarian' sees her self-world relationship options in a whole range of circumstances or by a bit of both. Either way, she will have differing conscious or unconscious views of her total or overarching self-world relationship and her experience and behaviour will be influenced in line with them in each situation encountered.

A group of people who have all learned to see themselves in the world as a Buddhist does will all tend to act, think, and feel in similar ways when faced with a similar set of situations. They will all tend to act, think, and feel in different ways in the same situations if they have all learned to see themselves in the world in different ways – some as Christians, some as Muslims, some as Atheists, and so on. Again, they may have acquired the total number of their optional views of their self-world relationship either at an overarching level or at the level of individual types of circumstances or of groups of such individual types, or through a mix of all of these. Either way, they will all end up having differing consciously or unconsciously held views of their total or overarching self-world relationship, and their experience and behaviour will be influenced in line with these in each situation encountered.

A particular person encountering a particular set of life circumstances will have one total or overarching behavioural and experiential relationship to the world if he has learned to see it as a Buddhist, liberal, flat-worlder does in any or all of these ways. He will have another if he has learned to see it as a Muslim, socialist, round-worlder does in any or all of these ways. Others in the group will be similarly influenced by their own learned views of their total or overarching self-world relationship, regardless of how it is acquired. Our behavioural and experiential relationship to both particular circumstances and the world generally depends not just on the situation or situations encountered but on how our various ways of viewing our self-world relationship interact with the situation or situations encountered.

Reflecting our Behavioural and Experiential Nature

The behavioural and experiential relationship of humans either to particular circumstances or to the world generally is not determined solely by our physical nature and that of the world at large, as is the case with mountains, mists, and molecules. If the case set out above is sound (as will be assumed in this book), it is also determined by how the range of our consciously or unconsciously held views of our own or the human self-world relationship interacts with particular circumstances and with the world at large. This is the same, in essence, as saying it is also determined by our overarching self-world relationship, or (see Chapter 7) self-view — the total set of views of the self-world relationship we hold and might apply to any situation encountered. It is also of evident significance in our search for a self-view that fully and accurately reflects our true behavioural and experiential nature, indicating that the views we hold of our self-world relationship help determine that nature, a point that will be developed further in the next chapter.

3

All Ideas Entail Self-World Perspectives

A Limitless Range of Narrowly Focused Perspectives

Any Idea About Anything

A key assumption made in the book – an assumption defended in the present chapter – is that the range of perspectives on our self-world relationship each of us has available to us is potentially very large. It is not limited to perspectives that specifically and evidently reference the self, the world, or the self-world relationship. Any conscious or unconscious idea, belief, or viewpoint we can have about anything – any idea, belief, or viewpoint we could possibly have in our repertoire – encompasses a perspective on our self-world relationship. Any and all of them can function to help determine how we act, think, and feel in any situation we encounter and thus to define our total or overarching relationship to the world. If the idea, belief, or viewpoint that encompasses the relationship is chosen and implemented as a situational response, it will interact with the situational circumstances to determine how we act, think, and feel in those circumstances and make the entailed relationship actual – operationally true.

This means that any conscious or unconscious idea, belief or viewpoint we can have about anything is a member of the range of views that can affect both our situational and overarching or total behavioural and experiential relationship. It also means that any overarching self-world perspective or self-view that reflects our full behavioural and experiential nature must encompass all such idea-based perspectives on our self-world relationship. All of them are potential determinants of how we act, think, and feel in the world and relatively narrow subsidiary elements of any comprehensive perspective on the total human behavioural and experiential relationship to the world.

Three Points Argued

Three points are argued below in this regard.

First, that any conscious or unconscious belief or viewpoint we can have about anything must reference something in human experience. Not only would a set of all ideas, beliefs, and viewpoints that referenced something in human experience be comprehensive, but it would be impossible to envisage, imagine, invent, express, communicate, or acquire a perspective that referenced something beyond human experience.

Second, that if these ideas, beliefs, and viewpoints all reference human experience, they must then reference either something of the self, something of the world, or something of the self-world relationship – which, according to Chapter 2, means they must all effectively encompass a view of the self-world relationship.

Third, that since all such ideas, beliefs, and viewpoints can make their inherent perspective on the self-world relationship actual if they are used as a situational response, all such ideas, beliefs, and viewpoints can help determine how we act, think, and feel in any situation where they are used. We can conclude both that they can all act to determine both our situational and overarching or total relationship and that an overarching self-world perspective or self-view that accurately reflects our full behavioural and experiential nature must encompass each and every one of them. We can conclude that they are all relatively narrow subsidiary views of our total self-world relationship that instantiate subsidiary aspects of that total relationship when used as situational responses.

All Such Ideas Must Reference Human Experience

Two Points

Any idea, belief, or viewpoint we can have about anything – any idea, belief, or viewpoint we could possibly have in our repertoire of perspectives on anything – must arguably reference something in human experience. It must either reference something we humans can have direct experience of, or it must reference something we can relate to something we can have direct experience of.

Two points can be made in support of this claim. The first is this. It seems incontestable that any set of ideas, beliefs, or viewpoints whose members reference things we humans can have direct experience of or things we can relate to such things would be a set of everything we could conceivably have an idea, belief, or viewpoint about. It would be a set that would include any idea, belief, or viewpoint we could possibly have in our repertoire of perspectives on anything.

Everything we can have direct experience of is fairly wide in scope. It encompasses things we can experience for real, things we can experience imagining, and things we can either experience or imagine but recognise (from experience) as falling into the category 'meaningless or nonsensical'. Everything we can *relate* to something we can have direct experience of is arguably much wider. It encompasses things we might envisage experiencing or imagining on the basis of things already experienced, imagined, or envisaged, including any successfully communicated to us by others on the basis of the relation of experiences to language or pictures, and any of the above falling into the meaningless or nonsensical category.

Ideas That Reference Human Experience: A Complete Set

On the face of it, such a set would encompass everything we can possibly have an idea, belief, or viewpoint about. It would encompass any viewpoint we might have on everything we have had or could have direct experience of, including imaginary, nonsensical, or meaningless things. It would encompass any viewpoint we could envisage having on the basis of such experiences and imaginings. It would encompass any viewpoint we might have on everything that might be successfully and meaningfully communicated to us by other humans by word of mouth, the written word (arguably – via translations – in any language), or by illustrative means. It would encompass any viewpoint we might have on everything we could not physically do at a particular moment in time or physically do at all but could imagine doing as humans. Things like walking on Mars, say, or being transported to another galaxy while some part of consciousness stays at home and experiences both viewpoints at once.

It would even encompass any viewpoint we might have on how the world would seem to a fox, an eel, a tree, or a stone, and experiences that might be communicated to us by an alien with a different range of senses to us (but a degree of commonality). All of these could either be assimilated and comprehended through comparing and contrasting similarities and differences with our own senses, experiences, and thoughts or would fall into the meaningless or nonsensical category.

It would, in short, be a wholly comprehensive set – one that could not possibly fail to encompass everything we could conceivably have an idea, belief, or viewpoint about.

It would encompass every possible idea, belief, or viewpoint we could have about anything we might experience or imagine, even those that happened to be nonsensical or meaningless. It would encompass every possible idea, belief, or viewpoint we could have about anything that every other human might experience, imagine, and communicate. It would even encompass ideas, beliefs, and viewpoints about things beyond direct human experience – the perspectives of aliens or animals we were able to compare, contrast, or otherwise relate to human experience, say. It seems incontestable that any set of ideas, beliefs, or viewpoints that all reference things we have direct experience of, or things we can relate to things we have direct experience of, would comprise a list of everything we could conceivably have in our repertoire of perspectives on anything.

We Cannot add Ideas Beyond our Experience

The second point in favour of this claim is that this is entirely as we would expect – or arguably so. We would expect a set of ideas, beliefs, or viewpoints that all reference things we have direct experience of, or things we can relate to such things, would encompass any idea, belief, or viewpoint we could possibly have in our repertoire. We would expect it because the claim seems self-evidently true.

An idea, belief, or viewpoint that did not fall into one of these two categories would be a perspective on something we had no experience of and no way of relating to anything we did have experience of. It would be an idea, belief, or viewpoint we could not, in any meaningful sense, envisage, imagine, invent, express, communicate, or acquire.

We could not add it to our repertoire by envisaging, imagining, or inventing it ourselves; it would be something entirely outwith our experience, real and imagined.

Other humans could not envisage, imagine, or invent it either, for the same reason. Even if they could, they would be unable to express it and communicate it to us, and we would be unable to acquire and understand it in any case.

Nor would there be any other way to add this or any other such perspective to our repertoire. There may be ideas, beliefs, or viewpoints in the universe that do not relate to some aspect of human experience (aliens totally unlike us might have them), but if so, they are ideas, beliefs, or viewpoints we would not and could not add to our repertoire. Even if we could somehow acquire them in a form the aliens themselves would understand, they would be acquired in an entirely indecipherable and untranslatable form. There could be no possibility of commonality if the perspectives they entailed referenced things fully and truly beyond human experience. We might acquire the form, but not the content; we could not acquire the ideas, beliefs, or viewpoints themselves. We could never add them to our repertoire. Any idea, belief, or viewpoint we can have about anything – any idea, belief, or viewpoint we could possibly have in our repertoire of perspectives on anything – must reference something of, or related to, human experience. We could not possibly envisage, imagine, invent, express, communicate, or acquire it otherwise. It is, quite simply, an impossibility.

All Ideas Encompass Self-World Perspectives
Referencing Self, World, or Self-World Relationship

This is clearly an important point in the present context. If true, it means that any idea, belief, or viewpoint we can have about anything must reference either something about the self, something about the world, or something about the self-world relationship.

These three categories – self, world, and self-world relationship – encompass everything in human experience. What we have within what we experience can only entail experiences that reference or relate to ourselves, experiences that reference or relate to the world outside ourselves, or experiences that reference or relate to the relationship between the two. If we divide the totality of our experience up in these ways, there is nothing else – either an experience relates to the self, or it relates to the world outside ourselves, or it relates to the relationship between the two (and, in a sense, encompasses both).

Some experiences may, of course, reference more than one of these, but such experiences nevertheless reference one or more of the three.

If we divide human experience up using these three categories, there is no experience that does not fall into one or more of the three. All of them necessarily reference something about the self, something about the world, something about the relationship between the two, or a mix of these. Any idea we can have about anything – any idea we could possibly have in our repertoire – falls into one or more of these categories.

Every Idea Holds a View of the Self-World Relationship

This is important. According to what was argued in Chapter 2, it means that every idea, belief, or viewpoint we can have about anything is essentially a view of the self-world relationship. Each and every one either relates directly to a particular view of the self-world relationship or it does so indirectly by referencing either the self, or the world, or both.

Any view of the self or of the world implies a particular self-world relationship. We cannot see ourselves as Buddhists, Christians, Muslims, Socialists, or Flat-worlders without this implying ways of acting, thinking, and feeling in the world. Nor can we see the world as flat or round, as a playground for our pleasure, as an exciting but dangerous place, or as our science or our religion regards it, without also implying ways of acting, thinking, and feeling in relation to it.

Any idea, belief, or viewpoint we can have about anything, whether conscious or unconscious, verbal or nonverbal, must reference something in human experience. This means it must reference either something about the self, something about the world, or something about the relationship between the two – which means, in turn, that it is, in essence, a view of the self-world relationship.

Relational Perspectives That can Become Actual

A View of the Relationship That can Become Operational

We can take it, moreover, that it is a view of the self-world relationship that can become actual or operational if used as a situational response.

If we are deeply attached to a God we believe made the world a pleasure garden for our enjoyment, we will have a particular view of the relationship of self to world and will act, think, and feel accordingly when we apply that viewpoint to particular situations we encounter. If we have learned to see ourselves as hedonists or to see the world as an exciting, enjoyable place, we will have a similar view of the self-world relationship and will act, think, and feel in a similar way if we apply that view in situations we encounter. Each of these viewpoints implies a similar – though not necessarily identical – view of the self-world relationship that can become operational or actual if used as a situational response.

Even ideas about narrow aspects of the world or the self – a belief that 'warm milk is full of germs', say, or that 'walking with a limp is unmanly' – will affect our self-world relationship and our consequent behaviour and experience in circumstances where they are a factor. Even meaningless or nonsensical notions will.

Imagine a man really does believe that warm milk is full of germs and that walking with a limp is unmanly. How will he react if he finds himself in a position where he has to walk across the room to a woman he finds attractive and wants to make a good impression on if he has just twisted his ankle? How will he react if he simultaneously sees his young son raise an old, open carton of tepid milk to his lips?

He may or may not react to the situation in terms of his two beliefs, but if he does, they will affect how he responds to the situation and will influence how he acts, thinks, and feels in it. His beliefs will interact with the circumstances of the situation itself to determine his actual behavioural and experiential relationship to the world in the circumstances in question. They will give him a particular view of his self-world relationship in that situation and essentially make that view of his self-world relationship his actual self-world relationship. He will act, think, and feel like a man who believes that warm milk is full of germs and that walking with a limp is unmanly.

Or imagine a woman has been doodling on a notebook cover and writes down 'rankorungs are really defilbubs' one day, then finds herself a few weeks later taking part in a psychology experiment. In it, she is asked to enter a room, read the message on the table, and do what it tells her to do. She walks in and finds only her notebook with her doodle on the cover – a nonsensical and meaningless idea that seems to say nothing about how she should react to it.

She does react, though. Perhaps she just stands there looking nonplussed, or maybe she responds like a suddenly enlightened student of a Zen master might and rips off the cover and begins to eat her words. Either way, even this nonsensical and meaningless idea made to dominate her acting, thinking, and feeling momentarily by the experimenter's instructions interacts with the circumstances to determine her behavioural and experiential relationship to the world.

It says nothing specific or meaningful about that relationship – or, rather, it says something empty and meaningless about it that causes her to react to an empty and meaningless view of her self-world relationship and act, think, and feel accordingly.

Available Self-World Perspectives: A Very Large Set

On this basis, the number of views of the self-world relationship each of us has available to us as possible behavioural and experiential determinants is potentially very large. Any conscious or unconscious idea, belief, or viewpoint we can have about anything encompasses a perspective on our self-world relationship that can help determine how we act, think, and feel if used as a situational response.

This applies even to views that relate to a narrow aspect of the world or the self or that are nonsensical and meaningless. Any such view, if used as a situational response, will interact with the situational circumstances to affect how we act, think, and feel in the situation in question. Any idea, belief, or viewpoint we can have about anything encompasses a view of the self-world relationship and can make that relationship operational if used as a situational response.

Meaningful and correct views like 'the world is round' will do this, as will incorrect views like 'the world is flat and a person can fall over its edge'. Even meaningless views like 'rankorungs are really defilbubs' will have this effect.

Nor is it necessarily the case that meaningless or incorrect views are valueless in this respect. A clown might usefully adopt the perspective and persona of someone who believes 'rankorungs are really defilbubs' to make people laugh at his consequent acting, thinking, and feeling. A teacher might usefully adopt the perspective and persona of someone who believes the incorrect claim that the world is made of blancmange in order to illustrate to children how science might go about testing the idea.

All Ideas can Impact our Self-World Relationship

If the case presented above is sound, any idea we can have about anything can affect our behaviour and experience in this fashion. Any and every idea, belief, or viewpoint we can have about anything is essentially a perspective on the self-world relationship that can become an actual behavioural and experiential relationship if used as a situational response.

On this basis, we can think of all of our ideas, beliefs, and viewpoints, conscious or unconscious, as potential self-world relationships that can become actual relationships. We can think of them as potential when they simply exist in the mental landscape as possible future situational responses – as idea-based self-world perspectives. We can think of them as actual when they – and the idea-based self-world perspectives they encompass – are chosen as operational responses in particular circumstances. As should become clear as we move forward, thinking of them in these terms is helpful and useful in the context of our attempt to establish the requirements of a self-view that accurately reflects our full behavioural and experiential nature.

Every Idea Helps Determine our Total Relationship

Every Idea a Potential Determinant

It will be assumed in what follows that the points argued in this chapter hold true. Any conscious or unconscious idea, belief, or viewpoint about anything is a view of our self-world relationship that can determine our actual relationship if used as a situational response.

We can then extend the conclusion drawn in Chapter 2 as regards the determinants of the human behavioural and experiential relationship to both individual situations and the world generally. We can add detail to the assertion that it is determined by how the range of our consciously or unconsciously held views of our own or the human self-world relationship interacts with our own physical state and that of the world. We can add that every possible idea, belief, and viewpoint we can have about anything is a potential member of that range. Every one of them is a potential determinant of both our situational behavioural and experiential relationship and our overarching behavioural and experiential relationship to the world, the latter relationship encompassing all of the idea-based self-world perspectives in our repertoire, whatever situation or situations they apply to.

If the example-based case made above is sound, any and every idea we can have about anything is a perspective on the self-world relationship that can have an impact on our behavioural and experiential relationship in any and every circumstance encountered by being instantiated and utilised as a situational response. Every possible idea we can have about anything is a potential determinant of our behavioural and experiential relationship to the world in any situation encountered, and hence to the world generally. They are all members of the range of views that can affect both our situational and overarching behavioural and experiential relationship and will be assumed to be so in what follows.

All Ideas Aspects of our Total Relationship

They are also, by extension, all aspects of any overarching or total perspective on the human self-world relationship that purports to be complete. An overarching self-world perspective or self-view that accurately reflects our full behavioural and experiential nature must encompass each and every one of them; it must entail every idea we can possibly have about anything. Every one of them entails a perspective on the human self-world relationship that can have a behavioural and experiential effect when it is used as a situational response; they are all potential determinants of how we act, think, and feel in the world. Every one of them is a perspective on the human self-world relationship that impacts some aspect of the actual human behavioural and experiential relationship to the world.

Collectively, they comprise the whole set of views of the human self-world relationship that determine and create the actual total human behavioural and experiential relationship to the world. Individually, therefore, we can think of them as relatively narrow idea-based subsidiary perspectives on the human behavioural and experiential relationship to the world – subsidiary perspectives that collectively determine the actual full relationship by making their relatively narrow perspective operational when used as a situational response. They are all subsidiary views of our total self-world relationship that instantiate subsidiary aspects of that total relationship when used as situational responses.

All Ideas Reflect Aspects of our Nature

This means that an overarching self-world perspective or self-view that accurately reflects our full behavioural and experiential nature must take account of each and every one of these idea-based subsidiary self-world perspectives. It means that any total perspective on the human self-world relationship must encompass each and every one of these subsidiary perspectives if it is to accurately reflect our full behavioural and experiential nature. To fail to do so is to fail to reflect the aspect of that nature determined by whichever subsidiary perspectives have been omitted.

If every idea we can possibly have about anything entails a perspective on the human self-world relationship that partially determines that relationship, they all make a contribution to our total or overarching behavioural and experiential relationship and must all be encompassed in any complete perspective on that relationship.

All Ideas are Aspects of a Self-View for Humans

Clearly, these various idea-based and narrowly focused subsidiary perspectives on the human self-world relationship play a key role in our attempt in this book to address the question of what an adequate self-view for humans should look like and be like. This should already be evident from the points discussed in this chapter and the last. It will become more so in the next chapter, where it will be argued that our overarching behavioural and experiential relationship (in essence, our self; see Chapter 7) can either be fixed or wholly-variable in nature. Our overarching behavioural and experiential relationship, or self, can be either fixed or wholly-variable depending on how many of these subsidiary (idea-based and narrowly focused) self-world relationships we have available to us and how we treat them.

Addendum: Knowing That and Knowing How
Both Entail Perspectives on our Self-World Relationship

Note that the distinction made between 'knowledge that' (that the world is round, or the sun is a star, for example) and 'knowledge how' (how to swim or turn a somersault, for example), much discussed and argued over in philosophical circles (see, e.g., Brandt, 2021; Ren, 2012;

Stanley and Williamson, 2001), is not seen as important here. Both types of knowledge are taken as included in the assertion that any conscious or unconscious idea, belief, or viewpoint we can have about anything encompasses a perspective on our self-world relationship that can help determine how we act, think, and feel in any situation we encounter. Any one example of either type can help determine how we act, think, and feel in a situation where they are available to us and are consciously or unconsciously selected as a situational response.

Knowing That

This is easiest to see where knowledge that is concerned. *Knowing that* Paris is an expensive place to holiday is a self-world perspective that might well come into play if a partner suggests a holiday there, indicating the need (say) to allocate a higher budget than usual to an agreed holiday. *Knowing that* Alice is better at fixing broken iPhones than Horace is a self-world perspective that might well come into play if a person's current iPhone was in need of repair and a new purchase was too expensive. *Knowing that* the moon's gravity is about 17% of Earth's is a self-world perspective that might well come into play when designing a spacesuit for a walk on the moon.

Knowledge that always expresses some fact that can only relate to the self, the world, or the self-world relationship (the only three possibilities) – one that can and sometimes will influence our acting, thinking, and feeling where it is relevant to a situation encountered. All possible instances of *knowledge that* encompass a perspective on our self-world relationship that can help determine how we act, think, and feel if we encounter a situation where the fact entailed has a bearing on how we might best react to that situation.

Knowing How

That *knowing how* encompasses a perspective on our self-world relationship that can help determine how we act, think, and feel if it is applied in a given situation is perhaps less evident, but no less true.

Knowing how to (say) play a trombone well in a practical sense is obviously different to *knowing that* a form of words and pictures in a book explains how to play trombone. The *knowing that* may lead to the *knowing how* after much repetition of an intelligent and informed form of trial and error, but it is not the same as the *knowing how* as such. Someone who we can describe as *knowing that* this is the way a trombone is played cannot be accurately described as *knowing how* to play trombone in the practical and practised sense purely on the basis of his *knowing that* it is played by following the instructions in the book.

That said, we can agree, surely, that someone we describe as *knowing how* to play trombone in the practical and practised sense is, when actually playing, exhibiting or instantiating a complex and nuanced experiential and behavioural self-world relationship comprising a set of sub-relationships that change as the playing proceeds. We can also reasonably assume that this is being driven and guided by a complex and nuanced associated self-world perspective set, which is probably largely unconscious most of the time, but must be in place all the same. The playing, we must presume, is not a random act, after all. Some form of brain-based programming is in control of how the player is relating to the world while playing – an algorithm that could be expressed in words and pictures as an admittedly very complex and extensive perspective on the player's dominant self-world relationship set when playing.

The book mentioned above on how to play the trombone would clearly and obviously describe in words and pictures how the player should relate to the world when playing. Adding a description of how the player is relating to the world when playing in the practised sense to the book and turning this into more detailed instructions would offer a more detailed account of how the player should relate to the world when playing. Neither version of the book would amount to *knowing how* to play the trombone, but they would both describe, at less and more detailed levels, the self-world perspective that needs to be in place as *knowledge how* when playing in a practical sense is occurring.

Knowing That and Knowing How: Similar in at Least One Sense

Knowledge that and *knowledge how* may or may not be different categories of knowledge in other respects, but both in some sense encompass a perspective on the self-world relationship that can determine how we act, think, and feel in particular situations. They are both included in the assertion that any conscious or unconscious idea, belief, or viewpoint we can have about anything encompasses a perspective on our self-world relationship that can help determine how we act, think, and feel in any situation we encounter. Any one example of either type can help determine how we act, think, and feel in a situation where they are available to us and are consciously or unconsciously selected as a situational response.

4

A Fixed or Wholly-Variable Total Relationship?

All Perspectives Equal as Possible Responses or not?

Wholly-Variable or Fixed Overarching Relationships

The conclusions drawn in Chapter 3 have an important bearing on the search for a self-view that accurately reflects our full behavioural and experiential nature. If every idea we can possibly have about anything is a potential determinant of our total behavioural and experiential relationship to the world in any situation encountered, and they must all be encompassed in any complete perspective on that relationship, the self-view we are seeking must reflect this. It must be designed so that, in any and every situation encountered, all such relatively narrow subsidiary perspectives are included in the self-view, and each initially has an equal chance of being chosen and used as a situational response – that there are no blocks in place preventing this. To put this more precisely, it must be designed to ensure that all such idea-based subsidiary self-world perspectives are possible responses *prior* to the circumstances of the situation in question being utilised as a means of (consciously or unconsciously) selecting the response most appropriate to those circumstances. In the terminology used here (as introduced in Chapter 1), it must be designed to permit and support a wholly-variable response.

A self-view that fails on this front – one whose design either blocks the use of some of these subsidiary self-world perspectives or entails a bias against their use prior to the operation of this response selection mechanism – fails to accurately reflect our full behavioural and experiential nature. By blocking the use of some of these subsidiary self-world perspectives *prior to the selection of a situational response*, it fails to reflect the fact that every conceivable one of them is equally able to act as a situational response in all situations. In the terminology used here, it supports an artificially fixed overarching response and self-world relationship rather than a wholly-variable one.

Wholly-Variable: Every Perspective a Potential Determinant

The case in favour of this position goes like this: If the conclusion drawn in Chapter 3 is valid, any and every possible idea-based subsidiary perspective on the human self-world relationship is a potential determinant of how we act, think, and feel in any situation we encounter. This means that our full behavioural and experiential nature is wholly-variable; it can and will vary according to which of the possible subsidiary perspectives on our self-world relationship is used as a response in any and every situation encountered. Any given member of this total set may or may not be an appropriate response to this situation or that, but it *is* a possible response – a potential response in any given situation encountered. A self-view whose design either blocks or entails a bias against the use of certain idea-based subsidiary self-world perspectives prior to response selection ensures that some of them cannot be chosen as a response, whether they are appropriate to a situation or not. It ensures that a response in any particular situation is determined by only a limited subset of all of the idea-based subsidiary self-world perspectives that could determine a given situational response.

A self-view that entails such blocks cannot be regarded as accurately reflecting our full behavioural and experiential nature because it artificially 'includes out' a range of subsidiary self-world perspectives that would otherwise be able to determine our behavioural and experiential response to situations we encounter. It takes a group of idea-based subsidiary self-world perspectives able to determine our behavioural and experiential nature and ensures they are unable to do so by including them out *prior to the selection of a situational response*. It ensures that our actual behavioural and experiential relationship in any and every situation encountered is determined by this artificially limited subset of all of the idea-based subsidiary self-world perspectives that could potentially be determinants of that relationship. It cannot be regarded as a self-view that accurately reflects our full behavioural and experiential nature because it allows that nature to be defined by a limited subset of the idea-based subsidiary perspectives that can be determinants of that nature (and therefore should define it).

A self-view without such blocks – one designed so that every conceivable idea-based subsidiary self-world perspective is a possible response prior to the operation of the response selection mechanism – *can* be regarded as a self-view that accurately reflects our full behavioural and experiential nature. It does not take a group of the subsidiary self-world perspectives able to contribute to the definition of our behavioural and experiential nature and ensure that they are unable to make that contribution by including them out prior to the selection of a situational response. It ensures that any and every idea-based subsidiary self-world perspective that can determine our response in any situation is potentially able to do so by not including any of them out prior to the operation of the response selection mechanism. Some of these will be appropriate responses to any given situation, and some will not, but a response selection mechanism that takes account of the situational internal and external environmental factors will take care of that.

If every possible idea, belief, or viewpoint we can have about anything is a potential determinant of our behavioural and experiential relationship to the world in any situation encountered, our behavioural and experiential nature is determined and defined by all of the subsidiary self-world perspectives inherent in these views. A self-view that prevents some of these subsidiary self-world perspectives from ever contributing to that relationship cannot be regarded as a self-view that reflects our full behavioural and experiential nature. A self-view that enables all such subsidiary self-world perspectives to be possible responses in any situation encountered prior to the operation of the response selection mechanism can be so regarded. It can be regarded as accurately reflecting our full behavioural and experiential nature in every situation encountered and therefore in the world at large. (We shall see later how it is possible to design a self-view so that all such idea-based subsidiary self-world perspectives are potential responses in any situation encountered, even though this means designing a self-view open to a near-infinite number of perspectives, including even unknown and undiscovered varieties.)

The kind of self-view labelled here as wholly-variable is an overarching self-world perspective or self-view able to fully reflect our behavioural and experiential nature by permitting and supporting a wholly-variable response. The kind we have labelled a fixed self-view is not. It supports a non-wholly-variable or fixed response.

A Fixed or Wholly-Variable Overarching Relationship?

Our Total Relationship: Either Wholly-Variable or Fixed

This distinction between a fixed and a wholly-variable response has a significant bearing on our search for a self-view that accurately reflects our full behavioural and experiential nature – on two counts.

The first is the obvious point that it helps us begin to define what is meant here by a self-view that accurately reflects our full behavioural and experiential nature. If, as is assumed in this work, the argument outlined above is sound, it is a self-view designed to permit and support a wholly-variable response.

The second is that comparing and contrasting this type of self-view with the fixed type helps us begin to pin down what permitting and supporting a wholly-variable response actually means in practice. It helps us draw out the first design requirement of a self-view that accurately reflects our full behavioural and experiential nature and also provides a basis for drawing out others.

We can say on the basis of the above that our total or overarching behavioural and experiential relationship to the world can be thought of as being one of two things. It can be thought of as either wholly-variable or fixed, depending on whether or not the whole range of idea-based subsidiary self-world perspectives is available for use in an unbiased way prior to the selection of a situational response. If the case made in Chapter 3 is accepted, every possible idea, belief, or viewpoint we can have about anything – any one of the full set of possible subsidiary self-world perspectives – can act to determine how any human acts, thinks, and feels in any given situation. This means that our real realisable total behavioural and experiential relationship to both the world at large and any individual situation encountered is one defined equally by every conceivable idea-based subsidiary self-world perspective, rather than just a limited sub-set or a set entailing a bias for one or more sub-sets over others.

Wholly-Variable in Theory; Fixed in Practice

In theory, every one of these subsidiary perspectives is a possible response choice in any given situation, and no one of them is more or less able to be used in this way than any other. In theory, all are equally valid members of the full set of response options able to be used in any given situation prior to the circumstances of that situation being utilised as a means of (consciously or unconsciously) selecting the response most appropriate to those circumstances. In theory, our full or total behavioural and experiential relationship to the world is defined and determined by all of them equally. In practice, however, artificial fixing caused by various factors – including our own mental habits, assumptions, and emotional attachments – is probably the norm given the way we usually develop.

More will be said about this over the next three chapters as we work towards drawing out the first design requirement of an overarching self-world perspective or self-view that accurately reflects our full behavioural and experiential nature. The aim in the remainder of the present chapter is to begin to clarify further what is meant here by the terms fixed and wholly-variable in respect of the range of idea-based subsidiary self-world perspectives equally available to us as possible behavioural and experiential responses.

Wholly-Variable and Fixed: Definitions
All Equally Valid Versus Limited and Biased

Put briefly, a wholly-variable total or overarching behavioural and experiential perspective or self-view is one that encompasses every one of the full set of all possible subsidiary self-world perspectives and gives no special weight to any one of them prior to the selection of a situational response. A wholly-variable total or overarching behavioural and experiential relationship is one supported by such a wholly-variable total or overarching behavioural and experiential perspective or self-view. A fixed total or overarching behavioural and experiential perspective or self-view is one for which these things are not true in some sense – where the options available as a response to any given situation encountered are either limited in some way, or biased in some way, or both. A fixed relationship is a human behavioural and experiential relationship that, instead of being wholly-variable as it can and should be, is to a greater or lesser extent (depending on the exact nature of the bias and limitations) relatively fixed. It is a behavioural and experiential relationship determined by a set of idea-based subsidiary self-world perspectives that is either limited, positively or negatively weighted in some way, or (more probably) both. An artificially fixed relationship.

What is meant here by a wholly-variable relationship is one that reflects our real realisable behavioural and experiential relationship to the world at large. A relationship supported by an overarching self-world perspective that encompasses the full set of all possible idea-based subsidiary self-world perspectives and gives no special weight to any one of them prior to the selection of a situational response (so that the relationship is defined by all of them equally). What is meant by a fixed or artificially fixed relationship is one that is not defined equally by all such subsidiary self-world perspectives in this way. One where the various influences mentioned above make the relationship less than wholly-variable, either by limiting the range of subsidiary self-world perspectives available as potential responses to a situation, or by introducing various kinds of bias and unequal treatment prior to or during the selection process, or both. Some perspectives that can affect behaviour and experience are either actually removed from the range of possibilities considered through non-inclusion or effectively removed through a bias against their use or for the use of others. They are taken out of the total or overarching self-world perspective or given an artificially low weighting within it, making it less than wholly-variable in the sense meant here; making it (and the overarching relationship it supports) fixed – restricted in some way.

Fixed-Self-Based Variability: Not Wholly-Variable

In a case where the resulting restriction is to a low number of viewpoints, this fixed rather than wholly-variable circumstance will tend to be fairly evident to the observer. The extreme example of someone who only and always sees the world in terms of the simple subsidiary self-world perspective that is the flat world theory and cannot do otherwise would be a case in point. A person like this will act, think, and feel in very limited ways – especially if he is unaware that it is just a way of seeing the world and actually just assumes that flat with an edge you can fall over is how the world is.

In cases where the level of restriction is determined by a more varied set of such subsidiary perspectives, the fixed nature of the total relationship may be less evident. An example of this type might be the kind of wide-ranging but still limited group of views on self and world we'd expect to find in a Buddhist and Socialist motorist with an open mind on the flat versus round world question. Here we might find that the wider and more varied set of idea-based subsidiary self-world perspectives entailed, together with a degree of actual response choice in some situations, would give the appearance of a variable relationship, particularly in situations where the flat versus round world question was at issue.

Any such appearance would be misleading, however; the degree of variability entailed is of a lower order. If the number of individual idea-based subsidiary self-world perspectives in play was restricted or biased in some way – as with someone with the viewpoints of a Buddhist and Socialist motorist but not those of a Muslim and Centrist, pedestrian, say – the circumstance would be the same in either case. The resulting overarching or total relationship would be fixed rather than wholly-variable in the sense meant here. It would be limited to the relatively small range of possible responses embodied within the restricted number of individual subsidiary self-world perspectives in play, and hence not what is meant here by wholly-variable. Some idea-based subsidiary relationships that are part of the total or overarching relationship – or should be because they can be – have been blocked out because the perspectives that support them have been blocked out.

The term wholly-variable – clarified further in later chapters – refers to circumstances where there are no blocks on the inclusion of all possible idea-based subsidiary self-world perspectives, not to the limited level of overall variability that may exist within a relatively varied but limited set of such perspectives. The degree of variability that any relatively varied but limited set of such subsidiary perspectives may entail represents only a less than comprehensive level of variability *within* that limited set of subsidiary perspectives. If the overall relationship is determined by a limited range of these subsidiary self-world perspectives rather than by all of them, then it is not wholly-variable in the sense meant here. It is artificially fixed – determined by only a limited subset of all of the possible idea-based subsidiary perspectives on the total human self-world relationship as described in Chapter 3, rather than by all of them.

A Fixed Self-World Relationship Tends to be the Norm

Having defined these terms, we can now examine the notion of artificial fixing and the fixed self in more detail. Various aspects of the question are looked at over the next three chapters, with three aims in mind.

The first is to argue that artificial fixing of our overarching self-world relationship through a restriction of the range of idea-based subsidiary self-world perspectives encompassed within the overarching self-world perspective or self-view that supports it can and probably does happen to most, if not all, of us as we develop.

The second is to argue that, if it does happen, the whole of the resulting artificially fixed perspective is effectively a self-view that misdefines us and makes that misdefinition operationally true (even though we may neither think of it nor have intentionally developed it as a self-view).

The third is to push forward with the main focus of this work – by using this misdefinition issue to draw out the first requirement of a self-view that accurately reflects our full behavioural and experiential nature and lay the groundwork for establishing some of the others.

5

Artificial Fixing can Happen as we Develop

Artificial Fixing: Causes and Effects

Chapters 5-7 examine artificial fixing in more detail. Chapter 5 looks at causes and argues that artificial fixing of our overarching self-world perspective and relationship can happen in the normal course of human development through the operation of a wide range of factors, including our own habits, assumptions, and emotional attachments. Chapter 6 argues that artificial fixing of this kind probably happens to most, if not all, of us in the normal course of human development and further strengthens the case presented in Chapter 5. Chapter 7 argues that such artificial fixing is something to be avoided, especially if we are designing a self-view that accurately reflects our full (wholly-variable) behavioural and experiential nature, and that this is true even if the point argued in Chapter 6 is not.

The case made on this last point is that, if it does happen, artificial fixing misdefines us and makes that misdefinition operationally true, and that this is something to be avoided, whether it probably happens to most of us or not. Recognising this misdefinition issue leads us to the first of several design requirements of the self-view for humans we are seeking – specifically, that it must be a self-view that makes an accurate definition, rather than a misdefinition, of our behavioural and experiential nature operationally true.

Routes to a Fixed Relationship: Programming the Brain

Overview

The case for the claim that artificial fixing of our overarching self-world perspective and the associated self-world relationship can happen in the normal course of human development rests on two things. The first is a known feature of the brain called neuroplasticity. This, in essence, allows the things we experience as we move through our lives to alter the structure and functioning of our brains in ways that help determine our subsequent acting, thinking, and feeling behaviours. The second is a set of readily imaginable examples of environmental circumstances that illustrate how artificial fixing of our overarching self-world perspective and relationship can happen as we develop via the effects of such environmental circumstances on our malleable brain. Not that it does happen necessarily, only that it can or might happen in the normal course of human development – all we are seeking to show at this stage.

Neuroplasticity Changes the Brain

Our brains are able to change structure and function in response to the internal and external things we experience as we develop, strengthening, weakening, or modifying existing neural pathways and networks and creating new ones as required (see, for example: Fuchs & Flügge, 2014; Medow, 2011; Shaffer, 2016). It is this 'neuroplasticity' that allows us to acquire new ways of acting, thinking, and feeling in response to situations we encounter and alter those already acquired when circumstances require it – to learn and recall new ways of experientially and behaviourally reacting to our environment as we develop.

Causes and Effects

Evidence suggests that our neuroplastic abilities are present throughout our lives, from childhood to our later years (see, e.g., Pauwels et al., 2018), that their effects can be both positive and negative (see, e.g., Peterson, 2012; Sale et al., 2014), and that the learning processes involved can be conscious or unconscious (see, e.g., Askenasy and Lehmann, 2013; Taschereau-Dumouchel et al., 2018). These abilities can allow us to acquire and embed habitual ways of acting, thinking, and feeling that can be bad, good, or indifferent in terms of their impact on both ourselves and the world at large. Experiencing rich and stimulating environments as we grow tends to have a positive impact on our behavioural and experiential capabilities and tendencies; experiencing poorer environments tends to have the opposite effect (see, e.g., Lipina & Posner, 2012; Noble et al., 2021; Sale et al., 2014).

Scientific evidence for neuroplasticity and a growing understanding of its workings have been acquired through research in a range of areas. Studies have shown its impact on the acquisition of musical skills (see, e.g., Münte et al., 2002), in the learning of languages (see, e.g., Li et al., 2014), in the treatment of depression (see, e.g., Brunoni et al., 2008), in learning computer programming (see, e.g., Hongo et al., 2022), and in a variety of other areas (game-playing (Lee et al., 2010), juggling (Malik et al., 2022), learning morse code (Schmidt-Wilcke et al., 2010), and others). Mental imagery can bring about neuroplastic changes, whether consciously or unconsciously applied (see, e.g., Doidge, 2008; Kuldas et al., 2013; Skottnik & Linden, 2019; Taschereau-Dumouchel et al., 2018).

Neuroplasticity-based brain changes induced by new experiences allow our brains to acquire new ways of acting, thinking, and feeling; they are how we learn and maintain our various ways of viewing and relating to the world. Whatever happens to our overarching self-world perspective and self-world relationship as we develop happens through the neuroplasticity-based effects of our experiences on our brains and our subsequent acting, thinking, and feeling behaviours. It is what underpins the development of an overarching self-world perspective and relationship, whether fixed or wholly-variable.

Rewiring or Programming?

Although there are exceptions (see, e.g., Albert, 2019; Slors, 2015), it is common in neuroplasticity research to talk about our experiences 'wiring and rewiring' the brain (see, e.g., Merzenich, 2013; Mitrovic et al., 2011; Sebastianelli et al., 2017), rather than programming and reprogramming it, which is the terminology employed below. The two terminologies refer to the same process but reflect a different focus.

The use of 'wiring and rewiring' reflects the fact that, as should be evident from the above notes on neuroplasticity, what we experience can actually update the hardware and software of our brains. Different neural pathways and networks 'form and fall dormant, are created, and are discarded' as we develop (Ackerman, 2018). The focus in such cases is on the *effects* of experience on brain structure and functioning. The focus with the 'programming and reprogramming' terminology used below is on the experiential *causes* of the wiring and rewiring.

An Important Distinction

The distinction is an important one for the case being developed here. When a teacher or trainer sets out to provide a learning or training environment to change the brains of the individuals who will take it, they are not thinking in terms of creating or moulding neural pathways, but in terms of giving participants experiences that will fashion new behaviours. The same is true of a person who participates in such training or teaching experiences. The aim is to acquire new acting, thinking, and feeling behaviours that will be useful or interesting in some future set of circumstances by participating in learning or training experiences fashioned with that aim in mind. The experiences are created and participated in with a view to programming the new acting, thinking, and feeling behaviours into the response sets of the participants. They are being used, in essence, to programme the brain to support these new acting, thinking, and feeling behaviours using a programming language the individual understands and the individual's brain responds to.

Neither group is setting out to wire and rewire brains in a direct sense, and could not effect the desired wiring and rewiring if they attempted to do so in this direct sense. They are setting out to 'programme' changes in acting, thinking, and feeling behaviours by inducing experiences that the brain will respond to by wiring and rewiring in ways that support the behaviours.

Rewiring is not the Immediate Aim

The distinction is important here because, as the arguments presented in the book develop, we will increasingly have a requirement to discuss circumstances where there is a conscious intention to fashion and use experiential circumstances to influence future acting, thinking, and feeling behaviours in particular ways.

In such circumstances, the focus of the conscious intention will tend to be things like mentally envisaging and rehearsing responding to certain situations with particular actions, thoughts, and feelings that cause neuroplasticity-based changes to our brains rather than mentally envisaging and rehearsing the associated wiring and rewiring as such. Mentally envisaging and rehearsing the associated wiring and rewiring would not have the desired effect, even if such envisaging and rehearsing were possible. Only envisaging and rehearsing the desired acting, thinking, and feeling behaviours themselves will have the desired effect – hence the need here to refer to the process in terms of programming the brain rather than in terms of the wiring and rewiring of the brain effected by this programming.

Not Quite Like Computer Programming

Although there is a degree of overlap, this is not quite programming in the sense meant when we refer to programmers writing code to have computers carry out certain tasks. What is meant by brain programming in the present context encompasses all of the aspects of neuroplasticity described above. It can even entail neurogenesis – the creation of new neurons from stem cells (Abdissa et al., 2020; Drigas et al., 2018).

Our experiences create neuroplasticity-based changes in our brains that programme us to act, think, and feel in particular ways in particular circumstances in ways that involve changes to the brain's physical form and structure as well as to the instructions encoded within it. They update the hardware of our brains as well as the software, but the impact is otherwise similar. The neuroplasticity of our brain allows the things we experience as we move through our lives to alter its structure and functionality in ways that help determine our subsequent acting, thinking, and feeling behaviours.

Things we Experience can Programme the Brain

This having been clarified, we can now move on to defending the claim that artificial fixing of our overarching self-world perspective and relationship can happen in the normal course of human development through the operation of a wide range of factors, including our own habits, assumptions, and emotional attachments. Of necessity, the case is based not on empirical evidence but on presenting examples that readers will recognise from general human experience as credible indications that the claim is true (although we can arguably find indicative evidence that this is so in the human population; see Chapter 6).

The case goes like this: As was argued in Chapter 4, our overarching behavioural and experiential relationship to the world can become fixed rather than wholly-variable when we become habituated to responding to it in terms of a subsidiary self-world perspective set that is either limited in scope, biased in some way, or both. This can happen if our brains can become wired or rewired – programmed in the sense outlined above – so that artificial fixing of our overarching self-world perspective (and, hence, of our overarching self-world relationship) is the end result. It can happen if our experience-based programming can result in us having only a limited subset of all possible idea-based subsidiary self-world perspectives available as possible responses in any situation encountered and blocks and biases in place that prevent a response from outwith that limited set.

We know the things we experience as we develop can change the brain in ways that can affect how we subsequently act, think, and feel in the world (see above). If we can identify circumstances in which the personal and external influences encountered as we develop could change our brains – programme them – so that our overarching self-world perspective and relationship becomes artificially fixed as defined in Chapter 4, we can conclude that the claim is true. We can conclude that artificial fixing of our overarching self-world perspective and relationship can occur in the normal course of human development if the circumstances we have identified can occur in the normal course of human development. Not that it necessarily does happen, just that it is possible that it could.

Factors That Might Programme the Brain

We can assume, both on the basis of the literature as sampled above and our own personal learning experiences, that the kinds of internal and external factors that might programme our brains for artificial fixing as we develop fall into one or more of three categories.

The first is conscious self-programming – we might consciously programme the brain via our own mental habits. We might create our own particular combination of a limited response set and blocks and biases that prevent moving beyond it by always rehearsing a particular view of ourselves and blocking out others by some means. We might, for example, habitually and consciously rehearse seeing ourselves as someone who acts, thinks, and feels (and is) like someone we admire and simultaneously block out any tendency to act, think, and feel like someone that person disapproves of (and do so till it essentially becomes true).

The second is unconscious, or semi-conscious, self-programming. Programming for the limited response set and the blocks and biases that prevent moving beyond it might occur in an unconscious or largely unconscious fashion. We might, for example, habitually rehearse being like someone we admire and unlike someone she disapproves of until it essentially becomes true, but be largely or wholly unconscious that we are doing it.

The third is conscious or unconscious programming by external agencies. The admired person might be a teacher who has consciously constructed a programme of experiences that induce particular ways of acting, thinking, and feeling and block out others, and the trainee might either be unaware he is being trained or may have consciously chosen to participate in the programme. One or more of these kinds of internal and external *factors* might programme our brains for artificial fixing.

How Artificial Fixing can Happen: Illustrative Examples

Can such factors programme the brain as we develop so that our overarching behavioural and experiential relationship becomes artificially fixed in the sense described in Chapter 4? Arguably, the answer is yes. The following examples illustrate the point.

Simple Fixing: Limited Knowledge Access and Skills

Imagine a relatively simple example, partly determined by external factors and partly by internal personal factors.

Imagine a person whose whole life is lived in a closed religious community where life is dominated by growing and harvesting food for the community, preparing and eating that food, keeping the community's buildings in good shape, taking care of the health of the community, and interacting with its other members. Imagine that this interaction is very largely ritualistic and that any other interactions centre around discussing their religion, other things from their daily life in the community, and aspects of the community's philosophical traditions, fictional output, and scientific understanding.

Imagine further that this person theoretically also has library access to all of the knowledge and other human output that ever existed – and so to every available idea-based subsidiary self-world perspective encompassed within it – but they cannot actually access it all because their skill set is too limited. Perhaps a range of digital age skills are required for access to the more recent elements, and these are not available to the person concerned, or there is some other impediment to accessing them. Imagine also that half of the documents she does have actual access to simply cover all aspects of life in the closed community – that all of the knowledge and other human output she might conceivably learn and use in her daily life is contained in them.

Imagine finally that the remainder of the documents she has actual access to relate to life, philosophy, fiction, and scientific understanding on a nearby island, where life is not identical but is nonetheless relatively similar. It does not cover life, philosophy, fiction, and scientific understanding in other, more developed areas of the planet, and especially not that of the most complex and advanced societies on the major landmasses.

Not Far-Fetched

This example is not far-fetched. We can readily imagine that the circumstances described might be encountered in the normal course of human development. We can also readily imagine that the result of developing in the circumstances described might be an artificially fixed overarching self-world relationship (i.e., one supported by an artificially fixed overarching self-world perspective encompassing only a limited subset of all possible subsidiary self-world perspectives). Not that it necessarily would be, but that it could be. The person described is only able to acquire a limited subset of all possible idea-based subsidiary self-world perspectives in the circumstances she is in, and her limited digital technology skills block the acquisition of any of the others from the total set.

We can, of course, imagine plausible circumstances in which this block would not be total. A book might wash up on the shore that would allow her to develop her skill set and access more of the library. She might encounter situations that might serendipitously teach her ways of seeing things that are otherwise only in the blocked part of the library. She might encounter a problem she does not have an immediate answer for but really needs to solve, and might find she has enough imagination and problem-solving skills to enable her to come up with new ways of seeing things that are otherwise blocked to her.

However, we can also imagine equally plausible circumstances in which the block on the extension of her acquired set of possible responses would be total. She may never encounter a means of extending her skill set. Life in her relatively closed community may never put her in circumstances where she learns new things; the response set she has learned in her closed community may have everything in it to allow an adequate response to every situation she encounters. She may never encounter a problem that acts as an impetus for imaginative or creative solutions from her own brain, or she may not have the mental abilities required to produce such solutions.

Even if she does add new ways of seeing things through serendipitous learning, or personal creative abilities, we can also imagine that there will be circumstances in which the expansion of her response set will in most cases be limited – that it will result in a slightly wider fixed set but still be artificially fixed in the sense meant here. Unless she has access by these means to all possible idea-based subsidiary self-world perspectives, the repertoire she has available will still be artificially fixed in the sense defined in Chapter 4. We can readily imagine plausible circumstances in which the example outlined above will not block the expansion beyond an initially artificially fixed overarching self-world perspective and relationship, but we can also imagine plausible circumstances in which it would.

This, of course, does not prove definitively that artificial fixing can occur in the normal course of human development. Proving this beyond doubt would require ensuring that the kinds of conditions described were in place in groups of humans who could then be compared with a control group in laboratory conditions, an impossible proposition at present. Arguably, however, it gives us reasonable grounds for concluding that it can occur. It shows us circumstances in which artificial fixing, in the sense meant here, can occur in the normal course of human development. It shows us it can occur in the entirely plausible circumstances described in the example above (and probably in other sets of circumstances similar to those in the example above).

Fixing can be Complex Too

The simple example above gives only a limited view of the factors likely to be involved in programming the brain so that our overarching self-world perspective and relationship becomes artificially fixed. A second example will add to the case presented above and also give a broader view of the factors in play.

In the first example, the limited response set entailed in the artificially fixed perspective and relationship had limited access to knowledge as its basis and extension of the set was prevented by the limited skill set of the person concerned. These are far from being the only possibilities, however.

The artificially fixed response set might be based on limited access to knowledge, and the block on extending the set might be based on the same thing – the limited access itself. Or the artificially fixed response set and the block on extending it might both be based on having only a limited skill set to draw on for building and extending the set rather than on limited access to knowledge as such. Or they each might be based on conscious or unconscious assumptions of completeness or truth, blocking any perspective outwith the set through an assumption that all necessary perspectives were already included.

A simple repetitive habit might be the problem – a situation where a person became so habituated to always and only using subsidiary self-world perspectives from one limited set that other subsidiary self-world perspectives were effectively blocked by the habit. Or perhaps just a science-, philosophy-, or belief-based intellectual preference for the limited set or a personal or interpersonal emotional preference for it (or both). The combination of an artificially fixed response set and the block on extending it required for artificial fixing might be based on any of the above – or, indeed, on a complex mix of some or all of them.

Complex Fixing: A Range of Factors and Influences

Imagine a person who habitually and determinedly makes a deliberate and conscious effort to always and only see themselves in one particular set of ways that blocks out all other possible ways. Imagine they make a habit of always mentally seeing themselves as Buddhist, not Christian, as Scottish, not Dutch, as left-wing, not right-wing, and so on, entirely basing their view of things on perspectives that block out others. Imagine they spend their lives continually rehearsing that view of themselves to the exclusion of all others, and that they ignore views of the self, the world, and the self in the world that fall outwith their preferred categories (Buddhist, Scottish, left-wing, etc.) entirely in their rehearsing.

Imagine, in addition, that they also make a habit of determinedly avoiding engagement with every possible source of ideas or viewpoints that do not fit into their rehearsed preferences – that they totally ignore people, communities, societies, countries, books, educational programmes, and so on, outside of these preferences. Imagine too that they inhabit a relatively closed society that makes such avoidance feasible, encourages it by blocking out offending ideas or viewpoints from schools, churches, libraries, communities, and so on, and ensures that every situation encountered can be adequately dealt with from within the person's rehearsed viewpoints repertoire. Imagine, in short, a person in very similar circumstances to the person in the simple example above.

Not Far-Fetched

As with that case, we can readily imagine that the circumstances described might be encountered in the normal course of human development. We can also readily imagine that the result of developing in the circumstances described might be an artificially fixed overarching self-world perspective and relationship – not that it necessarily would be, but that it could be. Since he is blocking out huge swathes of viewpoints in his mental rehearsing, the person concerned can only acquire a limited subset of all possible idea-based subsidiary self-world perspectives in the circumstances described, and his circumstances and personal prejudices would tend to block out any extension of that fixed set.

As with the simple example, we can, of course, imagine plausible circumstances in which this block would not be total. Some new threat might force him and his previously closed society to search through the perspectives of other societies and so widen their view of the world and their relationships to it, for example. Or something similar might cause him to encounter situations that might serendipitously teach him ways of seeing things that were previously inaccessible in his closed circumstances or spark his imagination and creative problem-solving skills to come up with perspectives on the world that were previously blocked out.

However, we can also imagine equally plausible circumstances in which the block on the extension of his acquired set of possible responses would be total. Circumstances in which his environment would not motivate a quest for new knowledge, where his imagination and creative solving skills would not be up to the task of extending his repertoire of perspectives, or where any extension would only result in a wider but equally fixed set. Unless he has access by these means to all possible idea-based subsidiary self-world perspectives, the repertoire he has available will still be artificially fixed in the sense defined in Chapter 4. We can readily imagine plausible circumstances in which the example outlined above will not lead to an artificially fixed overarching self-world relationship, but we can also imagine plausible circumstances in which it would.

Added Levels of Complexity

Now imagine that, in addition to the above, our left-wing Buddhist Scot does more than simply rehearse particular preferred ways of relating to the world.

Perhaps he grows up believing that his view of things tells him everything there is to know about the world and our relationship to it – that it is complete. Perhaps he grows up believing that it is not simply a 'view' but is how the world is. Perhaps he grows up believing both of these things, and these assumptions form an unconscious underpinning to the rehearsal of his fixed set of views.

Perhaps he attaches positive emotions to his preferred views and negative emotions to others – as a refugee saved from right-wing enemy soldiers at a young age, brought to his current closed society, and taught his Scottish, Buddhist, left-wing views by a beloved and now deceased teacher might.

Perhaps he simply uses his fixed viewpoints so regularly that using them and excluding perspectives not included becomes a habit hard or impossible to break – his brain so programmed by habit that it only has a set of more or less wholly fixed algorithms to operate within.

Perhaps he does all of these things simultaneously, basing his continuously rehearsed self-view on a clump of mental perspectives that limit his repertoire of subsidiary self-world perspectives, block its extension by avoiding circumstances that might add to it, and adding all of these other ingredients to the mix.

Extending the Fixed Set Made More Difficult

It is reasonable to assume, is it not, that if artificial fixing can happen without these additional factors in place in the circumstances described in the initial part of this second example, that adding these ingredients to the mix can act to make extending the fixed set more difficult? It is reasonable to hold that any and every possible mix of ingrained habit, positive and negative emotional attachments, and assumptions of truth and completeness might act as an additional barrier to seeking out new perspectives or discovering them through imagination and creative problem solving.

It is entirely plausible to argue that a brain programmed to habitually use certain perspectives, to assume that they offer a complete and wholly true view of things, and to feel emotionally positive towards them and negative towards others, might be less able to extend its preferred set. That it might be less likely to seek out new perspectives if the current set is assumed to be complete and wholly true, has positive emotional attachments, and is ingrained by habit. That it might be less able to see things in the new way required to discover new perspectives creatively if there are assumptions of truth and completeness, emotional biases, and ingrained ways of thinking and acting to block either discovery attempts or their success.

It is reasonable to assume, in other words, that adding these ingredients to the mix gives us additional reasons for holding that artificial fixing can happen in the normal course of human development. Not that these factors necessarily will increase the chances of artificial fixing, but that they might – there are plausible circumstances in which they might add to the likelihood of artificial fixing occurring in the normal course of human development.

None of this proves definitively that artificial fixing can occur in the normal course of human development any more than the simple example did. Once again, proving this beyond doubt would require ensuring that the kinds of conditions described were in place in groups of humans who could then be compared with a control group in laboratory conditions, an impossible proposition at present. Like the simple example, however, it arguably gives us reasonable grounds for concluding that it can occur. It shows us additional circumstances in which artificial fixing, in the sense meant here, can occur in the normal course of human development. It can happen as a result of the kind of conscious self-programming just described in the two examples above.

Other Types of Programming

It can also come about in other ways. As was suggested above, programming of an artificially fixed relationship need not come about as a result of conscious mental processes. It might equally arise as a result of unconscious or semi-conscious self-programming, as a result of programming by external agencies, or as a mix of these and of conscious efforts.

A person might create the same kind of artificially fixed perspectives and relationships as described above by regularly rehearsing their elements in ways he is wholly or partially unaware of. He might gradually assimilate the perspectives, attitudes, and philosophies of Buddhist, Scottish, or left-wing people he knows in his daily life, is impressed by, likes, and wants to impress, and simultaneously discard those of people he is unimpressed by, dislikes, and has no desire to emulate. He might, semi-consciously or unconsciously, strengthen these perspectives with positive and negative emotional elements, habitual use, and assumptions that the views held are complete, or are just how the world is.

Or he might become programmed in similar ways by external agencies of various kinds, with or without him being conscious that it is happening. A variety of external influences, negative, positive, or neutral, might lay down the brain programming that creates artificial fixing if repeated often enough, especially if the influences have sufficient impact to become viewpoints that are then regularly mentally rehearsed. A poor social learning environment that shows a person only a limited set of ways of seeing themselves and the world, blocks out the possibility of other points of view, and is experienced over a longish period might be one example. We can see, can we not, how it might leave him with a limited view of his relationship to the world and its challenges and be unable to see beyond it, especially if he worried over it a lot – habitually saw it as a self-defining thing?

Growing up in a small village that adhered strictly to some limited set of principles – one based on a particular religion, philosophy, or political colour, for example – might have the necessary effect and be wholly or largely unconscious. We can easily imagine how this might leave us with a limited set of responses to everyday events in our repertoire, a positive emotional view of adhering to these responses, and a negative emotional view of responding in a contrary fashion. We can also see how artificial fixing created in this way might come to be strengthened by habitual use, assumptions that the views espoused by the village are a complete set of possible views, or are just how the world actually is.

Other possibilities include a limited response set and associated blocks created by relatively long-term exposure to a teaching programme run by an inspiring teacher or parent consciously entered into, a sequence of dreams realised or dashed by external factors, apparently ongoing luck or ill-luck in love, and so on. External factors can also programme our brains so that our overarching self-world perspective and its associated behavioural and experiential relationship to the world become artificially fixed. We cannot argue that they always necessarily will, but it seems reasonable to conclude that they can.

A Greater Level of Complexity in Practice
A Complex Fixed Relationship Created in a Complex Way
Notice also that, if this fixing should occur, both the shape and form of any overarching fixed perspective and relationship created in these

ways and its mode or modes of creation are unlikely to be as simple and straightforward as is suggested by the examples offered above. The end result of programming by these various means is unlikely to be a simple one we can describe as a 'Buddhist, not Christian' fixed perspective and relationship or a 'left-wing, not right-wing' fixed perspective and relationship. It is far more likely to be a complex perspective and relationship where the result is better described as (for example) the overarching self-world perspective and relationship that defines 'Jo Jones, passport number 66534211, who is a Muslim, a Democrat, and a father, and has various individual idiosyncrasies too numerous to list'.

Nor can we necessarily assume the programming involved will itself be simple. Fixing due to the processes described in the examples above might or might not happen at the level of an overarching or total view of the self-world perspective. It might be that the result of these processes is to limit the response set to any and every situation encountered based on a limit learned at the overarching or total level of the whole organism, but it will not necessarily be so. It may be that the overall limit is set by a mix of subordinate groupings – preferences established at a variety of levels, from the overarching but circumstance-specific to the situation-specific (and encompassing all points in between). The result should be essentially the same regardless of the detail of how the processes operated – a response choice made in individual situations based on a limited set of subsidiary self-world perspectives rather than on the complete set of all possible subsidiary self-world perspectives. However, the detail of the fixed perspective and relationship itself and how it was formed will likely be more complex than the examples above imply.

The second example is a case in point. It is possible that the person described starts with a single overarching world-view that is Buddhist, not Christian, left-wing, not right-wing, and so on, and programmes his brain with repeated rehearsals to block out subsidiary self-world perspectives not included in this single view.

It is possible that he comes to use this single world-view habitually, to see it as complete and wholly true, and to develop an emotionally positive view of it, strengthening these blocks on subsidiary self-world perspectives not included in this single view. It is also possible, however, that this, or a similar artificially fixed end result, comes about in a more piecemeal fashion – that the overarching fixed relationship created is formed of, say, several subordinate groupings covering all Buddhist, all Scottish, and all political situations, and one covering something situation-specific. Imagine, for example, the person in the first example developing his Buddhist, Scottish, and left-wing fixed perspectives in entirely separate circumstances and also being a fisherman who has learned a fixed situation-specific flat-worlder perspective that applies only to fishing too far from shore.

Assuming that the outcomes in each case are artificially fixed, the end result will be roughly the same. In the case of the single overarching view, there might be what we can think of as a single algorithm in the brain blocking certain types of responses to situations encountered, whereas in the piecemeal version, there would be several. Assuming the blocks are total, however, the two circumstances would be roughly similar. The brain would be programmed so that when using the internal and external nature of a particular situation encountered to select a response, it would make the selection from a fixed subset of all possible idea-based subsidiary self-world perspectives rather than from all of them. Only a limited subset of all of the huge number of possible responses would be available, and the choice of a response from outwith that set would, in at least some encountered circumstances, be blocked by one or more of the various factors noted earlier. Assumptions of truth and completeness, positive emotional attachments, and simple habit would tend to favour responses from the preferred limited subset and tend to block out responses from outwith that set.

Programming and its Effects: Conscious or Unconscious?

Notice, moreover, that if this programming happens in the ways described, the person concerned might or might not experience either the resulting process of choosing a response in artificially fixed circumstances or the elements that contribute to the final choice consciously. Like their experiences of the factors that create their fixed selves, their experiences in these respects might be anything from wholly conscious to wholly unconscious to a mix of both and all points in between. If programmed in the various ways described above, a committed member of the Liberal Democrat Party consciously choosing between potential candidates for a forthcoming election might elect to vote for one rather than another based on a range of factors, some conscious and some unconscious. An unconscious dislike of an accent he unknowingly associates with a bad experience he had once might be one factor; a conscious disagreement on policy might be another.

A similarly programmed Christian, socialist, Scot who is also a devout Catholic and walks into a building without realising it is a church may immediately and automatically cross himself without consciously deciding to do so. His senses taking in information that allows the brain to identify a church without necessarily involving a conscious decision, and the brain's experience-based algorithm causing the action to occur without conscious thought. The same person who walks into the building knowing he is going into a church may consciously envisage crossing himself once inside before he opens the door, suggesting that the choice may have been conscious. However, it is also possible that the same algorithm simply made the choice automatically and only brought it to consciousness before the church was entered. The question of whether or not our decisions are conscious is a difficult area at best (see, e.g., Guggisberg & Mottaz, 2013; Mele, 2009), although there are undoubtedly some situations where a final decision on how to act requires conscious consideration. (When we determine that what we will do or say when we enter a room will depend on what and who we see when we do, for example.)

Conclusion

Regardless of how the process operates in detail in any individual case, it should be clear on the basis of the case presented above that the claim made at the head of the chapter is a reasonable one. Artificial fixing can happen in the normal course of our development as humans. It can occur in the entirely plausible circumstances described in the two examples above. We cannot claim that it will necessarily do so on the basis of these examples, but we can claim that it is possible that it might.

A further argument in favour of the claim that artificial fixing can happen in the normal course of human development will emerge in Chapter 6. The primary purpose there is to argue that artificial fixing of our overarching self-world perspective and relationship probably happens to most, if not all, of us as we develop, but the case made in the present chapter is strengthened in the process.

6

Artificial Fixing Probably Happens to Most

Fixing as we Develop

The claim that artificial fixing of our overarching self-world perspective and relationship as defined in Chapter 4 probably happens to most, if not all, of us as we develop is again difficult to prove definitively. As with the claim argued in Chapter 5, we would require scientifically acquired empirical evidence for this, and such evidence would almost certainly be impossible to obtain at present. There are, however, good reasons to take it as true, as will be shown below.

Gradual and Impractical by Normal Means

Gradual Acquisition: Part 1

The first point to note is that, in the normal way of things, we acquire new idea-based subsidiary self-world perspectives – new perspectives on the self, the world, and the self in the world – in a gradual fashion. This means that any attempt to avoid artificial fixing by adding all possible subsidiary self-world perspectives – any idea about anything – to our repertoire by normal means must, of necessity, be a gradual and ultimately impractical proposition (there being a close to unlimited number of them). And this, in turn, means that artificial fixing is probably the rule rather than the exception for all of us as we move through our lives.

There is no possible way in which our acquisition of even a subset of the huge numbers of perspectives on the self, the world, and the self in the world – any idea about anything as discussed in Chapter 3 – can be anything other than gradual. We cannot somehow magically acquire all of them at once in the normal way of things. It can only be done in a piecemeal fashion, and we all know that this is what happens. We acquire new ideas and perspectives in a gradual way as we develop. We cannot do otherwise. A mentally normal twenty-five-year-old man will have a wider range than his twenty-year-old self; his twenty-year-old self will have had more than his fifteen-year-old self; and so on.

With this in mind, think about a seven-year-old who moves to a new school. The teachers there want to discover what level of development he has reached, not just in terms of school work but in terms of his social development in the society he is growing up in. Over his seven years, he has gradually acquired a repertoire of some of the ideas that embody subsidiary self-world relationships – a relatively small number given that his experience only spans seven years. Clearly, he will have only a limited subset of all possible idea-based subsidiary self-world perspectives at his disposal as the teachers begin his assessment. Equally clearly, he will not have learned access to any subsidiary perspectives beyond that limited set. Access to these is effectively blocked since he has had no access to the experiences needed to programme the pathways in his brain that would give him this learned access. They cannot be used because they simply do not exist in his brain. Any access to subsidiary self-world perspectives outwith the limited set he has acquired would have to come about through an encounter with something hitherto beyond his experience.

A Limited Likelihood of Extension

There are various reasons why such an encounter might not occur in the assessment situation he is about to enter. We can assume that, if he knows he is to be assessed, he may well have been doing a good deal of revising of the idea-based subsidiary self-world perspectives he is likely to be tested on. In these circumstances, his focus will likely be on those and not on seeking out new experiences that will teach him something new. He will have a world-view oriented towards the experiences he has had and will be wondering which might be repeated during the assessment, rather than looking out for and hoping to learn from new experiences. He will be rehearsing what he has already learned on the assumption that the assessment will focus on past learning experiences.

Nor is he likely to be wrong in his assumption. We can also assume that his teachers are unlikely to lead him into circumstances where he will learn something new. They are aiming to test him on what he has learned and will be leading him into an environment that will require him to respond from the limited repertoire of perspectives he has already learned rather than in some new way.

It should be clear that in these circumstances, his perspective on and relationship to the world will be artificially fixed in the sense defined in Chapter 4. If his primary personal focus is on the limited subset of perspectives he has acquired, and the environment he then encounters only requires him to respond in terms of this limited subset, his responses will be determined by the environment itself and his limited subset of responses. While these circumstances persist, his behaviour and experience will be determined by his internal and external environment and a limited subset of all possible subsidiary self-world perspectives rather than by all of them. His overarching perspective on the world and its associated overarching self-world relationship will be artificially fixed in the sense defined in Chapter 4.

Artificially Fixed Before and After

What is perhaps less clear – but equally true – is that, even if what he experiences on entering the assessment situation does enable him to acquire a new idea-based subsidiary perspective, his relationship will have been artificially fixed before this acquisition and will continue to be so afterwards. Imagine he encounters circumstances he has never encountered before – maybe it is not a part of the assessment but just something he sees through the window of the classroom. Perhaps the experience itself teaches him a new way of seeing things, causes him to ask his teacher something that widens his limited set, or acts as an impetus that causes his imagination or problem-solving skills to dredge up a new perspective through his own creative efforts.

It is reasonable to assume, is it not, that the reason he regards the experience as new, the reason he knows something not already in his repertoire of responses is indicated, is because his brain has attempted to apply his limited set of responses and found it wanting? It is reasonable to assume that his relationship to the world was artificially fixed just before he acquired the perspective that extended his limited set, albeit momentarily, and that it was comparison of this limited set with new circumstances that caused the extension to occur.

Minor Extension Only

Now consider that this new acquisition will not have changed things very much. A previously artificially fixed overarching perspective will have been slightly extended, but only enough to allow it to encompass a slightly wider but still limited set of subsidiary self-world perspectives. It will only have been extended by one or a few self-world perspectives. Gradual acquisition means that what happens as we develop is that we are continuously jumping from one limited set to another. This, in turn, means that artificial fixing is the rule rather than the exception. It means that it happens again and again (and again) as we develop and gradually acquire new idea-based subsidiary self-world perspectives, suggesting that the claim that artificial fixing probably happens to most, if not all, of us as we develop is likely to be true.

Gradual Acquisition: Part 2

Now imagine the same person fifteen, twenty, or twenty-five years further along. He has acquired many more subsidiary self-world perspectives but still has nothing even remotely close to all of them in his repertoire. Perhaps he is well past the stage of his life where he is being assessed on some basis or another. However, he is increasingly in circumstances where the situations he finds himself in – at home, at work, at play – do not tend to require him to respond with perspectives that are not already part of the set he has learned reaching this stage of his life. As long as these circumstances persist, he will probably only respond in terms of his limited set. He will be like his earlier self in the assessment situation – his overarching perspective and relationship will clearly be artificially fixed in the sense meant here.

It will also be artificially fixed before and after any encounter with a situation he has no previous experience of.

Beforehand, his brain will recognise the need for a new response by comparing the situation encountered with the limited set already acquired. It will have been artificially fixed – albeit momentarily – just before acquiring the new perspective. Afterwards, his limited set will have been extended, but only in the sense of becoming an artificially fixed set slightly wider in scope. Gradual acquisition means that what happens as we develop is that we are continuously jumping from one limited set to another. It means that artificial fixing is the rule rather than the exception as we acquire new subsidiary self-world perspectives – which means, in turn, that artificial fixing probably happens to most, if not all, of us as our development proceeds.

Limited Intentions

We can also be reasonably certain that very few of us – if any at all – ever set out intending to attempt to add all of the huge number of ideas that encompass subsidiary self-world relationships as discussed in Chapter 3 to our repertoire. Some of us may well set out to acquire as wide a knowledge of everything as is humanly possible, but few of us set out to become all-seeing and all-knowing and acquire every perspective on anything we possibly could. We may not aim to acquire a limited subset of all possible subsidiary self-world perspectives and an artificially fixed relationship as we develop, but it is reasonable to suggest that unless we set out to acquire a complete set, an artificially fixed set is the most probable outcome. Artificial fixing of our overarching self-world perspective and relationship probably happens to most, if not all, of us as we develop if we do not set out to avoid this outcome. Our own personal experience will tell us whether or not this applies to most humans, but most would agree that it probably does.

Limits of Time and Effort

Even if we did set out to acquire all possible subsidiary self-world perspectives, an artificially fixed overarching self-world perspective and relationship might still be the end result. Obviously, we might give up our attempt, deciding we did not have the time or could not justify the effort, and end up with a fixed set as a result, but these are not the most telling points in this regard. The real point is that, even if we did set out to acquire all possible idea-based subsidiary self-world perspectives, the process would still be a gradual one. We would still be under the control of an artificially fixed overarching self-world perspective and relationship in all of the various circumstances our assessed student was and would still be jumping from one limited subset to another slightly wider one. Most of us probably do not set out to acquire a wholly complete set of all possible idea-based subsidiary self-world perspectives, but even if we did, the gradual nature of the acquisition process would mean that fixing would still be the rule rather than the exception. It would still be reasonable to hold that it probably happens to most, if not all, of us as we develop.

Impractical by Normal Means

In fact, even if we were to start out on our journey of development with the intention of adding all possible idea-based subsidiary self-world perspectives to our repertoire, we would be unlikely to succeed in our aim. Avoiding artificial fixing by normal means – which is to say, by gradual acquisition – is almost certainly impractical to the point of being unfeasible.

The claim argued in Chapter 3 was that any idea we can have about anything is essentially a subsidiary perspective on our self-world relationship. Adding all of them gradually by normal means is an impractically huge undertaking that would entail acquiring every idea ever known to any human, past and present. Such a range of ideas is probably infinite and certainly unimaginably large, especially given that scientists, philosophers, fiction writers, and even individual humans are probably inventing and presenting new perspectives on a daily basis. Acquiring all of them in the normal way of things would certainly require us to read every book ever written. It would also, most likely, require us to experience many of the situations the ideas referred to in order to fully comprehend the perspectives they presented.

Doing all this in a single lifetime is a self-evidently impractical and infeasible proposition. We could never have time to encompass all possible ideas about anything in our overarching self-world perspective. Acquiring such subsidiary self-world perspectives by normal means is not only a continuous process of moving from one artificially fixed perspective and relationship to another slightly wider one on an ongoing basis; it is a process that must inevitably fail through lack of time. Further grounds for holding that artificial fixing of the kind described probably happens to most, if not all, of us as we develop.

Further Evidence That Fixing can Happen

One further implication of the above arguments is worth noting before we move on. The case laid out above not only supports the claim made in this chapter – that artificial fixing probably happens to most, if not all, of us as we develop – it also lends further support for the claim defended in Chapter 5. Clearly, if it is true that gradual acquisition is a process of moving from one fixed relationship to another slightly wider one that can never succeed in encompassing all idea-based subsidiary self-world perspectives, it must also be true that artificial fixing can happen in the normal course of human development. The arguments above not only support the claim that artificial fixing probably happens to most, if not all, of us as we develop, they also provide further support for the claim argued in Chapter 5: artificial fixing can happen as we develop.

Preferences That Exclude and Other Blocks

Although the case presented above is probably sufficient on its own to justify the claim that artificial fixing probably happens to most of us as we develop, further support can be found elsewhere. A second point to note in this regard is that we are all probably subject as we develop to the various brain programming factors illustrated in the second example presented in Chapter 5.

Most would agree that, like the person in the example who made a habit of always mentally seeing himself as Buddhist, not Christian, as Scottish, not Dutch, as left-wing, not right-wing, we habitually prefer various groupings of viewpoints that block out others as we develop. Most would agree that the various blocking factors described in the second Chapter 5 example are probably present in our developmental environment. Most would agree that it is not uncommon for humans to assume that their view of things is a complete and true view, to become emotionally for or against particular viewpoints, or to end up doing the same thing so often that it becomes an unthinking habit.

Most would agree, in other words, that we are all subject to factors that can result in artificial fixing, as illustrated in the Buddhist, Scottish, left-winger example from Chapter 5, and that this gives us further grounds for holding that the claim argued here is true. Artificial fixing probably happens to most, if not all, of us as we develop.

Notice, moreover, that we can also reasonably assume that the assessed pupil from our earlier example may well be subject to these factors. We can assume that his overarching self-world perspective and relationship may well be artificially fixed, not just because of the gradual nature of the acquisition of new perspectives but also because these other factors are also acting to block the extension of his already limited set of possible responses. He may not only have acquired new perspectives as he developed, he may have acquired groups of perspectives that actively block out others; the society he is learning in may be teaching him to see things in Buddhist, not Christian, Scottish, not Dutch, left-wing, not right-wing terms.

The style of his teacher or the methods he himself uses when learning may be inculcating an unthinking habit of always automatically seeing things in a particular way. His teacher and society generally may be leading him to assume that the perspectives he is being taught are wholly complete and wholly true perspectives on whatever their focus is – that Buddhism offers a wholly complete and wholly true view of religious questions, for example. The gradual nature of acquiring new perspectives will itself ensure that he moves from one artificially fixed relationship to another as he develops, but these factors may operate to make the fixing that occurs more difficult to break out of.

If he is habituated to always seeing things in a particular A, not B fashion, assuming they are wholly true and wholly complete, and becoming emotionally attached to them, he will be less likely to react to new situations with new thinking that might expand his preferred fixed set. Indeed, it is arguably likely that at least one of these factors will have this impact unless he is specifically warned against it. If he is not specifically taught that the perspectives imparted to him by his teacher are probably something less than the whole story, he may well unconsciously assume that they are – that Buddhism is a wholly complete and wholly correct view of religious matters, for example. The absence of a conscious recognition that a perspective or group of perspectives is not wholly complete and wholly and exclusively true may well amount to an unconscious assumption that it is.

Evidence in the General Population

One final point that further strengthens the case is that we can arguably see evidence that artificial fixing probably happens to most, if not all, of us in the world around us. Most would agree that we encounter people who espouse one set of beliefs to the exclusion of a wide range of others on a daily basis. Most would agree that it often seems that the preferences of such individuals are somewhat cemented in place by habit, emotional attachments, and a belief that the views adhered to are how the world actually is rather than arguable points of view. In all probability, most of us are a little like this ourselves. Readers will no doubt judge these claims on the basis of their own experience of themselves and other people, but it seems reasonable to assume that most will agree they are true. We see evidence in the world at large that artificial fixing of our overarching self-world perspective and relationship as defined in Chapter 4 probably happens to most, if not all, of us as we develop.

Summary

Taken together, the various points made in this chapter arguably offer strong support for the claim that this artificial fixing of our overarching self-world perspective and relationship probably happens to most, if not all, of us as we develop, even if they do not prove it definitively.

The first of the points argued above seems particularly telling. If adding all possible ideas and their subsidiary self-world perspectives to our repertoire by normal means must, of necessity, be a gradual and ultimately impractical proposition, artificial fixing is probably the rule rather than the exception for all of us as we move through our lives. Not only does the process of acquiring more subsidiary self-world perspectives simply take us from one artificially fixed state to a series of other wider but equally fixed states, but there is no practical possibility of ever reaching a point where our repertoire encompasses all possible idea-based subsidiary perspectives.

It is arguably impossible or very, very unlikely that the gradual process by which we must acquire our repertoire of subsidiary self-world perspectives can ever lead to anything other than the creation of ever-widening sets of fixed perspectives and relationships with no all-encompassing endpoint. On this basis alone, it is reasonable to conclude that artificial fixing probably happens to most of us as we develop, even if we cannot provide empirical scientific evidence to support the claim.

More Definitive Support

More definitive support for this conclusion will be presented in some later chapters – Chapters 8 and 17 in particular. Chapter 8 will argue that avoiding artificial fixing by aiming to encompass all possible subsidiary self-world perspectives in our repertoire by normal means is not just impractical, as argued above, but actually impossible. Chapter 17 will argue that we can only avoid developing an artificially fixed overarching self-world perspective and relationship if we actively strive to adopt the transcendent self-view argued for in this book.

For the moment, we will assume that artificial fixing does happen to most, if not all, of us as a result of the various processes described above and move on to Chapter 7.

This argues that artificial fixing is something to be avoided, especially if we are designing a self-view that accurately reflects our full (wholly-variable) behavioural and experiential nature, and that this holds whether artificial fixing happens to most of us or not. The case made is that, if it does happen, artificial fixing misdefines us and makes that misdefinition operationally true, and that this is something to be avoided, whether it probably happens to most of us or not.

Recognising this misdefinition issue leads us to the first of several design requirements of the self-view for humans we are seeking – specifically, that it must be a self-view that makes an accurate definition, rather than a misdefinition, of our behavioural and experiential nature operationally true.

7

A Fixed Self Misdefines us and Should be Avoided

Fixed Perspectives are Essentially Incorrect Self-Views

The Fixed Perspective: Variations and a Commonality

If artificial fixing of our overarching self-world perspective and relationship does occur through the operation of the range of personal, societal, educational, and other factors described in the last two chapters, it may have come about in a variety of ways and may take a number of forms. The one factor common to all of them is that they are based on a fixed and limited subset of all possible idea-based subsidiary self-world perspectives. Within this commonality, however, a wide variety of forms are possible. It is tempting to think of the fixed and limited subset of subsidiary self-world perspectives as being made up of simple single perspectives on the self-world relationships humans can bear to all sorts of real-world situations, but things may not be so straightforward in practice.

For one thing, the notion of a simple, single perspective may be a relative thing. If we could create a list of all of them, we would likely find we could agree that some were 'simple' but would think that others were less so. For another, while it is possible that a given fixed perspective might comprise a straightforward summation of a limited and blocked group of 'simple' perspectives brought together simply by virtue of being active in a single person's mind, other groupings are also possible.

The fixed perspective might comprise a single overarching perspective on the self, the world, the self-world perspective, or a mix of these, with the included 'simple' self-world perspectives arising out of the application of this single overarching perspective to particular situations. It might comprise groups of what might be called conglomerates of idea-based subsidiary self-world perspective sets – interlinked and interacting subsets of 'simple' self-world perspectives that skew the use of individual members of the group, making them more or less likely to be used as responses in particular circumstances. It might comprise several circumstance-specific or even situation-specific subordinate groupings – subsets of subsidiary self-world perspectives with a particular focus, like Buddhism – that may be either complete in relation to their particular focus or fixed and limited, even in that regard. It might comprise mixes of these and other possibilities. All sorts of combinations are possible. The one thing they all have in common is that, measured against the yardstick of all possible idea-based subsidiary self-world perspectives, they comprise a fixed and limited subset of the total set.

The Fixed Perspective: Different Developmental Routes

As we have seen in Chapters 5 and 6, moreover, there are a variety of possible ways in which fixed perspectives and relationships, whatever their form, might come about.

They might come about via conscious self-programming, unconscious or semi-conscious self-programming, conscious or unconscious programming by external agencies, or a complex mix of these. We might create part of an artificially fixed overarching self-world perspective and relationship by regularly and consciously rehearsing a view of the kind of self we want to be in some specific set of situations – in the workplace, for example, or the local badminton club. We might create other parts of it by unconsciously or semi-consciously copying someone we admire – a particular writer or politician, for example – or by deliberately choosing to go through a particular educational course. We might create it through a single overarching view of the world, of the overarching self-world relationship, or even of the self that we then apply in every situation encountered, or we might do so piecemeal by learning fixed ways of responding to particular groups of situations or even particular situations. The possibilities are close to endless.

A Mistaken Notion of Self

Whatever its genesis, however, and whatever its final form, the end result will be essentially the same. It will not only leave us with a (sometimes partially or wholly unconscious) mistaken notion of self – an incorrect idea of who or what we are in the world – it will place us under the control of that mistaken notion of self. It will have us acting, thinking, and feeling according to its dictates. It will, in effect, take a misdefinition of who or what we are in relation to the world at large and make that misdefinition operationally true. This was hinted at by the definitions of the artificially fixed relationship and the fixed self-world perspective or self presented in Chapter 4, but some clarification of the detail of the relationship between the two will be helpful here.

A Left-Wing, Buddhist Overarching Relationship

We argued in Chapter 3 that any and every idea we can have about anything entails a view of the self-world relationship that can become an actual behavioural and experiential relationship if used as a situational response. If a person's overarching self-world relationship is artificially fixed, she only has a limited subset of these views of the self-world relationship that can become actual in her repertoire. Those not included in this limited subset cannot influence her behaviour and experience in the world; only those that are included can – so the artificial fixing ensures that a limited set of views of the self-world relationship control her behaviour and experience in the world.

Imagine someone who has learned only Buddhist and left-wing ideas about the self-world relationship (in various ways, conscious and unconscious) – she has an artificially fixed overarching self-world perspective and relationship based on these Buddhist and left-wing perspectives. Say she has come more or less unconsciously to absorb her Buddhist idea-based subsidiary self-world perspectives and Buddhist ways of acting, thinking, and feeling because a tutor she greatly admires sees, acts, thinks, and feels in these ways even though he never mentions Buddhism as such. Say also that she has learned her left-wing idea-based perspectives on the self-world relationship by acquiring left-wing beliefs and ways of acting, thinking, and feeling from others in her local community, some of which she is conscious of acquiring and some of which she is not conscious of acquiring. Assume that she lives in a society where the only responses usually called for are religious and political.

Her artificially fixed overarching self-world relationship based on these Buddhist and left-wing perspectives will control how she acts, thinks, and feels. Assuming it is fixed in the sense defined in Chapter 4, it will encompass all of the ways she has learned of responding to the only situations she usually encounters, which is to say, religious and political situations. Nothing outside of that set will influence her behaviour and experience in the usual way of things, since nothing outside of that set will have been programmed into her brain as a possible response to the situations she encounters.

Even if she happens to encounter a situation that leads to her extending her limited set of responses through serendipity or creative thinking, her artificially fixed Buddhist and left-wing set of idea-based subsidiary self-world perspectives will still be in control beforehand and will be largely in control afterwards. Her brain will recognise the new type of situation because it falls outside of the scope of her programming. If it adds a new response to her fixed set, it will probably only widen the set slightly. Her artificially fixed Buddhist and left-wing set of idea-based self-world perspectives will still be in control in most circumstances.

This, in effect, means that she has a Buddhist and left-wing view of her overarching self-world relationship, even if she may not necessarily have a conscious view of it as such. Her behavioural and experiential relationship to the world is controlled by an artificially limited set of Buddhist and left-wing perspectives that cause her to see the world and act, think, and feel in it in Buddhist and left-wing ways. Her overarching self-world perspective and relationship is made up of the combined set of these Buddhist and left-wing idea-based perspectives that cause her to see, act, think, and feel in the world generally in Buddhist and left-wing ways. It is reasonable to say that she has a Buddhist and left-wing perspective on her overarching self-world relationship, whether she consciously sees it in that way or not. We can say that, whether she is conscious of it or not, she has, in effect, a Buddhist and left-wing perspective on her overarching self-world relationship and that it has her acting, thinking, and feeling according to its dictates. A Buddhist and left-wing overarching self-world perspective defines who she is and determines how she acts, thinks, and feels.

From Overarching Perspective to Self-View

Now consider that we have seen (Chapter 2) that a perspective on any self-world relationship – and by extension, on the overarching self-world relationship – can also be expressed as a world-view or a self-view, and we can see why the claim made above is true. Artificial fixing will not only leave us with a (sometimes partially or wholly unconscious) mistaken notion of self – an incorrect idea of who or what we are in the world – it will place us under the control of that mistaken notion of self. It will have us acting, thinking, and feeling according to its dictates. We can say that someone who consciously or unconsciously has a Buddhist and left-wing view of her overarching self-world relationship controlling her behavioural and experiential relationship to the world essentially has a consciously or unconsciously held Buddhist and left-wing-oriented self-view controlling it. A view she could have learned consciously as a self-view if, say, her greatly admired left-wing and Buddhist mother taught her to consciously rehearse a view of herself as a left-wing Buddhist and to consciously encourage herself to act, think, and feel accordingly.

A Mistaken View of the Self-World Relationship

We can also say that this overarching self-world perspective that is essentially a self-view is an incorrect idea of who or what we are in the world – one that, being artificially fixed rather than wholly-variable (see Chapter 4), fails to accurately reflect our full behavioural and experiential nature. If what was argued in Chapter 4 is correct, our full behavioural and experiential relationship to the world is defined equally by all possible idea-based subsidiary self-world perspectives, not just a few of them – which means that an artificially fixed overarching self-world perspective is an incorrect view of who and what we are. Artificial fixing will not only leave us with a (sometimes partially or wholly unconscious) mistaken notion of self – an incorrect idea of who or what we are in the world – it will place us under the control of that mistaken notion of self. It will have us acting, thinking, and feeling according to the dictates of an incorrect view of our actual relationship to the world.

A Conscious Notion of Self but Only Part of the Whole

We might not necessarily think of this artificially fixed overarching self-world perspective as a notion of self – or even think of it at all. Since it potentially encompasses both consciously and unconsciously held views about the self, the world, and the self in the world, it may even include a conscious notion of self that is, in reality, only a small part of the whole. But a notion of self is essentially what the whole is.

It is a notion of self that we may be partially or even wholly unconscious of. One that might equally accurately be thought of as a view of the associated overarching self-world relationship but is otherwise not essentially different to a consciously held self-view that describes the same overarching self-world perspective in a slightly different form. Our Buddhist left-winger from above might have acquired her artificially fixed overarching self-world perspective in a mix of ways, both conscious and unconscious. However, the end result is not essentially different from an operational self-view she might just as easily acquire through regularly and habitually identifying herself with (i.e., repeatedly mentally rehearsing) the self-view of a Buddhist left-winger with the aim of producing the same resulting fixed overarching relationship. The end result is essentially the same in both cases.

Variations on a Theme

The devil would be in the detail, of course; acquiring the same fixed set of Buddhist and left-wing idea-based self-world perspectives expressed in self-form would not necessarily be enough in itself. Two people espousing exactly the same set of views might well react entirely differently when these views are aggressively challenged by another person. One may have developed a deep emotional attachment he is largely unconscious of to a set of religious views passed on to him by his mother. He may also be largely unconscious, either that they *are* just one set of views or that alternative views exist. Such a person may well react angrily and even violently if these views are challenged in an aggressive way, and may well be unable to help reacting that way. Another person with the same views learned from a book who is conscious of other views and has no emotional attachment to his preferred set will likely have more control and will probably be able to be more variable in his reactions in a similar situation.

Clearly, habitually identifying with the same fixed set of Buddhist and left-wing idea-based self-world perspectives expressed in the form of a self-view would only have a near identical result if other blocking factors – emotional attachments, assumptions of truth, and so on – were also part of the approach.

Habitual Identification as a Self Development Tool

As long as this was recognised, however, the end result could be identical – an important point here because this process of deliberate identification with a particular, regularly rehearsed, self-view is the main conscious and self-controlled tool we have at our disposal for changing our operational self-view. It is the main tool we have if our aim is to push away from an artificially fixed overarching view of the self, the world, or the self-world relationship towards a fully human, wholly-variable, transcendent self-view (a point we will return to in later chapters).

Complex Rather Than Simple

It is, of course, probable that a fixed self developed through the processes described in Chapters 5 and 6 will be much more complex than is implied by the left-wing Buddhist example used above. Most lives focus on topics and circumstances beyond the religious and political focus of our left-wing Buddhist and the range of human knowledge and creative perspectives is vast and growing. Clearly, if artificial fixing does happen as claimed, we would expect fixed selves encompassing a much wider range of idea-based subsidiary self-world perspectives and a greater degree of variability of response than is evident in the left-wing Buddhist example.

We would also expect greater complexity in detail. There could well be topics and circumstances where a fixed self entails a significantly large degree of variability in respect of possible responses, and others where the range is relatively narrow. There could be areas where a fixed self entails facets – sub-groupings of one or more idea-based subsidiary self-world perspectives with a particular focus – within which blocking factors like emotional attachments, assumptions of truth, and so on are commonplace, and others where they are minimal or entirely absent. There could even be variability in both of these respects from one fixed-self facet to another. A fixed self entailing a wide range of response options with no emotional attachments in areas like politics and professional expertise but a narrow range of response options with significant emotional attachments in the area of religion, for example.

Obviously, such complexity would be most likely in the modern, well-developed societies of today, where a label like 'John Smith passport number 8887321 with all of his various idiosyncrasies' might best describe the kind of self-view that might develop rather than something more limited like 'Buddhist' or 'Marxist'.

Artificial Fixing and Kinds of Human

None of this changes the various points made above, however. If our 'John Smith passport number 8887321' develops a fixed self via the processes described in Chapters 5 and 6, as we are supposing, he would still be similar to our left-wing Buddhist in all important respects. He would still ultimately bear a fixed behavioural and experiential relationship to the world embodied within what is essentially an operationally active notion of self defined by that fixed relationship, rather than a wholly-variable one.

He might be a complex individual – a Scottish, Buddhist, socialist, motorist, father of two from Dundee, say, with a range of individually unique fixed-self facet variations – but he will ultimately bear a fixed behavioural and experiential relationship to the world. It might well entail a degree of response variability, and this might vary from circumstance to circumstance, but the overall degree of this would nonetheless be a limited one. It would be determined by the (necessarily limited) range of idea-based subsidiary self-world perspectives he learned during his development and other factors such as his consciousness of them and his emotional attachment to some or all of them. He would have more variability of response inherent in his fixed self than some of the simpler fixed selves used as illustrative examples in this book.

Ultimately, though, his overall relationship would be as fixed as in these simpler examples – it would be broadly similar in terms of its characteristics and associated advantages and disadvantages. If we were observing his behaviour as scientists might, we would have to describe him as a particular fixed 'John Smith' human rather than as the (significantly different) wholly-variable, fully developed human (who might perhaps have 'John Smith'-like tendencies) referred to later in this book (Chapter 16). His experiential and behavioural relationship to the world would not be the wholly-variable relationship of the fully developed human we will define in more detail in the next chapter, but the artificially fixed relationship of one particular *kind* of human – a particular version of human, one might say.

Misdefining Ourselves
An Incorrect but Operationally True Self-View

This is significant here for two reasons. First, if it is true that artificial fixing probably happens to most, if not all, of us as we develop, then the end result is to make us into *kinds* of humans. Allowing it to happen leaves us with a complex but limited – and weighted or biased – repertoire of idea-based subsidiary self-world perspectives controlling how we act, think, and feel in the world. Rather than becoming fully developed humans with a wholly-variable relationship to the world, we become 'Buddhists' or 'Freethinker Scientists' or 'the individually unique John Smith, passport number 8887321' or some other limited view of what a human should be.

If we develop as suggested in Chapters 5 and 6 above (and most would accept that we probably do), then, without necessarily intending to, we develop a limited and fixed view of ourselves and essentially become that view. We habitually see our behavioural and experiential relationship to the world as fixed rather than wholly-variable and, in so doing, effectively make it just that. In essence, we misdefine ourselves and make that misdefinition actual – arguably something to be avoided. We essentially take a mistaken view of who we are – an incorrect, more or less incidentally arrived at, fixed self-view – and make it true by habitually allowing it to control how we act, think, and feel in the world.

A Self-View for Humans Must Avoid Such Misdefinition

Second – and this is true whether artificial fixing happens to most of us or not – the kind of self-view we are seeking in this book is quite clearly one that is the exact opposite of one that misdefines us and makes that misdefinition operationally true. The first of a range of requirements that a self-view that accurately reflects our full behavioural and experiential nature must meet is that it must not misdefine us and make that misdefinition operationally true. It must do the opposite of this – it must instead be a self-view that defines us (and our behavioural and experiential relationship to the world) accurately and makes *that* definition of us operationally true.

The self-view we must seek to identify ourselves with, rehearse, and put in place as our controlling self-view (and, indeed, encourage in our social, educational, and other external developmental programmes) must be the opposite of the artificially fixed self-views discussed in this part of the book. It must be a self-view designed to ensure that our response to any given situation encountered is determined equally and in an unbiased way by all possible ideas and the subsidiary self-world perspectives they encompass (as opposed to just a few of them). A self-view designed to support a wholly-variable response rather than a fixed self-view of the kind described above with a design that supports only a relatively fixed response. A self-view designed to support a wholly-variable response in an open-ended fashion, as discussed in the next part of the book.

PART 3

Further Design Requirements

Part 3: Outline of the Case Presented

A self-view able to accurately reflect our full behavioural and experiential nature must meet five additional design requirements:

It must be a self-view in which every possible subsidiary self-world perspective is not only seen as part of the whole self and as an equally-weighted potential temporary determinant of the actual relationship in any given situation, but one in which these things are also operationally true. Practically speaking, this means not that each must be included individually, but that they all must be included collectively in a descriptive sense in an open-ended, wholly-variable self-view that has no block or bias operating to prevent each of them being operationally available in any situation encountered **(Chapter 8)**.

It must be a self-view designed to avoid the negative but retain the positive aspects of fixed selves, that allows for personal uniqueness, does not block the wholly-variable response as the fixed self-view does, and (crucially) is not based on any one idea set, not even a wholly true and comprehensive scientific idea set **(Chapters 9-11)**.

It must be a self-view based on empty consciousness, the only aspect of our experience that does not entail a self-world perspective. Almost everything we know is known via its relationships to something else and can only be known indirectly and relationally. Knowing itself – and hence, empty consciousness – must be known more directly (which is to say, nonrelationally, as, or in terms of, itself). To assume otherwise is to be led into an infinite regress where the knower and the known must be linked by another (and another and another) way of knowing ad infinitum. Empty consciousness is the only aspect of knowing itself that is both directly and nonrelationally known and empty of other relational content. Since it cannot either be or entail a self-world perspective, it cannot be an idea, and it is therefore the only possible basis of a self-view that does not give undue weight to some fixed view of our overarching self-world perspective if we habitually identify with it. Habitually identifying with any idea-based self-view – even a scientifically based one – inevitably blocks out many other idea-based subsidiary self-world perspectives from the total relationship and thereby misdefines us **(Chapter 12)**.

8

An Open-Ended, Wholly-Variable Self-view

A Wholly-Variable Response?
Every Self-World Perspective a Determinant

So, what exactly is a self-view designed to support a wholly-variable response, as discussed here? What are its characteristics? The best way to begin to answer this is to first clarify further what the claim that the true human relationship to the world is a wholly-variable rather than a fixed one actually means. As should be evident from earlier chapters, it does not mean that it is ever-changing or in a constant state of flux. It means, rather, that it is a relationship defined not by one limited and weighted or biased group of the idea-based subsidiary self-world perspectives we can have access to, but by the total set of these operating without bias.

If every possible idea-based subsidiary self-world perspective can influence how we respond to every situation encountered if brought into play, our overarching self-world relationship can only fully reflect our behavioural and experiential nature if every possible one of them is equally able to influence our every situational response. Our relationship can only be said to be wholly-variable, as defined in Chapter 4, if there is no barrier or bias preventing every possible idea-based subsidiary self-world perspective having an equal chance of being brought into play in any given situation before the situational circumstances are taken into account. It can only be said to accurately reflect our actual behavioural and experiential nature if all possible idea-based subsidiary self-world perspectives are regarded and treated as equally valid potential aspects of the total self.

If some of them are seen and treated in ways that prevent them from having an impact on our total relationship in every situation encountered, the total human relationship is being determined or skewed by a weighted and limited (and so, fixed) set of the possible subsidiary perspectives and is not wholly-variable. If some are prevented from influencing the relationship, or there is a bias against one subsidiary perspective or another, the total human relationship is being determined by a biased and limited fixed set of the possible perspectives and does not accurately reflect our actual behavioural and experiential nature in the sense meant here.

Temporary Roles Rather Than Fixed Selves

Our true relationship to the world is one that can encompass and range across every one of the set of subsidiary self-world perspectives embedded in the various ideas and viewpoints on the self, the world, and the self in the world we have access to. It is one in which every one of them is equally capable of determining the actual relationship in any particular circumstance, and every one of them is equivalent in weight and importance as regards its contribution to, and role in, the total relationship. These are the factors that make it wholly-variable.

This implies a mutable relationship that can become briefly fixed when one or a limited group of all of the possible idea-based subsidiary self-world perspectives is given dominance as an appropriate response to a given situation, *but where that dominance is temporary*. One where this temporary dominance is relinquished once the situation is dealt with so that the response to the next situation can again be chosen from the complete set of all possible idea-based subsidiary self-world perspectives. It implies a relationship in which no one subsidiary self-world perspective is ever allowed to block a wholly-variable response and become the whole relationship – to become a fixed self-view – by being given long-term control of our total or overarching behavioural and experiential relationship to the world.

Put more briefly, it implies a relationship that can vary according to which of the full set of subsidiary self-world perspectives embedded in our various ideas and viewpoints on the self, the world, and the self in the world is given dominance at any given point in time. One where no one of them is more important than any other in terms of its potential impact on the total relationship or the possibility of being chosen and used as a response to specific circumstances. It implies a relationship where all individual idea-based subsidiary self-world perspectives are temporary, inter-changeable roles rather than the basis of a fixed self.

Descriptive and Operational Characteristics of the Self-View

Descriptive Inclusion

What does this mean as regards the characteristics of the self-view we would have to adopt to support a wholly-variable relationship of this kind? What features are we looking for in a self-view that would support full variability of response of the type just described – a truly wholly-variable self-view? Clearly, it would be a self-view seen as including the whole set of all possible idea-based subsidiary self-world perspectives, rather than just a subset of them – a self-view in which any and every possible one of them was seen as part of the whole self. One in which every possible subsidiary self-world perspective was seen as being equally capable of temporarily determining the actual relationship in any particular situation encountered and where every possible subsidiary self-world perspective was again able to determine the actual relationship in whatever circumstances were encountered next. This much is readily obvious from the description given above regarding what wholly-variable means in the context of the human behavioural and experiential relationship to the world.

Operational Inclusion

What should also be evident is that it would be a self-view where these things had to be operationally as well as descriptively true. If the relationship was to be not just seen as wholly-variable but actually so in practice, it would have to be a self-view constructed so that it *worked* in the ways just described. It would have to be a self-view that operated in these ways in practice. It would have to be one in which every possible subsidiary self-world perspective was equally capable of temporarily determining the actual relationship in any given situation and of relinquishing its controlling role in each new situation so that the same wholly-variable response was again possible in the new circumstances.

Equal Before, but not After, Situational Considerations

Includes Even Fantasy and Nonsense Views

Does this imply that what is being proposed is a self-view that treats even perspectives as widely divergent as scientific views of self and world and fantasy or nonsense views of self and world as equally valid possible human behavioural and experiential responses to the world? Yes, it does – and this is surely as it should be. Even a nonsensical perspective where self and world were seen as being made of blancmange might have value to a comedian entertaining children at a Christmas party or to a teacher trying to make some scientific point, after all.

Any and every perspective on self or world that a human might adopt is a possible human behavioural and experiential response that might well have value in some situation and should be freely available as a possible response for that reason.

Possible Rather Than Necessarily Appropriate

Does it imply that what is being proposed is a self-view in which every subsidiary self-world perspective is regarded as an *adequate* or *appropriate* response to every situation? No – what is implied is that they should all be available as possible responses prior to the situational circumstances being consciously or unconsciously taken into account. The actual choice made in any given instance would be made on the basis of the requirements of the situation being responded to, and the various options would no longer be equivalent once those requirements were considered. It is simply that things would be so arranged that the initial relationship was always wholly-variable in the sense defined above – that all options were equally available in an unbiased way prior to the requirements of the situation being responded to being used to determine a response.

Internal and External Situational Factors

Situational circumstances are obviously taken to include external environmental aspects of the situation faced – whether it calls for a scientific approach, a teaching approach, or a comedic response, for example – factors that would act to remove possible situational responses as inadequate and inappropriate to the environmental circumstances faced. They are also taken to include internal personal aspects of the situation a person is in at a given moment. What their relevant mental, emotional, and physical skills and limitations are at that point in time, what their relevant life experiences are, whether current legal circumstances such as being banned from driving are relevant, whether they are ill or hungover, and other considerations in that vein. More detail on how this would work in practice is presented later in the book (see Chapter 13). For the purposes of this chapter, it is necessary only to note that the suggestion is not that all of the subsidiary self-world perspectives embedded in any and every idea we can have about anything are appropriate or adequate to every circumstance, only that they are *possible options*. Options whose adequacy and appropriateness will be determined consciously or unconsciously by the situational circumstances encountered at any given moment – situational circumstances that entail both external environmental elements and internal life experience and other physical elements.

An Infinity of Self-World Perspectives?
Not Just a Significant Practical Challenge...

One final point worth addressing is this: It may appear from the above that the position proposed is one where someone looking to adopt the wholly-variable self-view would be faced with seeking to habitually identify themselves with a self-view incorporating every conceivable idea-based subsidiary self-world perspective in an individual rather than a collective sense. It may appear they would be faced with the task of regularly rehearsing every possible way of looking at the world, the self, or the self in the world until the use of all possible subsidiary self-world perspective-bearing conscious and unconscious ideas and viewpoints was second nature. This would be a significant difficulty in that it would be an entirely impractical and all but impossible task. Even the set of all idea-based subsidiary self-world perspectives ever known to humans is probably infinite and is certainly unimaginably large. No one is likely to have actual learned access to all of them, especially so since it is safe to say that scientists, philosophers, fiction writers, and even individual humans are discovering new varieties every day. Even if they did have such access, they would probably find rehearsing them all a huge difficulty and choosing between them in given circumstances an unmanageable challenge.

...A Wholly Impossible Task

This apparent need to identify habitually with a self-view encompassing an infinity of idea-based subsidiary self-world perspectives or an infinity of roles or viewpoints is not the whole of the difficulty, however. Learning and encompassing any and every idea-based self-world perspective ever known to humans individually, even if it were practical and manageable, would be insufficient to ensure full variability of response as defined in Chapter 4. The set of all possible idea-based self-world perspectives is larger than the set of every such perspective ever known to humans; it also includes those idea-based self-world perspectives yet to be discovered by humans. Any conceivable idea-based self-world perspective can contribute to the actual real and realisable behavioural and experiential relationship to the world, even those as yet undiscovered – which means that even those undiscovered are a potential part of the total relationship. Achieving full variability of response by a route based on individually encompassing every conceivable idea-based self-world perspective is thus not just an impossibly impractical and close to impossible enterprise; it is actually wholly impossible. How are we to encompass idea-based self-world perspectives we do not yet know of or that have not even been discovered yet? We cannot, of course; it is simply not possible to do it in the normal way of things.

Including Everything by Excluding Nothing

Fortunately, this is not the only approach possible, nor is it the approach proposed. We can deal with the problem in a different way – one that *is* practical and *can* be claimed to deal adequately with the issue of undiscovered ideas and the self-world perspectives they encompass. Self-world perspectives unknown to the individual human can be accessed via imagination, creative problem solving, looking up a book or a website, phoning a friend, or conducting scientific research. Even those not yet discovered by humans generally can be acquired through research and creative thinking. As long as there is no block or bias in place to prevent every possible idea-based self-world perspective, known or previously unknown, being a potential response, a person's relationship can at the very least be said to be as wholly-variable as it is possible to be. On a descriptive level, all idea-based subsidiary self-world perspectives can be seen as part of the self-view, at least in a general way – even undiscovered ones. On an operational level, if there is no bias or barrier to any and every subsidiary self-world perspective being brought into play, then even undiscovered subsidiary self-world perspectives – if they can be discovered when needed – can be brought into play.

Close to Wholly-Variable or Actually so

At worst, this is as close to full variability of response as it is possible to get, given that we cannot ever *guarantee* that undiscovered ideas encompassing self-world perspectives can be discovered and included. It enables *theoretical* full variability of response by ensuring there is no barrier to any such perspective – even a relevant undiscovered one – being brought into play and *actual* full variability where any relevant undiscovered idea-based self-world perspective can, in the event, be discovered and brought into play. It permits even undiscovered idea-based self-world perspectives to have an impact on our total relationship to the world, provided they can be picked up via imagination, creative problem solving, cross-fertilisation of ideas, or conducting scientific research in circumstances where they might provide the best response to a situation faced.

There is, however, a case for claiming that this can offer a truly wholly-variable, overarching self-world relationship in the sense defined in Chapter 4. If a brain is programmed not to force a response based on a limited set of idea-based subsidiary self-world perspectives but to be both open and conducive to the discovery and use of even unknown future possibilities, we can reasonably claim it is programmed to be wholly-variable. We can reasonably claim that these future possible idea-based self-world perspectives are having a real influence on the total relationship of the person in question, even if they are unknown and may never become known. If the algorithm in place in the brain is such that there is a programmed path open and conducive to such future possibilities being brought into play, then the availability of that path will be part of what determines the person's response in a given situation. We can reasonably claim that even unknown and undiscovered idea-based self-world perspectives that never become known, discovered, or used are nevertheless having an impact on the person's total relationship.

Illustrating the Point

Imagine two sailors who have both been taught that the world is flat and that they will fall off the edge to their doom if they sail too far out to sea. One has a brain programmed so that when the fish stocks close to shore run out, the only possibility that presents itself to him as regards feeding himself and his family is to go out into the woods to hunt rabbits. The other has a brain programmed so that, although the flat world-view is the only world-view in his repertoire and is a view he assumes is true, the algorithm in place is also open and conducive to the possibility that what he has been taught is wrong. He knows his view of the world as flat is just that – one particular (and possibly wrong) perspective on things. He knows that other views might exist and has a brain programmed to be conducive to their discovery where necessary – he has both creative problem solving and library information discovery skills in his repertoire, say.

In times when the fishing is good close to shore, he never ventures very far out – why take the risk? However, if the fish stocks run out, he and his family are starving, and he has not heard there are rabbits in the woods that are good to eat, the chances are that he might well venture further out to sea to try his luck with the fishing there. His behavioural and experiential relationship may not be directly determined by the round world-view, but it is being partially determined by the possibility of such a view (and its inherent self-world perspective) existing. His brain has been programmed, both to allow for the possibility of such a view and to be conducive to its discovery. His total relationship is being partially determined by idea-based self-world perspectives presently outwith his learned or known repertoire of responses – or arguably so.

Wholly-Variable in an Open-Ended Sense

A self-view that is designed in this open-ended way is what is meant here by a self-view able to instantiate and support a wholly-variable response. If the arguments above are valid, it is a self-view that can reasonably be regarded as accurately reflecting our full behavioural and experiential nature by enabling even unknown and undiscovered idea-based subsidiary self-world perspectives to act as determinants of our overarching behavioural and experiential relationship to the world. It also, on the face of it, avoids the practicality problem touched on above: avoiding any requirement to rehearse a possibly infinite number of the ideas and viewpoints that encompass self-world perspectives. There are good grounds for holding that it offers the only practical and achievable way of instantiating and supporting a wholly-variable response.

The Second Requirement of a Self-View for Humans

An Open-Ended, Wholly-Variable Self-View

This is the view taken here at any rate: that the arguments presented above are sound and that the second requirement of a self-view that accurately reflects our full behavioural and experiential nature is that it must support wholly-variable self-world interaction in this open-ended, barrier-free sense. It is assumed, on the basis of the case presented above, that this open-ended design offers the only practicable way of ensuring that all possible idea-based subsidiary self-world perspectives – even those unknown to individuals or undiscovered by humans generally – are potential situational responses. To put it more definitively, it is assumed that only a self-view designed to support a wholly-variable self-world relationship in this open-ended, barrier-free sense can be the basis of a self-view that accurately reflects our full behavioural and experiential nature. Note that this second requirement is further clarified at the end of Chapter 10 under '**The Fourth Requirement: Avoid Fixed-Self-Type Blocking**'

Descriptive and Operational Parameters

Understanding what meeting this requirement means in terms of the descriptive and operational parameters of a self-view for humans is the key to finding a self-view that is an adequate alternative to the fixed self-view. It is the key to finding a self-view that accurately reflects our full behavioural and experiential nature. It is also the key to answering the related set of questions that are the focus of this book. *What self-view should we identify with? If a fixed definition is a misdefinition, how should we humans see and define ourselves? How do we become wholly developed variable-response humans rather than kinds of humans with a complex but limited repertoire of self-world perspectives controlling how we act, think, and feel in the world?*

Drawing out a detailed answer to this clutch of questions and justifying that answer is a process that will stretch out over the remainder of this third part of the book. A process that begins in the next chapter with an examination of the negative and positive effects of the fixed self-view and what they tell us about the further requirements of the open-ended, wholly-variable self-view we are seeking.

Additional Points

Implied Aspects of an Open-Ended Design

Before we move on to this, two further points are worth noting as regards a self-view that is wholly-variable in this open-ended sense. These are implications of the design requirements of the kind of self-view we are seeking rather than design requirements as such, but they are worth mentioning here for clarity's sake.

Long-Term Responses

The first is that there may be circumstances in which viewpoints entailing unknown and undiscovered idea-based subsidiary self-world perspectives that are ultimately brought into play may, on occasion, be brought into play in a longer-term rather than an immediate sense.

If bringing some of these unknown and undiscovered perspectives into play is dependent on things such as conducting research, creative problem solving, and the like, then clearly, identifying a correct response and bringing it into play may sometimes be a less than immediate process. We can think of a scientist or a philosopher looking to solve a particularly intractable problem regarding the nature of the human organism as an example – the so-called hard problem of consciousness tackled in Chapters 23-26, perhaps. If the kind of self-view described above is in place, there will potentially be an open path to a solution as described above. However, solving the problem and successfully bringing the right way of seeing it into play may still require significant long-term thought and analysis.

Non-Biased Implies Disaggregated

The second implication is that, while all of the various possible idea-based subsidiary self-world perspectives may and often will inter-relate at the point when a situational response is selected, they will do so as individual, separate, and equally valid aspects of a whole disaggregated self. The kind of self-view described above assumes that all such idea-based subsidiary self-world perspectives are treated equally – that there is no bias in place prior to the selection of a situational response. This means that they cannot exist within either the descriptive or operational aspects of the self in a way that creates such bias. If they exist within the self as separate, wholly disaggregated aspects of the total self, then, all other things being equal, bias should be avoided. If they exist there as subordinate and integrated parts of more complex views of the self, the world, or the self-world relationship, there is, as the example below will illustrate, at least a possibility that this will introduce bias into the mix.

Imagine a person who reveres all life as part of being a Buddhist but only applies that self-world perspective when she is actively engaged in Buddhist activities, not when she is out driving. When she is out driving, she inhabits her own particular brand of motorist persona instead. This tells her never to brake when a cat runs in front of her, as this will cause an accident and hurt both herself and other drivers.

Arguably, she will get the ideal response to a situation where a cat runs in front of her car if these two self-world views exist and interact as individual self-world perspectives. Then she might run the cat down if that is the safest thing, but she might brake if she sees there is no real danger to herself or others. In effect, the situation will interact with both self-world perspectives, and the decision will be made depending on the specifics of the situation.

If, on the other hand, her *revere life* self-world perspective is tied up to her wearing her Buddhist persona and her *never brake for a cat* self-world perspective is tied up with her motorist persona, she will likely kill the cat even if it is safe not to. Her overarching self-world perspective will entail a bias. It will be biased in favour of the *never brake for a cat* response, regardless of whether this is the best response to the situation. It will not be the kind of open-ended, wholly-variable self-view described above. This would, by definition, not entail a bias in favour of one response or the other. It would treat both responses equally, allowing the situation itself to be the deciding factor between the two – something that would not be possible if they were both subordinate and integrated parts of different, more complex views of the self, the world, or the self-world relationship.

9

Fixed Self: Negatives, Positives and Possibilities

Of necessity, the case presented in this chapter is again based on presenting examples and drawing out their implications. It is based on hopefully plausible combinations of particular fixed selves and situational circumstances which most readers will accept as indications that the claims made as regards positive and negative effects and related issues covered below are supportable. The claims made here about fixed selves may one day be thought worth testing under scientifically controlled conditions. For now, however, the case must rest primarily on shared human experience and logic and the example-based arguments presented below. This approach is also an essential prerequisite for drawing out much of the detail of what is being argued here regarding the issues surrounding fixed selves, their positive and negative effects, and the factors that influence them.

The chapter has four aims. The first is to argue that fixed selves can sometimes have positive effects – that their limiting effects can sometimes be advantageous, especially when they also encompass emotional, habitual, and perspectival barriers that prevent change. The second is to argue that they can also (unsurprisingly) have negative effects, that these are strengthened by emotional attachments, harder to escape when emotional, habitual, and perspectival barriers are involved, and are caused when a conflict between an entailed perspective and reality becomes an issue. The third is to argue that the wholly-variable self-view described in Chapter 8 should be able to avoid the negative but retain the positive effects while also optimising responses generally and encompassing personally unique aspects of a fixed self. The fourth is to posit that encompassing such characteristics should therefore be regarded as a further requirement of the self-view for humans we are seeking.

A Fixed Self-View can Sometimes Have Positive Effects

Examples: Advantages as Well as Disadvantages

It is important to note that the limiting effects of fixed selves can sometimes be advantageous. A pair of examples will illustrate this.

We can readily imagine, can we not, soldiers able to fight with more determination and perseverance because their fixed self comprises a limited repertoire of self-world responses all focused on the notion that they are God's heroes and the enemy are evil soldiers of the anti-prophet. We can imagine, too, that they will likely be even more effective in this regard if there are emotional, habitual, and perspectival barriers preventing them from seeing beyond this perspective on things – if the beliefs they have are emotionally charged, habitually and unconsciously rehearsed, and seen as unquestionably true. This is one example of circumstances in which being under the influence of a fixed self might be regarded as having a positive effect – if only among the leaders of the soldiers in question.

Effects From Fixed Self not Just Individual Beliefs

Notice that it is the fixed self that has this effect, not simply the belief at its core. Clearly, if the self-view was less fixed in some way, the effect regarded as positive by the commanders would be weakened. It would be weakened if the belief at its core was only one view of the conflict among others and there were no emotional, habitual, and perspectival barriers preventing soldiers from seeing beyond this perspective on things (to thoughts about the humanity of the enemy, say). The effect the commanders see as a positive feature is caused by the fixed self, not by the core belief as such, although this is obviously also a factor, in that a fixed self based on a different belief would have a different effect.

This, clearly, is an instance where a fixed self's positive impact would likely have a negative effect on other humans, but it is not hard to come up with a scenario where that is not the case. One example might be a circumstance where everyone in the world had a Buddhism-based fixed self (say) and habitually and consciously or unconsciously saw other Buddhists as friends they felt positive towards, thereby making both conflict in the group and alienation in the individual less likely. Notice again that it is not simply the Buddhism-inspired belief set that is having the positive effect but the fact that it is at the heart of a fixed self. Having Buddhism at the core of the fixed self is important to the positive effect, which would likely vanish entirely if replaced by a belief set antagonistic to other humans. The fixed nature of the self is important too, however. If the various believers were able to move from this belief at its core and latch on to others antagonistic to other humans, the likelihood of avoiding conflict in the group and alienation in the individual would be reduced.

We know that individual beliefs can sometimes have positive effects, even when they can also have negative effects (see, e.g., Gunn & Bortolotti, 2018; Koenig, 2012), but this is not the same as a fixed self having positive effects. The positive effects in the examples above come, at least in part, from the fact that other ways of relating to the described situations are blocked out and that this has a positive effect in certain situations, even if not in others. They come, in short, from the fixed nature of the self in question, not from the belief at its core. What is being argued here is that fixed selves can sometimes have positive effects, not simply that individual beliefs do.

That said, it is arguably possible to claim some indirect evidential support for the claim that fixed selves can have positive effects – indirect in that its focus is beliefs as such rather than fixed selves based on the beliefs. We can argue there is evidence in work mentioned earlier on the effects of having either a fixed or malleable view of personal intelligence (Dweck, 2013; see also Gál et al., 2022; King, 2017; Mueller & Dweck, 1998; Smiley et al., 2016). Learners with a malleable view tend to seek out opportunities to learn and develop and to react to setbacks by working to find ways to overcome them; their belief has a positive effect. Learners who regard intelligence as fixed tend to regard setbacks as reflections on their own presumed lack of innate intelligence and to react in a more floundering fashion as a result; their belief has a negative effect. We can argue on this basis that a fixed self that favoured the malleable view and blocked out its opposite would evidence a positive effect; one due partly to the malleable belief having a positive effect and partly to the fixed self blocking out its opposite view of intelligence. A self-view that consciously or unconsciously applied both views in different circumstances would have less of a positive effect overall, and a fixed self that favoured the fixed view of intelligence would have a negative effect. We can therefore take it that the positive effect in the first of these instances is due, in part at least, to the impact of the fixed self.

A Fixed Self-View can Often Have Negative Effects

Fixed Self-Views may not be Negative...

Arguably, therefore, the effects of the fixed self-view can, at times, be positive; it is not necessarily an entirely negative thing. The point being made in this chapter is not that habitually allowing a limited set of subsidiary self-world perspectives control over how we act, think, and feel in the world will *always* have negative effects on ourselves and others. It is, rather, that there is a good case for claiming that it can often have such negative consequences. The implication being that, if the practice can be avoided without losing the potential positives (as will be argued in Chapter 16), it ideally should be avoided, especially if this is done in a way that also begins to address the misdefinition problem alluded to in Chapter 7.

...But They can be Negative

We now turn to the case for the claim that a fixed self can also have negative effects – that these arise when a conflict between an entailed perspective and reality becomes an issue and are strengthened and harder to escape when emotional, habitual, and perspectival barriers are involved.

The case, once again, is based primarily on examples, with the main focus being another version of our fisherman with a flat world belief, and this and other examples being used to illustrate conflict-based negative effects in a range of environments.

Before we turn to the first of these examples, however, it is worth noting that, as with the positive effects dealt with above, we can also claim some evidential support for the claim that fixed selves can have negative effects. This is again indirect in that its focus is on beliefs as such rather than fixed selves based on the beliefs. However, it is arguably indicative nonetheless. As with the positive effects, we know that individual beliefs can sometimes have negative effects (see, e.g.,

Gibbs, 2015; Kaanders et al., 2022; Scheffer et al., 2022), but this is not the point here. What is required is support for the claim that the fixed self can have negative effects, not simply that the belief at its core can have negative effects.

As may be evident, the support claimed above for the assertion that the fixed self can have positive effects can be readily repurposed to support the case that it can also have negative effects. We can argue that the same work referenced there regarding the effects of having either a fixed or malleable view of personal intelligence (Dweck, 2013; Gál et al., 2022; King, 2017; Mueller & Dweck, 1998; Smiley et al., 2016) can also give indirect support for the claim regarding negative effects. This work shows that learners with a malleable view tend to seek out opportunities to learn and develop and to react to setbacks by working to find ways to overcome them; their belief has a positive effect. It also shows that learners who regard intelligence as fixed tend to regard setbacks as reflections on their own presumed lack of innate intelligence and to react in a more floundering fashion as a result; their belief has a negative effect.

We can argue on this basis that a fixed self that favoured the fixed view of intelligence and blocked out its opposite would evidence a negative effect, one due partly to the belief having a negative effect and partly to the blocking out of the malleable view of intelligence. A self-view that consciously or unconsciously applied both views in different situations would have less of a negative effect, and a fixed self that favoured the malleable view of intelligence would have a positive effect.

A similar argument can be built around Subhi and Geelan (2012). Most members of Christian groups that regarded homosexuality as a sin suffered negative effects when they realised they themselves were homosexual, except for a few who had by that time given up their association with the group. This suggests that anyone with a fixed self based on the belief that homosexuality is a sin for a Christian, so that they could not move beyond this view, would inevitably suffer negative effects on discovering that they themselves were homosexual, arguably offering further indirect support for the claim that fixed selves can have negative effects.

Examples: Negative Effects

The primary case for negative effects depends on examples, however, with the first of these again focused on our fisherman who believes the world is flat.

Imagine a man who lives on an island in the middle of a huge ocean. His (recently deceased) parents taught him everything he knows about living in their island community: his mother about the ways of his fellow islanders, his father about fishing, and so on. Between them, though, they only taught him two things about the world beyond the island. He has spent his whole life hearing these stated, alluded to, or hinted at every other day. From his mother, he has heard that a man from a neighbouring island killed her father and raped her mother, and that 'blue-skinned devils' like him are evil and not to be trusted. From his father, he has heard that it is an absolute fact that the world is flat and that he cannot sail beyond their normal fishing grounds, or he will go over the edge of the world and fall to his doom. He is so used to hearing these things that he has a deep-seated fear of both blue-skinned people and fishing too far from his island, considers his views on them undeniably correct, becomes hurt or angry if they are questioned (especially by blue-skinned people), and habitually avoids both. He is, moreover, largely unaware that there are other points of view on these issues, seeing his views as facts, not points of view.

Is it not probable that when our fisherman suddenly finds one day that his usual fishing grounds are exhausted, he will be too afraid to go fishing further out, to the detriment of himself and his family? Is it not also likely that claims by a fellow fisherman who is a 'blue-skinned devil' that the world is round and that fishing further out is a safe and fruitful pursuit will be rejected and seen as an evil plot to send him to his doom? Even if we allow that some aspect of his greater self-view may eventually ensure he will be able to break out of this particular bind, is it not likely that he would take longer to do that than he might otherwise do and that he and his family would suffer as a result? Is it not also likely that he himself would suffer higher levels of anxiety as he forced himself out towards what he assumed was the edge of the world? These are the kinds of considerations that underpin the claim that allowing a limited set of subsidiary self-world perspectives control over how we act, think, and feel in the world can sometimes have negative effects on ourselves and others.

Emotional, Habitual and Perspectival barriers

Is it not also likely that the negative effects our fisherman experiences will be stronger because his views about the world and about blue-skinned people are emotionally charged via their associations with his mother and father? If the conflicting situation challenges and contradicts not just a long held world-view but the strong feelings he has about that view because of its association with his much-loved parents, can we not reasonably presume that the negative effects he experiences will probably be magnified? Does our own experience of being human not tell us that this is the likely outcome? It is generally accepted that emotions can strengthen beliefs (see, e.g., Frijda et al., 2000; Lao & Young, 2019; Memon & Treur, 2010; Mercer, 2010). If a fixed self entails and deploys an emotionally charged belief that has a negative effect in certain circumstances, is it not reasonable to suggest the negative effects will also be strengthened?

Is it not similarly likely that the negative effects will be harder to escape if there are emotional, habitual and perspectival barriers in place that make it harder to change the perspective that is at the heart of the negative effects and replace it with a better alternative? If escaping the negative effects means changing perspective – switching from a flat world-view to a round world-view, for example – can we not presume that this will be more difficult if there is an emotional attachment to the perspective that strengthens the belief? Can we not also presume that changing the perspective will be more difficult if there are perspectival barriers to change – if, for example, there is an unconscious assumption that the perspective is not a perspective but simply reflects the reality of how the world is? Can we not additionally presume that changing it will also be more difficult if seeing the world in this way is a much-used habitual way of viewing it? There is research that suggests that each of these barrier types can operate to block a change of perspective (see, e.g., Frijda et al. (2000), on how emotions affect resistance to belief change, De Aldecoa et al. (2021) on how habits can impede creativity, and Öllinger et al. (2008), on how mental set can sometimes block insightful thinking). This, on the face of it, supports the view that the assertion is likely true.

Features That Affect Control and Negativity...

We will move on to other examples presently, but it is worth noting first of all that the level of control – and the consequent extent of an associated negative effect – is likely to be a matter of degree. Imagine that, just as the fish stocks run out, our fisherman meets his future wife. Her own much-loved and dearly-departed father taught her a couple of things too, things she passes on to her new friend. First, that both fathers and ways of seeing things can be wrong, and that sometimes our beliefs and feelings about both need to change. Second, that her own father believed that the sea went on forever – that a person could never fall over an edge, however far out they fished.

It is probable, is it not, that hearing these notions from his future wife changes the fisherman in two ways? On the one hand, it adds an additional way of seeing the world to his repertoire, showing him there are alternatives to the flat world-view his father taught him. On the other, it gives him a way of, as it were, 'rising above' his flat world-view and his beliefs and feelings about it and opens up at least the possibility that they could be wrong. Between them, these two changes likely move him slightly in the direction of the kind of wholly-variable self-view described in Chapter 8, offering both an expansion of the views available to him and an increased ability to free himself from one subsidiary self-world perspective and adopt an alternative.

On the face of it, this should mean that the possibility of a different response to the fish stocks running out is increased – that the hold of the flat world-view is weakened. First, because the fisherman now has an additional perspective that increases the chances of him seeing the flat world perspective as a point of view and changing his beliefs and feelings about it. Second, because he now has a repertoire of possible responses entailing an alternative way of seeing the world.

And, of course, the inverse of the point also holds. Presumably, the unavailability of an alternative world-view and an inability to see the flat world notion as a point of view strengthens its hold somewhat. The presence of these features makes it a little bit more likely that our fisherman will be able to break out of the bind that his parents have put him in and be more able to escape its negative effects. Their absence (a move in the direction of more absolute control by the fixed flat world self-world view and away from the wholly-variable self-view described in Chapter 8) will make it a little less so. Twin points that will be important in the next and subsequent chapters as we begin to discuss our proposed alternative human self-view in more detail.

Two Conditions: Conflict That Becomes an Issue

As indicated above, the view taken here is that the negative effects of the fixed-self habit will arise whenever two conditions are met. First, where there is conflict between the limited set of subsidiary self-world perspectives in operation and the actual nature of the world; second, where circumstances bring that conflict to the fore. A fixed set of perspectives that conflict with the reality of the world may work without difficulty in a range of common circumstances – especially so in these days where science is such a dominant influence on our view of the world – but have a negative impact in others.

This is another area where it can be reasonably claimed that there is a certain amount of indirect support from the literature on beliefs for the assertion being defended here. Subhi and Geelan (2012), for example, report results showing, among other things, that subjects growing up with a positive view of Christian teachings encompassing the view that homosexuality is a sin only experienced negative outcomes when they realised that they were homosexual themselves. Dweck (2013) reports various studies indicating that praising the intelligence of students who see intelligence as fixed (rather than able to be improved with effort) can have a positive effect on self-esteem but turn negative when challenging tasks are encountered (see, e.g., Mueller & Dweck, 1998). Baumeister (1990), in a discussion of 'suicide as an escape from self', reports that painful self-awareness caused by conflict between relatively high self-regard based, among other things, on past achievements, can lead to suicidal thoughts and suicide attempts when something arises to damage their self-esteem.

These results relate to individual beliefs rather than fixed selves, but they do imply that a fixed self encompassing such beliefs and deploying them in circumstances that expose a conflict between them and how the world is will have a negative effect in those circumstances. They offer indirect support for the claim that the negative effects of the fixed-self habit will arise when a conflict between a world-view entailed in the fixed self and how the world actually is becomes an issue.

That said, however, the primary basis for this claim is again a set of examples – plausible combinations of particular fixed selves and situational circumstances most readers will hopefully find supportive of the claim. Examples covering various conflict situations possible in our outer and inner environments.

Examples: Conflicts With the Outer World (1)

Our fisherman above is the simplest of the examples. Before he meets his wife, there is a conflict between his fixed self and the world. The only view of the world he has in his fixed self is the view that the world is flat and he can fall over it to his doom if he sails too far out. There is a conflict between this fact and the fact that the world is actually round, with no edge to fall over. The conflict only becomes an issue, however, when the fish stocks run out and there is pressure to fish further out. Moreover, it is only an issue in the first place because his fixed self only entails this one view of the world. Once his wife introduces him to an additional world-view, the conflict can potentially be avoided by adopting the new world-view.

We can say that the negative effects arose for two reasons. First, because there was conflict between the limited set of subsidiary self-world perspectives in operation and the actual nature of the world; second, because the failing fish stocks brought that conflict to the fore. The negative effects of the fixed-self habit will arise whenever two conditions are met. First, where there is conflict between the limited set of subsidiary self-world perspectives in operation and the actual nature of the world; second, where circumstances bring that conflict to the fore. A limited set of subsidiary self-world perspectives may operate happily without negative impact in most circumstances, yet still have negative consequences in others. The fisherman in our example might live quite happily with his mistaken view while fish stocks remain high close to shore; the negative consequences will hit him only if the nearby fish stocks run low or if he encounters some other circumstance where his conflicting view becomes a problem.

Examples: Conflicts With the Outer World (2)

Another similar example might be someone from the entirely flat and climatically temperate country X who has grown up watching videos about country Y that appear to show that it too is completely flat and temperate. He has no reason to doubt any of this and has no experience of anywhere that is not flat and does not have a temperate climate. He has never encountered a mountain and has no idea what a mountain is. He essentially has a fixed self that consists only of a response set suitable for a flat country with a temperate climate, one that only has one other facet. He has also grown up with a religion that tells him that when bad things happen, they happen because of evil spirits, and he believes this without question. He decides to visit Y and to travel across it from one side to the other. He goes off on his trip unaware that he will have to cross extremely high mountains to complete it and entirely unprepared for the fact that it gets murderously cold up there for a person who only has clothes suitable for the temperate lowlands.

He is fine with these beliefs until the path starts moving upward. When it does and he moves into the higher regions, though, he starts to shiver. The previously hidden conflict between the subsidiary self-world perspective or perspectives in his fixed self and reality is revealed, and he suffers the negative consequence of starting to freeze. Believing this to be the work of evil spirits, he sinks to his knees and prays and prays. The weather spirits fail to heed him, though, and he eventually suffers the ultimate negative consequence of dying of cold. As with our fisherman, he has a limited set of subsidiary self-world perspectives that operates quite happily without negative impact in most circumstances, yet still has negative consequences in others. To reiterate, the negative effects of a fixed self arise whenever two conditions are met: when there is conflict between the limited set of subsidiary self-world perspectives in operation and the actual nature of the world, and when situations arise that make that conflict an issue.

Examples: Conflicts With the Inner World (1 & 2)

Fixed sets of subsidiary self-world perspectives that apply to or have an impact on the inner mental and emotional world are arguably no different. Whether conscious or unconscious, emotional attachments to aspects of an overarching fixed self that conflict with each other, with innate inner needs, or with outer pressures may co-exist quite happily in some circumstances but have negative psychological and emotional effects on us in circumstances where the conflict becomes important. A person brought up to believe that someone who steals is always 'a bad person' no matter what may rub along quite happily in times of plenty but struggle in circumstances where she is regularly going hungry unless she steals. She may then suffer the negative consequences of hunger if she does not and the negative consequences of feeling like 'a bad person' if she does. A person who sees herself as 'creative and diligent' and also as a great writer may not suffer any negative effects while she is too busy to write. She may suffer mental and emotional distress when she suddenly does have time and finds these two beliefs in conflict – that she often has 'writer's block', for example, and 'just can't be bothered applying herself' when it hits.

Examples: Conflicts Between Different Inner Worlds (1 & 2)

The same sort of thing applies to conflicts between differing views held in the inner worlds of different individuals. Emotional attachments to particular views in one person can co-exist quite happily with a conflicting view in another in some circumstances but cause feelings of pain in other circumstances. Belief that an emotional partner is a soul mate for life may actually have positive consequences – make the person happy – as long as she does not tell her partner this. It may cause her hurt and misery when she tells her partner this and discovers he sees their relationship as 'just a bit of fun for the summer'.

This last example highlights a final point worth noting about negative effects and conflict (and also adds an additional example to the list above). We can say that the probability of negative consequences arising from the fixed self will increase – at least in the population as a whole – by the extent to which humans generally cede control of themselves to different fixed sets of subsidiary self-world perspectives that conflict with each other.

Imagine a world with ten countries in which every citizen of each is brought up believing he or she is of the race chosen to rule the whole world by God 1 in country 1, God 2 in country 2, and so on. Imagine, further, that they are each taught it is their duty to kill all unbelievers and that a place in heaven is only guaranteed to those who pursue such a course of action with passion and determination. The outcome is fairly predictable, is it not? Only allow ten fixed and limited emotionally charged sets of subsidiary self-world perspectives that all conflict with each other to control groups of competing humans, and the potential for conflict with the world (and associated negative effects) is increased at least a hundredfold. (This may well be a real issue in the religious field, see, e.g., Eidelson and Eidelson, 2003; Svensson & Nilsson, 2018; and aspects of Wright & Khoo, 2019).

This is an additional reason why it seems reasonable to claim that, while allowing a fixed self control over how we act, think, and feel in the world may not always be a bad thing, it often can be. It may often have the negative effects on ourselves and others suggested here, and it is reasonable to consider whether a better alternative exists.

Features of a Better Alternative to the Fixed Self-View

Wider Access And An Ability To Switch Viewpoints

Some indication of the nature of this better alternative has already been touched on above in the example of the fisherman for whom the world is flat and his future wife. We can presume that the fisherman's acquisition of an additional perspective weakened the hold of the flat world-view. It added an alternative way of seeing the world to his repertoire, increasing the chances of him seeing the flat world-view *as* a point of view, of changing his beliefs and feelings about it, and of replacing it with the alternative. These changes move the fisherman's perspective on things in the direction of a wholly-variable self-view of the kind described in Chapter 8 by offering both an expansion of the views available to him and an increased ability to free himself from one subsidiary self-world perspective and adopt an alternative.

They also show us something about the specific kinds of mental and emotional features needed in a self-view that allows the negative effects of the fixed self-view to be avoided. Having access to alternative ways of seeing the world and an ability to switch from a view that gives rise to negative consequences because it conflicts with how the world actually is will increase the chances of avoiding such negative effects. (This might be characterised as an ability to shift mindsets or behavioural repertoires (Dajani & Uddin, 2015), one aspect of the notion of psychological flexibility (Kashdan & Rottenberg, 2010). Having higher levels of psychological flexibility is of positive value on a number of fronts, including adult creativity levels (Chen et al., 2014) and an improved ability to cope with negative situations (Genet & Siemer, 2011)).

Maximising the Possibility of Avoiding Negative Effects

What matters in individual cases, of course, is not simply having access to any old additional way of seeing the world. Our fisherman with the flat world belief would only find it easier to avoid the negative effects of his world-view if the additional world-view he attained access to was one that assisted him in avoiding the negative effects. A new world-view that suggested that the sea went on forever – that a person never came to an edge he could fall over, no matter how far out he fished – would be likely to help in this respect. However, one that told him that the sea went on forever with no edge to fall over but that a person could not turn back once he went beyond the horizon probably would not.

Access to one additional perspective will only be of value if the additional perspective is one that helps resolve the conflict between the fixed self-view and how the world actually is. Access to one or a few additional subsidiary self-world perspectives would not ensure the possibility of avoiding the negative effects of even one such conflict. Even access to subsidiary self-world perspectives at the level entailed in a self-view with the general characteristics described in Chapter 8 – a self-view open to the possible inclusion of any and all possible subsidiary self-world perspectives – might not be guaranteed to do this.

It would maximise the possibility of it, however. If a subsidiary self-world perspective that would resolve the conflict exists or could be discovered, it would be included in the group of all possible subsidiary self-world perspectives and so could be brought into play if the conflict arose. Nor would its ability to do this be limited to conflicts arising from only one particular subsidiary self-world perspective. We can expect that a wholly-variable self-view of the kind described in general terms in Chapter 8 would maximise the possibility of avoiding conflicts of this kind created by *any* subsidiary self-world perspective. Again, if a subsidiary self-world perspective that would resolve the conflict exists, it would be included in the group of all possible subsidiary self-world perspectives and could be brought into play if the conflict arose. The possibility of avoiding negative effects associated with any given subsidiary self-world perspective would be maximised because the possibility of switching from that subsidiary self-world perspective to a better alternative subsidiary self-world perspective would be maximised. It would not guarantee avoiding the negative effects of any given conflict, but it would greatly improve the chances of doing so.

Optimising Responses, Retaining Positives and Preferences

There is, moreover, another slant to this that is worth noting. Having access to all possible subsidiary self-world perspectives could be expected to do more than just assist in the avoidance of negative effects of the kinds described above. It could also be expected to help optimise responses in circumstances where all that was needed was a best choice between positive responses rather than an avoidance of conflict with the world. Indeed, it would be reasonable to argue that blocking such an optimisation of response could be seen as an additional negative of the fixed self-view and, by extension, an additional point in favour of the kind of wholly-variable self-view outlined in Chapter 8.

Notice also that the ability to switch away from one subsidiary self-world perspective to an alternative one without hindrance would also support two other features of interest to us here.

On the one hand, it would potentially allow us to avoid negative consequences while also retaining the positive features of the fixed-self habit described above. A soldier, for example, might be totally emotionally immersed in the notion that she was God's hero and the enemy were evil defenders of the anti-prophet while in combat, but be able to switch away and see them as humans just like her in non-combat situations. An ability to switch to an alternative subsidiary self-world perspective without hindrance should theoretically permit such emotional immersion yet still avoid any negative consequences entailed when a conflict with how the world actually is arises.

On the other hand, it would also allow us to retain another feature of the fixed-self habit we can expect to want to retain in our alternative human self-view: those personally unique aspects we particularly associate with ourselves as individuals or with our membership of particular groups. An ability to become immersed in a subsidiary self-world perspective but discard it in favour of an alternative as circumstances demand would potentially allow us to be immersed in and emotionally attached to such personally favoured perspectives without permitting them to become the basis of a fixed self-view.

The Third Requirement: Avoiding Negatives, Retaining Positives

These, of course, are nothing more than indications at this stage – pointers to the direction of travel as regards a wholly-variable self-view for humans. They do, however, highlight an important point as regards the requirements that our alternative human self-view must meet. If a self-view with the general characteristics described in Chapter 8 can, in theory, offer a means of doing these various things (by instantiating and supporting a wholly-variable response), it is reasonable to require that our alternative human self-view should do so also. If a self-view with those characteristics can theoretically allow us to avoid the negative effects of conflict with the world, optimise responses generally, and retain both the positive effects and personally unique aspects of a fixed self-view, we can reasonably require the same of our alternative human self-view.

This, at any rate, is the position taken in what follows: that we are seeking a self-view we can all identify ourselves with (and rehearse till it becomes operational) that offers the various features just outlined as well as others touched on in Chapters 7 and 8. The third requirement of our alternative human self-view is that it should allow us to avoid the negative effects of conflict with how the world is, optimise responses generally, and retain both the positive effects and personally unique aspects of a fixed self-view. A further requirement – that our alternative human self-view should avoid blocking the open-ended, wholly-variable response in various ways that are features of fixed selves – will be identified in the next chapter.

10

Fixed Self: Blocking the Open-Ended Response

The Open-Ended Response: No Barriers or Bias

Requirements of the Open-Ended Response

It was argued in Chapter 8 that a key requirement of a self-view that accurately reflects our full behavioural and experiential nature is that it should be a self-view that supports a wholly-variable response to all situations encountered. This, as was pointed out there, implies two things. First, that it must be a self-view in which every possible subsidiary self-world perspective entailed in our various ideas, beliefs, and viewpoints has an equal and unbiased chance of being chosen as a response in any given situation *before the situational circumstances are taken into account.* Second, that it must be a self-view in which any subsidiary self-world perspective so chosen is only permitted control on a temporary basis so that every possible subsidiary self-world perspective is again able to determine the actual relationship in whatever circumstances are encountered next. This, in practical terms, it was argued, requires a self-view so constructed and instantiated as to ensure that there are no blocks in place to prevent any and every possible subsidiary self-world perspective – even those as yet unknown or undiscovered – being encompassed and utilised in these ways.

An Open-Ended Response: No Barriers

What that means in terms of the descriptive and operational parameters of the alternative self-view for humans we are seeking is a self-view so constructed and instantiated as to ensure three things. First, that there is no barrier to replacing whatever subsidiary self-world perspective is in use at a particular time with an alternative when a need for change arises. Second, that there is no barrier to having any possible subsidiary self-world perspective available as a possible alternative, either by being included in the known subsidiary self-world perspectives in the person's repertoire or by being potentially available via the use of imagination, viewing websites, or employing creative problem-solving skills. Third, that there is no barrier to any and every possible subsidiary self-world perspective initially being given equal weight as a potential response to a particular situation.

The various varieties of fixed self criticised in this book tend to block the barrier-free, wholly-variable response in a variety of ways we will touch on below, creating blockages in all three of these areas. They get in the way of the wholly-variable response in ways that we should aim to avoid in a self-view that accurately reflects our full behavioural and experiential nature.

Blocking The Open-Ended Response: Simple Example

Although some of them are better than others in this respect, fixed self-views of the kind discussed in this book will tend to block the open-ended response on the three fronts noted above. This is easiest to see if we take a very simplistic example as an initial illustration.

Example: The Extreme Flat World Believer

Imagine someone whose only view of the world is that it is just obviously flat. He has grown up with people who assume this, and the evidence of his senses seems to him to confirm it. He is entirely unconscious of the notion that it is a view, unconsciously assuming that the world is just like that. Moreover, his upbringing has left him with various feelings and emotions – some positive, some negative – that are all tangled up with this take on the world. It is a view taught to him by his beloved late father, say. He has positive feelings about it he is barely conscious of, and tends to get angry and emotional if anyone casts doubt on it. Plus, he has been warned from an early age that he will fall off the edge of the world if he goes too far in any particular direction, and actually gets very nervous if it looks like he is moving too far in one direction or another. He has negative feelings about doing so; he has learned to fear going too close to the mountains behind his village, for example, or too far out to sea.

He has what might be called a flat-world-believer fixed self, is unconscious of having it, and has negative feelings and emotions attached to doing anything that is at variance with the view of the world it entails. If he finds himself in a situation where he needs to change tack – because, for example, the fish stocks close to shore are running low and he is facing starvation – his fixed self will tend to block the change of perspective he needs to resolve his problem. There will be barriers in place, creating resistance to the change needed.

The Barrier-Free Wholly-Variable Response

Someone capable of the kind of barrier-free, wholly-variable response described in Chapter 8 ought to have no difficulty dealing with the circumstances our flat-world believer encounters. The brain of such an individual would be able to swap away (consciously or unconsciously) from the flat-world perspective currently in play. It would be able to (consciously or unconsciously) 'consider' every possible known and unknown subsidiary self-world perspective as a possible alternative. It would be able to (consciously or unconsciously) 'select' the best one for the circumstances in an environment, giving no undue weight to any one of them.

His brain would be programmed to be open to any possible perspective in the person's repertoire being (consciously or unconsciously) 'considered' as a possible response. It would also be programmed to be open to seeking out and finding perspectives as yet unknown to him and even undiscovered; he would have the knowledge and skills to find these either via books, websites, other individuals, or through creative thinking. His brain would be optimised for sourcing a worldview that solved his problem, even if starting from a position where the solution was unknown or undiscovered.

The Fixed Self Flat-World Believer: Set Against Change

Our flat-world believer with his fixed self is, at best, less likely to have these options. His mind is, in a very real sense, set against them. He only has a very limited set of subsidiary self-world perspectives in his repertoire; he has always seen himself and the world only in terms of his one flat-world-oriented perspective on himself and the world. He is emotionally set against a change (fearful of going out too far in any direction and sensitive to any suggestion that the view – and therefore his father – is wrong). He is unconscious that the perspective that encompasses his one subsidiary self-world perspective *is* a perspective that *can* be changed (assuming that flat is just how the world is). He does not have a mind programmed to be open to and conducive to seeking out and finding perspectives as yet unknown to him or those as yet undiscovered by humans generally.

All of this means that a change to a subsidiary self-world perspective that might allow a better response to his situation is difficult, if not impossible. He is blocked from choosing a better subsidiary self-world perspective in the three ways mentioned above. There is a barrier to him replacing the subsidiary (flat-world believer) self-world perspective he has in place. Change is blocked by having only one possibility in his repertoire and none of the skills required to extend it – and because it is, in any case, emotionally and habitually preferred and assumed to be just how the world actually is. There is a barrier to selecting any possible subsidiary self-world perspective as an alternative for the same reasons: a limited repertoire of known perspectives and no skills that would allow him to extend it. There is a barrier to each and every possible subsidiary self-world perspective being given equal weight as a possible alternative, not only because he has only the one available to him but also because he has a habitual, emotional, and perspectival bias in favour of it or against changing it.

Fixed-Self Habits Inimical to the Wholly-Variable Response

This obviously cannot be taken to mean that the fixed self blocks or gets in the way of the barrier-free, wholly-variable response in the case of our flat world believer – he never had a self-view of this kind in place to block. It can, however, be taken to mean that the kind of mental environment that creates and supports a fixed self can block or get in the way of the barrier-free, wholly-variable response as such. The factors that underpin a fixed self can block the various elements that are conducive to the barrier-free, wholly-variable response, creating a mental and emotional environment where the habits, emotional preferences, assumptions, and limited set of self-world perspectives in place get in the way of those elements. Having a fixed self in place is therefore inimical to the existence of the barrier-free, wholly-variable response. It gets in the way of having a mental and emotional environment conducive to a barrier- free, wholly-variable response – or tends to, at any rate.

Barriers not Necessarily Conscious

Notice, moreover, that it may well do this in a way that the person who has a fixed self is wholly unconscious of. Some of the harder choices our brains make undoubtedly *require* conscious consideration and *must* come to consciousness as a result (when we realise that the best choice may be one of two options, for example, and can only decide which by researching the alternatives on the internet). However, many may well take place at an unconscious level (see, e.g., Libet et al., 1983; Soon et al., 2008; Wegner, 2002 – but, see also, Mele, 2009; Guggisberg & Mottaz, 2013).

Assuming what was argued in Chapter 5 holds, the various factors underlying the fixed self – habitual use, emotional attachment, unconscious assumption of truth, limited response repertoire – can get in the way of the brain's response-choosing mechanisms at all levels of consciousness. They can create neural pathways and algorithms that limit and bias response possibilities prior to a consideration of situational circumstances at both a conscious and unconscious level.

Blocking the Open-Ended Response: Complex Example

Example: The Multifaceted Fixed Self

Most of the fixed selves in place in humans are more complex than is illustrated by our extreme flat-world-believer example, of course. Clearly, the extent to which there is a tendency to block out or get in the way of perspective change, limit the repertoire of subsidiary self-world perspectives available, and give undue weight to those in the repertoire over all others will vary from example to example. Imagine, for instance, that our flat-world believer, as described above, had a range of additional subsidiary self-world perspectives in his repertoire – a range of fixed-self facets each comprising a set of one subsidiary self-world perspective. Imagine that, in addition to having a fixed flat world-view tied to the way the world is seen as regards fishing, he also had similar fixed world-views applicable to city living, social situations, religious situations, and so on. Imagine that, in the circumstances they applied to, the status of these single subsidiary self-world perspective sets was similar to that of his flat world-view when out on the ocean. Imagine that, like the flat world perspective, they were the only view he had of the circumstances they were applicable to, were habitually used in those circumstances, were assumed to represent how the world is, and were emotionally charged in some way.

Multifaceted Barriers

Moving away from the use of any one of these subsidiary self-world perspectives if the need arose would likely be just as problematic as it was in our simpler example of the flat-world believer faced with vanishing fish stocks. More subsidiary self-world perspectives would be available to him in theory, but his mind would be set against using them in anything other than the city living, social, or religious circumstances he learned to apply them to. For each of these sets of circumstances, his brain would be programmed only to consider the one subsidiary self-world perspective learned for that situation. That one perspective would, in the circumstances concerned, be emotionally preferred, habitually used, and assumed to be just how the world actually is. The same three barriers to the open-ended response would still be in place in every set of circumstances.

Thus, there would be a barrier to replacing the subsidiary self-world perspective in place for the circumstances concerned. Change would be blocked both by having only one possibility in his repertoire for those circumstances and none of the skills required to add others, and because that one possibility would be emotionally and habitually preferred and assumed to be just how the world actually is. There would be a barrier to selecting any possible subsidiary self-world perspective as an alternative for the same reasons. And there would be a barrier to giving the others in his repertoire equal weight in any selection process – not only because they are blocked by his fixed preference, but because he has a habitual, emotional, and perspectival bias in favour of that perspective in the circumstances concerned.

In all probability, the availability of additional perspectives in these circumstances would not improve things at all as regards the open-ended response. Indeed, we can imagine it might make things worse – that the brain would have a wider variety of fixed paths to get lost in and that these would get in the way of the open-ended response to an even greater extent than in the simple flat world believer example.

Any Improvements Limited

That said, it is also possible to imagine other possibilities that would improve the situation in this respect. The availability of a range of alternative subsidiary self-world perspectives might help the person who had this more varied fixed self realise that his various views of the world *were* actually perspectives – that how the world actually is is not as fixed as he had assumed. This might lead to the realisation that several of them might, for example, be applicable as alternatives to his flat world-view in the falling fish stocks situation. This would make a variable response slightly more likely – cause him to be more open to other alternatives.

It would still be severely limited, however. He would not be open to all possible subsidiary self-world perspectives as possible responses, only to a limited set; his habits, assumptions, and emotional attachments would still get in the way of anything even approaching a fully variable, open-ended response. Indeed, this would still be true even if he acquired a wider, but still limited, set of preferred *optional* responses to one set of circumstances or another. He would still not be open to all possible subsidiary self-world perspectives as possible responses in the circumstances in question, only to a limited set; his habits, assumptions, and emotional attachments would still get in the way of anything even approaching a fully variable open-ended response.

Fixed Selves Tend to Block the Open-Ended Response

It is possible, of course, that any revelation regarding his views being perspectives on the world rather than invariable facts as to how the world is might take him even further. It might also draw him to learn more about different ways of seeing the world and to acquire the skills required to find them in libraries, on websites, or in classrooms. It might even encourage him to start looking for new perspectives himself and have him trying to develop his own imagination and learning skills to this end. Such developments would make his mind more conducive to acquiring unknown and undiscovered perspectives and would certainly improve his ability to be more variable in his responses from within his artificial fixed-self environment, even if they did not take him the whole way in that direction.

The point to take from these examples is not so much that fixed selves block out every option and facility entailed in the wholly-variable response entirely, uniformly, or in every instance. It is that the kinds of habits, assumptions, and emotional attachments illustrated in the flat-world believer example *tend* to block the various aspects of the open-ended response and probably can block them entirely in some circumstances. They tend to get in the way of the brain choosing the appropriate and best option from the range of all possible idea-based subsidiary self-world perspectives, even if they do not necessarily do so entirely, uniformly, or in every instance.

The Fourth Requirement: Avoid Fixed-Self-Type Blocking

The significance of this is that it not only suggests a fourth requirement of the alternative human self-view we are seeking, it also allows us to further clarify the second requirement we identified in Chapter 8. In respect of the first of these – the fourth requirement – it suggests that our alternative human self-view should be such that it does not block the open-ended wholly-variable response in the various ways the fixed self can. It should not get in the way of the brain choosing the appropriate and best option from the range of all possible subsidiary self-world perspectives in the way that the fixed self can. In respect of the Chapter 8 requirement, it allows us to be more precise about the nature of a self-view able to support a wholly-variable self-world interaction in the open-ended, barrier-free sense identified there. It allows us to specify that such a self-view should be the polar opposite of a fixed-self – a self-view able to support a wholly-variable response, rather than block it in the ways a fixed self can. It allows us to specify that it should be a self-view so constructed as to permit the deployment of a situationally appropriate response from a repertoire of all possible responses utilising bias-free response switching and selection mechanisms rather than one that has barriers in place to prevent these things. To restate the second requirement identified in Chapter 8 in these terms.

We shall see when we come to consider the detailed workings of the transcendent self-view we are moving towards (Chapters 13-17) that, assuming what is argued in Chapter 12 regarding empty consciousness is true, meeting all of these requirements (and more) is entirely possible. Before we move on to that, however, it is sensible to raise an obvious question – one we will address in the next chapter. Is it really the case that any and every fixed self-view should ideally be avoided? If it is conflict between the fixed self and how the world actually is that is the cause of the various negative effects outlined above (Chapter 9), might a fixed self-view based on a wholly complete, wholly correct, wholly scientific world-view provide us with an exception?

11

A Science-Based Overarching Self-World View?

Can a Science-Based Fixed Self be an Exception?

A Science-Based Fixed Self Will Not Do

So, is it really the case that any and every fixed self-view should ideally be avoided? If it is conflict between the fixed self and how the world actually is that is the cause of the various negative effects outlined in Chapter 9, might a fixed self-view based on a wholly complete, wholly correct, wholly scientific world-view provide us with an exception? This would consist of every scientifically correct view we could possibly have about anything in the world and would, on the face of it, avoid conflict with how the world actually is on all fronts. Might this provide us with a self-view that reflects our full behavioural and experiential relationship to the world? The answer to this question – even for science itself, arguably – is an unequivocal no.

Practical and Scientific Barriers; The Main Problem

There are, of course, practical difficulties with the notion. Even if we could currently pin down something we could all agree was a wholly complete, wholly correct, wholly scientific world-view, how could we all hope to acquire such an extensive viewpoint and make it the basis of our self-view? The idea is simply not practical. Even if it were, the idea is likely to encounter significant resistance from the scientific community itself. For one thing, our scientific world-view is still developing. There are many areas where our knowledge is known or thought to be incomplete or is still argued over (see, e.g., *The Biggest Questions in Science*, 2018). For another, the whole ethos of science goes against regarding even the most tried and tested scientific hypothesis as any kind of unchallengeable and final truth (Popper, 1963; see also Ebringer, 2011). Creating a fixed self based on some final scientific view – making this view the fixed basis of how every human saw and related to everything, perhaps one that also entailed emotional attachments and an unconscious assumption of truth and completeness – flies in the face of this.

These issues are far from being the main problem, however. There are other considerations that must lead us to reject the scientific world-view as a controlling, overarching self-world perspective for the human self, even if it were practical and consciously seen as a provisional scientific view of the world held without emotional attachment.

A Science-Based Relationship: Still Fixed with Negative Effects

The Fixed Relationship of the Scientist

It was argued in earlier chapters that the actual behavioural and experiential relationship of humans to the world is wholly-variable, not fixed. It was further argued that allowing any one subsidiary self-world perspective set overarching control of the human self to the extent that our habits make it the only view of self, world, or self in the world we ever use turns this on its head. It effectively takes that variable behavioural and experiential relationship to the world and makes it fixed.

It is tempting to assume that a wholly complete, wholly correct, wholly scientific world-view – being, presumably, all-encompassing in respect of the knowledge it contains of anything in the world we might encounter – would prove an exception to this rule. This is not the case, however. Such a perspective would entail everything there is to know in terms of the nature of the things we encounter in the world: the sun, a flower, ourselves, other people, a waterfall, an electricity pylon, and so on. What it would not do is encompass all of the possible behavioural and experiential relationships to these things available to us as humans. Instead, it would only encompass one – that of the scientist.

A person with only the scientific subsidiary self-world perspective set in her repertoire to the exclusion of all else would only ever experience the world from a scientific viewpoint and react accordingly. Roles that allowed her to act, think, and feel in the world as a poet, a sunworshipper, or a silly comedian at a children's party claiming the world was made of blancmange would be outwith her repertoire. Assuming the relationship was truly fixed – or so ingrained as to be something very close to that – she would be something less than fully human in the wholly-variable sense meant here.

By habitually assuming the scientific world-view to be the only world-view she would have effectively defined herself, not as a fully developed human with a variable behavioural and experiential relationship to the world, but as a *kind* of human. She would effectively have misdefined herself as what we might call the scientist kind of human and have made that misdefinition actual. She would not have a self-view that fully reflects our true, wholly-variable behavioural and experiential relationship to the world.

She would be able to adopt varying perspectives on even individual aspects of the world as seen by science, of course, but all of them would ultimately be based on the self-world relationship of the scientist. The relationship entailed would be effectively the same in all cases, at both an overarching and a subsidiary level. It would be the relationship of the wholly objective outside observer of the things in the world. It would neither encompass nor be able to instantiate other views of the self-world relationship.

Negative Effects Reduced not Eliminated

As a container for our knowledge of the nature of the world, a wholly complete, wholly correct, wholly scientific world-view would presumably be all-encompassing. But as a definition of who we are as humans, it would represent only one of the many behavioural and experiential relationships we are able to bear to the world. Adopting it as the basis of our self-view would not have the effect we are aiming for. The likelihood of negative effects would probably be reduced somewhat because conflict with the nature of the external world is less likely – this is, after all, assumed to be a wholly complete, wholly correct, wholly scientific world-view. Reduction of conflict with the nature of the internal world is another matter, however. Our scientific world-view would presumably recognise the variable nature of the human behavioural and experiential relationship to the world, but making it the basis of a fixed self would, through that very act, create conflicts in respect of that variable nature. It would block out impulses to be poetic, religious, humorous, or just plain silly, and this would presumably give rise to negative effects by frustrating these impulses. It would also negatively affect our interactions with the internal worlds of others following similar impulses, in that our ability to interact effectively with someone who is being humorous or poetic would be hampered by our solely scientific relationship to the world. It would do both of these things at both an overarching and a subsidiary level.

A Better but Still Limited Basis for a Self-View

The scientific world-view would undoubtedly make for a better, more flexible, fixed self than something more limited and limiting, such as the flat world-view we discussed earlier, but it would still be limiting and incorrect as the basis of the human self-view. It would fix our behavioural and experiential relationship to the world just as other limited sets of subsidiary self-world perspectives would if adopted as the basis of our self-view. It would not allow the kind of variable response we are seeking and could not be the basis of our alternative human self-view. We would always and only relate to anything and everything in the world, including ourselves and other humans, via our scientific view of it. We would block out humorous, poetic, religious, political, and other ways of seeing and relating to such things. Our self-view would not be a true reflection of our wholly-variable behavioural and experiential relationship to the world.

Conflict with Science Itself

Two Areas of Conflict

There are, moreover, other issues to consider. Arguably, allowing a wholly complete, wholly correct, wholly scientific world-view a controlling role in the human self puts us in conflict with science itself – on two counts.

The first relates to the scientific world-view itself. If it is true that the actual behavioural and experiential relationship of humans to the world is wholly-variable, not fixed, then a wholly complete, wholly correct, wholly scientific world-view must presumably reflect that. This means that allowing that scientific view to fix our relationship to the world would be at variance with the scientific world-view itself. We would be fixing our behavioural and experiential relationship to the world using a world-view that says that relationship is wholly-variable and making something we hold to be true operationally false in the process.

The second relates to an erroneous conclusion that might well be reached through the introduction of bias into a scientific study of the human self-world relationship. In a world where everyone took a scientist's perspective on things all of the time, scientists studying the human self-world relationship might well conclude (wrongly) that the relationship was fixed, not wholly-variable, simply because everyone adopting the scientist's perspective all of the time would make it seem true.

This would be an issue for science on two fronts.

First, because assuming the relationship is wholly-variable, as argued in this book, it would lead science to draw an erroneous conclusion that nevertheless appeared to be well supported by the observational evidence. Everyone would act, think, and feel as though the relationship was a (relatively) fixed one.

Second, because the reason for the erroneous conclusion would be the introduction of something we can think of as a form of self-fulfilling prophecy bias into the equation (see, e.g., Stukas & Snyder, 2016). In essence, the conclusion would appear to be true because the subjects studied took it to be true and made it true by adopting a self-view based on a fixed view of the human self-world relationship. Scientists do and must strive to avoid the introduction of bias into their attempts to discover the true nature of things (Arias et al., 2023; Scribbr, n.d.), but this would be a case of erroneous results arising from the introduction of a bias whose source, ironically, would be science itself. It would be an erroneous result arising from the simple fact that the subjects studied had adopted and habitually used a perspective on the world espoused by the scientists observing them. Arguably, a slightly unusual form of self-fulfilling prophecy bias.

A Temporary and Replaceable Self-World Perspective

Assuming that the human behavioural and experiential relationship to the world is indeed wholly-variable as has been argued above, each of these conflicts implies a single thing. Both mean that, even from a scientific viewpoint, the scientific world-view and the outside observer's objective self-world perspective it entails must be consciously recognised as a temporary perspective on the world. If it is always used as the only view of the human self-world relationship, there are two possible negative outcomes for science.

If the situation is such that scientists have already established that the human relationship is wholly-variable, it creates a situation where a scientific view of the human self-world relationship that sees that relationship as wholly-variable actually makes it fixed. If the situation is such that scientists are still seeking to discover the human self-world relationship, it will likely lead them to draw an erroneous conclusion based on a form of self-fulfilling prophecy bias, whose source ironically is an acceptance by all humans of the scientist's perspective on the world.

These problems only arise if the scientific world-view is *always* used as the only perspective on things and allowed to fix the human self-world relationship as a result. Even from a scientific viewpoint, therefore, the scientific world-view and the outside observer's objective self-world perspective it entails must be consciously recognised as a temporary perspective on the world. It must be recognised at both an overarching and a subsidiary level as one of many self-world perspectives that can define who and what we are and determine how we act, think, and feel. It must be consciously recognised as one of a range of possibilities that can include anything from religious, political, and philosophical perspectives to fantasy and even nonsense perspectives.

If the arguments presented in this book are valid, the human behavioural and experiential relationship to the world is wholly-variable, not fixed. Our focus on the scientific world-view must reflect that. It cannot be the basis of our alternative human self-view. The result would still be limiting and incorrect. In this respect, at least, it is no different to any other self-world perspective.

The Fifth Requirement: No Idea-based Perspective Adequate

This is not to suggest that the scientific view is on a par with the blancmange view of the world mentioned earlier in all circumstances, or even in most. As our best way of arriving at a detailed and accurate understanding of the world, including ourselves, science is unmatched; it stands alone. As might be expected – and as we shall see as we proceed – there are sound reasons for giving the scientific viewpoint and approach a very significant role in our alternative human self-view.

That said, the question of the relationship between our scientific world-view and our alternative human self-view is a complex one best left for more detailed consideration in later chapters of the book. In particular, it will be dealt with further as we move through Chapters 22-26.

Chapter 22 will focus on the key role a scientific outlook and education have to play in a wholly-variable self-view, particularly as regards ensuring that response choices are adequate and appropriate to situations where the true nature of the world is an important consideration.

Chapters 23-26 will seek to show, among other things, that failing to recognise the scientific outside observer's viewpoint as a *perspective* on reality rather than reality as such can even block progress in science itself where the question of the relationship of consciousness to the physical world is concerned.

These questions need not concern us at present, however. All we need note for now is that a fifth requirement of our alternative human self-view is that it should not have any self-world perspective or self-world perspective set as its basis – not even one based on a wholly complete and wholly correct objective observer's scientific world-view. On the one hand, using any limited set of ideas as the sole basis of how we relate to the world blocks out the range of subsidiary self-world perspectives outwith that limited set, so no approach based on a limited idea set will do. On the other, attempting to build a wholly-variable response based on adding every possible subsidiary self-world perspective to our repertoire is, as we have seen earlier (see Chapter 8 under **An Infinity of Self-World Perspectives?**), impractical in terms of volume and impossible because it cannot encompass as yet undiscovered perspectives. For each of these reasons, an idea-based approach cannot work; it cannot be the basis of a wholly-variable relationship and cannot provide us with a self-view that fully reflects our true behavioural and experiential nature.

Something else must act as the basis of our alternative human self-view. Something that will not create one of the various varieties of idea-based fixed self discussed earlier if placed in that role. Something that is arguably the one thing in our experience that neither is, nor entails, a self-world perspective – and so, cannot be an idea that encompasses a self-world perspective. Something labelled here as 'empty consciousness'.

12

Empty Consciousness

Empty Consciousness as the Core of the Self

The aim in this chapter is to begin to make the case for placing empty consciousness at the core of our alternative human self-view. Five points are made in favour of the position.

The first is that, provided it is known directly as itself and not indirectly via another perspective, empty consciousness is the only aspect of our experience that neither is, nor entails, a self-world perspective, and so cannot be an idea. It is also an experience outwith or beyond all possible viewpoints, feelings, and other sensory events.

The second is that this makes it the only possible basis of a self-view that avoids giving undue weight to some idea-based fixed view of our overarching self-world relationship if we habitually identify with it as the preferred and repeatedly rehearsed central hub or resting state of the self. (Always provided it is known directly and nonrelationally as itself and not via another perspective.)

The third is that it is, in addition, generally suitable as the core of our alternative human self-view and is a real and distinguishable aspect of our experience that we *can* make the central hub or resting state of the self.

The fourth is that it is also a unique aspect of our experiential nature in its own right and must, of necessity, be included in a self-view able to fully reflect our behavioural and experiential nature for this reason.

The fifth is that, in view of these various points, the sixth and final requirement that our alternative human self-view must meet is that it must be a self-view built around the nonverbal, nonrelational essence of conscious experience, labelled here as empty consciousness.

The chapter also covers some additional points about qualia and argues that, while the various arguments made for the points noted above assume that indirect realism is true, the same conclusions can be drawn even if it is not – if direct realism is true instead.

Empty Consciousness Defined
The Essence of our Every Experience

As defined here, empty consciousness is the one element of our mental and emotional landscape – of what we know of ourselves and the world – that is common to our every experience. It is that aspect of our experiential landscape – everything we sense, feel, or think about the world inside and outside ourselves – that makes our experiences conscious. More specifically, it is the essence of our every conscious experience with every way in which individual conscious experiences differ from each other removed – conscious experience without content: empty consciousness. Everything we experience – seeing stars, tasting tea, hearing music, thinking creatively, smelling gas, anything sensed, thought, or felt – is experienced in consciousness, and empty consciousness is the one thing they all have in common, however different they may be in terms of individual character.

The Underlying Essence of our Experienced Self

Empty consciousness, as the term is used here, does not include the individual character of the various experiences it is common to. It is empty. It does not encompass anything at all other than empty consciousness itself. It is the underlying essence that itself contains or encompasses the individual character of our every experience. The underlying essence of every subsidiary self-world perspective, every feeling, emotion, and sensation we have ever encountered and ever could, and every experience of self, world, and self in the world we can have. It is the common element underlying all of these experiences – the empty consciousness that remains when the individual character of our various experiences is removed. Identifying with a self that has empty consciousness as its core is arguably like identifying with the underlying essence of ourselves as experienced, suggesting that it is a good candidate for its proposed core role in our self-view. At any rate, it is if, as is argued below, it is the one aspect of our experiential landscape that neither is nor entails a self-world perspective and would not give undue weight to some idea-based fixed view of our self-world perspective if we habitually identified with it.

Empty Consciousness as Nonrelational: A Summary

Seven Points

The case for this claim about empty consciousness (that it neither is nor entails a self-world perspective) is presented in detail below, but can be summarised as follows:

1. Almost everything we know is known via its relationships to other things. We can only know most of the things we know of ourselves and the world indirectly and relationally – we can only know them from the outside via a way of knowing or in terms of how they relate to other things in the world.

2. Knowing itself (conscious experience – everything we experience) is the one possible exception to this. In theory at least, knowing itself can be known directly and nonrelationally – it can be known *as* itself and in relation to nothing but itself.

3. Observation of our own experiential world seems to support the notion that knowing is known directly in this way; we seem to know a red, a sweet, or a whimsical experience by direct acquaintance with the experience itself.

4. There is, moreover, a more compelling argument in its favour. Assuming that we do *not* know everything we experience directly and nonrelationally leads to an infinite regress. If we do not know it directly and nonrelationally, we are forced to think in terms of knowing it via another way of knowing, then another and another and another (and so on ad infinitum). Assuming knowing itself or everything we experience *is* known directly and nonrelationally is the only way of resolving this infinite regress and is arguably the only reasonable conclusion on that basis. Ergo, everything in our conscious experience, including empty consciousness, must be known directly and nonrelationally as and in terms of itself.

5. This means that, as an aspect of experience defined as having no content other than empty consciousness itself, empty consciousness cannot entail a relational view or self-world perspective (it is empty) and cannot itself be relational (it is empty consciousness known directly and nonrelationally *as* empty consciousness). It is direct nonrelational knowing of nothing but (empty) direct nonrelational knowing and cannot entail anything relational.

6. This does not apply to anything else in our conscious experience. Although we must have direct and nonrelational knowledge of everything in conscious experience to resolve the infinite regress, the content of every experience other than empty consciousness is indirect and relational in nature. Even simple experienced redness

expresses a relationship between light of a particular wavelength and aspects of the human visual system.

7. Empty consciousness is therefore the one aspect of our experience that neither is nor entails a self-world perspective, and so is the one aspect of our experiential landscape that would not create the kind of fixed self argued against in this book if used as the core of a self-view. Habitually identifying ourselves with it would not create a fixed self by giving undue weight to some idea-based fixed view of our self-world relationship – not being an idea, the habitually preferred core could not become the basis of a fixed self.

Indirect Realism

It will be evident as we proceed that the detail of these seven points is presented in a way that assumes that the view of perception and the external world labelled *indirect realism* is true (see, e.g., O'Brien, n.d.). This, in essence, is the view that we know the world indirectly via our sensory constructs – that, as Russell (1912, p. 74) puts it, '... knowledge of the table as a physical object... is not direct knowledge... it is obtained through acquaintance with the sense-data that make up the appearance of the table'.

Indirect realism is a position disputed by philosophers who espouse *direct realism* (see, e.g., Huemer, 2018; Le Morvan, 2004), but is taken as correct here on the grounds that it is generally accepted in the neurosciences as being in accord with the empirical evidence on perception and related topics (see, e.g., Smythies & French, 2018, pp. 8-10; Kent, 2018; Lehar, 2018; Brown, 2008; see also Griffiths, 2021). That said, it will be argued later in the chapter that accepting direct realism does not substantially affect the case for the claims made here.

Indirect and Relational Knowledge is the Norm
We Know Things Outside of us Indirectly

There are reasonable grounds for holding that we can only know most aspects of our universe indirectly in relation to something else.

In its simplest form, the argument goes as follows:

In almost every case where we know some aspect of our universe, there is a physical gap between the thing known and our knowing of it – a gap bridged by information passing from the thing known to the aspect of us that knows it (a sensory system, say). The existence of this physical gap means that the thing known cannot be known directly. It can only be known indirectly via the medium of the information passed being interpreted by one or more of our sensory systems. The thing known is not known directly; the physical gap makes that impossible. It can only be that we know it indirectly *via* one or other of our ways of knowing it. Our knowing of it is indirect knowing.

In most cases – where the things known are outside of our physical body – the physical distinction is clear. The sun, the moon, the hill on the horizon, the car in the garage, the flower in the garden, the other people in the world, the cups in the cupboard, and so on, are all clearly things that are physically distinct from us as knowers. We know them via our senses and our senses as extended by our ideas; we can only know them via these information-bearing ways of knowing them, no other possibility is open to us.

The sun (and anything else external) we see is not the sun itself; it cannot be. Rather, it is *an image* of the sun itself constructed within us from information carried to our brain via our eyes and visual system (cf. Russell, 1912, p. 74). The soap we smell is not the soap itself, but the effect that physically distinct object has on our smell-oriented systems. The bell we hear and the softness of the fabric we feel are the same. We do not – cannot – know them directly; only indirectly, *via* a way of knowing them.

We Also Know Things Inside of us Indirectly

In most other cases – where the things known are within our physical body – the distinction is perhaps less evident but no less real. Most of our senses – those involved with sight, sound, touch, taste, and smell – are outward-looking in any case. In these cases, we know even parts of our physical body externally – we know them *via* the associated ways of knowing. Data is picked up from these parts of ourselves as sensed from the outside, and we know them via the associated construct in the same way as other things outside our sensory apparatus.

In the remainder of cases – those involved with inner feelings such as pleasure or pain – it is still the case that the knowing is essentially indirect; that it is known via our sense of feeling. The pain we feel when we break a toe is something other than the toe itself – a feeling that can only be a construct of our brain and central nervous system, built out of information transmitted to us as knowers *from* the toe. There is still what amounts to a physical distinction between us as knowers and the thing known. The thing known is still known indirectly via our way of knowing it on the basis of sensed information. The phantom limb phenomenon (see, e.g., Hill, 1999) seems to support this view in that we can apparently still experience a limb when the limb itself is gone; the experience is something distinct from the limb itself; we know the limb via our way of knowing it.

Indirect Knowing is Relational Knowing [1]

The significance of this is that things known indirectly in this way can only be known *relationally*; the thing known cannot be known directly *as itself*; it can only be known indirectly *in relation to* other things. The sun we see and feel is not the sun as such; it is the sun known *in relation to* our sensory systems; we know it via the visual and other data transmitted from it and the images and feelings we construct from that data. This is true even of the sun understood in more scientific terms – via verbally and mathematically expressed theories and models. We know it not as itself but *via* those theories and models.

Indeed, since much of science is constructed by observing how things behave in particular physical circumstances – which is to say, by observing their behaviour in relation to other things in the physical world – this indirect and relational tag applies for another reason. It applies, not just because our theories and models sit between us and the sun itself, but because the detailed content of these theories and models is itself indirect and relational in nature. It tells us not what the sun is in itself but rather what it is in relation to other things in the universe – planets, moons, photons, gravity, and so on. Our entire external observer's scientific knowledge of the world at large can only comprise entirely indirect and relational knowledge. Through it, we know not what things are in themselves but what they are in relation to other things in the universe – in relation to scientific models and theories, in relation to our own senses, in relation to the instruments used in our measurement of them, and so on.

Indirect Knowing is Relational Knowing [2]

In the context of the present work, this claim regarding the relational nature of our scientific knowledge rests solely on the arguments presented above. It is, however, a perspective on scientific knowledge that finds echoes in views expressed elsewhere. Russell, for example, is known for taking a similar view of physics (see, in particular, Russell, 1927). Chalmers (2003, p. 130) puts it like this: 'Russell pointed out there that physics characterizes physical entities and properties by their relations to one another and to us.'. Botin (2023, p. 1831) echoes Russell: 'we know about the properties of the world through the way that they affect us, either immediately, as in perception, or indirectly, via our measuring instruments').

Russell used this view of physics as a partial basis for a case in favour of his neutral monist position on the problem of consciousness, but this is not our direction of travel here. In the longer run (see

Chapters 23-26) we will argue for a different position on the problem of consciousness, best thought of as noneliminative physicalism. More immediately, the point made is simply that the view of scientific knowledge as relational expressed above is neither especially new nor is it necessarily controversial.

In an earlier work, Russell (1914, Lecture II 5, p. 60) notes that 'A complete description of the existing world would require not only a catalogue of the things, but also a mention of all their qualities and relations.' This is arguably tantamount to saying that a complete knowledge of the world is, as argued here, relational in nature. The one aspect of it that does not specifically mention the relations between things relates to the things themselves and their qualities. However, since we can only identify these things indirectly via our senses and by noting how they and their qualities are distinguished from other things and the qualities these have, this aspect is relational also. Our entire external observer's scientific knowledge of the world at large can only comprise entirely indirect and relational knowledge.

Knowing Must be Known Directly
The one Thing we Might Know Directly

Note that this is not just applicable to our scientific views. As has been indicated above, most of the things we know in our world – almost everything we have an experience of, or a thought about, including most of what we know of ourselves as experienced internally – are things we know in this indirect and relational way. Our knowledge of most of the objects and facets of the world known to us is always indirect and relational in nature; it cannot be otherwise. We know these things in terms of how they relate to our sensory systems, to each other, to our instruments, and to our ideas and theories. We know them indirectly and relationally.

The only circumstance in which our knowing of the objects and facets of the world can be other than indirect and relational is where the knower and the thing known are not distinct in the ways outlined above but are one and the same thing. Which means that it is only possible when knowing *is* the thing known. Knowing itself – all of our conscious experience – can, in theory at least, be known in a more direct and *nonrelational* way.

Clarification: Intrinsic and Extrinsic Properties

A point of clarification is perhaps necessary here. Some philosophers distinguish between intrinsic and extrinsic properties, seeing the latter as relational in nature and the former, by extension, as nonrelational (see, e.g., Lewis, 1983; Sider, 1996). They take the view that objects in the world have intrinsic or nonrelational properties. The size of a solid brass cube, for example, or the area of a concrete square are intrinsic or nonrelational in this parlance. They do not depend on their relationship to other things in the way that, say, the properties of water change with (and so are relative to) temperature.

This view may seem to contradict the claim that most things in the world are only known in an indirect and relational way, but it does not. In using the term nonrelational here, we are applying it to ways of knowing. In the example just noted, the size of the brass cube and the area of the concrete square may be intrinsic or nonrelational properties of these objects, but they are still relational ways of knowing the objects in question. Knowing the cube in terms of its size or the square in terms of its area means knowing them in terms of their relative size or area in relation to other things, to ways of measuring size and area, and to the notions of size and area.

Our knowledge of most of what we know is always indirect and relational in nature; it cannot be otherwise, with the one exception of knowing itself. Knowing itself – all of our conscious experience – can, in theory at least, be known in a more direct and *nonrelational* way.

Experience Suggests That it is Known Directly

This is not to say, of course, that knowing itself *is* known directly and nonrelationally, but there are good grounds for taking the view that this is indeed the case. Aside from anything else, observation of our own experience suggests that this is not just theory: that, provided we are not actively 'standing apart from' and taking a particular perspective on them, we do know the aspects of our experiential world in this direct way. Our own personal experience suggests that they are – or, at least, can be – known directly as themselves and not indirectly via or in relation to another way of knowing.

This seems evident when we observe our own experiential landscape. The logic outlined above may tell us that experiences like an image of the sun or a sweet taste provide us with indirect knowledge of things beyond themselves – like the sun itself or things with a sugary taste – but things appear to be different as regards the experiences themselves. These, it appears, are 'just there' before us when we know them and are known directly as themselves, not in relation to anything else. We may know a red sunset and a spoonful of sugar indirectly via these ways of knowing them, but we know a red sunset experience *as* a red sunset experience and sweetness *as* sweetness – we know the experience itself directly as itself.

We know each and every aspect of our experiential world by acquaintance with the thing itself (cf. Russell, 1912, pp. 73-4; Duncan, 2021); we have direct knowledge of what a red experience or a sweet experience is in itself. We may compare them with other experiences, of course – take a relational view of them for some reason or another – but, in the normal run of things, we know them directly as themselves, in relation to nothing else. Our own experience arguably confirms the notion that knowing itself – all of our conscious experience – can, as claimed here, be known in a more direct and *nonrelational* way.

Logic Suggests That it Must be Known Directly

There is, moreover, a more compelling argument in favour of the position. If we ask ourselves the question, 'How do we know knowing?', there are only two possible answers. Either we know each way of knowing via another way of knowing, which leaves us asking how we know that way of knowing (and the one we know that through and the one we know that through) ad infinitum, or we know it directly by being it. Either we assume the knower and the known are in some sense separate and need to be linked by another (and another and another) way of knowing, in which case we are led into the infinite regress just described (cf. Cameron, 2022). Or we assume that the knower and the known in this case are one thing and the knowing is known directly – that it is known directly and (hence) nonrelationally, as, or in terms of, itself by the experiencer who essentially is the experience in that experiential moment.

Viciousness Through Explanatory Failure

We really only have two options. The first is to live with an illogical and nonsensical infinite regress where we know knowing via another (and another, and another) way of knowing in an endless series of knowings of knowing. (A vicious regress, arguably, exhibiting an example of what Huemer (2016, pp. 236-7) calls 'Viciousness through explanatory failure'.) The second is to accept the only other logical alternative: to accept the conclusion that our knowing of knowing itself is direct and nonrelational knowing; that all of our knowledge of everything – the whole of our conscious experience – is known directly and nonrelationally *as itself*.

Empty Consciousness: Wholly and Uniquely Nonrelational

Empty Consciousness: No Relational Content

And this, of course, supports the claim that empty consciousness has no relational content – that it neither is nor entails a self-world perspective. Since it is defined as having no content other than empty consciousness itself, it follows that it is 'nothing but' empty consciousness with no relational content added. If all of conscious experience must be known directly and nonrelationally to avoid the infinite regress mentioned above, then, since empty consciousness is clearly an aspect of conscious experience as a whole, it must itself be known in a direct, nonrelational way as nothing but what it is. If the case made above is sound, empty consciousness must be nothing but an empty conscious experience known directly and nonrelationally as nothing but an empty conscious experience. It can neither be nor entail anything relational and so cannot be a self-world perspective.

Empty Consciousness: Uniquely Nonrelational

It is, moreover, unique in this regard. We may be able to argue that all aspects of conscious experience must be known directly and nonrelationally if we are to avoid the infinite regress mentioned above, but we cannot argue that all other aspects of conscious experience have no relational content. Only empty consciousness is direct and nonrelational knowledge of nothing but empty experience, known directly and nonrelationally *as* direct and nonrelational knowledge of nothing but empty experience. Most of the content of our conscious experience is indirect and relational in nature – or arguably so.

Some of it is simply indirect and relational knowledge of the world, including ourselves, known from the outside. All of it, other than empty consciousness itself, can be seen to be indirect and relational knowledge of the landscape of inner experience itself, known in a direct and nonrelational way – indirect and relational knowledge of our inner landscape, known directly and nonrelationally.

When we know the sun, the moon, a house across the road, or other humans (including ourselves viewed via our externally focused senses), we know the actual things indirectly and relationally via our sensory and other ways of knowing them. Viewed in relation to the things known, the ways of knowing are indirect and relational ways of knowing these things, and only indirect and relational ways of knowing these things.

There is, however, a very real sense in which these ways of knowing the world indirectly and relationally from the outside can also be regarded as directly and nonrelationally known indirect and relational ways of knowing conscious experience itself. To avoid the infinite regress, we must accept that they are directly and nonrelationally known aspects of conscious experience – ways of knowing conscious experience directly and nonrelationally – but there is also a sense in which they also contain indirect and relational knowledge of conscious experience.

When we know the sun, the moon, or other humans indirectly and relationally via our sensory systems, there is a very real sense in which we also know conscious experience indirectly and relationally. We know what conscious experience is like in relation to seeing and feeling the sun, the moon, the house across the road, and so on. These experiences are indirect and relational knowledge of conscious experience itself.

And the same is also true of the remainder of our conscious experience (other than empty consciousness itself). When we experience ourselves in particular ways – while swimming in the sea, dreaming of home, feeling sad, having a whimsical thought – there is a sense in which we know our conscious experience, not directly *of itself* but indirectly *in relation to* these various experiential circumstances. We know it through its relationships with other things – which is to say, indirectly and relationally.

We must apparently accept that we know these ways of knowing – all of our conscious experience – directly and nonrelationally if we are to avoid our infinite regress. But what we know directly and nonrelationally as regards all such ways of knowing (aside from empty consciousness itself) is indirect and relational knowledge.

Empty Consciousness Unique

On this basis, empty consciousness is unique in being direct and nonrelational knowledge of nothing but direct and nonrelational knowledge. All other aspects of conscious experience, including, obviously, our idea-based subsidiary self-world perspectives, are directly and nonrelationally known ways of knowing that *do* entail indirect and relational content. When we know ourselves, the world, or the self-world relationship in terms of (say) some Buddhist, scientific, or atheistic viewpoint, we know them *in relation to* that idea. The view we have expresses a relationship, which is why it instantiates that relationship when used as a controlling situational response.

This makes empty consciousness the one thing in our experiential landscape that neither is nor entails an idea-based self-world perspective. It cannot be something that expresses and entails a possible relationship between self and world that can become an actual relationship if used as a situational response, such a thing being self-evidently relational in nature. It is, therefore, the one thing in our experiential world that would not create the kind of fixed self argued against in this book if used as the habitually rehearsed core of a self-view – or it is if the case presented above is offers us an accurate view of things.

Empty Consciousness: An Experience Beyond all Others

Notice, moreover, that if experiences like pain encompass indirect and relational knowledge of other (hurt) parts of our bodies, and experiences like redness or sweetness encompass indirect and relational knowledge of things in the external world, this means they are experiences outwith empty consciousness as defined here. This, in turn, means that a core of the self based on empty consciousness is one that sits outside of everything else in our experience. It means that it not only sits outside of all of the various views we have of everything, but even sits outside of – stands apart from – feelings like pain and pleasure and emotions like love and hate.

Identifying with empty consciousness as the core of our self-view means identifying with an experience beyond viewpoints, feelings, and emotions. It means identifying with something empty of such things – a point that will be important later when we discuss the core of the self as the *rest state* or *resting state* we habitually return to after using any particular temporary perspective as a situational response. (Although no specific claim is made here in this regard, this 'experience beyond viewpoints, feelings, and emotions' sounds very similar to the mental state described in Desbordes et al. (2014) as 'equanimity'...an even-minded mental state or dispositional tendency toward all experiences or objects, regardless of their origin or their affective valence (pleasant, unpleasant, or neutral).' The mindfulness-related work described in this area arguably suggests that 'an experience beyond viewpoints, feelings, and emotions' is at least possible.)

The Significance and Nature of Empty Consciousness
The Key to the Case Made in This Book

As may already be evident, the case made above regarding the nonrelational nature of empty consciousness is key to the claims made for the transcendent self-view argued for in this book. Readers must decide for themselves how they view this case and the conclusion drawn, but it is assumed in what follows that the argument made is sound. All aspects of conscious experience, including empty consciousness, must be known directly and nonrelationally if we are to resolve the infinite regress noted above. Most of what we know in this way has relational content – the knowledge known directly and nonrelationally is itself indirect and relational in nature. Empty consciousness is the one exception. It is (empty) direct and nonrelational knowing of nothing but (empty) direct and nonrelational knowing. It neither is relational nor entails relational content. It is an experience outwith relational perspectives on the world, outwith sensations like redness and sweetness, and outwith emotions like love and feelings like pain – an experience that is nothing but the essence of experience itself.

This makes it the one aspect of our experience that cannot become the basis of a fixed self through any of the mechanisms identified in this book. It is not a self-world perspective that can become a fixed relationship through habitual use – it does not entail a relational perspective. It is not a view of anything other than itself that can be mistaken for how the world is, rather than just a view of it. It is not something we could normally become emotionally attached to in the normal way of things. (It is an experience that sits outside of our feelings and emotions. If we are truly experiencing it as it should be experienced, it is an experience beyond any possibility of emotional attachment that might make it the basis of a fixed self. Moreover, even if we should somehow become emotionally attached to it, it is not something that would create a fixed self in any case since it does not entail a self-world relationship. It is empty of anything relational and does not and cannot entail a relational perspective.) It cannot, on this view, ever become the basis of a fixed self in the sense outlined in Chapter 4.

What Empty Consciousness Really is

Note, however, that it is important to be clear about what is meant by the assertion that empty consciousness is known directly and nonrelationally – and thereby to be clear about what empty consciousness is; about the actual aspect of experience the label refers to.

As should be clear from the notion of direct and nonrelational knowing itself (this being what is meant by direct and nonrelational knowing: how it is defined), it does not mean that empty consciousness is known *via* some other way of knowing. It does not mean that empty consciousness is known *via* some other way of knowing called 'direct and nonrelational knowing' with the thing known sitting beyond the way of knowing and only being known via it (as with the sun and the image of the sun example above). It means, rather, that it *is itself* direct and nonrelational knowing, empty of all content other than direct and nonrelational knowing.

Empty Consciousness: Direct and Nonrelational Knowing Itself

This implies that it *just is* the direct and nonrelational aspect of conscious experience with all other experiential content taken away – and that, of course, is exactly what it is. As defined above, empty consciousness is the underlying essence of consciousness itself. It is consciousness emptied of all other experiential content. It is what makes our experiences conscious. If all of conscious experience is, by the infinite regress argument, known directly and nonrelationally, then empty consciousness is what is left when all of the indirect and relational aspects of the conscious experiences we know directly and nonrelationally are removed (consciousness emptied of all other experiential content). It is nothing but direct and nonrelational knowledge of nothing but direct and nonrelational knowledge. It *just is* the (directly experienced) direct and nonrelational aspect of conscious experience, with all other experiential content taken away.

Empty consciousness is the one thing that is left if we remove everything that makes our various experiences different from each other. Direct and nonrelational knowing is too. They are both the same aspect of our experiential world. If we take all of the relational knowing away from conscious experience, we are left with direct and nonrelational knowing of nothing but direct and nonrelational knowing – we are left with empty consciousness. The two labels have the same referent; both sets of words refer to a single aspect of conscious experience. Empty consciousness is direct and nonrelational knowing (empty of relational content), known directly as direct and nonrelational knowing (empty of relational content). It is simple consciousness of empty consciousness itself.

To know empty consciousness is to know the thing itself directly – to experience it directly as itself in a nonrelational way. It does not involve standing apart from empty consciousness and knowing it indirectly from the outside via another way of knowing. There is an awareness involved, but only in the very slender sense of having empty consciousness as the dominant focus at the core of any given experiential landscape and having a minimal level of awareness of the fact.

Knowing empty consciousness is not a matter of standing apart from it and knowing it indirectly via the perspective taken. It is simply a matter of knowing it from inside the experience itself and knowing it (and being minimally aware of it) because it is an experience and one cannot *but* know an experience (simply because it is an experience, and experiences are ways of knowing). To experience is to know – and therefore to be aware of in that minimal sense.

As long as this is recognised, empty consciousness is the one aspect of our experience that is not and does not entail anything relational and is the one thing in our experience that cannot be a self-world perspective – always assuming the case made above is sound. As long as we do not confuse actual directly known empty consciousness with a particular indirect and relational view of it, it is the one aspect of our experience we can habitually identify with without creating the kind of fixed self we are aiming to avoid.

An Ideal and Distinguishable Core for the Self
An Underlying Essence of Ourselves as Experienced

Assuming we can single it out from our experiential landscape and focus on it as a discrete aspect of experience – a point we will return to below – this makes empty consciousness ideal as the core of our alternative human self-view.

It was suggested earlier that seeing ourselves in terms of empty consciousness is like identifying with the underlying essence of ourselves as experienced – with the 'container' for everything we experience of ourselves and the world, the aspect of our conscious experience that makes it conscious. Provided it is also true (as just argued) that it neither is nor entails a self-world perspective, this makes it an entirely sensible proposition as the core of our self-view.

It makes sense to habitually see ourselves in terms of the underlying 'container' of everything we experience; there is nothing illogical, nonsensical, or difficult to imagine about a self-view built around this. And if it is not a self-world perspective, then doing so does not entail the drawbacks of allowing one or a group of such relationships to dominate the self.

Evidential Issues: Personal Experience

It is, of course, only possible to make empty consciousness the central basis of the self if it is a real and distinguishable aspect of our experiential world that we can both be cognisant of and set at the core of our every experiential landscape. That this is possible is difficult to prove definitively. It should, however, be possible to convince the reader that this is not an unreasonable suggestion.

A Real and Distinguishable Aspect of our Experiential World

It should be evident to most that there is something real we can call empty consciousness – the aspect of our mental and emotional landscape that all of our experiences have in common and that makes them conscious. It should be evident that we can mentally distinguish this something from the rest of our experiential landscape by noting this one thing they all have in common and recognising that it is something other than the things that make them different. And it should be evident that by the very act of making and noting this distinction, we make empty consciousness something that, in that instant, is the aspect of our experience that is the centre of our attention and something we are cognisant of. This is arguably a straightforward thing, evident to any one of us. This common essence of our every conscious experience is just self-evidently 'there' in our experiential landscape. It is something we can recognise and distinguish and thereby make the centre of our attention and be cognisant of – something that we can distinguish from the rest of our experiences and label as empty consciousness.

The Momentary Core of our Experiential Landscape

Setting empty consciousness at the core of our every experiential landscape is something that requires practice, and mental exercises that recognise this and support the process will be suggested in later chapters. Achieving it *momentarily* is arguably quite feasible, however. We can manage it in two ways (both of which, incidentally, should also provide further indications that empty consciousness is a real and distinguishable aspect of our experiential world).

The first of these is somewhat indirect. Since we can view empty consciousness as an extended substrata common to all experiences, we can arguably set it at the core of our experiential landscape momentarily when we cease momentarily to focus on what distinguishes individual experiences from each other. We can do it by ceasing to focus on any one aspect of our experiential landscape – by letting the underlying substrata common to all experiences become our 'focus' momentarily (although it is arguably more accurately described as an absence of mental focus). Since the underlying essence of our every experience is always there, a mind not focused on anything else must, in that instant, arguably then have the experience labelled here as empty consciousness at its core. If we are briefly not focused on anything else in consciousness but still aware in the minimal sense described earlier, then empty consciousness is the kind of nothingness that is nonetheless experientially real then at the core of our experiential landscape – or arguably so.

The second way of momentarily setting empty consciousness at the core of our experiential landscape is to use a variation on the famous Zen koan that asks, 'What is the sound of one hand clapping?' (Editors of Encyclopaedia Britannica, 2017, April 24). The exercise has three steps. The first is to employ our own hands so that we experience the sound of two hands clapping enough times so that the sound of it is in memory. The second is to internalise the experience so that when we ask ourselves to mentally answer the question, 'What is the sound of two hands clapping?' the mind will then move automatically towards our memory of the sound. The third is to then attempt to follow the same kind of mental action in answer to the Zen koan question, 'What is the sound of *one* hand clapping?'. Since this question can have no memorised experienced sound we can answer it with, an attempt to answer it should have the mind moving towards an experiential answer to a question that has no experiential answer and should take it momentarily to an empty 'space' in the experiential landscape. It should take the mind briefly to an experience that is empty of all content other than what remains in experience when all other content is removed. It should put empty consciousness momentarily at the core of our experiential landscape – briefly move the mind to an experiential place where empty consciousness is the dominant focus and core.

Viewing Empty Consciousness and Being it

Note that there is a difference between being cognisant of empty consciousness and setting it at the core of our experiential landscape. While identifying empty consciousness entails focusing on that aspect of our experiential landscape, identifying *with* empty consciousness – making it the dominant focus of an experiential landscape – does not. In the former case, we are effectively on the outside looking *at* empty consciousness; in the latter, we are viewing our mental landscape from the vantage point of *oneness with empty consciousness itself*. The latter is a matter of avoiding focusing on any identifiable aspect of our experiential landscape so that what we identify with and make the central core of our mental state is the one thing all of our conscious experiences have in common: empty consciousness.

Empty Consciousness Need not Exist in Isolation

Notice, incidentally, that it is not claimed here that it is possible to experience empty consciousness in the absence of other experiential content, nor is it necessary that this should be possible for it to be used as the core of the self-view as described in this work. All that is necessary here is that empty consciousness should be a distinguishable aspect of experience when we are conscious, not that it should be possible for it to be experienced in the absence of content.

It may or may not be possible to experience empty consciousness alone with no other content present. Perhaps without additional experiential content, there would still be something there we might be minimally conscious of; perhaps not. No position is taken on this here, one way or another; it has no bearing on the claims about empty consciousness made in this book. What matters is that empty consciousness should be a distinguishable aspect of our conscious experience when we are conscious, not that it should be possible to experience it with nothing else there to experience.

Evidential Issues: 'Minimal Phenomenal Experience'

It is worth noting, as an aside, that there is some evidence in the psychological and philosophical literature that some thinkers accept the existence of such a state.

Metzinger (2020), for example, notes that 'pure consciousness,' which he calls 'minimal phenomenal experience,' is 'probably an experience every human being knows' but that the 'most explicit reports come from contemplative traditions' (see also Metzinger, 2010).

Gamma and Metzinger (2021) report an attempt to map the phenomenal character of this type of experience using an online questionnaire and describe it in ways that suggest it may be the same experience as our empty consciousness.

Blanke and Metzinger (2009) argue for a research focus on 'minimal phenomenal selfhood' relating it to 'the *simplest* form of self-consciousness' and appear to be suggesting that something similar to empty consciousness, as defined here, as a basic underlying basis for the experienced self.

Travis and Pearson (2000) report an attempt to examine 'subjective reports and physiological correlates of... consciousness itself", describing it as 'self awareness isolated from the processes and objects of experience during Transcendental Meditation practice'.

Yaden et al. (2016, p. 286) note that the Buddhism-related meditation practice of mindfulness emphasises 'judgement-free awareness and simply being present.', while Sauer et al. (2013, p. 9) note general agreement among researchers that mindfulness consists of attending to 'momentary experience' with 'a genuine non-judgemental, open, and accepting attitude'.

Josipovic and Miskovic (2020) urge caution on equating 'minimal phenomenal experiences' too closely with 'consciousness-as-such,' suggesting that the latter is 'first and foremost' a 'nonconceptual, nonpropositional, and nondual' or 'nonrepresentational' form of awareness.

Srinivasan N (2020) notes that 'practitioners in various contemplative traditions' have reported the existence of a state of 'consciousness without content', and that, while many current conceptions of consciousness do not consider its existence as a possibility, the continuity of conscious experience may make its existence a theoretical necessity.

None of this is evidence for the existence of empty consciousness, of course; it simply indicates that there are other thinkers whose focus is conscious experience who think that it, or something very like it, may exist. As was indicated above, the view taken here is that the existence of such a state is easily verified by personal experiential observation, as described in this chapter. As with many aspects of this work, readers must decide for themselves whether this position is justified.

Clarifications

Nonrelational as Used by Colour Relationalists

A couple of points of further clarification are worth noting at this point.

The claim made here that experiences, including experiences of colours, entail indirect and relational knowledge is similar in essence to views espoused by colour relationists such as Cohen (2004), who takes colours 'to be constituted in terms of relations between objects, viewers, and viewing conditions'. Arguably, there is no significant difference between this view of knowing colour and the above claim that our knowledge of the red colour of a sunset is indirect and relational knowledge – that what is known is a relationship between human sensory organs and light of a particular wavelength.

What Cohen's paper is arguing against, however, is a nonrelational view of colour, and it is probably important, for the sake of clarity, to distinguish between nonrelational as used in that context and nonrelational as used above (and in the present book generally). The nonrelational view of colour that Cohen is contesting is one that takes colour to be independent of the perceiving mind – in effect, as a characteristic of external objects that have that colour.

Nonrelational as Used Here

Nonrelational, as used here, signifies something quite different. As should be clear from the earlier parts of this chapter, it is used here to indicate a particular way of knowing – a direct way of knowing where experiences like redness are known by the knower by virtue of being aspects of what he experiences as himself. A way of knowing in which the knower and the known are, in effect, one thing – where redness is known as redness and sweetness as sweetness by virtue of being directly experienced aspects of our experience of self. One where the thing known is not known indirectly in relation to other things but directly in relation to nothing other than itself, i.e., nonrelationally. Where the thing known is known simply because it *is* a way of knowing that the knower has access to because it is an aspect of his experienced self, and he (experientially speaking) is that self.

Direct Nonrelational Knowledge and Acquaintance Knowledge

Direct nonrelational knowledge, as may be evident, is essentially the same as what philosophers call knowledge by acquaintance in respect of our experiences (see, e.g., Hasan & Fumerton, 2020). However, it is important to be clear about what is meant by this term. Putting what acquaintance knowledge is into words is fraught with difficulty. Russell (1912, pp. 73-4) famously puts it like this: 'We shall say that we have acquaintance with anything of which we are directly aware, without the intermediary of any process of inference or any knowledge of truths. Thus in the presence of my table I am acquainted with the sense-data that make up the appearance of my table—its colour, shape, hardness, smoothness, etc… the sense-data which make up the appearance of my table are things with which I have acquaintance, things immediately known to me just as they are'. This is essentially what is meant here by having direct nonrelational knowledge of redness or sweetness and is accurate enough as its verbal expression as long as we are clear about what is implied by the word 'aware'. In particular, we must be clear (as Russell is) that we are not referring to the kind of awareness we have of something and being aware of it in an outsider looking on sense – that the word 'direct' implies a more intimate acquaintance with experiences like redness or sweetness.

Other writers tend to echo Russell in their verbal expressions, either using the phrase 'directly aware' (e.g., Duncan, 2021; Giustina, 2022) or something similar like (being familiar with) 'the known entity in the most direct way that it is possible… to be aware of that thing' (Conee, 1994, p. 144). Conee perhaps gets closer with 'Knowledge by acquaintance of an experience requires only a maximally direct cognitive relation to the experience.' (1994, p. 136) but the word 'cognitive' also has the potential to mislead.

The point is that direct nonrelational knowledge, as meant here, is acquaintance knowledge, as referred to by these and other writers, as long as we are clear that the awareness entailed is limited. Giustina (2022, p. 1) probably comes closest to the sense intended here with her 'conscious mental states there is something it is like to be in'. Direct nonrelational knowledge, as used here, only involves the minimal awareness entailed because it is impossible to have an experience like redness or sweetness without being at least minimally aware of it.

A Unique Aspect of our Behavioural and Experiential Nature

One final point about empty consciousness should be noted before we move on. If it is uniquely nonrelational, as argued above, this makes it a key aspect of our alternative human self-view from another perspective. If it is a nonrelational view of ourselves as experienced and unique in that regard, then it is an aspect of our experience of ourselves that cannot be included within a self-view encompassed entirely within self-world perspectives but cannot be ignored either.

This means (see Chapter 17) that it has a key role to play in any self-view that purports to accurately reflect our full behavioural and experiential nature, over and above the fact that it is the only alternative to basing that self-view on a self-world perspective. It is arguably a unique nonrelational experience that such a self-view must actively and knowingly encompass as an aspect of that behavioural and experiential nature – a unique aspect of human experience that any self-view that purports to accurately reflect our full behavioural and experiential nature must encompass.

The Sixth Requirement: A Self With a Nonrelational Core

These and other topics will be revisited in Chapter 13 as we begin to outline the alternative human self-view we have been seeking.

In the meantime, note that, if the arguments presented in this chapter hold (as will henceforth be assumed), we have a sixth requirement that our alternative human self-view must meet. In addition to meeting the requirements outlined in Chapters 7-11, it must also be a self-view built around the nonverbal, nonrelational essence of conscious experience labelled here as empty consciousness. If it is the only aspect of our experience that is not and does not entail a self-world perspective, it is the only possible basis of a self-view that does not give undue weight to some idea-based fixed view of our self-world relationship if we habitually identify with it. Habitually identifying with any idea-based self-view – even a scientifically based one – inevitably blocks out many self-world perspectives from the total relationship and thereby misdefines us. Only by making empty consciousness the core of the self-view we habitually identify ourselves with can we avoid this.

Addendum on Qualia-Related Questions

Before we progress to a description of the transcendent self-view itself, two further points are worth noting. Both are challenges for any attempt to give a scientific account of consciousness experience (cf. Tye, 2020; Chalmers, 1996, p. 7; Nagel, 1974), an issue considered under the hard problem of consciousness in **Part 6** of the book.

The first is the need to answer questions such as (for example), 'Why is experienced redness like this?' (rather than like a blue experience or a sweet one). The point worth noting here with regard to this type of question is that the referent of any given example of the 'Why like this?' type of question is a particular example of the directly and nonrelationally known indirect and relational knowledge of conscious experience mentioned above (redness and sweetness, for example).

The second is the need to answer the related (single) question, 'Why is conscious experience like anything?' (rather than just being information in non-conscious form). The point worth noting here with regard to this question is that the referent of the 'Why is conscious experience like anything?' question is the direct nonrelational essence of conscious experience labelled here as empty consciousness.

Final Note: Does the Case Hold if Direct Realism is True

A Case not Based on Either Version of Realism

Arguably, the case for the claim that empty consciousness is the only aspect of human experience that is direct and nonrelational knowledge of nothing but direct and nonrelational knowledge still holds if we accept direct realism as true rather than indirect realism. The case for the claim that empty consciousness is direct and nonrelational knowledge of nothing but direct and nonrelational knowledge holds regardless of which flavour of realism we accept as true.

It is based on a logic that says three things. First, that only knowing itself – experience – can be known directly and nonrelationally because knowing itself is the thing known. Second, that knowing itself is known directly and nonrelationally for the reasons given earlier. Third, that since empty consciousness is defined as the underlying basis of experience with no other content, it can neither be nor contain anything that is not direct and nonrelational knowledge. These elements of the argument do not depend on which of the realisms is adopted. The element that does is the claim that empty consciousness is unique in this respect – that all other experiences do encompass indirect and relational knowledge. This, on the face of it, appears to conflict with the direct realist claim that we have direct knowledge of the external world.

Direct in an Indirect Way?

Two points can be set against this, however. The first is that, if the case made earlier in this chapter is valid, knowing something directly and nonrelationally is only possible if the knower and the knowing are the same thing. If this is true, we can never know something in the external world directly and nonrelationally in the sense meant in this book. Since we are physically distinct from an external world thing known, we can only know it indirectly and relationally in the sense meant here.

It appears, however, that direct realists must mean it in a different sense to that meant here. In addressing the first of the eight arguments against direct realism he attempts to refute, Le Morvan (2004, p. 5) argues that direct realists must accept that perception is indirect in one sense if they are to rebut the argument against direct realism successfully. He argues that they must accept that, in line with the empirical evidence, 'perception is indirect in the sense that it involves a series of causal intermediaries between the external object (or event) and the percipient'. This means, he suggests, that direct realists can argue that it does not follow from the fact that perception is indirect in this sense, that it is indirect in the indirect realism sense that the external object (or event) is only known via a sensory construct of some kind.

Accepting this causal indirectness, however, is arguably tantamount to accepting that (contrarily) any external object (or event) is known indirectly and relationally, as claimed in this chapter, even if direct realism holds and there is no sensory construct involved.

This is evident if we think of a situation in which the percipient of an external object perceives it via several of his senses – sight, touch, and smell, say. Even if it is true, as direct realists claim, that the object is known directly in their sense of the thing itself rather than a sensory construct being known, it is nonetheless known indirectly and relationally. It is known indirectly in Le Morvan's causal sense via three different neurological and external world routes in relation to the percipient's visual sense, his sense of touch, and his sense of smell. Even if it is not known indirectly in the sense of being known via a sensory construct, it is still known indirectly and relationally in the sense meant in the present chapter. All aspects of human consciousness other than empty consciousness, including our experiences of the outside world, still entail indirect and relational knowledge.

Arguably, the case for the claim that empty consciousness is the only aspect of human experience that is direct and nonrelational knowledge of nothing but direct and nonrelational knowledge still stands. The assumption here is that indirect realism is the correct view as regards our perception of the external world, but the claims made in this chapter for empty consciousness are not necessarily in conflict with direct realism.

PART 4

The Transcendent Self-View

Part 4: Outline Of The Case Presented

A self-view with empty consciousness as its core offers the basis of the self-view for humans we have been seeking. Individuals who adopt this self-view recognise and treat empty consciousness as the core of the self – a nonverbal and nonrelational resting state or hub they are mentally continually returning to. They also recognise and treat any and every possible self-world perspective as initially equivalent, equally-weighted, subordinate aspects of that core self sitting within and under empty consciousness and able to be used temporarily and replaced as changing circumstances require (similar, but not identical to, an actor's roles). In addition, they learn to store and categorise life experiences as useful information rather than as a basis for fixed-self-type habits and further develop this initial **baseline transcendent self-view (Chapter 13)** into a **first-pass transcendent self-view**. They work to facilitate switching between self-world perspectives, to widen the range of perspectives available for switching to, to facilitate access to unknown and undiscovered perspectives, and to ensure that any choice of a replacement perspective is bias-free **(Chapter 14)**.

Being based on empty consciousness rather than even a scientifically-based idea set, this self-view self-evidently meets two of the requirements of our sought-after self-view. There are, moreover, good grounds for holding that it also meets all of the others. It can be argued that fully adopting it successfully instantiates the wholly-variable self-view described in Chapter 8 and avoids the fixed-self blocks on it outlined in Chapter 10 **(Chapters 13, 14, and 15)**. It can be argued that this creates a mental and emotional environment that entails the positive, but not the negative, aspects of the fixed self-view, as well as its personally unique elements **(Chapter 16)**. Finally, it can be argued to be a view of the self that not only avoids the misdefinitions inherent in fixed self-views, replacing them with an accurate (and operationally true) reflection of our behavioural and experiential relationship, but is the only self-view that can **(Chapter 17)**. This latter point supports the assertion made in Chapter 1 that, unless we each personally adopt this transcendent self-view by habitually identifying ourselves with it, we cannot claim to be fully developed humans. It also supports the assertion made in Chapter 6 – that adopting it fully and correctly is the only way we can avoid adopting some variety of fixed self.

13

The Baseline Transcendent Self-View

The Transcendent Perspective on the Self

A Self-View Based on Empty Consciousness

If everything argued in earlier chapters is sound, empty consciousness – the nonverbal, nonrelational essence that makes our experiences conscious and is the only thing in our experience that is not a self-world perspective (see Chapter 12) – is the only possible basis for the self-view we are seeking. It is the only possible basis for a self-view that does not misdefine us, does not entail the negative effects of the fixed self, and does not block the open-ended response in the ways that the fixed self does. If everything argued in earlier chapters is sound, a self-view with empty consciousness as its core – the transcendent perspective outlined in Chapter 1 and described in detail over this chapter and the next – will arguably meet every requirement of the self-view for humans we have been seeking. Chapters 15-17 below present the case for this claim. They also argue (Chapter 17) that the self-view not only accurately reflects our full behavioural and experiential nature but is the only self-view that can.

Baseline to First-Pass and on

Since key elements of the transcendent self-view are experiential and operational, it is best described in detail by mapping out both the mind – the working mental and emotional landscape – of someone who has instantiated it and the mental tasks she has undertaken to create and support it. Two sets of steps are involved, one covering the *baseline transcendent perspective*, presented in the present chapter; the other its extension to form the *first-pass transcendent perspective*, presented in Chapter 14. The baseline perspective forms the underlying basis of the transcendent self-view, but has an incorporated aide memoire that verbally describes the details of both the baseline perspective and those of the more developed first-pass perspective. The operational aspects of the latter version are covered in Chapter 14, which builds on the baseline perspective to create the first-pass transcendent perspective, the self-view that is the full basis of the assertions made in subsequent chapters (although further clarifications are subsequently added over the remainder of the book).

Key Assumptions

The claims made for the transcendent self-view over the next five chapters are underpinned by two general assumptions. More specific assumptions will be detailed as we proceed, but these two are worth mentioning up front. The first relates to earlier points argued. There is an assumption that everything argued in earlier chapters – particularly points covering any idea about anything and the true human relationship to the world, fixed and wholly-variable selves and responses, undiscovered perspectives and the open-ended response, and the nature and existence of empty consciousness – is sound. The second relates to the transcendent self-view itself. A key assumption made is that the self-view described over Chapters 13 and 14 can exist - that it can be instantiated by the mental exercises described and will, if it is, have the operational features claimed for it (some of which depend on assumptions about earlier points argued). It is assumed, in other words, that – partly because of assumptions based on earlier arguments put – the various exercises described will have the effects claimed for them. They will first fashion a self-view that looks and operates like the baseline transcendent self-view as described below, then build on that to fashion the first-pass transcendent self-view as described over this chapter and the next.

It should hopefully be clear to readers assessing earlier points argued and examining the mental exercises detailed in what follows that, based on their own experience of the human mind, there are sound reasons for holding that the characteristics will be as described. However, proving it definitively at this stage is not feasible. Scientific testing of actual programme outcomes is the only real way of doing this, and this is impossible at present. Aside from anything else, we can assume that no one has yet gone through the programme of mental exercises described, so there is, at present, nothing to test.

As ever with the case being developed in this book, readers must form their own judgement as to whether this assumption about the development programme and the characteristics of the self-view it puts in place has a sound basis. The assumption here is that it does, and the case presented in Chapters 15-17 is a case in favour of the self-view described in this chapter and the next as being the result of the associated mental-exercise-based development programme.

A Conjecture That Needs Testing

This is seen here as an entirely valid position to take in the circumstances. In terms of the widely accepted viewpoint that science proceeds by making conjectures about the world and gains knowledge by examining whether they can survive attempts to empirically refute them (Popper, 1963; see also Ebringer, 2011), we can see the assumption as a part of a conjecture that requires testing.

The book aims to show that a particular conjecture about the behavioural and experiential nature of humans is of sufficient potential interest to science to make it worthy of detailed scientific scrutiny. It makes the case for the conjecture that the transcendent self-view it describes is the one self-view that fully and accurately reflects the true human behavioural and experiential relationship to the world. Part and parcel of this conjecture is the notion that the self-view described can exist; that it can be programmed into the human brain by the mental exercises outlined in this chapter and the next and will have the characteristics claimed for it. If the conjecture as a whole is deemed worthy of detailed scientific scrutiny, it is reasonable to see this assumption about the mental exercises and their effects as being one element of the conjecture that requires testing.

The Baseline Transcendent Self-view: A Brief Description

Baseline Beginnings: The Aide Memoire

Describing the detail and workings of the operational baseline version of the transcendent self-view as envisaged here - a self-view intentionally designed to meet the various requirements specified in Chapters 7 through 12 - is a long process that will take up the remainder of this chapter.

Imagine a person who, with the active community support of parents, teachers, and other instructors, learns at an early age to accept that the basic human self should take the form of the transcendent self-view as described in this book.

In line with this, she aims to adopt it as her own self-view. To develop the habit of seeing and experiencing herself, not in terms of a limited set of ideas encapsulating her personal, political, social, philosophical, religious, and other allegiances as in a fixed self, but in terms of the aforesaid transcendent self-view – initially, the baseline version described in this chapter.

She understands from her instructors that this has a core or resting state aspect and an interactive role-playing aspect, and that a key element of the core is a form of words outlining the primary details (baseline *and* first-pass) of her chosen self-view. This form of words, her instructors explain, is a brief verbal description designed to act in the working self as an aide memoire to remind an adopter of the self-view's form, content, structure, and underlying logic when the instantiated working self is in its core or rest state.

Her instructors explain that she must memorise this aide memoire before moving on to tackle the mental exercises designed to put the self-view in place. They inform her that it consists of the four primary points detailed below, but tell her she should also note that the fourth point refers to the first-pass transcendent self-view rather than the baseline version as such.

Aide Memoire: Core and Interactive Role Playing Elements [1]

As envisaged here, the transcendent self-view is an operational perspective on the self with two interworking elements. One is a core and rest state in which empty consciousness is both the dominant focus and an experiential container seen (via a verbal aide memoire) as encompassing all imaginable ways of seeing and relating to the world - all possible idea-based self-world perspectives - as its subordinate facets or roles. The other is an interactive role-playing element able to deploy all such roles. In the working self, these two elements interoperate through an ongoing process of switching control back and forth between individual subordinate facets or roles deployed for particular situational purposes and a core or resting state where the self is seen and experienced as encompassing empty consciousness plus every possible facet or role. Each facet or role is held to be both a perspective on and a determinant of one aspect of the total human self-world relationship, with the whole human self-world relationship held to be determined by all of them. All are therefore seen as aspects of a transcendent self-view held to reflect the full human behavioural and experiential relationship to the world.

Aide Memoire: Temporary Whole-Self Facets and Roles [2]

Every possible idea-based self-world perspective is seen and treated as a potential way of relating to whatever circumstances an adopter encounters, able to be used in a temporary situation-specific way and replaced by a new idea-based self-world perspective when a new situation is encountered that makes replacement necessary. All of them are seen and treated within the working self in two ways. First, as temporary roles to play when required before control returns to the core self; second, as facets of the whole or total self rather than the whole or total self as such (which encompasses and is defined by all idea-based self-world relationships). In line with these points, each facet or role is viewed and controlled in a way similar, but not identical, to how an actor views and controls his onstage roles, with deploying a facet seen as enacting a limited but real facet of the subject's whole self. Any idea any human can have about anything is held to be a possible subordinate facet or role, in that even fantastic, nonsensical, and meaningless perspectives on the self, world, or self-world relationship can affect how we act, think, and feel in some situation or another (as can unknown and undiscovered perspectives – see [3] below).

Aide Memoire: All Responses; Bias-Free Switching and Selection [3]

When a new situation calls for a change of response, it is selected through the interaction of the environmental circumstances with a self designed to support a wholly-variable response as described in Chapter 8 and clarified at the end of Chapter 10 under the fourth requirement – a self open to every possible human response rather than one set to limit and bias selection in the ways that a fixed self does. All possible facets or roles are seen and treated as being equally valid as potential situational responses prior to the situational circumstances themselves being used to consciously or unconsciously select and deploy a situationally appropriate response from this all-encompassing repertoire utilising bias-free response switching and selection mechanisms.

This is ensured at a baseline level in two ways. First, by replacing the limited definitions of self, emotional attachments, habitual preferences, and erroneous assumptions of truth that characterise fixed selves with a wider, more accurate self-view – a self-view that does not entail practices that limit the response repertoire, block response switching, and bias response selection. Second, by habitually moving control back to a core self dominated by empty consciousness where there is a recognition that all possible idea-based self-world perspectives are regarded as equally possible responses. By moving control back to a core self not dominated by a restrictive fixed-self-style mental set that would block a switch to a new response, block out or bias possible responses when switching, and bias response selection, but by empty consciousness, argued here to transcend or sit outside of any biasing mental set. By moving control back to a core self held, for reasons detailed later, to support a wholly-variable response because its empty-consciousness-dominated core ensures bias-free switching and selecting from an all-encompassing response repertoire.

The notion that all possible facets or roles are potential responses in any situation encountered and are elements of this all-encompassing response repertoire is taken to include responses currently unknown to the adopter and even undiscovered by humans generally, implying and pointing up the possibility that discovering and deploying the most appropriate response in a given situation may entail knowledge acquisition, creative thinking, or both. They are verbally included in the recognition that all (collectively envisaged) subordinate facets or roles are seen and treated as limited or partial aspects of the whole self.

Aide Memoire: Wholly-Variable and Personal Enhancements [4]

The extension of the baseline transcendent self-view to the first-pass transcendent self-view enhances the position described above in various ways. It puts in place mechanisms and routines that strengthen switching perspective capabilities, widen the range of subsidiary perspectives available for switching to when a switch is required, and ensure that any choice of a replacement perspective in any situation encountered is bias-free. The enhancements include the development of associated information seeking, imaginative problem solving, and creative thinking skills that facilitate the discovery of unknown and undiscovered responses when known responses fail to solve a particular need. They also encompass a mental skill that allows the adopter to maintain any personal uniqueness she might value through the use of an 'immersion level control facility' covered in Chapter 14 (see Chapter 16 for details of how this operates). These responses related to personal uniqueness are not regarded as more important than any of the other equally valid potential situational responses at an overarching level. The third point above still holds.

Aide Memoire: Beyond the Brief Version

Our adopter's instructors also stress that the aide memoire is only an outline of the full verbal description of the transcendent self-view, a brief outline required as a key part of the functioning self she is aiming to adopt. In the longer term, they stress, she will ideally aim, with their help, to acquire a more detailed verbal understanding of the form, content, structure, and reasoning behind her adopted self-view (everything in this book, potentially, or as much as she needs to meet her own everyday operational requirements). She will ideally work to mentally link this to the various elements of the aide memoire, partly to enhance its operational influence on her adopted self-view and partly to ensure that it becomes a retrieval route into the wider description and understanding as required.

They tell her she should not worry about these points for now, however – they will take care of themselves in time. She should simply determine to regularly check that her aide memoire is in place and readily retrievable before moving on.

Instantiating the Baseline Transcendent Self-View

Instantiating the Core: Empty Consciousness Identified

Having memorised this aide memoire, she sets out to put in place the self-view it describes, working with her support community to instantiate and maintain the baseline aspect of her adopted self-view using the set of mental exercises outlined below.

Her first step in this is to identify empty consciousness - the self-view's central core - in her own experiential landscape. After some effort, she succeeds (with the help of her support community) in identifying this nonrelational experience within herself and learns to move her mental perspective at will so that empty consciousness is momentarily her dominant focus. Her support community helps her do both of these things by using 'the two hands clapping' method outlined in Chapter 12. First, they help her learn to move her mind repeatedly to a memory of the sound of two hands clapping. Next, they help her learn to make the same mental move to the experience of empty consciousness by having her internally address the question, 'What is the sound of one hand clapping?' as described in Chapter 12, to move to the experiential emptiness this question inevitably throws up. Finally, having achieved this, they help her learn, after much repetition, to develop the mental skill of momentarily making it (i.e., empty consciousness) her dominant focus at will and to consolidate her progress using the 'absence of mental focus' method outlined in Chapter 12 as an alternative way of achieving the same end.

Instantiating the Core: Adding the Aide Memoire

This having been achieved, the adopter then starts working to acquire the habit of seeing herself in terms of a core self with empty consciousness as the dominant focus and the aide memoire, as outlined above, as a subordinate perspective mentally sitting under and within this dominant focus. Having first transcribed the aide memoire from words on a page to words in her mind, she practises moving from this to a position where empty consciousness is the dominant focus but the aide memoire is still in mind within or beneath that dominant focus. A position where she is, so to speak, 'sitting mentally apart' from the aide memoire but still has it in mind. A position where she is, in that instant, mentally within the perspective at the empty-consciousness-dominated core of the self-view she is working to adopt.

Instantiating the Core: A New Habitual Self-View

Achieving this makes it possible for our adopter to begin work (with the help of her instructors) on making this experience the core of how she habitually sees herself. She becomes able to see herself in terms of the experience of empty consciousness and an aide memoire that tells her that every possible idea-based self-world perspective, including those unknown to her and even to humans generally, is an equally valid aspect of that self. She begins to view her self in this way and to repeatedly rehearse the experience as her preferred self-view until she has made it – rather than some limited set of ideas encapsulating various personal, political, social, and other allegiances – the core of how she habitually sees herself.

She habitually identifies herself, not with some limited set of ideas that then form the basis of a fixed self, but with a self-view whose core is the nonrelational experience of empty consciousness. She develops and practises the habit of seeing herself in terms of the one thing in her experiential landscape that (if the arguments put in Chapter 12 are sound) is not an idea and so cannot form the basis of a fixed self. (Not only is no idea set blocked, because no idea set is preferred, but her aide memoire, the subordinate verbally expressed perspective within her empty-consciousness-dominated core, makes it clear that all possible idea-based self-world perspectives are recognised as aspects of the self-view she has adopted.)

She thereby comes to see and experience her self in terms of an essentially unlimited (collectively envisaged) set of roles set within a nonrelational substrata that potentially contains and transcends all such relational views and the feelings, emotions, and perspectives they can entail (see Chapter 12 on empty consciousness). She comes to see and experience her self in terms of all possible idea-based ways of relating to the world plus empty consciousness – a nonrelational experience that sits outside of or above them, and a focal point seen and experienced as the core of who she is.

Our adopter has completed the programme of exercises aimed at ensuring that the core element of the baseline transcendent perspective is in place.

Instantiating the Interactive Role-Playing Element of the Self

Our adopter knows, of course – and her instructors affirm – that a verbal description that tells her that she is adopting the self-view described in her aide memoire is only the beginning. To fully adopt and instantiate the self-view, she must programme her brain so that her operational self *works* in the way her aide memoire describes in all respects. She must programme it so that each idea-based self-world relationship in her all-encompassing repertoire is *actually* treated as a facet of her whole self and as a temporary role to play when required before control returns to the (already programmed) core of her adopted self. She must programme it so that in a new situation requiring a new perspective, her response is wholly-variable in the sense described in Chapter 8, as clarified in Chapter 10. She must programme it so that, when required by a situational change, there is always a barrier-free switch from the currently deployed perspective to a mental state where empty consciousness is dominant and her brain can select a new response in a bias-free way from an all-encompassing repertoire.

With this aim in mind, she undertakes two sets of exercises in parallel: one aimed at ensuring she avoids the fixed self habits that limit her response repertoire and block switching and bias-free selection of responses; the other at putting in place a working self designed to support a wholly-variable response.

Handling and Processing Life Experiences

Using the first set of exercises, she adopts and practises ways of handling and processing life experiences so that, rather than becoming building blocks for a limiting fixed self, they instead become ways of informing future responses in a non-fixed-self environment.

When she encounters a situational response that either works, does not work, or works relatively well or poorly, she processes it in a way that will inform response selection in later situations rather than in a way that will lead to the creation of a fixed self and fixed-self habits. She avoids indulging in the kinds of habitual preferences, incorrect assumptions, and emotional attachments that can lead to the creation of a fixed self and fixed-self habits and simply files the information away for future reference instead. She focuses on creating what we can think of as a life-experiences databank that can aid her brain's selection of appropriate responses in future. She actively shuns the creation of a fixed-self environment through the habitual use of preferred perspectives, assumptions as regards their truth and falsehood, and positive or negative emotional attachments to their view of things, and instead simply notes their possible value or otherwise as regards particular future situation types. She explicitly avoids any tendency to make a habit of always using them as a preferred response in particular types of circumstances, to associate positive or negative emotions with them, or to see them as how the world is rather than just perspectives on how it is. She processes them so that, rather than create a fixed self with a limited response-choice repertoire and related barriers, they create an information bank that informs future conscious or unconscious choices. A life-experiences databank that will end up containing details of her skills, education, knowledge, and ability levels and will steer her away from or towards certain choices in consequence. She thereby avoids putting a fixed self or any fixed-self habits or barriers in place.

A Wholly-Variable Response: Temporary Roles; Whole-Self Facets

Using the second set of exercises, she works repeatedly (with the help of her instructors) to ensure that the various ways of relating to her everyday world she has learned before taking on these exercises are habitually seen and treated as described in her aide memoire. She works to identify the range of idea-based self-world perspectives she uses in aspects of her everyday life and undertakes a series of mental exercises designed to ensure that her operational self treats them as temporary roles. She repeatedly practises moving in and out of these idea-based perspectives and roles in everyday situations, seeing them as facets given temporary control, returning to her core self afterwards, and seeing it as her core or controlling self, ultimately in control of these facets. (Repeatedly moving into the empty-consciousness-as-dominant-focus state with its subsidiary aide memoire has already become 'second nature', so these exercises are merely an extension of her work with her core self.)

As part of this process, moreover, she works to ensure that she sees and treats these facets her whole self deploys as something less than her whole self – they are only limited roles her real self deploys – but also as aspects of that whole self. She works to ensure that she sees and treats them as limited aspects of her total self – aspects that, as individual facets, do not reflect its full nature, but do reflect a real part of that nature in that all such facets taken together define it entirely.

A Wholly-Variable Response: Return to the Core

She also works to develop two other mental skills: returning internally from a perspective in current use to the core self when her response needs change suddenly, and putting her mind in its resting state just before a new response to a new challenge is selected.

In respect of the first of these, she practises jumping out of an in-use perspective and returning to her core self under all sorts of circumstances, particularly unexpected ones, where she must then respond to a new situation with a new response. Her support community subjects her over and over to situations where she is immersed in some whole-self facet but encounters some unexpected event like a fire alarm, which she knows is a signal to quickly switch her mental focus out of the facet and back to her core self. In respect of the second, she practises returning to her resting state just before opening a door she knows will present her with some new and unknown challenge to respond to.

A Wholly-Variable Response: Aide Memoire Linkups

She also does work with her aide memoire. She uses it to regularly remind herself of five things when returning to her core self. First, that the various perspectives she has practised moving in and out of are facets of her whole self. Second, that each facet or role is both a perspective on and a determinant of one aspect of the total human self-world relationship, and that all of them together are elements of the full human behavioural and experiential relationship to the world. Third, that any idea any human can have about anything – even fantasy, nonsense, and meaningless notions – can be part of her repertoire of roles. Fourth, that even perspectives currently unknown to her personally – including those as yet undiscovered by humans generally – are part of this repertoire that defines and determines both her own total self-world relationship and that of humans generally. Fifth, that all such roles should be seen and treated as possible ways of responding to any situation encountered – as temporary determinants of her acting, thinking, and feeling in a situation encountered that can and will be replaced when new situations require it.

A Wholly-Variable Response: Undiscovered Perspectives

Aware of the need to build the use of unknown and undiscovered perspectives into her repertoire of responses, her instructors also construct exercises to train her in these areas. They deliberately put her in positions where she knows she has to come up with unknown and undiscovered responses and has to apply herself to finding them or inventing them from tools and sources her instructors have placed near at hand in the exercise environment. They teach her to expect to encounter situations requiring her to identify and use previously unknown and even as yet undiscovered perspectives as situational responses.

A Wholly-Variable Response: Repetition and Completion

She repeats these various exercises until the new habits become second nature, and she has programmed her brain so that it only ever cedes control temporarily to what she sees as facets of her whole self and always returns control to her core self when a new response is required. She repeats them until she can consciously assure herself that she has instantiated the kind of self she understands is necessary to support a wholly-variable response. One where control always switches back to an empty-consciousness-dominated core before a new response to a new situation is selected, where deployed facets are always seen and treated as temporary departures from the core, and where return to the core is an expected and much practised event. She practises to such an extent that the process of switching away at need from a perspective in current use to her core self dominated by empty consciousness, and then to a new response to a new situation, can often be automatic and semi or wholly unconscious. She practises until her operational self works as described in her aide memoire. Until it works in a way she understands is necessary if it is always to operate in a wholly-variable fashion – utilising bias-free response switching and selection mechanisms to identify and deploy situationally appropriate responses from a repertoire so all-encompassing that even unknown and undiscovered perspectives are possible options.

Our adopter has completed the programme of exercises aimed at ensuring that the role-playing element of the baseline transcendent perspective is in place and is interoperating with the core element.

Operational Baseline Self-View And Actors #1: Not Play-acting

Assumptions

Assuming these mental exercises (together with any associated assumptions that depend on arguments put in earlier chapters) have the effects claimed for them above, it is reasonable to hold that the end result of this development programme for our adopter is as intended. The claims made below for the shape, form, and functioning of the resultant self-view are based on the assumption that all of the following are true:

1. That everything argued in earlier chapters is true. Particularly as regards experiences programming brains, any idea about anything determining the true human relationship to the world, the distictions between fixed and wholly-variable open-ended selves and responses, and the various points regarding empty consciousness revisited below.

2. That regularly repeating a mental process in response to particular circumstances will result in it becoming the habitual response to those circumstances. One example might be repeatedly rehearsing jumping out of a particular response to a particular situation and returning mentally to a core self to make that response to a change of circumstance habitual. Another might be repeatedly experiencing situations where an appropriate response requires

coming up with unknown or undiscovered solutions to a problem through knowledge acquisition or creative thinking.

3. That avoiding habits that have one effect and replacing them with alternatives that have the opposite effect - as, for example, with the life experiences exercise described above - avoids putting the effect of the first set of habits in place and puts the second set in place instead.

4. That empty consciousness exists, can be identified in our experiential landscape as argued in Chapter 12, and has the characteristics claimed for it there (being nonrelational, being an experience that sits outside of feelings, perspectives, and any kind of mental set – see Chapter 12 for supporting arguments on this).

5. That the 'two hands clapping' exercise described above and in Chapter 12 will allow us to identify empty consciousness in our experiential landscape and provide a means of learning to move our mind towards it and ultimately make it the dominant focus and habitual core of our working self as described. See Chapter 12 for supporting arguments on this.

6. That to switch mental functioning to a core self with nonrelational empty consciousness as its dominant focus is to switch to a mental environment free of any biasing or restrictive mental set at an overarching or brain-wide level.

7. That a brain will operate in either a balanced or an unbalanced fashion, depending on its programming. A brain with barriers in place either through an overarching mental set that creates restrictions or bias or with similar issues at lower, more specific, levels will operate in an unbalanced way, with preferred aspects having a magnified effect and non-preferred aspects having a reduced effect. A brain programmed to ensure that such barriers are not in place and that operations take place with no overarching mental set in place will work in the opposite fashion, with all of its various programmed elements treated equally, working

together in a balanced fashion, and having unweighted effects on the processing outcome (see the heading '*Switching: Whole Self Control*' below for an example of this).

8. That if an actor can learn the level of control he has on stage, our adopter can too. She can learn to control the various facets of her self as roles her whole self enacts as required but retains ultimate control of, seeing and treating them as limited but nonetheless real aspects of her whole self as described in the associated exercise.

An Operational Version Of The Aide Memoire Self-View

If these assumptions are sound (as is taken to be the case here), it is reasonable to hold that the adopter's programme does what it was intended to do. It puts in place an operational version of the self-view described in the first three sections of the aide memoire – a working self with the three sets of characteristics described there. A working self with interacting empty-consciousness-based core and multifaceted role-playing elements as described in the first section. A working self entailing an all-encompassing repertoire of whole-self facets similar but not identical to an actor's onstage roles as described in the second section. A working self capable of supporting a wholly-variable response as described in the third section – of selecting and deploying a situationally appropriate response from an all-encompassing repertoire of whole-self facets utilising bias-free response switching and selection mechanisms. A working self referred to in this work as the baseline transcendent self-view and described in detail below.

The case goes like this:

Facets Similar To An Actor's Roles

If the above assumptions are sound and the exercises have the effects claimed for them, then, by working through them with her support community, our adopter programmes her brain in a way that ensures two things. First, that she avoids – through her life experiences work

– the fixed-self-type tendency to cultivate a limited set of preferred idea-based self-world perspectives she might otherwise habitually return to as the core of who she is, be emotionally attached to, and assume are the right way of always seeing things. Second, that – through repeatedly working through the various exercises aimed at putting in place a core self and a wholly-variable response – she instead puts in place a self-view with two interoperating elements. The first being a core self in which empty consciousness is the dominant focus and hub and her aide memoire is a subordinate subset that reminds her that all possible ideas about anything are facets of her whole or total self. The second being an interactive role-playing element able to deploy all such roles and of always moving her mental focus to her empty-consciousness-dominated core self before a new perspectival response to a new situation is consciously or unconsciously selected and deployed.

She puts in place a self-view where her core self is a kind of mental and emotional hub dominated by the nonrelational experience of empty consciousness – a hub that is the normal or habitual rest state of her mental and emotional functioning. A hub with a nonrelational dominant focus beyond views, emotions, and feelings (see Chapter 12) that she habitually returns to after using particular self-world perspectives for particular purposes. A hub that is the experiential place she returns to whenever she ceases being in circumstances where she needs to be 'Dr Brown, scientist', 'Jo Brown, kitemaker', or 'JB, football supporter' – and accordingly returns to a core self where she is all of these whole self facets and none of them. A core self where she is empty consciousness and sees and treats all of the self-world perspectives referred to in her aide memoire in a way similar to how an actor might see and treat the parts he plays when on stage. Where she sees each as a temporary role she adopts for a while as circumstances demand, relinquishes when the situation changes, and replaces with a new perspective and role appropriate to the new situation after first returning control to her whole or total self.

By following the programme organised by her instructors, our adopter avoids putting any of the fixed self habits in place and puts the alternative self-view and its various parts and interoperations in place instead. If the assumptions listed above as regards repeating mental exercises creating habits, empty consciousness existing, being identifiable, and having the characteristics claimed, control similar to an actor's roles being possible, and so on, are sound, it is reasonable to assume that the results are as claimed above. It is reasonable to assume that the mental exercises put in place the working self outlined above.

Different to an Actor: A More Nuanced View of Roles

Our adopter's resulting mental landscape is not entirely like an actor's, however. If the exercises have the effects claimed for them, then it differs from it in two ways, the first being a difference between how an actor sees the parts he plays and how our adopter sees her temporary roles. She views the various total self facets she enacts as circumstances require in a way similar, but not identical, to how we can assume an actor views the roles he plays on stage.

We can assume the actor has a particular perspective on the roles he plays. We can assume he recognises them as play-acting, as pretences – as 'parts', that are, in some sense, not who he really is, just who he is pretending to be, distinguishing them in these ways from the everyday self he regards as more truly himself. We can assume that, even when he becomes wholly and emotionally immersed in an onstage role, his brain still retains a knowledge of this, ensuring he can, at need, 'snap out of it' and return control to his everyday self no matter how involved and immersed he has become. We can assume that this will happen when a fire alarm goes off during a performance, for example, and he can see or smell smoke.

Unless our adopter is acting in an onstage sense herself (a possibility we will ignore, as it would serve no useful purpose to explore its consequences here), her perspective on the roles she takes on is similar to the actor's in some ways but different in others. As is the case with the actor, she sees them as roles she takes on for a purpose then relinquishes again as the occasion requires. However, she does not see them quite the way the actor does – as play-acting, as pretences, as 'parts' that are, in some sense, not who she really is, just who she is pretending to be. Instead, she sees them in a more nuanced way – the way she learned to see them when using her mental exercises to put them in place as part of her working self. She sees them in a way that recognises them as valid aspects of her real self but also notes that they are not the whole of that self, only one part of the total relationship, one role among many, an aspect of the truth about the whole relationship.

Unlike the actor, she does not see them as pretend roles that are not who or what she really is; she is not acting, thinking, and feeling as though she is just pretending when she takes them on. She is not like the actor in that respect. This is not how her exercises have taught her to see them and treat them. She is, however, similar in another important sense. When she is in the rest or resting state of her core self, she sees all possible individual self-world relationships as something less than her real self. She sees them as aspects of her real self that she can adopt when needed but also pull out of when needed; she sees them as something less than what she fully or wholly is.

Moreover, if the exercises have the effects claimed for them, this perspective will persist beyond her self's rest state. She has worked with her roles over and over in various kinds of circumstances until seeing them and treating them as facets under the control of her whole self is a commonplace everyday event, and she is practised at jumping out of them at will. Even if she becomes fully engaged in a role in the immersed sense of the onstage actor described earlier, some part of her mental landscape continues to recognise that the role is something less than her real self – that it is just a role she is temporarily playing. Some part of her knows – just like the actor does – that the role is something less than her whole self, ensuring that she can (like the actor) 'snap out of it' if she needs to, no matter how involved and immersed in the role she has become.

In consequence, these self-world relationships or roles are never in full control of who and what she is. She is practised at ensuring they relinquish the control they are temporarily given when used as situational responses, just as an actor is with his roles. Because she has learned to always see every self-world relationship as a temporary role and a limited aspect of her full self (and is practised in ensuring her brain sees and treats them as such), she is not play-acting in the sense that an onstage actor is. However, she does still have control of her roles in the same sense that the actor on stage has control of his roles and parts (if an actor can learn this mental skill, we can presume that any human can). They are alike in that respect, but different in the sense that our adopter does not see her roles as play-acting or pretending. She sees them as something less than her real or whole self, but as aspects of her real self her whole self enacts at need – real, not pretend, aspects of who she is. Limited but real facets of her whole or total self.

Operational Baseline Self-View And Actors #2: Not A Fixed Self

A Difference in Controlling Selves

The second way in which our adopter's mental landscape differs from the actor's relates to the nature of the self that controls these various roles. Given all that we have argued in earlier chapters regarding the likelihood that most of us probably develop a fixed overarching self-world relationship, it is reasonable (and useful in the present context) to assume that the actor's controlling self will be a fixed self. The adopter, on the other hand, has striven to avoid adopting a fixed self and worked to instantiate an alternative self-view instead. If the exercises work as claimed (and the associated assumptions are sound), the controlling self put in place is quite different to the actor's fixed self. It differs in the various ways outlined below – and a look at the detail of how it differs will both clarify the notion of a self-view able to support a wholly-variable response and finalise our description of the baseline transcendent self-view.

How a Fixed Self Operates

Assuming the points made in Chapter 10 hold true, someone with a fixed self controlling his acting, thinking, and feeling in the world will have an operational self with the kinds of features described in that chapter. When his brain reacts to the internal and external environments he encounters in a particular situation to select an appropriate response to that situation, it will be the algorithms inherent in his fixed-self-dominated brain that do the selecting. This means (cf. Chapter 10 on blocking the wholly-variable response) that there will likely be barriers operating that block switching away from a self-world perspective in current use, block finding a better alternative from the set of all possible self-world perspectives, and block selecting a replacement in an unbiased way. The shape and form of these will depend on the exact nature of the fixed self in place, but there will assuredly be some or all of these blocks in evidence.

There will likely be resistance to switching to a new perspective, either because the current perspective is regarded positively or any alternatives available are regarded negatively (or both), a circumstance that may be due to individual biases, or because of positive or negative weightings given to the perspectives at an overarching level within the fixed self itself. There may, for either of these reasons, be habitual, perspectival, or emotional resistance to changing the current perspective or to adopting any available alternatives.

There will certainly be a barrier to finding a better alternative from the set of all possible subsidiary self-world perspectives. The controlling fixed self will be based on only a limited subset of all of the possible idea-based self-world perspectives that humans can ever envisage, and those included will likely have positive and negative weightings.

It is also likely there will be bias within the selection mechanism itself, either because the fixed self itself skews the selection (partly by blocking some options out entirely) or because the perspectives entailed in the limited repertoire of the fixed self will have individual habitual, perspectival, or emotional weightings attached.

These blocks and barriers will likely skew the response of our everyday fixed-self person. A required change of situational perspective may be resisted by biases inherent in the self itself or attached to individual perspectives, and the choice of an alternative will be limited to the subset of perspectives in the fixed self and biased by either fixed-self preferences or individual weightings. There is also the possibility that a perspective that is chosen as a response to a new situation will entail a habitual, perspectival, or emotional weighting of its own. If so, this will tend to limit or bias the next requirement to consider, select, and switch to a new response to a new situation.

How a Baseline Transcendent Self Operates

Our adopter, of course, has not programmed her brain in the same fashion as our offstage fixed-self actor has. She and her instructors have worked through the development programme described above, aiming to put a different kind of operational self in place – one that reacts in a way controlled by algorithms inherent in a brain programmed by the set of mental development exercises described above. When she encounters a need to change her currently operational self-world perspective, then – always assuming the mental exercises have the effects claimed for them – her operational self differs from a fixed self in the various ways outlined below as regards perspective switching, response repertoire scope, and response selection.

Switching: Barrier-Free

As was noted earlier in the book, fixed-self-type habitual, perspectival, or emotional resistance to changing the current perspective or to adopting any available alternatives can come into play at both the level of individual perspectives and the level of the overarching or total self. If the exercises have the effects claimed for them, the factors that cause these kinds of resistance are absent in our adopter's self. The kinds of things that might tend to prevent switching or skew the operation of the switching mechanism from these sources are not programmed into her brain.

There is no inbuilt resistance to switching away from a perspective in current use or towards any that might replace it at the level of individual perspectives. Assuming they work as claimed, her mental exercises relating to life experiences processing have made sure of that. She avoided associating the habitual preferences, incorrect assumptions, and emotional attachments with individual self-world perspectives that cause such problems in the fixed self.

Nor is such resistance in place at an overarching or total self level. In addition to dealing with the issue at the level of individual perspectives, her life experiences exercises – if they work as claimed – have also ensured that she avoids the mental habits that create a fixed self that resists and biases perspective switching at an overarching level. She has avoided putting a fixed self in place to resist and bias perspective switching, partly through using the life experiences exercises themselves to avoid this, partly by focusing her mental efforts on creating a wholly-variable self-view instead.

She has, moreover, done something else as regards avoiding resistance to switching at an overarching level. If the mental exercises have the effects claimed for them, she has put in place a working self in which the initial habitual reaction to a need for a new response to a new situation is to switch control back to a core self dominated by empty consciousness. This means a switch to a mental landscape where, if empty consciousness has the characteristics claimed in Chapter 12, the dominant focus is a nonrelational experience that sits outside of the various kinds of relational perspective that create resistance to switching in a fixed self at an overarching level. It means, in effect, a switch to a mental landscape where the kind of limiting fixed-self mental set that creates resistance to switching is entirely absent – replaced by an empty, nonrelational experience sitting outside of every kind of skewed or limited viewpoint that might cause such resistance.

The overarching or total self our adopter switches back to when encountering a new situation is the polar opposite of the kind of fixed-self environment with its inbuilt resistance to switching. It does not entail a fixed-self-style limited and biased mental set that blocks out response options and can entail resistance to switching from or to particular responses. Its core is a perspective where she is mentally sitting outside of any preferences, emotional attachments, and perspectival assumptions that might create barriers to switching (and, moreover, has an aide memoire in place that reminds her that no perspective is preferred over any other at an overarching or total self level).

If the exercises have the effects claimed for them, the kinds of things that cause resistance to switching in the fixed-self mind at an overarching level are not present. Her programme of mental exercises ensures that the algorithms programmed into her brain do not entail barriers to switching away from a perspective currently in use or to some particular alternative at an overarching level, any more than they do at the level of individual perspectives.

Switching: Assumed, Facilitated, Whole Self Controlled

This absence of resistance is not the only difference as regards switching, however. Our adopter has also worked to ensure, not just that switching is not resisted by her mental make-up, but that it is both expected and facilitated by it. She has practised switching mental control out of a perspective in current use and back to the core or resting state aspect of her operational self until that reaction to a new situation has become second nature. She therefore has mental habits and skills in place that facilitate switching away from a perspective in current use rather than operating in a way that tends to block the switch.

She has also worked through her development programme so that her whole self retains a level of control whenever a perspective is allowed dominance as a situational response. She has practised seeing and treating perspectival responses in a way similar to how an actor sees and treats the parts he plays on stage (see above). She is therefore practised at ensuring her situational responses are seen and treated as roles she plays and controls in essentially the same way that an actor controls his roles. She is also practised at actively seeing and treating them as temporary choices and at ensuring they do not entail positive or negative weightings. In consequence, she is able to 'jump out' of them and switch to an alternative just as an actor can; she has practised ensuring her overarching or whole self retains a level of control.

Switching control back to the core self in the fashion programmed by her mental exercises effectively gives her whole self control – or arguably so. It ensures that every possible facet of the whole self can potentially be the next response. An actor's everyday self has overall control of any role he plays; he can switch control back to his everyday self more or less at will. If her mental exercises work as claimed, our adopter has a similar level of control. Her brain is programmed to return control to the core self and, thereby, to a mental landscape where all possible facets of the whole self have an influence on the next response. Returning control to the core self essentially returns it to the whole self by returning it to a point where no one facet of the total self has dominance.

Not only is her mental landscape programmed in ways that ensure that there is no resistance to switching, it is also programmed in ways that ensure that switching is an expected and much-practised event under the habitual control of her total or whole self.

Barrier-Free, All-Encompassing Response Repertoire

A person with a fixed self in place has a limited set of perspectives available as response options. Because he habitually rehearses seeing his self-world relationship in limited ways and also gives individual perspectives positive and negative weightings through habitual use or non-use, perspectival assumptions, and emotional preferences, he limits his response repertoire to a sub-set of the possibilities available and biases options within those. Any and every choice of a new response for a new situation takes place in a mental context where many options are excluded by fixed self habits and where the mind is set to block out any options not habitually preferred.

Assuming the mental exercises she works on have the effects claimed for them, the adopter of the baseline transcendent self-view successfully avoids doing these things. Her approach to processing life experiences avoids putting a fixed self and fixed self biases and blocks in place. It ensures that the mental practices she does adopt avoid preferences for this idea or that and regard all of them as possible, equally valid responses. Moreover, assuming that empty consciousness has the characteristics claimed for it in Chapter 12, her practised habit of always switching control back to her core self comprising an aide memoire dominated by empty consciousness ensures two things. First, that her mind is not set to block out options in the way that a fixed self mind is – in the view taken here, empty consciousness is essentially the absence of a restrictive mental set. Second, that she has an aide memoire at the forefront of her mind reminding her to treat every response option equally in the first instance as possible responses to any given situation encountered.

Assuming the related exercises all act as claimed, her efforts in these areas ensure that the blocks on options evident in a fixed-self mental landscape are not put in place. Her mind is open to all possibilities. Her response repertoire is all-encompassing. Being programmed not to block out options and not to give those that are in her repertoire positive and negative weightings ensures that nothing is put in place to stop the brain allowing every known option in her repertoire an equal chance of being a possible response to an encountered situation. Switching her focus away from a perspective in current use ensures that *it* (the perspective in current use) does not set the mind to block out options (as it might otherwise do) and that no fixed self mental set is in place. Assuming empty consciousness consists of the kind of nonrelational experiential emptiness as argued in Chapter 12, switching to a core self dominated by it ensures that there is no other limiting mental set in place to block out possibilities (as there would be in a mind dominated by a fixed-self-style dominant perspective). It is reasonable to claim that a brain programmed so that it does not block options and is not dominated by a limiting mental set will work so that every known possible option is given equal consideration as a possible response, especially with an associated aide memoire reminding the adopter that this is how it should be. (Hence the claim above that control by the core self is control by the whole self. The whole self is programmed into the brain; how could it be otherwise? We can assume that the brain, and hence the whole self programmed into it, will be in control if there is nothing preventing it from being in control. Returning control to the core self ensures that it is not at that point dominated by a limiting mental set but by nonrelational empty consciousness. It therefore ensures that the whole self has control. Control by the core self is control by the whole self.)

It is also reasonable to assume that a brain programmed in these ways will work so that even unknown and undiscovered self-world perspectives are possible responses. Our adopter practised mental exercises focused on learning to expect and deal with situations where new knowledge acquisition or creative thinking is needed and on learning embryonic skills in these areas. She also worked to memorise an aide memoire that reminds her that unknown and undiscovered self-world perspectives are possible responses in any situation encountered and that therefore new learning or creative thinking may be required to acquire a suitable response in some situations. She has, moreover, worked to ensure that her brain is not programmed to block out any possible option - only empty consciousness is habitually preferred and fixed-self-type barriers have been avoided. It is reasonable to assume that her brain is open to every possibility. It is reasonable to assume that if it exhausts known responses, it will flag this up to the adopter, who will recognise that an option unknown to her or even one as yet undiscovered by humans generally is indicated and that she should engage her embryonic skills in these areas.

We can take it that her response repertoire is barrier-free and all-encompassing – even unknown and as yet undiscovered perspectives are possible responses. Everything is included in because nothing is included out.

Selection is Core-Self Dominated and Bias-Free

Response selection from within a fixed self will not usually be bias-free, either because some responses are not included in the first place, or because some options are preferred to others within the limited repertoire, or because some included perspectives will have individual habitual, perspectival, or emotional weightings attached. If the mental exercises have the effects claimed for them, these types of bias do not exist within the self-view instantiated by our adopter.

Assuming empty consciousness consists of the kind of nonrelational experiential emptiness claimed in Chapter 12, setting empty consciousness as the dominant perspective ensures that there is no mental set in place to bias the selection mechanism by blocking some possibilities out. Ensuring the aide memoire is also part of the core gives the adopter a verbal indication that all possible responses are initially regarded as equally valid responses prior to a consideration of the encountered environmental circumstances (which the brain then interacts with to select an appropriate response). These considerations, plus the mental exercises aimed at handling life experiences so as to avoid giving perspectives positive and negative weightings through habitual use or non-use, perspectival assumptions, and emotional preferences – either individually or within the total self – ensure that response selection within the adopter's self-view is bias-free. The brain is programmed in such a way as to avoid the creation of algorithms that block out options. Any perspectival response is a possible choice, with selection between them dependent solely on the environmental circumstances of the situation being responded to. Even unknown and undiscovered options are possible choices if the situational circumstances seem to require it; they are possible choices if and when the adopter's known options are examined and found wanting.

Operational Baseline Transcendent Self-View: Summary

This, then, is what is meant by the baseline transcendent self-view as referred to here. Not simply a particular way of seeing the self as described in the first three points of the aide memoire, but the instantiated operational self-view or working self as put in place by the adopter's programme of mental exercises and outlined in the last part of this chapter. A working self with the operational characteristics just described above.

A working self with both a core element and an interactive role-playing element: a core element in which empty consciousness is both the dominant focus and an experiential container seen as encompassing all imaginable ways of seeing and relating to the world as its subordinate facets or roles; an interactive role-playing element able to deploy any and all of these roles.

A working self that operates through an ongoing process of switching control back and forth between individual subordinate facets or roles deployed for particular situational purposes and a core or resting state where the self is seen and experienced as encompassing empty consciousness plus every possible facet or role.

A working self in which the subject has a perspective and level of control over her various roles similar to those an actor has when playing his parts on stage – except that there is no question of play-acting; roles enacted are seen as limited but nonetheless real facets of the subject's total self.

A working self controlling these roles that differs from a fixed self on three fronts. First, in that there are no barriers in place to block a switch away from a perspective in current use to the total or overarching self. Second, in that the total or overarching self is not based on a limited set of ideas that block out those not included and bias those that are. It is an empty-consciousness-dominated self encompassing all possible self-world perspectives, known and unknown. One in which every possible perspective any human could possibly envisage is potentially available as a possible new response – even those unknown to the adopter and undiscovered by humans generally. Third, in that it is a self in which response selection is bias-free.

A working self that meets the requirements of a self-view able to support a wholly-variable response as defined in Chapter 10 (following Chapter 8). A self 'so constructed as to permit the deployment of a situationally appropriate response from a repertoire of all possible responses utilising bias-free response switching and selection mechanisms', a point we will return to briefly in Chapter 15.

A working self that is the self-view referred to here as the baseline transcendent self-view – a self with the characteristics described above, characteristics that make it the polar opposite of a fixed self.

Caveat

As indicated at the head of this chapter, it is, of course, impossible to prove at this stage that the mental exercises described above (and in Chapter 14) will have the effects claimed for them and will put in place an operational self with these characteristics. However, it should hopefully be clear to readers that this assumption is a reasonable one and that the characteristics of the resulting self-view will be as described (providing the points argued in earlier chapters are also valid). We know our mental habits programme the brain in ways that affect how our brain works in future instances and our subsequent acting, thinking, and feeling in those instances. It is reasonable to hold that the exercises described will have the outcomes claimed (at least as a working hypothesis – see *A Conjecture That Needs Testing* near the head of the chapter). It is reasonable to hold that they will put in place an operational instantiation of the self-view outlined in the aide memoire and its related verbal description – that they will put in place the position meant when the baseline transcendent perspective is referred to in this work.

This, at any rate, is the view taken here and assumed in what follows: that the self-view put in place by the adopter's development programme and labelled here as the baseline transcendent self-view looks and operates as described above. The case presented in Chapters 15-17 assumes that the exercises have the effects claimed for them and that the resulting self-view has the characteristics described above (and as extended in the next chapter, Chapter 14).

14

The First-Pass Transcendent Self-View

Enhancing the Baseline Self

This chapter covers the second set of mental exercises worked through by our adopter to instantiate the self-view described in her aide memoire – the set aimed at building on the baseline-related exercises described in Chapter 13 to implement the first-pass transcendent self-view. It also summarises the first-pass transcendent self-view and the operation of its situational response selection mechanism. Two assumptions are made in what follows. First, that the baseline transcendent self-view is in place and has the characteristics claimed for it in Chapter 13. Second, that, as with those detailed in Chapter 13, the mental exercises outlined in the present chapter also have the effects claimed for them as regards their impact on the adopter's working self.

In her efforts to instantiate the baseline transcendent perspective as described in Chapter 13, a large part of our adopter's programme of exercises was focused on avoiding the mental habits that create the fixed self. On the one hand, she focused her efforts away from fixed-self habits, directing them towards alternative habits designed to fashion the baseline transcendent self-view instead. On the other, she practised alternative ways of processing new life experiences so that they would not result in the creation of a fixed self.

Her focus in seeking to build on this by instantiating the first-pass transcendent self-view covered in this chapter is to take her efforts on this front a step further – aiming to develop practices that actively work against barriers to switching, response repertoire restrictions, and biased response selection. These practices are covered under the corresponding headings below. Assuming they work as claimed, they enhance the baseline self outlined in Chapter 13 in the ways detailed below. Their main focus in this is on improving the operation of the interactive role-playing aspects of the self-view described in Chapter 13. Their only impact on the core self is to validate the part of the aide memoire that refers to the effects of exercises covered in Chapter 14.

Actively Combating Barriers to Switching

Under this first heading, our adopter develops and sustains two practices that actively work against barriers to switching. On the one hand, she develops and sustains a wary attitude to the practices that tend to create such barriers, focusing on ongoing activities in her everyday life rather than just on her ways of processing new life experiences. On the other, she develops a facility for relaxing this wariness in a controlled and controllable way when desired or needed, using something we can think of as an 'immersion level control facility'.

Developing An Ongoing Wariness to Switching Barrier Creation

Our adopter practises the habit of always being wary of – and avoiding – any conscious or unconscious tendency towards emotional attachment, habitual bias or preference, and unqualified assumptions of truth in regard to the various idea-based self-world perspectives in her repertoire in her everyday life and functioning. She learns to be wary of and avoid these fixed-self tendencies that can block a switch away from a self-world perspective in use. She learns to avoid emotional attachment, habitual bias or preference, and unqualified assumptions of truth in regard to any verbal or nonverbal viewpoint that encompasses a self-world perspective, whether it is expressed as an idea about the self, an idea about the world, or a mix of the two. She learns to avoid it, not just in her processing of new life experiences, as covered in the last chapter, but on an ongoing basis during her everyday thinking and functioning.

Just as an actor throwing himself into a role will retain some awareness that he is play-acting and will be able to shake off the role at need, no matter how immersed in it he becomes, so our adopter learns similar levels of awareness and control. She works to actively strengthen the awareness she has already cultivated that any subsidiary self-world perspective adopted is only a temporary aspect of her full self via a practised wariness of any conscious or unconscious tendency towards emotional attachment, habitual bias or preference, and unqualified assumptions of truth.

Aware that emotional attachment to a self-world perspective, the habit of using it automatically, or a tendency to assume it is always wholly true in every situation can block her brain's ability to switch to and from self-world perspectives as required, she works to prevent such blocks. With the help of her support community and appropriate mental exercises, she develops an ability to spot and be wary of the dangers of such tendencies and to avoid falling into the traps of emotional attachment, habitual preference, or assumption of truth. She develops a mental and emotional environment that is, at some level, aware and wary of such dangers and acts to weaken the grip of any self-world perspective chosen as a temporary role might otherwise have, thereby improving her ability to switch subsidiary self-world perspectives when she needs to. She works to resist any tendency to allow emotional attachment, habitual preference, or assumption of truth to create the fixed-self tendency to block switches to other perspectives at need and cause negative effects as a result.

Developing An Immersion Level Control Facility

Having worked towards developing this wariness for a while, she comes to realise two things. First that, despite developing this wariness, she may nevertheless sometimes become so immersed in one of the roles or facets of the self she adopts that she consciously or unconsciously falls into the traps of emotional attachment, habitual bias or preference, and unqualified assumptions of truth regardless. Second, that there may well be occasions in which immersion of this kind would be an attractive prospect, albeit a short-term one. With these points in mind, she works to establish a means by which she might control the immersion process; she learns to develop and become adept at operating what we shall call here an *immersion level control facility*.

Our adopter recognises that becoming wholly detached from the roles she plays in her everyday life may be difficult to always achieve in practice and is not necessarily a wholly beneficial thing in any case. She is unlikely to be able to wholly avoid emotional, perspectival, and habitual involvements with her friends, for example, and probably would not wish to live her life like that, even if she could. Her enjoyment of events such as Christmas, an exciting foreign holiday, or a walk in the countryside in spring would also be diminished without a degree of emotional, perspectival, and habitual involvement. Plus, full detachment might be impossible anyway, given the excitement that such events tend to engender and the extent to which we look forward to them. Some level of immersion in some roles could be a desirable thing, she realises, and the mental skill her support community calls an immersion level control facility could probably help provide it.

Most would agree that the best actors can be so involved in roles when onstage as to be entirely immersed in the actions, perspectives, and feelings of the character they are playing at a given time. This can apply even to the extent of knowing (and acting out) the pain or anger they are feeling in particular circumstances and becoming, to some extent, unconscious of being in a play at all, albeit briefly. We can assume, however, that this immersion is temporary. If a fire alarm goes off in the theatre, for example, they will immediately 'snap out' of their role, stop being the passionate lover or the evil murderer, and head for the exit. They will have within their actor's self a kind of safety valve mechanism that pulls them out of the role they are immersed in when this becomes essential (or, indeed, when the play ends and they have to be someone else to deal with their everyday issues).

The actor essentially has an overarching perspective in place in respect of some self-world perspectives – those he has learned as roles he plays in the theatre. One that sees those particular self-world perspectives as temporary points of view with limited emotional importance that can and should be replaced as controlling self-world perspectives when circumstances require. He also has a mechanism in place – again in regard to these particular self-world perspectives – that is practised at pulling him out of these roles as and when required (when a fire alarm goes off in the theatre, for example). He can immerse himself in a role so that he almost forgets while playing it that it is a role, but quickly pull himself out of it and back into his overarching perspective when required. The fixed self he regards as his real self recognises that the role he is immersed in is, in fact, a temporary point of view with limited emotional importance that can and should be replaced as a controlling perspective when circumstances require.

This kind of mechanism is an example of what is meant here by the notion of an immersion level control facility. It is not something new that any one of us would have difficulty learning and using. It is simply the sort of commonplace thing we would expect an actor immersed in a role as described above would have in place to ensure that his real self takes back control when necessary – when a fire alarm goes off in the theatre, for example. Nor is this a mechanism unique either to the actor's onstage life or to actors as such. Most of us will already have a similar mechanism in place within whatever fixed self we have in place – to pull us out of one role and into another as circumstances demand. We, too, will jump to respond to fire alarms or whatever in the middle of being a plumber, a manager, or an engineer, should circumstances demand it. There is nothing unusual or remarkable about a mechanism of this kind. It is a normal part of our everyday lives – a mechanism our adopter realises she can as easily learn to adopt (and adapt) as anyone else.

So, she does just that. Recognising that a degree of immersion may often be unavoidable and may sometimes be desirable, she works to develop and practise operating an immersion level control facility along these lines, understanding that it will tend to facilitate switching between subsidiary self-world perspectives, but will also allow for a degree of immersion. She identifies various circumstances in her life where a degree of immersion is desirable, but the ability to jump out of the immersion is also important. She teaches herself to become practised at combining the two, undertaking a programme entailing two appropriate sets of experiences. In the first set, she acquires a degree of experience of actual onstage acting to teach her immersion in roles and experience jumping out of them when a fire alarm sounds, a play ends, or a director breaks in. In the second, she gets a partner or flatmate to startle her away from immersion that happens in her everyday life by clapping his hands loudly in her face when he notices she is immersed in some task or other.

After practising in these ways for a period of time, she becomes skilled at allowing herself to become immersed in certain subsidiary self-world perspectives while ensuring she also has a working safety valve in place to pull her out and back to her core self as and when required. She has improved her ability to facilitate switching between subsidiary self-world perspectives and weakened any tendency towards fixed-self habits not only by learning to be wary of emotional attachment and so on, but also by developing and practising the use of this immersion level control facility.

Combating Response Repertoire Limitations

Under this second heading, our adopter takes steps to develop a practised skill set that improves and supports access to a wider range of self-world perspectives, including unknown and undiscovered examples of such self-world perspectives. She takes the kind of steps we can imagine an actor might take to develop his acting capabilities, working to ensure she has as wide a range of perspectives in her repertoire as possible and a developed ability for acquiring new perspectives and seeing things in novel ways.

Widening Access and Support for Self-World Perspectives

Under this heading, she works on an ongoing basis to widen her repertoire of known idea-based self-world perspectives, adding as many perspectives on the self, the world, and the self in the world as she can manage to find time for. By various means – reading books and websites, listening to lectures and podcasts, watching films and performances, taking educational courses, talking to others with differing views – she adds as wide a range of known idea-based self-world perspectives as possible to her repertoire. As a result, she ensures that the range of known self-world perspectives she can switch to is as wide as possible and that her skill set in respect of finding and using these various sources, and extracting, learning, and using new known self-world perspectives from them is well developed.

Developing A Practised Ability for Seeing Things in Novel Ways

In a similar way, she also develops her abilities in respect of learning, developing, and discovering novel and imaginative perspectives on herself and the world at large, and for seeing things as others see them. She explores imaginative fiction and practises coming up with her own imaginative tales. She explores all kinds of weird and wonderful philosophies and works to develop her own. She works to understand the problems and possible solutions to certain scientific issues and to acquire the thinking and analytical skills and research capabilities needed to tackle them. She engages in discussion and debate with others who have a different mindset to hers in these various areas she delves into, and so on. By these means, she develops and encourages a facility for discovering not only self-world perspectives unknown to herself but even those as yet unknown to humans generally (undiscovered by science or philosophy, say). If she ever encounters circumstances where her brain tells her that nothing in her repertoire of known perspectives will successfully address what she faces and makes her realise that she needs either to add to her known repertoire or apply creative thinking to the problem, she will be ready. She will have the skills to search for fresh perspectives, new to her but known to other humans, or to apply creative thinking to the problem if what is needed is as yet undiscovered.

Through these two sets of processes, she widens the range of subsidiary self-world perspectives available to her for switching to at need, even to the extent of potentially encompassing not only self-world perspectives unknown to herself but also those as yet undiscovered. As we shall see in future chapters, she thereby improves her chances of avoiding the kinds of negative effects described in Chapter 9 as a feature of the fixed-self habit.

Combating Biased Response Selection

Under this third heading, our adopter takes steps to develop a set of practices, perspectives, and mental and emotional states that allow a replacement subsidiary self-world perspective to be selected in a fashion not biased by habits, emotional attachments, and assumptions. She trains her mind to avoid external response selection bias and be aware of the pros and cons of individual perspectives.

Practise Avoiding External Response Selection Bias

She knows that much of the work needed to avoid bias in the response selection mechanism has been done in the context of her efforts to instantiate the baseline transcendent perspective. In that context, she focused all of her mental activity towards processes designed to avoid the mental habits that create the fixed self and its inherently biased response selection processes and worked instead to create an alternative self that does not entail such biases. She strove to create a mental and emotional environment free of the bias that operates in the fixed-self mind by avoiding the practices that create that bias and adopting others in their place.

She knows that this should be sufficient to ensure that the biases created in the fixed-self mind are not present in her own mental landscape. Just to be sure, though, she adds an additional set of mental exercises to those she already follows. Recognising that there are times when bias can be introduced by external factors and that these might sometimes confuse the issue and result in biased response selection despite her best efforts, she works to train her mind to recognise and mitigate externally introduced response selection bias. She has her support community create a training programme that teaches her to recognise such situations and develop the skills she needs to see beyond them. With their help, she learns how to identify and deal with bias in the way something she must respond to is worded, for example, or in the way a situation is presented to her by another individual who is either biased, ill-informed, or confused. She learns to become practised at avoiding response selection bias, even when its source is the world external to herself.

Learning the Pros and Cons of Individual Perspectives

As well as taking the steps noted above to avoid bias, our adopter also takes other positive steps to help encourage and support a bias-free choice. She works to be adept at seeing the potential value of all self-world perspectives in a wide range of situations and to recognise, in addition, that every perspective has its limits and does not necessarily offer the best response in every situation. She teaches herself to recognise, for instance, that even the most wide-ranging scientific theory might not be the best answer to the requirements of an entertainer at a children's party, whereas a silly-sounding idea like the world being made of blancmange might be just the thing. In fact, silly or not, it might also be of value to a teacher trying to illustrate some scientific point (what the world would be like if some particular law of physics did not hold, say) or to an actor playing the role of a court jester. She teaches herself to recognise this and a range of other similar things in a wide variety of areas, making sure she has a sound grasp of both the value and the limitations of as wide a range of subsidiary self-world perspectives as possible.

Through these two sets of processes, she trains her mental and emotional environment to support bias-free perspective switching beyond the baseline level in two ways. Through learning to recognise external issues that might bias response choice in various ways and through learning to see that any given self-world perspective can often have value in a range of situations and that no one self-world perspective is necessarily always the best response in every situation. In essence, she learns to recognise and avoid various possible sources of internal and external bias in selecting responses.

The First-Pass Transcendent Self-View: An Overview

The First-Pass Transcendent Self-View in Summary

Imagine all of the above added to the baseline perspective presented in the previous chapter, and we have a first pass at the transcendent self-view proposed in this book – a first pass at a position that will be clarified further as the book proceeds. Assuming everything claimed for it above is true, it is a self-view with the various key features outlined above. A self-view that includes and gives pride of place to nonverbal, nonrelational empty consciousness – the underlying nonrelational substrata of our every conscious experience – rather than to a fixed set of subsidiary self-world perspectives. A self-view that sees and treats any and every possible subsidiary self-world perspective as an equally-weighted aspect of the total self, able to be brought into play and relinquished as and when required, with control being returned to the total self afterwards. A self-view designed to facilitate switching between self-world perspectives, even where a degree of emotional and other immersion has been indulged in, to encompass access to as wide a range of subsidiary self-world perspectives as possible, and to facilitate a non-biased response to new situations encountered.

It is, moreover, a self-view where the person who has adopted it 'transcends' (sits above or stands apart from) subsidiary self-world perspectives in general, including those encompassed within feelings and emotions – in two senses.

First, in the sense that the mental hub and rest state of the person who has this self-view is an experiential perspective in which all possible subsidiary self-world perspectives, known and unknown, are seen as subordinate aspects of consciousness and equally-weighted parts of the total self. One whose dominant focus is empty consciousness itself, the one thing in our experience that is not an idea-based self-world perspective, that sits outside of or transcends all of the subsidiary self-world perspectives it encompasses, and is the one thing they all have in common.

Second, in the sense that it operates in a way that, while control is ceded to some particular subsidiary self-world perspective when a situation requires it, that control is temporary and always returns to the total self afterwards, ensuring that all subsidiary self-world perspectives are again potential situational responses. In consequence, we can expect that the level of control habitually accorded to individual subsidiary self-world perspectives will tend to be much weaker than that accorded to the total self – the total self transcends individual subsidiary self-world perspectives in the second sense that it is always in overall control. Even when control is ceded to an individual subsidiary self-world perspective, the habits of the person holding the self-view ensure that its control is always temporary and that there is a practised habitual pathway back towards the rest state of the total self – to the transcendent self-view – afterwards.

Designed to Meet the Identified Requirements

This first-pass transcendent self-view was intentionally designed to meet all of the requirements of the alternative human self-view we have been seeking and self-evidently meets those identified in Chapters 11 and 12. It is clearly a self-view based, not on a limited set of subsidiary self-world perspectives (not even a scientifically-based one), but on the nonverbal, nonrelational substrata of all of our experiences we have called empty consciousness.

The question of the remaining four requirements is dealt with in Chapters 15-17, which present the case for holding that a full and correct adoption of this transcendent self-view meets all of them.

As has already been touched on in Chapter 13, the self-view arguably avoids blocking the open-ended response in the way that the fixed self does, as covered in Chapter 10, and successfully instantiates, at both a descriptive and operational level, the wholly-variable self-view described in Chapter 8. The Chapter 13 case in this respect, together with additional points added based on extensions implemented in Chapter 14, is summarised below (Chapter 15).

The self-view also arguably creates a mental and emotional environment that avoids the negative aspects of the fixed self while additionally optimising responses generally and supporting retention of both its positive effects and any personally unique aspects we might wish to retain as per the requirement identified in Chapter 9 (Chapter 16).

Finally, it not only replaces the various fixed-self-view-based misdefinitions of who and what we are as outlined in Chapter 7 with a self-view that accurately reflects our full behavioural and experiential nature, but is the only self-view that can achieve this end – or arguably so (Chapter 17).

In addition to the above, Chapter 17 also argues that, unless we each personally adopt and instantiate this transcendent self-view, we cannot claim to be fully developed humans, and that adopting it fully and correctly is the only way we can avoid adopting a variation on the fixed self.

Taken together, these various points mean that the perspective will provide the best possible answer to the group of questions considered in this book. *What self-view should we – all humans – identify with? How do we become fully developed variable-response humans rather than kinds of humans with a complex but limited repertoire of subsidiary self-world perspectives controlling how we act, think, and feel in the world? If a fixed definition is a misdefinition, how should we humans see and define ourselves?*

Situational Response Selection in Practice
From all Possibilities to Adequate and Appropriate Responses

Before we consider these remaining requirements, it is worth looking first of all at what is assumed in all of this as regards how this first-pass transcendent perspective on the self will operate in practice to select situational responses that are both appropriate and fit for purpose.

The assumption is that the starting point as regards response selection will be all possible subsidiary self-world perspectives, known and unknown, but that this essentially infinite set of possibilities will then be narrowed down by an algorithm that measures their effectiveness and appropriateness against three elements of the adopter's environmental situation. The first of these, obviously, will be the external world situation the adopter is in. The second will be the adopter's inner environmental state (is she well, or ill, or tired, or fresh, and so on). The third will be the contents of her life-experience databank and will encompass a range of things based on her life experiences. Personal skills, education and knowledge levels, moral thinking, relationships to places, events, and people, current or general state of health, temporary or long-term aims, work or personal or group roles, among other things.

The assumption is that, in practice, this will result in responses that are appropriate to the situation and adequate to the person's needs, despite the initial starting point being the whole wide range of possible human subsidiary self-world perspectives. Operating at a largely unconscious level, with consciousness brought into the process only where it is required for final response selection or for behavioural reasons, it is assumed that the adopter's brain will select a situational response without interference from algorithms that bias and limit the options available. It will narrow down the range of possible responses based on information coming from the three sources mentioned above, using these various sources of information to limit the choices to appropriate and adequate ones.

The considerations concerned may well be complex. Situational circumstances will be movable feasts, with both internal and external factors changing from moment to moment and the situational factors that make a response choice changing with them. An external world situation may be encountered that is recognised as potentially meeting the adopter's needs (as determined by her internal state) in some area, provided she can control the outcomes of developing events through her response. This may require a response that is an accurate reflection of how the world actually is and result in a standard and accepted scientific response choice being considered, but other factors may also come into play before a final choice is made. Personal and social considerations may deflect response choice down a different path. Known caveats to the position of science on the issue may come into play a moment later. If the science is uncertain, the result may be a response that entails a long-term search for new and unknown scientific positions. If the situation involves the health, welfare, or rights of others, initial considerations may result first in a range of wholly practical responses, then follow these with a complexity of moral perspectives that rule out some or boost others, perhaps at a conscious level, perhaps not. And so on.

In simpler circumstances, a situation where a nonsense response is required (a comedian performing at a children's party, for instance) may throw up the persona of a pretend scientist who has decided that the world is made of blancmange or something similar. If an optimum response in some area of her expertise is required in some situation or another, the adopter may respond as required on most occasions but call off if she is ill, has a hangover, or is simply exhausted. In a situation where the response required is one that requires intervention by a specialist of some kind – a mechanic, say, or a health professional – the response is likely to depend on whether or not the person concerned has these skills or not. If a doctor is needed, she may either respond by intervening herself if she is one or by telephoning someone who is if she is not. The situation, including her own recognition of her personal skills and limitations from her life experiences, will determine which response her brain will select from the range of all possible subsidiary self-world perspectives.

Life Experiences: Informing but not Predetermining Responses

The upshot ought to be a circumstance in which life experiences form part of this first-pass transcendent perspective, but only as an information-bearing adjunct to a core self based on empty consciousness and all possible subsidiary self-world perspectives. A circumstance where they do not provide a basis for the creation of a fixed and limited self-view but a mechanism for informing choices in the kind of self-view described earlier as wholly-variable. A circumstance where life experiences help inform response choices but do not predetermine them as a fixed self does.

Any and every possible subsidiary self-world perspective will be part of the total self of an adopter of this first-pass transcendent perspective, but their use in practice will depend on external and internal circumstances, with the latter including information from this life-experience databank.

This is as it should be. Selecting out (excluding) a role before the situational circumstances are taken into account – as the fixed self does – is unnecessary, artificially limiting, and encompasses an inaccurate view of our relationship to the world.

It is unnecessary because inadequate and inappropriate responses to a situation can be selected out by ensuring that the final selection of a response choice is determined by the situational circumstances as just described; they need not be preselected.

It is artificially limiting because not seeing roles like surgeon as potential aspects of our self-view – removing them as a possibility before situational considerations are taken into account – might stop us using them for other purposes such as acting, teaching, comedy, or an aspirational educational route. The surgeon self-world perspective is a role we might adequately and appropriately take on in a wide range of circumstances and should therefore not just be part of how we see humans generally but also of how we see ourselves.

It is inaccurate because, even if we are untrained and disastrously bad at it, the role of an actual surgeon is one we might conceivably adopt. The results might well be dreadful, but we could and might nonetheless do it; indeed, it is possible to imagine extreme circumstances where adopting the role might save a life (cutting off someone's foot to free them from a burning car, say). It is also not entirely beyond the bounds of possibility that even those of us with absolutely no talent in respect of the role of the actual surgeon might one day find that advances in robotics, artificial intelligence, and nanobot technology might well allow us to overcome these limitations.

In short, as long as responses that are inadequate or inappropriate to a situation encountered are selected out by the use of the external and internal circumstances of the situation itself, as described above, this approach to response selection is better than the fixed-self-based alternative. It is better and more accurate to have the possibility of adopting such roles open prior to the application of situational circumstances, as the transcendent perspective described above arguably allows. All possible roles being of possible value in some set of circumstances, all possible subsidiary self-world perspectives are seen and treated as possible aspects of the whole self. Situational circumstances, including the life-experience databank, then determine which aspect of the total range of subsidiary self-world perspectives in the total self is chosen as a temporary role to play at any given time.

Final Point

The one point worth adding here is that, as touched on in Chapter 8, there may be times when the best option as a response will be one that is only discoverable in a long-term rather than an immediate sense. In such instances, the immediate response thrown up by the situational circumstances, including the life-experience databank, will be an awareness that no response immediately known to the person concerned quite fits the current requirement and that more research or thought is required to find an appropriate response. In such instances, an open neural path to a possible solution will arguably be part of the outcome (see Chapter 8).

15

A Self-View Hospitable to the Wholly-Variable Approach

Aims and Assumptions

As previously noted, the self-view described in Chapters 13 and 14 self-evidently meets two of the requirements of the self-view we have been seeking, being built around empty consciousness rather than even a scientifically-based idea set. The aim in the present short chapter is to argue that it also meets two others: that a full and correct adoption of the first-pass transcendent perspective outlined above meets the requirements of the self-view for humans we have been seeking as identified in Chapters 8 and 10. More specifically, it is to argue that it both instantiates and supports an open-ended, wholly-variable self-view as outlined in Chapter 8 and clarified at the end of Chapter 10 and also avoids creating the blocks on the wholly-variable response a fixed self exhibits as outlined in Chapter 10. The claims made in this regard assume that the arguments made in Chapters 8, 10, 13, and 14, together with any associated assumptions specified in these chapters, are sound and valid. They also assume (in line with this) that the first-pass transcendent perspective looks and operates as laid out in Chapters 13 and 14.

Meeting The Requirements

The Baseline Transcendent Self-View

Much of the work necessary to show that the requirements identified in Chapters 8 and 10 are met by the first-pass transcendent self-view has already been done in Chapter 13. It was argued there that – always given the various assumptions made are sound – the mental exercises described put in place an operational self-view that is the polar opposite of a fixed self. They put in place a working self-view of which two things relevant to the present point are true. First, that the mental habits that put in place the various varieties of fixed self and the associated barriers to a wholly-variable response detailed in Chapter 10 are avoided. Second, that the self put in place as an alternative to a fixed self is a working self that meets the requirements of a self-view able to support a wholly-variable response as defined in Chapter 8 (and clarified in Chapter 10). It is a working self with the operational characteristics defined at the end of Chapter 10 (unsurprisingly, since it was designed to be such a working self). A working self so constructed as to permit the deployment of a situationally appropriate response from a repertoire of all possible responses, utilising bias-free response switching and selection mechanisms.

It is, in short, a working self that meets both of the requirements we are considering here. The requirements identified in Chapters 8 and 10 are met by the baseline transcendent self-view – which means, in turn, that they are also met by the first-pass transcendent self-view.

The First-Pass Self-View Encompasses The Baseline Self-View

As previously indicated, the baseline transcendent self-view underpins the first-pass transcendent self-view, with the latter version of the transcendent self-view being merely an extension of the former. If the baseline version meets these requirements, then – provided the first-pass extensions to the baseline do not somehow reverse the effect – the first-pass version also meets them.

First-Pass Extensions Enhance Basleine Abilities

In fact, as will no doubt be evident to the reader, the first-pass extensions to the baseline version actually enhance the extent to which the two requirements are met.

The baseline level life experiences exercise works to ensure that the blocks on the fully variable response entailed in the various varieties of fixed self as outlined in Chapter 10 are not put in place. The first-pass level exercises described in Chapter 14 actively work against putting such blocks in place. They strengthen rather than weaken the extent to which the Chapter 10 requirement is met.

The same is true of the Chapter 8 requirement. The exercises aimed at putting the core and interactive role-playing aspects of the baseline self-view in place work to instantiate and support a wholly-variable response, as described above and in Chapter 13. The first-pass exercises described in Chapter 14 work to enhance the baseline capabilities in this area. They work to further facilitate the extent to which the baseline level transcendent self-view supports the (wholly-variable-style) deployment of a situationally appropriate response from a repertoire of all possible responses utilising bias-free response switching and selection mechanisms. They strengthen the ability of the self-view to meet the Chapter 8 requirement as clarified in Chapter 10.

Enhancements: First-Pass Exercises 1 and 2

The first two exercises in Chapter 14 – working to avoid the emotional attachments, habitual preferences, and assumptions of truth that block switching away from individual perspectives and to practise the mental skill of breaking free from any perspective the adopter *has* become emotionally, habitually, or perspectively immersed in – impact on both requirements. They not only work against any tendency towards fixed-self-style barriers to switching; they also help facilitate switching when necessary even where immersion is involved, thereby strengthening the wholly-variable response in the switching area.

Enhancements: First-Pass Exercises 3 and 4

Exercises three and four from Chapter 14 – the acquisition of as many new perspectives as possible from both factual and fictional sources and the development of a practised ability for creative and imaginative thinking – also have this dual effect. They not only actively work against any tendency towards fixed-self-style response repertoire restrictions, they also help widen both the known response repertoire and the adopter's abilities as regards undiscovered response possibilities. They, too, strengthen the wholly-variable response in the response repertoire area.

Enhancements: First-Pass Exercises 5 and 6

Exercises five and six from Chapter 14 – working to develop an experienced understanding of the value and limitations of individual perspectives and to become practised at avoiding external factors that might cause response selection bias – have a similar impact. They not only actively work against any tendency towards fixed-self-style selection bias, they also help ensure that any choice of a replacement perspective in any situation encountered is bias-free. Again, they strengthen the wholly-variable response in respect of bias-free response selection rather than weaken it.

Far from damaging the ability of the baseline self-view to meet the requirements identified in Chapters 8 and 10, the Chapter 14 enhancements work to strengthen the extent to which the transcendent perspective can be claimed to meet them.

Conclusions

On the basis of the above, it is reasonable to suggest that the first-pass transcendent self-view outlined in Chapters 13 and 14 meets both of the requirements discussed above. Fixed-self-style habits are not only avoided, there is an active programme in place that works against such habits. Moreover, the mental exercises described over Chapters 13 and 14 instantiate and support an open-ended, wholly-variable self-view as outlined in Chapter 8 and clarified at the end of Chapter 10.

They put in place a self-view so constructed as to permit the deployment of a situationally appropriate response from a repertoire of all possible responses utilising bias-free response switching and selection mechanisms, rather than one that has barriers in place to prevent these things.

When a new situation requiring a change of controlling subsidiary self-world perspective is encountered, there are, on this view, no barriers in place to block the open-ended, wholly-variable response.

There are no barriers in place to block the move away from a currently used subsidiary self-world perspective to a new one. On the contrary, a well-practised and much-used switching mechanism is in place to facilitate what is a commonplace event: a switch away from one subsidiary self-world perspective to a new one more appropriate to the new situation.

Nor are there barriers in place to prevent any and every possible subsidiary self-world perspective being included in the repertoire of possible new responses, even those unknown to the individual and undiscovered by humans generally. On the contrary, there is a good case for claiming that all possible subsidiary self-world perspectives are 'included in' to the range of response possibilities by ensuring that none are 'included out'. As we saw in Chapter 13, there are grounds for holding that the adopter's response repertoire will be all-inclusive. If her brain fails to find a suitable response among the possible responses known to her, it will indicate this somehow to the adopter, who will then go looking for possibilities unknown to themselves and ultimately for those undiscovered by humans generally.

Finally, there are no barriers in place to block a bias-free choice between these possible responses. The brain's choice will be made in the bias-free environment of empty consciousness, an environment that sits outwith emotions, limited perspectives, and habitual preferences and operates on subsidiary self-world perspectives that are equally-weighted – untainted by emotional attachment, habitual bias or preference, and unqualified assumptions of truth.

In short, whereas the practices that underpin the fixed self act to block the open-ended, wholly-variable response as described in Chapter 10, there are sound reasons for holding that the first-pass transcendent self-view meets both of the requirements addressed above. It ensures that those practices that create the blocks detailed in Chapter 10 are not put in place and replaces them with practices that – assuming the arguments presented above are sound – instantiate and support an open-ended, wholly-variable self-view as described in Chapters 8 and 10. They instantiate and support an open-ended, wholly-variable self-view of the kind we have been seeking in this book.

Conscious Intention: A Final Point

One final point is worth noting before leaving this chapter. It is reasonable to suppose that the practices underpinning the first-pass transcendent self-view outlined in Chapters 13 and 14 will be applied more successfully if the person applying them is doing so with the conscious intention of adopting a self-view designed to support the wholly-variable response, as discussed above. If they take the steps described in Chapters 18 to 20, knowing the various points made in this chapter, and with the conscious and informed intention of instantiating the wholly-variable response at an operational as well as a descriptive level.

The next chapter, Chapter 16, deals with the third requirement of a fully human self-view, as identified in Chapter 9. Specifically, that it must maximise the chances of avoiding the negative effects of conflict between any subsidiary self-world perspective and how the world is, optimise responses generally, and support the retention of both the positive effects of the fixed self and important personally unique aspects of a person's self-view.

16

A Self-View That Improves on the Fixed Self

Meeting the Chapter 9 Requirements

The aim in this chapter is to present the case for holding that a full instantiation of the first-pass transcendent perspective outlined in Chapters 13 and 14 meets the requirements of a self-view that accurately reflects our full behavioural and experiential nature as identified in Chapter 9. Specifically, that it maximises the chances of avoiding the negative effects of conflict between any subsidiary self-world perspective and how the world is, optimises response validity generally, and supports the retention of both the positive effects of the fixed self and important, personally unique aspects of a person's self-view. A key element in the case is the assumption that the transcendent self-view works in an open-ended, wholly-variable fashion, as argued over Chapters 13, 14, and 15.

Maximising Avoidance of Conflict-Based Negative Effects

A Barrier-Free Mental Environment

We saw in the Chapter 9 example of the flat-world-believer fisherman and his future wife how having additional subsidiary self-world perspectives available could allow him to break free from one subsidiary perspective and adopt another he could use to avoid the negative effects of his fixed self-view. This illustrates a general point of relevance to this question. A person who can break free of a subsidiary self-world perspective that is in conflict with the world at large in some way in some situation encountered and replace it with a subsidiary self-world perspective that resolves that conflict can thereby avoid the negative effects of the conflict.

Assuming it works in an open-ended, wholly-variable fashion, as argued over Chapters 13, 14, and 15, the first-pass transcendent self-view outlined in Chapters 13 and 14 optimises the chances of this happening in any and every situation that could ever be encountered. It optimises an adopter's chances of being able to switch away from a subsidiary self-world perspective in current use, find a better alternative from the set of all possible subsidiary self-world perspectives, and select a replacement from this set in an unbiased way.

If the case presented in Chapters 13, 14, and 15 is sound, the practices, perspectives, and emotional attitudes that underpin the first-pass transcendent self-view do not block the open-ended, wholly-variable response in the way those entailed in the adoption of a fixed self do. The practices that block the wholly-variable response in a fixed-self environment are not only not in place in the environment created by the transcendent perspective on this view; they are replaced by practices that actively instantiate and support the open-ended, wholly-variable response we detailed in Chapters 8 and 10. This means that there are no barriers in place to prevent switching away from a subsidiary self-world perspective in current use, finding a better alternative from the set of all possible subsidiary self-world perspectives, and selecting a replacement in an unbiased way.

More than this, it means that the environment that entails these barriers in a fixed self is replaced with its polar opposite. One in which switching away from a subsidiary self-world perspective in current use, finding a better alternative from the set of all possible subsidiary self-world perspectives, and selecting a replacement in an unbiased way is an expected and much-practised everyday process. This optimises the chances of a person with this self-view in place being able to switch away from a subsidiary self-world perspective that is in conflict with the world at large in some situation and replace it with a subsidiary self-world perspective that resolves that conflict.

Switching

Not only are there no barriers in place to block switching when the need arises, our adopter has taken steps to facilitate such switching. She has taken steps to ensure that switching from a currently used subsidiary self-world perspective to an empty-consciousness-based core or controlling self, then from there to a new subsidiary self-world perspective appropriate to a new situation is an expected, much-practised, and routinely repeated everyday function. She has also practised other skills that enhance her abilities in this regard, as described in Chapter 14. Not only has she replaced the fixed-self tendencies towards emotional attachment, habitual bias or preference, and unqualified assumptions of truth that can block a switch away from a subsidiary self-world perspective in use, she has actively learned to be wary of and avoid them.

She has also, additionally, learned the mental skills involved in the immersion level control described in Chapter 14, ensuring that she is able to switch away even from subsidiary self-world perspectives she has temporarily become more deeply involved in. The possibility of switching when a conflict arises is optimised because there are no blocks in place to act against switching, a practised mechanism in place to effect a switch away from the subsidiary self-world perspective causing the conflict, and other skills in place that further facilitate the process.

All-Encompassing Repertoire

Nor is this the whole of it. When a new response is required, not only are there no barriers in place to prevent the choice of a replacement subsidiary self-world perspective being made from the set of all possible subsidiary self-world perspectives, but our adopter has worked to make her repertoire as all-encompassing as possible. As indicated above under the switching mechanism, switching from a currently used subsidiary self-world perspective to a core or controlling self based on empty consciousness, and then from there to a new subsidiary self-world perspective appropriate to a new situation, is an expected, much-practised, and routinely repeated everyday function. This means that whenever a replacement perspective is required, the selection mechanism operates in circumstances where the core or resting state self is the controlling perspective.

This controlling perspective has two elements, comprising the experience of empty consciousness – the dominant focus – and a verbally expressed subordinate aide memoire perspective that tells our adopter that her whole or total self is made up of the totality of all possible equally-weighted subsidiary self-world perspectives. This means that the selection mechanism operates in circumstances where the dominant perspective – empty consciousness – is the one thing in our adopter's experience that is not a subsidiary self-world perspective. Assuming that the case made in this regard in Chapters 13 and 15 is sound, this in turn means that the dominant perspective prior to response selection is not one that sets the mind so that all but a few preferred subsidiary self-world perspectives are blocked out by a dominant fixed self. It is the opposite of that – a mental landscape where the dominant perspective is not one or more subsidiary self-world perspectives that block out those not included in the preferred set, but something that is not a self-world perspective and does not, therefore, block out any by preferring some.

We can assume that there will be no blocks in place to prevent known possibilities in the adopter's repertoire being thrown up as possible responses; the mental processes that create the fixed-self type blocks have been replaced by others that do the opposite. We can therefore assume that if the brain fails to find a suitable response among the possible responses known to our adopter, it will indicate this somehow to the adopter. We can further assume that, since the adopter's aide memoire notes that situational responses will sometimes have to come from unknown and undiscovered sources, our adopter will then go looking for possibilities unknown to themselves and ultimately for those undiscovered by humans generally. Nothing will be blocked out. The response repertoire will be all-inclusive. Either a known response will be found, or an unknown or even undiscovered response will be sought.

This, plus the fact that our adopter also has a practised skill set in place (see Chapter 14) that works both to widen immediate access to known subsidiary self-world perspectives and to facilitate discovery of unknown subsidiary self-world perspectives, optimises the potential for resolving conflict with the world in situations encountered. The possibility of accessing a subsidiary self-world perspective that will resolve the conflict is optimised on three counts. First, because there are no blocks in place to prevent any and every possible subsidiary self-world perspective – even those unknown to the adopter or undiscovered by humans generally – being considered as a better alternative to the conflict-causing subsidiary self-world perspective. Second, because there is a practised skill set in place that works to widen and continually extend the range of known subsidiary self-world perspectives immediately available for resolving the conflict. Third, because there is a practised skill set in place that works to improve access to undiscovered subsidiary self-world perspectives through facilitating novel and imaginative thinking.

Bias-Free Selection Mechanism

A similar case can be made for the response selection mechanism being free of bias. Not only are there no barriers in place to prevent the choice of a new response being bias-free, there are replacement practices in place that ensure three things. First, that individual subsidiary self-world perspectives are not given either a positive or a negative weighting through emotional attachment, habitual bias or preference, or unqualified assumptions of truth. Second, that response selection takes place in a bias-free mental and emotional environment based on empty consciousness. Third, that steps have been taken to avoid creating bias in response selection processes and to strengthen recognition of both the potential value and the limitations of all subsidiary self-world perspectives in a wide range of situations.

Not only are there no barriers in place to prevent the choice of a replacement being bias-free, there are replacement practices in place that – assuming what was argued in Chapters 13, 14, and 15 under this heading is sound – instantiate and support a bias-free selection process.

On this view, there will be no bias associated with individual subsidiary self-world perspectives. Our adopter has worked to ensure that these are not given either a positive or a negative weighting through emotional attachment, habitual bias or preference, and unqualified assumptions of truth. Assuming her efforts have been successful, there will be nothing in her repertoire of known subsidiary self-world perspectives to introduce bias into the response selection process via weightings given to individual self-world perspectives.

There will be no bias either from a fixed self dominating her response selection environment on this view. In the case of our adopter, the mental practices that create the fixed-self environment have been avoided and replaced by alternatives. Not only will a fixed self not be there to skew response selection by ensuring it takes place in an environment where many of the possible responses are blocked for one reason or another, it will have been replaced by an alternative designed to be bias-free. Since our adopter has become habituated to always returning to a core dominated by empty consciousness prior to making a new situational response choice, response choice will take place in an environment dominated by a perspective that, in essence, transcends bias – or arguably so.

If the arguments presented in Chapter 12 are correct, the person concerned momentarily sits outside of emotions and other biasing factors that can set the mind so that response selection takes place in a fashion skewed by such biases. Response selection takes place instead in a mental environment momentarily free of bias; it takes place in a mind that momentarily sits outside of all emotions and relational perspectives, one that is not mentally set for bias. It also takes place in an environment in which the dominant focus of empty consciousness also entails a subordinate verbal aide memoire that reminds our adopter that every conceivable subsidiary self-world perspective is seen and treated as an equally-weighted element of her total self.

Taken together, these factors should mean that she has successfully ensured that her response selection mechanism is bias-free. Especially so given that she has also taken the additional steps described in Chapter 14 to avoid creating bias in response selection processes and to strengthen recognition of both the potential value and the limitations of all subsidiary self-world perspectives in a wide range of situations. The possibility of making an unbiased selection of a replacement subsidiary self-world perspective from the whole range of possibilities is optimised. The practices that prevent a bias-free response in a fixed-self environment are gone, replaced by a set of mental practices and an associated environment that facilitate bias-free response selection in the various ways described above.

Conflict Resolution Possibilities Optimised

What this all means is that the possibility of avoiding the conflict-based negative effects of any given subsidiary self-world perspective is optimised by the adoption and instantiation of the transcendent self-view. It not only replaces the barriers inherent in the fixed self as regards switching self-world perspectives, includes all possibilities in the repertoire of possible replacements, and selects between these in an unbiased way (with practised mechanisms that facilitate and optimise performance in these areas), it also adds additional enhancements. It facilitates a switch away from any conflict-causing subsidiary self-world perspective in current use by removing barriers and strengthening skills in this area. It also removes barriers and strengthens skills in respect of selecting an alternative subsidiary self-world perspective in an unbiased way from the range of all possible subsidiary self-world perspectives. If there is a subsidiary self-world perspective, known, unknown, or undiscovered, that will resolve the conflict, it can potentially be brought to light and accessed in a mental and emotional landscape shaped by the open-ended, wholly-variable first-pass transcendent self-view as described in Chapters 13 and 14.

A person who has adopted and instantiated this self-view will have no blocks in place to prevent any one of the whole set of possible subsidiary self-world perspectives being fairly considered and put in place as a replacement for a conflict-causing subsidiary self-world perspective. More than this, she will have a practised skill set in place that will facilitate change and unbiased selection from an all-encompassing range of replacement possibilities. She will also have a wide range of actively learned subsidiary self-world perspectives in her immediately available repertoire and a developed set of skills in areas such as novel and imaginative creative problem solving that will assist in the discovery of new, previously undiscovered, subsidiary self-world perspectives. Her chances of finding a conflict-resolving subsidiary self-world perspective and putting it in place at need are as good as they can possibly be made. By adopting and instantiating the first-pass transcendent self-view, she will have optimised her chances of replacing a conflict-causing subsidiary self-world perspective with an alternative that resolves the conflict and allows her to avoid its otherwise negative effects.

Because of these various considerations, when a person with the transcendent self in place encounters a conflict situation, she is in a different position to a person with a fixed self in place in the same situation. As was indicated previously, negative effects are caused when the practices, perspectives, and emotional attitudes that underpin the fixed self get in the way of the brain finding and putting in place an alternative subsidiary self-world perspective that resolves the conflict. They block a move away from the subsidiary self-world perspective that is in conflict with how the world is, block out a huge range of possible alternatives, one or more of which might resolve the conflict, and block the possibility of a bias-free choice among those alternatives that are considered.

A person with the transcendent self in place is in a different position. Her operational self does not block a move away from this conflict as a fixed self does, but instead actively facilitates a switch away from the conflict-causing subsidiary self-world perspective. When it does switch away from the conflict-causing subsidiary self-world perspective, it does not switch away from the subsidiary self-world perspective in place to a fixed self based on a range of subsidiary self-world perspectives that artificially limits the choice of a replacement subsidiary self-world perspective. It switches away to a controlling self where, since the only habitually preferred perspective is one dominated by the nonrelational experience of empty consciousness, there are no blocks in place that stop any and every possible subsidiary self-world perspective, discovered and undiscovered, being entertained as a possible replacement subsidiary self-world perspective. It switches away to a controlling self where this open-ended, wholly-variable response is further strengthened in respect of finding a conflict-resolving alternative subsidiary self-world perspective by a practised skill set aimed both at widening immediate access to known subsidiary self-world perspectives and facilitating discovery of unknown subsidiary self-world perspectives. Moreover, once it does act to choose a replacement subsidiary self-world perspective, it does so in an environment that has no barriers in place to prevent the choice of a replacement being bias-free. One that also encompasses a practised skill set that enhances a person's ability to see that a subsidiary self-world perspective can often have application in a wide range of situations and that no subsidiary self-world perspective is useful in every situation.

In essence, the fixed-self brain has practised pathways and algorithms in place that operate at a conscious or unconscious level to block its ability to escape the negative effects of a conflict-causing subsidiary self-world perspective by blocking the open-ended, wholly-variable response outlined in Chapter 8 as extended by Chapter 10. The brain organised along the lines of the first-pass transcendent self-view does not have these pathways and algorithms in place. It has alternative practised pathways and algorithms in place that not only do not encompass the blocks that are a feature of the fixed self, but fully instantiate and support the open-ended, wholly-variable response, optimising the chances of identifying and using a conflict-resolving alternative subsidiary self-world perspective. The possibility of avoiding the negative effects of a conflict-causing subsidiary self-world perspective is optimised. The brain's practised pathways and algorithms actively support a move away from the conflict-causing subsidiary self-world perspective and facilitate and enhance the possibility that all possible subsidiary self-world perspectives, discovered and undiscovered, can be considered as possible alternatives in an unbiased way. As previously indicated, these processes can be conscious, unconscious, or somewhere in between, depending on an individual's internal circumstances and the nature of whatever situations he encounters.

How This Works in Practice

A look at the impact of the transcendent self-view on someone whose starting point is one similar to that of the flat-world-believer fisherman from Chapter 9 will help illustrate how this would operate in practice and also help clarify this aspect of the transcendent perspective.

Imagine that a person who has adopted and instantiated the transcendent self-view suddenly finds himself forced to make a living as a fisherman and work alongside the kind of extreme fixed-self-flat-world-believer fisherman we saw under this conflict type in Chapter 9. At first, he accepts his co-worker's view that the world is flat – and that they'll fall off the edge if they fish too far out; he has no previous experience of this question, and his senses seem to confirm the flat world notion.

Then one day the fish stocks run out close to the shore, and he and his colleague are faced with a conflict situation: they need to fish further out, but their view of the world says they cannot safely do that. Up till now, the transcendent self fisherman has had no reason to question the flat world-view, but now he has. His colleague cannot break out of the belief that they dare not fish further out. He cannot shift away from his flat world-view subsidiary self-world perspective. He is emotionally attached to it and also thinks it is just obvious that flat is how the world is. In any case, he cannot choose a replacement subsidiary self-world perspective; he only has the one in his repertoire. Worse, even if he did have others to choose from, he is strongly biased in favour of his flat world-view. In his (admittedly very extreme) circumstances, he is stuck in the conflict situation with no way of avoiding its negative consequences.

His transcendent partner is different, however. Although he has not had reason to question his flat-world viewpoint until now, he is otherwise in a better position. He has no strong attachments or unwarranted assumptions in place that make switching away from the flat world-view difficult. On the contrary, he has a self-view that sees all subsidiary self-world perspectives as temporary and replaceable ways of relating to the world. And, while he does not have an alternative to the flat world-view in his repertoire of known subsidiary self-world perspectives in the first instance, he does see his self-view as encompassing every possible subsidiary self-world perspective, known by himself, known by others, and as yet undiscovered. He also has a set of skills that will facilitate him finding an alternative by checking for possibilities known to others or by using his own abilities to see things in novel and imaginative ways so as to come up with an alternative himself.

Wondering whether the flat world-view might be wrong, he comes up with a number of possible alternative views and tells his partner about them. His partner now has other possibilities he can consider, but his bias towards the flat world-view quickly has him ruling them out as views that seem to him not to fit the facts as he sees them. The transcendent fisherman, however, has no such bias; he is able to consider all of them as possible alternative views, optimising his chances of finding a way out of the conflict situation.

Immediate vs Long-term Problem Solving

Notice that, as previously indicated, our transcendent self adopter will not necessarily come up with the right alternative to the flat world-view immediately, nor will he necessarily come up with all of the possible alternatives, including one that resolves his problem, right away. It is just possible that he will. As he struggles with the problem of the fading fish stocks, he may overhear someone else talking about the notion that the sea goes on forever with no end and no edge to fall over – and that this will free him from the conflict situation. It is equally possible, however, that he will not – that the course of events will be more involved than this.

The claim about the transcendent self-view is not that it lets every possible subsidiary self-world perspective in immediately, but rather that it does not block out any possibility and entails other features that improve the chances of finding a suitable alternative. It entails active attempts to widen a person's known repertoire and develop skills that will provide routes to source new known alternatives when required and others that will aid in acquiring undiscovered possibilities through novel and imaginative thinking and problem solving. The fisherman as described in the example would not have an alternative view in his learned repertoire, so he would have to fall back on his skills in these areas to find alternatives. This would almost certainly take time and be an iterative process that might well involve considering possibilities for a while, then dropping them in favour of new ones as they proved inadequate to the task. We can imagine that he hits the conflict situation with his flat world-view in place. Since his mind is open to new possibilities, it automatically responds by looking for new options. Not finding any, it throws up the possibility of looking in the library. That throws up some possibilities that add to his repertoire of known subsidiary self-world perspectives, and the prevailing subsidiary self-world perspective – the flat-world subsidiary self-world perspective plus the knowledge of the conflict – selects one from these that seems better than the others.

If there is a reason to also reject that, he may go on to look for others, either from known sources or by applying his novel and imaginative thinking skills. Perhaps some of these will also be rejected as he moves along. Every time an option is rejected, the situation he is facing changes because his prevailing subsidiary self-world perspective has changed. From just being the flat-world subsidiary self-world perspective plus the related conflict perception, it moves to new subsidiary self-world perspectives that also fail to resolve things. Eventually, though, his efforts throw up an alternative to the flat world-view that does solve his problem and lets him see how the world might look like it does but still not have an edge he can fall over. The point is that having a mental and emotional landscape that is open to all possible subsidiary self-world perspectives does not necessarily mean all of the options are immediately available. It only means that there are no blocks on any one of them being considered. Actually finding the better option may require a long-term effort.

The transcendent fisherman will still be able to select an alternative perspective from the whole range of all possible subsidiary self-world perspectives, optimising his chances of finding a way out of the conflict situation. It is simply that this will not necessarily be an immediate or simple process. The necessary subsidiary perspective may not be immediately available, but the path towards finding it – and finding a way out of the conflict – is open, not blocked.

Conflict and Negatives Less Likely and Optimum Response

Two further points are worth noting here. The first is that someone with the transcendent self-view in place is actually much less likely to encounter a conflict situation in the first place and much less likely to suffer negative effects in a conflict situation if he does.

Our transcendent fisherman, of course, will encounter the conflict situation, but he is less likely than his partner to suffer the negative effects of it. Even if his initial perception as a fisherman starts from the viewpoint that the world is obviously flat, he will still have the transcendent perspective on self and world in overall control. This will tell him that all subsidiary self-world perspectives are temporary perspectives subject to change. It will also make him aware of a range of other perspectives. Even if none of these apply to the fishing situation, the combined result will be to allow him to see more or less immediately upon hitting the conflict situation that his view of the world being flat might be wrong, even if he cannot immediately see how. This will predispose him to look for an alternative subsidiary self-world perspective rather than suffer the negative effects of the conflict.

The person with a flat-world fixed self in place will either suffer the negative effects of not being able to feed himself and his family or, at best, will probably be very much more afraid if he does venture further out to fish. The fisherman with the transcendent self in place will be less likely to suffer these effects. He will still encounter the conflict, but will be more likely to avoid its negative effects.

That said, a fisherman with the transcendent view in place is also much less likely to encounter this conflict in the first place. Even if his initial assumption when he starts fishing is that the world is flat and he might fall off the edge if he sails too far out, he has a mind that knows that subsidiary self-world perspectives are all explicitly *perspectives*. He will not necessarily accept the flat world-view uncritically. More likely, he will go to the library when he has a spare moment and discover that alternative views of the world exist well before he encounters what his fellow fisherman with his flat-world fixed self in place will experience as a conflict situation. If so, he will probably already have put a better alternative subsidiary self-world perspective in place before he encounters the problem of fish stocks running out close to shore. He will be less likely to experience the conflict situation in the first place.

The second point to note is that having the transcendent self-view in place will also allow an optimum response in a situation where there are no immediate negatives but there is a need to find the best way forward on some issue where a range of options need to be looked at. The person tackling this will have a wide range of learned options in his repertoire, no blocks on considering any other possible options, and no bias for or against any one view or group of views. He will also have skills in place to allow him to identify other possibilities, either through researching collections of options known to others but not to him or through novel and imaginative thinking that might allow him to discover options previously unknown to anyone. The chance that his ultimate choice will be the best way forward should be optimised as a result [see also **Appendix A** on the transcendent perspective and the notion of free will].

In summary, assuming the case presented in Chapters 13, 14, and 15 is sound, the practices and perspectives that underpin the transcendent self-view create a mental and emotional environment that improves on the fixed-self environment in the ways outlined above. An environment in which conflict and negative effects are easier to escape and avoid if they occur, where they are less likely to occur in the first place, and where, in addition, an optimal response to any situation encountered is more likely. The transcendent self-view meets the first part of the requirement identified in Chapter 9 in these areas.

Retaining Positive and Personally Unique Fixed-Self Aspects

Positive Effects and Immersion Level Control

The remainder of the requirement noted in Chapter 9 is also met. A particular feature of the transcendent self-view environment is a practised ability to permit a level of emotional, perspectival, and habitual immersion in a particular subsidiary self-world perspective but pull out of it more or less automatically where a change in the circumstances faced requires it (using the immersion level control facility described in Chapter 14). This feature allows for the retention of both the positive effects of the fixed-self habit and those important personally unique aspects of a fixed self-view we particularly associate with ourselves as individuals or with our membership of particular groups or communities.

There are inevitably some limitations on the extent to which the positive effects can be retained. The immersion possible under the transcendent self-view is likely to be less extreme than can occur at times in a fixed self, simply because it is of a type ultimately under the control of the transcendent self. Everyday examples of the type of immersion mentioned in Chapter 9 – immersion in the emotional and perspectivally romantic aspects of Christmas, a foreign holiday, or a walk in the country on a spring morning – should not be a difficulty. We would simply learn to let ourselves slip into them for a while and return to the core of our transcendent self when the event was over.

The same kind of immersion and subsequent extraction would be possible up to a point in the more extreme case mentioned in Chapter 9, but it would be more limited. A soldier who can fight with more determination and perseverance because he is emotionally, perspectivally, and habitually attached to a viewpoint that paints his own side as the righteous soldiers of God and the enemy as the soldiers of the evil anti-prophet might still be feasible up to a point. In the overall context of a controlling transcendent self, however, it would have a much weaker hold on the individual concerned and be that much less effective as a result. Although some would undoubtedly disagree, this is arguably a positive thing. Do we really want to be creating soldiers with the level of extreme immersion outlined in the example in Chapter 9? Would anyone want, agree, or seek to become such a soldier?

Immersion at this transcendent level could still entail negative effects, of course. Another example from Chapter 9 mentioned the case where one partner in a relationship saw it as a serious long-term thing and the other 'just a bit of fun for the summer'. The partner who saw it as serious would probably still be more immersed in the relationship and more easily hurt by its demise than her partner. She would still probably suffer the negative effects of a conflict between her view and his. In the transcendent style of immersion, however, the immersion would likely be less extreme and the negative effects easier to escape than those in the fixed-self scenario would be. The more deeply involved partner would be practised at pulling herself out of situations like this and focusing on her core self with the non-relational, emotion-free experience of empty consciousness at its core.

Another area where negative effects would likely still occur but be reduced is in the kind of situation illustrated in the 10 gods example from Chapter 9. This envisaged a world with ten countries in which every citizen of each is brought up believing he or she is of the race chosen to rule the whole world by God 1 in country 1, God 2 in country 2, and so on. It envisaged a world in which each person in every country was taught that all unbelievers were evil people to be actively shunned and fought against. If all of the people concerned had these views as a key element of a fixed self, conflict between those of different countries would be inevitable, and the negative effects on all of them easy to imagine. Immersion in such a context would be deep and difficult to escape.

In a world where all of these citizens had transcendent self-views in overarching control, however, and where their immersion in their religious outlook was of the looser, less deep transcendent variety, conflict would be less likely and the knock-on negative effects less severe. Even if the people chose to immerse themselves in the emotions and perspectival romance of their various religions in a relatively habitual way, it would be an immersion of the weaker, more limited transcendent type. Conflict situations would still arise, but they would be easier to escape before negative effects were encountered. The protagonists might be immersed in their opposing religious views at the moment of conflict, but they would be practised at relinquishing immersion in them and returning to a transcendent level with a much wider perspective on things before the negative effects went too far.

Personal and Collective Selves

A practised ability to permit a level of emotional, perspectival, and (to a degree) habitual immersion in a particular subsidiary self-world perspective set but pull out of it more or less automatically where a situational change makes this advisable also has another positive aspect. It allows us to retain those important, personally unique aspects of a fixed self-view we particularly associate with our individuality or with our membership of particular groups or communities.

Although it is not necessarily invariably true, personal and community-related preferred aspects of fixed selves we might want to have an emotional, perspectivally romanticised, and habitual attachment to will usually be complex matrices of interacting simple subsidiary self-world perspectives. Examples might be a complex subsidiary self-world perspective matrix associated with being a surgeon, a plumber, a teacher, or a member of a neighbourhood religious community. Others might include having an attachment to a particular set of moral beliefs, being what the local society would regard as a model citizen, or a variation on this (a dissident, say). These are all aspects of fixed selves we would likely prefer to retain in the context of adopting the transcendent self-view.

This should not be a difficulty in the context of adopting the transcendent self-view as our overarching self. The assumption in the context of the transcendent perspective is that all such simple subsidiary self-world perspectives would be encompassed in the total self in a disaggregated fashion and be used as responses when a situation called for this. They would be brought together as complex, interacting matrices only by virtue of the person concerned operating for an extended period of time in a situation or set of situations that called for this. A surgeon's matrix being brought together when he was operating might be an example, or a plumber's when she was installing a central heating system.

As should be clear from the points made above on the retention of the positive effects of fixed selves, this would not prevent a person becoming immersed in or emotionally, perspectively, and (up to a point) habitually attached to these aspects of their total selves. Letting them become entirely dominant as a group to the exclusion of all others would, of course, produce a fixed self. However, treating them as aspects of the transcendent self that we sometimes become emotionally, perspectively, and even, to a limited extent, habitually, attached to and immersed in (but nevertheless retain overall control of within the overarching transcendent self-view) would avoid this issue.

As long as they are actively regarded as nuanced aspects of the real self intended for temporary use and not as the whole self for sole and permanent use, there should not be a problem. A degree of immersion in them will then allow them to be treated and used as especially personally important aspects of the whole self. Personally important aspects that will not impact in a negative way on the overall transcendent self, provided the practised immersion level control facility described in Chapter 14 is in operational place.

In these circumstances, a conflict encountered by any element of these personally important aspects of the whole self should cause a return to the empty-consciousness-centred core of the transcendent self. There should never be any question of these groups of simple subsidiary self-world perspectives taking over complete control and becoming the basis of a fixed self. The practices, perspectives, and emotional attitudes that underpin the transcendent self on an ongoing basis will work to prevent that happening. With a transcendent self and this approach to individual preferences in place, our one-time fixed-self-based 'individually unique John Smith, passport number 8887321' might be best described as a wholly-variable, fully developed human with occasional 'John Smith, passport number 8887321' associated preferences and tendencies. He would still have the uniqueness but would be able to mentally and emotionally jump out of that particular aspect of his whole self as and when required, without any of the barriers created by fixed-self habits.

Summary

Requirements met

In summary, the transcendent self-view not only meets the requirements of the fully human self-view set out in Chapters 8, 10, 11, and 12. Given that the case presented in Chapters 13, 14, and 15 is sound, it also meets all aspects of the additional set of requirements identified in Chapter 9. It creates a mental and emotional environment in which the chances of avoiding the negative effects associated with fixed-self-type conflicts are optimised and in which negative effects of this kind are both easier to escape and avoid if they occur and less likely to occur in the first place. It also creates an environment where an optimal response to any situation encountered is more likely, as well as an environment that allows for the retention of the positive effects of the fixed-self habit. Finally, it creates an environment in which those important personally unique aspects of a fixed self-view we particularly associate with ourselves as individuals or with our membership of particular groups or communities can be maintained.

This means it meets most of the requirements of the fully human self-view we set out to identify. That it also meets the final requirement of this fully human self-view – the resolution of the misdefinition issue as highlighted in Chapter 7 – is a point we will turn to in the next chapter.

Conscious Intention

As with the previous chapter, one final point is worth noting before we move on. It is reasonable to suppose that the practices underpinning the first-pass transcendent self-view outlined in Chapters 13 and 14 will be applied more successfully if the person applying them is doing so with the conscious intention of instantiating the features described above. If the person applying them is doing so with the conscious intention of creating an environment that avoids the negative effects of the fixed self and retains its various positive aspects, as described in the current chapter.

Addendum on Inherent Nature and the Transcendent Self-View

One final point is worth touching on here before we move on. The question of personally unique aspects of a person's self raises questions about how the transcendent self-view interacts with our inherent nature. Can it encompass and control instinct-driven responses to situations we encounter?

The assumption here is that the answer to this question is yes – such responses can be encompassed and controlled. We can learn the mental and emotional skills required to ensure that even instinctive responses can be mediated via the same learned brain algorithms as responses acquired through learning. Most of us appear to be able to acquire and maintain control over such things as angry reactions, violent tendencies, and sexual urges – even (at times) those who struggle to do so (see, e.g., Deffenbacher et al., 1996; Guerra & Slaby, 1990; Kärgel et al., 2016; Sari et al., 2020). This arguably suggests that our more deep-seated urges can be mediated through the more developed aspects of the socialised brain and might be as susceptible to being encompassed and controlled by the transcendent self-view as any learned response. It is difficult to prove this definitively, of course, but it is arguably a reasonable assumption. That said, it is not really a question that can be examined closely here. The best we can do in the context of the present work is to highlight it as an area of what is claimed in the book that is best marked down as a position that requires investigation and research in the longer term.

17

The Best Alternative to Misdefinition

The Aims of This Chapter

The primary aim in this chapter is to present the case for holding that a fully correct adoption of the first-pass transcendent perspective outlined in Chapters 13 and 14 meets the requirements of a self-view that accurately reflects our full behavioural and experiential nature identified in Chapter 7. More precisely put, it is to argue that it not only replaces the various fixed-self-view-based misdefinitions of who and what we are as outlined in Chapter 7 with a self-view that accurately reflects our full behavioural and experiential nature, but is the only self-view that can.

A supplementary aim is to justify two claims made in Chapters 1 and 7, respectively. The first being that, unless we each personally adopt this transcendent self-view by habitually identifying ourselves with it and building our operational self around it, we cannot claim to be fully developed humans. The second being that adopting it fully and correctly is the only way we can avoid adopting some variation of the fixed self.

In arguing these points, it is assumed that various previously presented arguments and conclusions are sound. First, that the behavioural and experiential relationship of humans to the world is wholly-variable, as argued in Chapter 4. Second, that this means it must be an *open-ended*, wholly-variable relationship rather than one based on the infinity-of-roles view, as argued in Chapters 8 and 10. Third, that the transcendent self-view presented in Chapters 13 and 14 instantiates and supports such an open-ended, wholly-variable relationship as was argued in Chapters 13, 14, and 15.

Sole Reflector of our Full Behavioural and Experiential Nature
Not Fixed – Wholly-Variable

If the case presented in Chapter 4 is sound, the behavioural and experiential relationship of humans to the world is not fixed but wholly-variable. If any and every subsidiary self-world perspective is equally able to determine our behavioural and experiential response to the world in any given circumstance, only a self-view that allows this in practice can be claimed to reflect our full behavioural and experiential relationship to the world. It must be so constructed as to ensure that every possible subsidiary self-world perspective, including even those unknown to an individual and those as yet undiscovered by humans generally, always has an equal chance of determining our behavioural and experiential relationship to the world in any situation encountered.

A self-view so constructed as to prevent this, either by blocking out or by creating bias for or against some subsidiary self-world perspectives, cannot be claimed to reflect our full behavioural and experiential relationship to the world on this view. Only a self-view where any and every subsidiary self-world perspective has an equal chance of being consciously or unconsciously chosen as a response in any given circumstance can accurately reflect our full, wholly-variable behavioural and experiential relationship to the world.

This, we can assume, applies even to those subsidiary self-world perspectives unknown to an individual or undiscovered by humans generally. These, too, can determine our behavioural and experiential relationship in a given situation if, through the acquisition of new information or creative thinking, they become known when the situation is encountered. Ergo, any self-view that prevents their inclusion fails to accurately reflect our full, wholly-variable behavioural and experiential relationship. Only a self-view that allows every possible subsidiary self-world perspective to be an equally-weighted potential determinant of our response to any given situation – even the unknown and undiscovered ones – can be said to be an accurate reflection of our actual behavioural and experiential relationship to the world.

A fixed self-view based on a limited set of subsidiary self-world perspectives cannot, by definition, do this, even for already-discovered subsidiary self-world perspectives. No matter how complex it is, it will still be a self-view based on or biased towards a limited set of these subsidiary self-world perspectives known to humans generally and, hence, will not support even the level of variability possible with discovered subsidiary self-world perspectives.

Nor are there any exceptions to this. As we saw in Chapter 11, even a fixed self-view based on a wholly complete, wholly accurate scientific world-view fails in this respect. It limits us to a scientist's eye view of the world and blocks out both other perspectives known to humans generally – those of the poet, the philosopher, or the clown, say – and those that are as yet undiscovered, either by scientists or by anyone else.

The Infinity-Of-Roles View: Impractical and Ineffectual

A self-view based on what was called in Chapter 8 the infinity-of-roles view – a self-view based on seeing and rehearsing every conceivable subsidiary self-world perspective known to humans generally as part of our self-view – can theoretically solve this problem for discovered subsidiary self-world perspectives. However, it is a far from achievable proposition, even in this limited sense. Rehearsing defining ourselves in terms of each one of a near-infinite and always-growing number of subsidiary self-world perspectives known to humans generally on an individual basis is not only an impossibly impractical task but one that is probably doomed to fail in any reasonable imagined world.

Our attempts to define ourselves in terms of all such subsidiary self-world perspectives would require us to know every subsidiary self-world perspective ever known to any human at any time. It would require us to keep pace with the continuous addition of new subsidiary self-world perspectives by every human alive. It would require us to have time to rehearse seeing ourselves in terms of all of them in a habitual way – to rehearse seeing them as an aspect of our total self until they became just that. This is arguably an impossible task in any reasonable world we can imagine, especially if we still hope to have enough of our lives left to allow us to use them for everyday living.

There is, moreover, a further, insurmountable, difficulty with the infinity-of-roles view. Even if it could work as required for known subsidiary self-world perspectives, it will not and cannot deal with the problem of as yet undiscovered subsidiary self-world perspectives. The infinity-of-roles view cannot be used to instantiate a self-view that accurately reflects our full behavioural and experiential relationship to the world by supporting a fully wholly-variable relationship because it cannot encompass as yet undiscovered subsidiary self-world perspectives. We cannot rehearse seeing ourselves in terms of undiscovered subsidiary self-world perspectives; it is simply impossible; for how are we to do this with idea-based subsidiary self-world perspectives as yet undiscovered by humans generally?

Self-Views That Misdefine us

Identifying ourselves with a self-view that does not reflect and instantiate this wholly-variable relationship in this way misdefines us. As we saw in Chapter 7, this is the case with any of the various varieties of fixed self; they take a limited view of our possible behavioural and experiential relationship to the world. The relationship is assumed, consciously or unconsciously, to be a fixed one and is used continuously as if it were the true relationship (and so becomes it). The effect is the same as it would be if we took a particular fixed view of ourselves – saw ourselves as only a Buddhist, a flat-worlder, or a scientist – and made that self-view true by regularly rehearsing it as a view of who we are. We effectively take a limited view of our true relationship to the world – a misdefinition of who we truly are in relation to it – and make that misdefinition operationally true.

The same is true ultimately of the infinity of roles view. Even if it were a practical proposition, which it clearly is not, the best it would manage to do would be to instantiate what was, in the last resort, a broadly based and potentially very variable fixed self. It would not and could not encompass every possible subsidiary self-world perspective, because identifying ourselves with undiscovered subsidiary self-world perspectives (or even with those that were only unknown to us personally) would remain an impossibility.

The end result – if such a thing were possible at all – would still be a misdefinition of who and what we really are. At best, it would define us not in terms of all possible subsidiary self-world perspectives (as it should according to the position presented in Chapter 4), but in terms of discovered subsidiary self-world perspectives only. At worst, it would not do even this but only define us in terms of those subsidiary self-world perspectives known to us personally. However variable such an end result might be, the relationship instantiated would still be relatively limited and fixed. It would not give us a self-view that accurately reflected our full, wholly-variable behavioural and experiential relationship to the world.

Reflecting and Instantiating our Actual Relationship

The transcendent self-view is not based on and biased towards a limited set of subsidiary self-world perspectives in the way that a fixed self is, nor is it based on an impossibly impractical task ultimately doomed to fail as the infinity-of-roles view is. Assuming that what was argued in Chapters 13, 14, and 15 holds true, it does what it was designed to do – it both reflects and instantiates our actual behavioural and experiential relationship to the world. Since it is based on identifying with empty consciousness and recognising that all possible subsidiary self-world perspectives can be possible responses to a given situation – even unknown and undiscovered ones – it arguably includes all self-world perspectives in by including none of them out.

On a descriptive level, it recognises all possible subsidiary self-world perspectives as potential, equally-weighted, ways of relating to the world, albeit in a collective sense. On an operational level, it avoids preferring any limited set of subsidiary self-world perspectives over any others through a focus on the only thing in our experience that is not a self-world perspective – the nonrelational empty consciousness that is the core of our every experience. It therefore resolves both the fixed self problem and the infinity-of-roles difficulties. The former because no limited set of subsidiary self-world perspectives is habitually preferred over any other; the latter because no subsidiary self-world perspective – not even those unknown to the individual or as yet undiscovered by anyone – is blocked as a possible response to any situation encountered.

On this basis, the transcendent self-view not only reflects and instantiates our actual behavioural and experiential relationship to the world – all possible subsidiary self-world perspectives are both seen as part of the total relationship and operationally encompassed as possible roles – it is the only self-view that can. It supports and instantiates a wholly-variable self-view as outlined in Chapter 8 in the only way it can be supported and instantiated. By making the core of the self we aim to identify with the one and only thing in our experience that is not a self-world perspective and so ensuring that we do not give undue weight to any one subsidiary self-world perspective or any limited group of subsidiary self-world perspectives. By this means, all subsidiary self-world perspectives, even those that are unknown or undiscovered, are encompassed as possible responses and as part of our total or overarching relationship, either immediately where known relationships are concerned or via an open path to possible future discovery through creative thinking or research where unknown relationships are concerned.

Including Empty Consciousness

It also has another feature important to a complete and accurate reflection of our actual behavioural and experiential relationship to the world: it actively and consciously includes empty consciousness itself in the self-view that defines that relationship. If this is a unique aspect of our experience, as was argued in Chapter 12, then it is a unique aspect of our experience that should and must be actively and consciously included in any self-view that aims to reflect and instantiate our full behavioural and experiential nature. If it is the only aspect of our experiential world that is nonrelational – the one aspect common to every experience that, experienced directly as itself, sits outside of and beyond relational experiences like emotions, feelings, and relational points of view – it must be part of such a self-view. A self-view that fails to actively and consciously include it would not be a fully accurate reflection of our behavioural and experiential nature.

Of course, given that it is an experience common to every other experience, it is, self-evidently, an experience that is never absent, even in a fixed-self mind. It could be actively and consciously added to either a fixed or an infinity-of-roles-based self-view without difficulty and thereby improve those self-views in this one respect. We need not adopt the transcendent perspective to achieve this end. Adding it in this way to these self-views would not improve them in other ways, however. Fixed self-views would still be limited in respect of variability of response and would still misdefine us, and the infinity-of-roles position would still be impractical and ultimately inadequate to the task of achieving a wholly-variable relationship.

The transcendent self-view is the only self-view that reflects and instantiates our actual behavioural and experiential relationship to the world, encompassing empty consciousness in this way *and* using its unique nonrelational properties to support and instantiate a wholly-variable response and self-view as outlined in Chapter 8. It is thus the only self-view that can be considered a complete and accurate reflection of our behavioural and experiential relationship to the world – a full and correct answer to the problem of misdefining ourselves by adopting some variety of fixed self. A way of defining ourselves that accurately reflects our full behavioural and experiential nature and thereby makes that true definition operationally as well as descriptively true.

A More Reasonable Alternative to the Infinity-Of-Roles View

There are, moreover, two further points in its favour. Seeing ourselves in terms of a self-view that has empty consciousness as its core and that collectively includes every possible subsidiary self-world perspective as a subordinate aspect of the total self is a reasonable proposition in the same way that identifying ourselves with a fixed self-view is. It is a reasonable proposition in a way that identifying ourselves with the close-to-impossibly large and ever-growing set of subsidiary self-world perspectives of the infinity-of-roles perspective is not. We are envisaging ourselves in a way that is simple to understand and implement, rather than in a way that involves seeing ourselves in terms of every conceivable perspective on self and world under the sun on an individual basis, as we would with the infinity-of-roles perspective.

Implementing the transcendent perspective has its difficulties; see Chapters 18 onwards. However, seeing ourselves in terms of a self-view that has empty consciousness as its core, that collectively includes every possible subsidiary self-world perspective as a subordinate aspect of the total self, and that is open to even unknown and undiscovered subsidiary self-world perspectives is a reasonable, easily-envisaged proposition. It is a reasonable, easily-envisaged proposition in a way that identifying ourselves with a close-to-infinitely large and ever-growing set of subsidiary self-world perspectives on an individual basis – as in the infinity-of-roles perspective – is not. It is a coherent, manageable, and effective way of addressing the misdefinition issue identified in Chapter 7.

Individual and Collective Differences Included

It also has a further point in its favour as regards reflecting our behavioural and experiential relationship to the world in a complete and accurate way. If what was argued in Chapter 16 is sound, it is a self-view that not only supports and instantiates a wholly-variable response as described above but also facilitates the inclusion of individual and collective differences without diminishing the comprehensive and wholly-variable nature of the overarching transcendent self. In short, it not only allows us to transcend the limitations of the fixed self, it also allows us to retain those aspects of it we might see as important to our own self-definition without diminishing the scope or level of control of the transcendent self.

The Best Basis for a Self-View for Humans

It should now be clear why the transcendent self-view offers us the best basis of a first-pass answer to the multi-faceted question this book aims to address. If the arguments presented in Chapters 13-17 are sound, the position outlined in Chapters 13 and 14 meets all of the requirements of the alternative human self-view we have been seeking.

It meets the twin requirements identified in Chapters 11 and 12: it is clearly a self-view based, not on a limited set of subsidiary self-world perspectives (not even a scientifically based one), but on empty consciousness, the one thing in our experience that is not a self-world perspective. It instantiates, at both a descriptive and operational level, the open-ended, wholly-variable self-view described in Chapters 8 and 10, while also meeting the related requirement added in Chapter 10 that it should not block the open-ended, wholly-variable response in the way that fixed selves do (see Chapters 13, 14, and 15). It meets the requirement identified in Chapter 9: creating a mental and emotional environment that entails the positive, but not the negative, aspects of the fixed self-view and also encompassing personally preferred aspects of an individual's self (see Chapter 16). Last but not least, it also meets, as detailed in the present chapter, the requirement identified in Chapter 7. It replaces the various fixed-self-view-based misdefinitions of who and what we are with a self-view that not only accurately reflects and instantiates our full behavioural and experiential nature but is the only self-view that can.

It thereby provides the best possible answer to the group of questions considered in this book: *What self-view should we identify with? How do we become fully developed variable-response humans rather than kinds of humans with a complex but limited repertoire of subsidiary self-world perspectives controlling how we act, think, and feel in the world? If a fixed definition is a misdefinition, how should we humans see and define ourselves?*

A Self-View for the Fully Developed Human

This raises the question of the claim made earlier in the book: that we cannot consider ourselves fully developed and educated as humans until this transcendent perspective is instantiated. The logic behind this claim should now be evident. Our self-view develops as we grow. If our behavioural and experiential relationship is variable, but our habits can make it fixed, there are two possible endpoints to human personal development and education: one fixed and one wholly-variable. The fixed one is an inaccurate reflection of who and what we truly are on this view; the wholly-variable one is an accurate reflection of who and what we truly are. If our personal development and education does not go beyond the development of a fixed self-view, it has not gone far enough. We are not fully developed and educated as humans until we see ourselves as we truly are and make that self-view the determinant of our behavioural and experiential relationship to the world.

Moreover, since our behavioural and experiential relationship to the world is determined by our self-view, this means that we are not fully developed humans until the self-view that has operational control of our behavioural and experiential responses reflects and instantiates our true, wholly-variable relationship. We are not fully developed as humans until we both see ourselves in terms of the kind of transcendent, wholly-variable self-view described above and ensure it has operational control of our behavioural and experiential relationship to the world. We are not fully human unless and until we personally realise this transcendent perspective on ourselves and the world – the only possible way we have of avoiding making a misdefinition of ourselves actual and making an accurate definition actual instead. We are not fully human unless and until we personally put in place the mental and emotional environment described in this book as the first-pass transcendent self-view – even if it is true, as some would hold, that, in structuring the human self, we are structuring an illusion.

The transcendent self-view described above is a self-view we should arguably all adopt – a standardised self-view for all humans that nevertheless allows us to retain our preferred personal uniqueness as well as realising our full behavioural and experiential relationship to the world. On the view argued in this book, we cannot claim to be fully developed as humans unless and until we adopt it personally.

Final Proof That Fixing Happens to all

Notice, moreover, that if (as was argued above) the transcendent self-view is the only self-view that can reflect our true nature, we can only avoid fixing by actively adopting it. Final confirmation that, as claimed in Chapter 7, fixing probably happens to all of us as we develop unless we aim instead to instantiate the transcendent self-view. If it is the only self-view that can allow us to avoid developing some form of fixed self, it follows that anyone who does not actively set out to adopt it as they develop must inevitably develop some form of fixed self instead.

Informed Adoption and two Caveats

Informed Adoption

Again, as with the two previous chapters, one final point is worth noting before we move on. It is reasonable to suppose that the practices underpinning the first-pass transcendent self-view outlined in Chapters 13 and 14 will be applied more successfully if the person applying them is doing so with the conscious intention of instantiating the features described in this present chapter. They will be applied more successfully if the person applying them is doing so with the conscious intention of putting in place a mental and emotional environment that accurately reflects our full behavioural and experiential nature.

Caveat #1: Scientific Testing

Two caveats should be noted as regards the position stated above.

The first is that, as previously indicated, the claims made above as regards the transcendent perspective are clearly based on the author's own personally applied chain of observation and logic rather than anything approaching definitive proof. They only hold true if the observations and assumptions made are accurate, if the logic is sound, and if nothing vital to the chain or the conclusions has been missed under any of these headings.

In the last analysis, of course, the only definitive basis for acceptance of the position is an assurance that all of the claims made are able to survive a rigorous and sustained regime of scientific testing. As was noted in Chapter 1, this is not impossible to envisage; the position presented entails behavioural and experiential assertions that can, in theory, be examined and shown to be either false or unrefuted by science. However, it does entail a range of difficulties that suggest that achieving scientific acceptance can only be a very long-term possibility.

How do we attain full instantiation of the transcendent self-view and of representative fixed selves in sufficiently large groups of subjects to allow adequate testing? How do we design and determine the validity of verbal tests to establish full instantiation of both transcendent and fixed selves in individual subjects? How do we design and implement physiological and neurological tests to determine a subject's mental and emotional states in respect of both transcendent and fixed-self subjects and the beliefs and perspectives they entail? How, in particular, do we manage this in respect of the key claim about empty consciousness? How do we test the claim that it is an experiential state beyond and outwith all things relational, including self-world-perspective-based tendencies to act and feel in particular ways and relational emotions like hate, relational feelings like pain, relational experiences like colours, sounds, tastes, and so on?

These and other similar questions will have to be addressed and resolved if scientific testing is to be feasible – no minor matter if the literature on the kinds of problems faced when researching inner states is any guide. (De Gelder, 2010; Kitson et al., 2020; Krueger & Grafman, 2012; Larsen & Fredrickson, 1999; Mauss & Robinson, 2009; Meier, 2023; Scholtz et al., 2020 give a flavour of the difficulties likely to be encountered. Difficulties sufficiently significant to suggest that, in the short to medium term at least, readers can only assess the arguments presented in earlier chapters and decide on the strengths and weaknesses of the case for themselves through a critical examination of the position as presented.)

Caveat #2: Beyond the First-Pass Perspective

The second caveat relates to the description of the transcendent perspective presented in this section of the book. While the position as outlined above (Chapters13-17) is a good first pass at a complete account of the nature and detail of the transcendent self-view, it does not represent the final word on the position. Further clarification of the detail of the first-pass perspective described above is presented in the remainder of the work.

Assuming the case made for it in this book is correct, adopting the first-pass transcendent self-view described above fully and correctly is the one way we have of ensuring we become fully developed humans, accurately bearing a wholly-variable behavioural and experiential relationship to the world. It is the one way we have of ensuring we do not allow ourselves to become *kinds* of humans with a fixed behavioural and experiential relationship to the world that misdefines us – the one way of ensuring we become fully and truly human.

Adopting this transcendent self-view fully and correctly is a relatively complex process, however. It entails tackling a range of issues beyond instantiating the perspective and giving it operational control – points that will be taken up in the remainder of the book.

These (as we shall see) include applying the perspective to other humans and recognising the key role of science in the perspective (and of the perspective in science). They include dealing with the problems of hidden fixed-self facets in general and those relating to the hard problem of consciousness in particular. They include recognising and accepting the impact of the perspective on religious views. Most important of all, they include remaining aware that achieving and maintaining the perspective is an ongoing mental struggle, especially in a world where most will not have adopted and instantiated the perspective.

PART 5

Instantiation; Seeing Others; Science

Part 5: Outline of the Case Presented

Further clarification and additional detail is required to bring the first-pass transcendent perspective described above closer to the final position proposed. In particular, it should be recognised that:

The self-view as described will only have the merits claimed for it and only be correctly understood if implemented fully at a personal level as an operational experience of self. This entails moving beyond mere verbal understanding of the position described to actual personal transcendence. It means knowing its various aspects as actual experiences – particularly empty consciousness, which must be grasped and utilised as a nonrelational nonverbal experience (not a verbally expressed idea) if it is to play the key operational role assigned to it in the functioning transcendent self-view. Achieving personal transcendence means struggling internally (in ways suggested in **Part 5** of the book) to replace current mental and emotional habits with alternatives, aiming to subdue a resident fixed self and instantiate the transcendent self-view instead **(Chapters 18-20)**.

The self-view should also be utilised as a way of seeing and relating to other humans – for two reasons. First, because this is an accurate way of seeing a person who has adopted the perspective. Second, because to see others habitually as *kinds* of humans is to fix our relationship to their aspect of the world and block the full instantiation of the transcendent perspective in ourselves. Handling this requirement in the short term will be difficult because of the likely preponderance of nonadopters in current circumstances **(Chapter 21)**.

The self-view should be understood as implying a strengthening of the role of science in human affairs. Despite the requirement to see and treat the scientific world-view as one of a range of possibilities ranging from religious, philosophical and political viewpoints to fantasy and even nonsense perspectives, there is no implication that it is weakened. Scientific perspectives must be possible responses in situations where an accurate view of the true nature of the world is required – and should inform the degree of wariness with which a nonscientific self-world perspective is adopted in circumstances that suggest a nonscientific approach is best **(Chapter 22)**.

18

Instantiating the Core Perspective

Changing Mental Habits

The Problem

How does someone who has some variety of fixed self in place set about replacing it with the transcendent self-view? How are we to set about replacing the mental and emotional practices, perspectives, and attitudes that created and support our fixed self with a new set that sweeps these away and creates instead the kind of transcendent, wholly-variable self-view outlined and discussed in this book? How can we achieve personal transcendence? Adopting this new perspective on ourselves is straightforward enough in essence. It is merely a matter of dropping a set of mental and emotional habits centred on an old self-view and replacing them with another set focused on a full and accurate understanding of the new alternative self-view. A matter of ceasing to habitually see oneself in one way and beginning to habitually see oneself in another, something we all know how to do.

The primary barrier to managing this is that old habits die hard, even when they can be readily identified and tackled, and the process is made more difficult when there is either emotional attachment involved, or the habits are partly or wholly unconscious, or both. How do we break old habits when some have been in place for so long they have become second nature to us, when we are emotionally attached to the associated view of ourselves, and when many of them – including some we are emotionally attached to – are partially or wholly unconscious?

No Magic Pill

Not without a long-term struggle is the short answer. Not without wrestling over a significant period of time with all of the various complexities addressed in Chapters 13 and 14 above and discussed further over this chapter and the following two. There is no escaping this. There is no magic pill or mystical revelation that will short-circuit the process and allow us to instantiate this transcendent self-view more easily by some quicker, more direct route.

Approach #1: A 'Quick' Route in

That said, two approaches are probably possible – the first of which may at least appear or feel more direct. Some readers may be attracted by the possibility of taking a shorter route into the problem. This involves following their own path and tackling issues in their own way with the following outline plan as a rough guide:

1. Armed with an understanding of Chapters 1-17, use the 'two hands clapping' exercise described in Chapters 12 and 13 (and again below) to learn the mental habit of moving the mind to a point where empty consciousness is the core and dominant focus of the mental landscape.

2. Work to memorise a brief version of the aide memoire that simply specifies that any idea about anything – including possibilities

unknown to the adopter or even undiscovered by humans generally – should be seen and treated as facets of the self and as equally valid possible responses to any situation encountered.

3. Build on the habit of moving the mind to a point where empty consciousness is the core and dominant focus of the mental landscape to make this aide memoire a subordinate perspective in a landscape in which empty consciousness is the core and dominant focus.

4. Learn the habit of experiencing the result of this empty-consciousness-dominated landscape with the aide memoire in place as the preferred view of the self and its hub and rest state – habitually identify with this experience as the preferred view of the self and its rest state and hub.

5. Work on a case-by-case basis to ensure that perspectives used in everyday life come to be seen and treated as facets of the total self rather like an actor's roles. Work on them until they come to be seen and treated as roles enacted by the core or whole self with control returning to that core or whole self before a new role is selected and deployed in a new situation. Work in this way to eventually put in place an embryonic transcendent self-view in a mind otherwise still dominated by a fixed self.

6. Work both to recognise fixed self habits spotted in use in everyday life and reprocess them as stored information about their value or otherwise in specific circumstances, and to consciously aim to avoid creating any new fixed self type habits. Aim in these ways to gradually decrease the influence of the fixed self while building on the embryonic transcendent self.

7. Work to build on all of the above until every aspect of the transcendent self-view as described in Chapters 12 and 13 (and again below) is fully encompassed in the adopter's operational self.

Approach #1: Not so Quick, Perhaps

The problem with this 'quick route in' approach is that it is unlikely to shorten – and may even lengthen – the overall process. Indeed, there is every likelihood an adopter following this route may find it difficult to complete the process and deal with all aspects of the above-mentioned complexities without at some point turning to the longer alternative plan presented below for detailed help and guidance. This does not negate its possible value as an approach, however; it may still be an attractive and valid option for those drawn to it.

Approach #2: A Detailed, Step by Step, Plan

The second possible approach is to follow the alternative plan presented below from the first. Some readers may prefer taking a short route into the problem, even if this ultimately makes for a longer struggle; others may be more attracted to the more detailed, step-by-step approach suggested in what follows.

For these readers, implementing the set of mental and emotional exercises outlined below and doing so as part of a conscious attempt to put in place a mental and emotional landscape that has the various merits ascribed to the transcendent self-view in Chapters 15-17 should hopefully have the effect desired. It should ultimately replace legacy fixed-self habits with the alternatives needed to put in place the kind of transcendent, wholly-variable self-view outlined and discussed in this book and achieve personal transcendence.

It should also help clarify the transcendent view itself. Full comprehension of the perspective is only realisable when a person moves beyond mere words on a page, puts the working self-view in place, and experiences it for themselves. It is only realisable when they transcend their old self by instantiating the transcendent perspective on who and what they are and relate to the world as they arguably can and should. There are a variety of reasons for this, but the main one relates to empty consciousness, the core of the self-view. This is a nonverbal experience that can only be accurately known for what it truly is and can only have the operational effect claimed for it if it is known in situ as an experience and is included within the transcendent self-view *as* this experience.

Understanding why

An essential first step is to assimilate an understanding of the position itself, a knowledge of the benefits claimed for it, and a detailed comprehension of the arguments that support these claims. To start with a clear view of the whats, the whys, and the wherefores of the aim of adopting and instantiating the transcendent self-view. Chapters 1-17 cover these points in detail. Would-be adopters should consider taking steps to fully comprehend and absorb the various arguments and perspectives covered in these chapters before attempting to use the guidelines set out below to set about adopting and instantiating the transcendent perspective themselves. It is reasonable to suppose that the practices underpinning the first-pass transcendent self-view will be applied more successfully if the adopter applies them with the conscious intention of instantiating a self-view that will meet the various requirements and achieve the various ends identified between Chapters 7 and 17. An awareness of the perspectives that underpin the position as set out in the chapters preceding Chapter 7 is also likely to be of value, if only as background.

Old Habits and New: A Struggle

The primary problem likely to be encountered lies in the fact that any would-be adopters will differ from the adopter described in Chapters 13 and 14 in one crucial respect. There, we imagined someone starting, if not from scratch, then at least at a very early stage in her personal development, learning the new perspective as she grew. This is unlikely to be a position enjoyed by any would-be adopters reading this book. They will not be starting their efforts from the same early stage.

Instead, they will likely be starting from the position of a person who has, over many years, developed the kind of mental habits found in the fixed-self mind and will be seeking to successfully expunge these habits as well as to instil the habits and perspectives that underpin the transcendent self-view.

This will not be easy. Nor will it be quick, uncomplicated, or frustration-free. Old habits do indeed die hard, especially when there is either emotional attachment involved or the habits are partly or wholly unconscious (or indeed, if they are both emotionally charged and partially or wholly unconscious).

There are, moreover, two secondary problems. The first is that the adopter described in Chapters 13 and 14 had the active support of a knowledgeable community of instructors to guide and direct her efforts. This is unlikely to be true of any reader of this book who sets out to adopt the transcendent self-view. They will be on their own to a far greater extent as they struggle to put in place new habits and expunge those learned in the past. A possible solution to this is for one or more would-be adopters to work together and support each other, and some of the exercises proposed below assume some level of collaboration with others. Such collaboration is probably not essential, but it would very likely be helpful.

The second is that it is impossible in a book such as this to personalise the steps required to instantiate the transcendent self-view so that they deal with each would-be adopter's existing individually unique operational self. The steps set out below are necessarily generic. Would-be adopters must read, understand, and then adapt them to their own individual circumstances before beginning to work towards instantiation. Although the steps relating to empty consciousness and the aide memoire are an exception, others cannot simply be followed as is. Would-be adopters must adapt them to their own individual circumstances - a point that should be kept in mind when reading the points set out below.

Mental Exercises for Instantiation

Since the adopter utilising them is not starting from scratch like the adopter described in Chapters 13 and 14, the mental exercises proposed in what follows as a means of instantiating the transcendent perspective are organised differently from the exercises undertaken by the adopter as described in Chapters 13 and 14. Instead of aiming to instantiate, first the baseline perspective, then the first-pass extension, the aim here is to instantiate the core self first, then move beyond the core to complete the whole first-pass transcendent self-view by tackling its response repertoire, switching mechanism, and selection mechanism elements. There will also be an attempt under these headings to tackle the problem of dealing with older mental practices and habits. The best approach to working through the various exercises towards full instantiation is probably to tackle them in sequence in the initial stages, although it is likely that the work will start to become a parallel and even, to some extent, an overlapping process in time.

Core Self: Envisaging the Core

Anyone aiming to adopt and instantiate the transcendent self-view should begin by reminding themselves that the core of this self-view has two aspects, each integrated within a single experiential landscape. The first of these – the core or underlying substrata of the self – is empty consciousness, known directly as itself, a nonverbal, nonrelational experience. The second is a verbal reminder or aide memoire of how adopters should see and treat the total self they are aiming to instantiate – a total self seen as encompassing all possible self-world relationships, each having equal weight in the total self. The two aspects – empty consciousness and the aide memoire – are integrated within a single experiential landscape, one where the actual nonverbal experience of empty consciousness is the dominant focus and the verbally expressed aide memoire is tagged as a perspective subordinate to that dominant focus.

Core Self: Identifying Empty Consciousness

Empty Consciousness

According to the view put here, we can only successfully instantiate the transcendent perspective by identifying and experiencing the actual experience of empty consciousness and putting that experience at the core of our self-view. Confusing it with anything else in our experience and putting that at the core in its stead will, by definition, put something relational at the core of the self. Identifying ourselves habitually with this relational substitute for empty consciousness would be no different from identifying ourselves habitually with any other self-world relationship; it would put in place another fixed self rather than the wholly-variable self-view of the transcendent perspective. It would put in place a self-view that would fail to fully reflect our behavioural and experiential nature in two senses. First, in the sense of not being wholly-variable: only habitual identification with empty consciousness itself ensures that there are no blocks on the open-ended, wholly-variable self-view and actively works to prevent the unintentional creation of such blocks. Second, in the sense of failing to encompass the actual experience of empty consciousness as a unique aspect of that behavioural and experiential nature.

Only by identifying, experiencing, and encompassing the actual experience of empty consciousness in our self-view and habitually identifying with its nonrelational reality rather than with some relational substitute can we avoid these outcomes on this view. Only by identifying with the actual experience of empty consciousness rather than confusing it with something relational.

Identifying Empty Consciousness: two Hands Clapping

Fortunately, confusing it with a relational substitute is the main difficulty as regards identifying and experiencing the actual experience of empty consciousness. As long as this pitfall is recognised and avoided, there is nothing particularly difficult about identifying and experiencing it, and most will find it relatively easy to do. The thing to avoid as regards confusing it with a relational substitute is the adoption of a perspective where the adopter's mental focus is a point outside of empty consciousness itself. To adopt this perspective is to ensure that what is known is not empty consciousness itself, but empty consciousness as known by an outside observer. To know empty consciousness itself, we must adopt a mental perspective where empty consciousness is *itself* the vantage point and dominant focus – a perspective where we are looking out at everything *from* the perspective of empty consciousness. Then and only then are we mentally sitting at the heart of the experience rather than viewing it relationally from the outside.

The two-hands-clapping exercise referred to in Chapters 12 and 13 is probably the best way of both identifying the actual experience of empty consciousness and avoiding confusing it with a relational substitute. This should take the mind directly to the nonrelational experience itself, at least momentarily. It should also help in the development of a mental skill that has a key role in the operational transcendent self-view – that of moving the mind towards the situation in which empty consciousness is the dominant focus.

As will be recalled from earlier chapters, the first step is for the would-be adopter to actually experience the sound of two hands clapping by clapping their hands enough times to be sure they know what the sound is like and can retain it in memory. The second step is then to internalise the experience – the would-be adopter should close their eyes, ask themselves, 'What is the sound of two hands clapping?', and move their mind to the memory of the sound. They should repeat this several times until this mental move and its endpoint become second nature – then proceed to the key step, step 3, which involves following the same mental process just practised with the Zen koan question, 'What is the sound of *one* hand clapping?'

This should send the mind seeking for the answer to a question that has no answer, except an experience empty of all content other than what remains in experience when all other content is removed. Doing this should take the adopter to the contentless experience that is the only possible answer to the question, 'What is the sound of one hand clapping?' – the experience of consciousness itself with everything else in experience taken out: of consciousness of nothing but consciousness. It should take the mind momentarily to an experience that not only has empty consciousness as its dominant focus and core but that is, in that instant, nothing but empty consciousness.

By repeating this process a number of times, the would-be adopter should come to know the experience we have called empty consciousness, not as words on a page or via or through another (relational) experience, but as the nonrelational experience of empty consciousness itself. They should also have learned the mental habit they need to make this nonrelational experience the habitual core of the self-view – the mental or experiential process of moving the mind from some other experiential place to a point where empty consciousness is the dominant focus and core. By mastering this process, the adopter should have both identified empty consciousness itself and learned the mental process of making this nonrelational experience its dominant focus and core, at least momentarily.

Identifying Empty Consciousness: Slippery And Elusive

Notice that identifying empty consciousness in this sense means knowing it in the minimal sense of momentarily knowing the experience by being that experience; it does not mean knowing it in the sense of sitting mentally outside of it and knowing it via another perspective. This may well seem like a slippery and elusive thing for the mind to grasp, but that is as it should be. It is as expected. The point is not to have the mind turn around and view empty consciousness; it is to take the mind to an experiential place where empty consciousness is the core and dominant focus. It is to take the mind to an experiential place where it (the mind) is, as it were, 'looking out from' the vantage point of the core and dominant focus of empty consciousness, not turning around to view it externally.

Identifying Empty Consciousness: An Alternative Method

Should it be necessary, Chapter 12 outlines a second way of achieving the same end – the end, that is, of making empty consciousness the core and dominant focus. Since we can view empty consciousness as an extended substrata common to all experiences, we can arguably set it at the core of our experiential landscape momentarily when we cease momentarily to focus on what distinguishes individual experiences from each other. We can do it by ceasing to focus on any one aspect of our experiential landscape – by letting the underlying substrata common to all experiences become our momentary mental focus (although it is arguably more accurately described as an absence of mental focus). Since the underlying essence of our every experience is always there, then a mind not focused on anything else must, arguably, in that instant, then have the experience labelled here as empty consciousness at its core. If we are briefly not focused on anything else in consciousness, but are still aware in the minimal sense described earlier, then, at that instant, empty consciousness is a kind of nothingness that is nonetheless experientially real at the core of our experiential landscape – or arguably so.

Core Self: Empty Consciousness a Much Visited Perspective

Once the empty consciousness state has been identified and experienced, the next step should be to practise moving into the state on a regular basis, until doing so becomes second nature. The specific mental skill involved in doing this will differ slightly, depending on which of the two methods of identifying empty consciousness described above is preferred by the adopter. That said, the first method based on the Zen koan already entails the action of moving the mind towards empty consciousness, so it may be that it will provide the best starting point for the learning of this skill. However, adopting the second method outlined above does provide a possible alternative approach for those who find they need or prefer it.

Core Self: Aide Memoire: All Self-World Relationships

The next step is to transfer the details of the aide memoire perspective from the printed page into the mind of the adopter. The aide memoire has two primary elements. The first is a reminder that the total self is made up of empty consciousness and the (collectively envisaged rather than individually rehearsed) totality of every self-world relationship any human can conceive of, including those unknown to the adopter personally and undiscovered by humans generally. The second is a reminder that each of these conceivable self-world relationships is seen and made to operate as an equally-weighted facet of the total self under the control of an empty-consciousness-dominated core. A more detailed description of it is given in Chapter 13, however, and it is this more detailed version that the adopter should work to acquire as the second element of the core of the self (see the four points outlined under the heading '*Baseline Beginnings: The Aide Memoire*').

Core Self: An Integrated Core of the Self

Having put the two elements in place, the next step for the adopter is to integrate them into a single whole with empty consciousness as the dominant focus and the aide memoire reminding the adopter of the self-view being adopted as a peripheral subordinate perspective within it. This should be relatively simple for an adopter already adept at moving into the empty consciousness state on a regular basis. To achieve it, the adopter need only begin with the aide memoire viewpoint as the dominant mental focus and practise moving from this to the empty consciousness state while retaining an awareness of the aide memoire as a subordinate perspective within it.

This is simply a slight variation on the mental skill of moving into the empty consciousness state already acquired. It simply involves practising moving from a situation where the aide memoire is the initial focus to one where empty consciousness is dominant, while retaining a peripheral awareness of this reminder of the self-view being instantiated that the adopter is then mentally sitting outside of or transcending. It involves practising this slightly altered perspective until retaining the aide memoire as a peripheral subordinate adjunct to the empty consciousness state becomes an integrated part of the skill of moving mentally to make empty consciousness the dominant focus – until this slightly adjusted skill itself becomes second nature.

This having been achieved, the next, and crucial, step is to practise habitually seeing this empty-consciousness-dominated mental landscape – and the subordinate aide memoire verbally describing the self-view being adopted – as the core of the self. To practise habitually identifying with that view of the self in the same way that a person with a fixed self might make a mental habit of regularly rehearsing a view of herself as 'Joey, the gay Buddhist psychologist with expensive tastes'. To do this until experiencing this empty-consciousness-dominated landscape as the core of the self becomes habitual.

Having acquired the habit of habitually experiencing this as the core of the self, the need then is to practise regularly moving in and out of this core self from all sorts of everyday situations as a reminder that this is the core of the self-view being adopted. To practise visiting this core experience for both short periods and longer, more meditational sessions, ensuring that it becomes the habitual rest state when the adopter is not engaged in anything else. To consciously programme the brain so that moving in and out of this core of the new self-view – and consciously seeing it *as* the core of the self – becomes an almost unconscious habit.

Core Self: Avoiding Rehearsing the Resident Fixed Self

One final step is then required as regards cementing this new core of the self in place. It is to actively discourage the older habit of habitually identifying with the fixed self still in place in the areas of the mental landscape developed prior to the attempt to put the transcendent self-view in its place. There are two elements to this. The first is to learn to spot when the mind slips into the older habit of identifying with particular limited idea-based views of the self. The second is to learn to respond to such incidents by focusing instead on identifying with the new core of the self learned through the exercises above. Ideally, the adopter should first determine what ideas the mind is identifying with. Then they should practise moving away from the mental position where these ideas are dominant to the newly developed core of the self, habitually identify with that instead, and repeat the exercise until they have replaced the older habit entirely.

The next two sets of steps for the adopter are covered in Chapters 19 and 20 below.

19

Beyond the Core: Switching

Overview: Core Self Controlled Switching

The next step is to develop the mental habit of seeing and treating every experiential departure from this core self as a temporary excursion into the interactive role-playing aspect of the transcendent self-view being adopted. To see it as a temporary excursion that always ends with a return to the empty-consciousness-dominated core self. This entails working on mental exercises focused on two interrelated aspects of the interactive self, aiming to bring them all together under the central control of the empty-consciousness-dominated core self.

The focus of the first set is on new roles adopted to cope with circumstances never encountered before – roles based on newly acquired subsidiary self-world relationships to cope with either new variations on previously encountered situations or situations that are more or less wholly new. The focus of the second is on aspects of the would-be adopter's current fixed self – life roles the adopter enacts regularly under the auspices of the fixed self, where switching to alternatives tends to be blocked by barriers created by habitual or emotional attachment or perspectival blindness.

The aim is to ensure that both sets of roles, new and old, are brought under the control of the core self, and thereby the total or whole self. Specifically, it is to ensure that they each come to be seen and treated as being similar to an actor's roles as played by the core (and so total) self, but in a more nuanced way. The difference being that there is no pretence or play-acting involved, only temporary episodes of acting out limited aspects of the real or total self adopted as required for this circumstance or that while continuing to ensure that the core self is the start and end point of each episode.

Almost Acting: Processing New Roles and Life Experiences

New Subsidiary Self-World Relationships

The aim under this heading is to begin to create the interactive role-playing aspect of the transcendent self-view by focusing first on learning a new approach to processing new roles and life experiences – to create an area of the mental landscape that is more transcendental self than fixed self. To create an area where new habits hold sway before tackling the harder problem of mastering older fixed-self habits.

There are two elements to the process, although both can be handled using a single set of mental exercises.

The first aims to ensure that roles based on newly acquired subsidiary self-world relationships – roles appropriate for use with either wholly new situations or partially changed previously encountered situations – are brought under the control of the core self, and thereby the total or whole self. It aims to ensure that they each come to be seen and treated as being similar to an actor's roles as played by the core (and so total) self, but with the difference that there is no pretence or play-acting involved. Just temporary episodes of acting out limited aspects of the real or total self adopted as required for this circumstance or that, with the core-centred whole self being both the start and end point of each temporary episode.

The second aims to align the ways in which we process the subsidiary self-world perspectives acquired as we encompass these new roles in our repertoire, ensuring that this entails both avoiding any tendency towards habitual use and adopting a wary attitude towards attachment, bias, and assumptions about the world.

Tackling Untried Roles and Associated Perspectives

The mental exercises here focus on experiencing and handling new roles and circumstances and require a certain amount of input from the individual concerned. The adopter must either identify new situations likely to be encountered in the foreseeable future or deliberately seek out such situations as a basis for the focus of the various aspects of the exercise. The latter approach may be the more practical of the two and is recommended here, but this is a matter of individual choice. The specifics of the exercises must also be a matter of individual choice; the adopter must adapt the approach outlined below to whatever list of new roles applies in their particular situation.

The aim should be to tackle various untried roles and associated perspectives – roles and perspectives a poet, a priest, or a scientist, say, might adopt in particular circumstances – and train the brain so that each is mentally seen as a temporary role-playing departure from the core and behaves and is experienced as such in the circumstances in question. It should be to ensure that, in the various limited circumstances where the roles are possible responses, switching between them via the core self to meet whichever specific circumstances they apply to – circumstances concocted by the adopter to fit the chosen roles – becomes second nature.

To achieve this end, the adopter should mentally rehearse – habitually imagine themselves into – each previously untried role tackled while holding two aims in mind as regards what is being imagined (and acting out any associated physical expressions and actions where this is appropriate).

The first should be to avoid habitually imagining actually being a poet, priest, or scientist and instead imagine being like an actor playing a part in whatever circumstances they apply to (but doing so in a way that does not entail seeing this as play-acting or pretending). The adopter should imagine being someone whose core (and therefore total or real) self has an actor's level of control over a role (and the switching mechanism) but who sees the role as a valid but limited facet of the real or total self rather than as a pretence.

The second should be to avoid allowing the role to become the only role seen as appropriate to a situation, to avoid becoming emotionally attached to it or developing a bias for or against it, and to avoid allowing it to be the only role used through simple habit. The adopter should not do the fixed-self-type things we tend to do when we imagine ourselves actually being a particular role being adopted, but simply note the usefulness or otherwise of the role in question in particular circumstances. Creating an emotional attachment by imagining our significant other being impressed by us in our new role, for example; always using the role in a situation even though other possibilities exist; or assuming the world shown to us by the role is the world as such. These all lead us into fixed-self practices and need to be avoided when seeking to adopt the transcendent self-view. The adopter should avoid them and instead aim to simply memorise the usefulness or otherwise of a particular role in a particular situation.

Training the Brain

We can take it that mental rehearsals of this kind – and the perspective taken when they are rehearsed – will effectively train the brain in their image. An adopter who habitually mentally rehearses being like an actor playing a role will come to act, think, and feel in that way. An adopter who, either simultaneously or later, adjusts their perspective to see the role as similar to play-acting but as more accurately regarded as an aspect of the real or total self will come to act, think, and feel in that more nuanced way. An adopter who actively avoids emotional attachment and the like when rehearsing a role, simply noting its characteristics instead, will not put in place the fixed-self habits that block the open-ended, wholly-variable self-view but only memorise the value or otherwise of the role in question. There is nothing innovative, special, or complicated about this. It is simply a matter of refocusing our normal approach to adopting roles to serve a slightly altered purpose – that of bringing a new role into being in a controlled way and adding information on it to our life-experiences database.

A Transcendent Area in a Fixed-Self Mind

Once a reasonably wide range of previously untried roles are acquired in this fashion, the next step should be to then work on them to create an area of the adopter's fixed-self mind that can be the basis of a developing transcendent self-view.

Suppose the roles practised are those of a novice, an informed layperson, an accomplished academic, and an experienced practitioner in particular areas of poetry, religion, and science and are identified as being possible responses in a series of interactions with staff in a library. The adopter should practise with these roles until switching back and forth between them via the core self in response to certain types of situation – interactions with staff in libraries about books on the topics concerned – becomes second nature. They should practise until they can readily switch between them when interacting with librarians in response to a texted request from a friend to apply a randomly chosen group of three of the twelve possible combinations in quick succession in various different libraries.

Obviously, the exact nature of the roles and circumstances where they apply would have to be adjusted to suit the adopter's own chosen new roles, but the basic approach would be similar and the endpoint essentially the same. There would be an area of the mind where switching between the newly acquired roles via the core self in certain types of situation in a fashion similar to that envisaged for the full-blown transcendent self-view would be second nature.

Key Building Block

A development of this kind serves only a limited purpose in its own right, but provides a key building block as regards the development of the interactive role-playing aspect of the transcendent self-view. The end result should be an area of the mind that can be built on to create the full-blown transcendent self-view by following the further exercises presented below. Much of the adopter's mental landscape will still be dominated by a fixed self that operates in most of the adopter's usual life situations, but there will be a part of it that is not so dominated. There will be a part where a core self based on empty consciousness and an aide memoire holds sway and where it can, in the limited circumstances implied by the chosen roles themselves, readily switch between this role and that in response to changes in those circumstances. A part of the adopter's mind where roles will not dominate the switching mechanism as in the case of the fixed self, but will themselves be dominated and controlled by an empty-consciousness-based core self. A part that can ultimately be the basis of a fully developed transcendent self-view.

From Building Block to Full Transcendence

Once this has been achieved, the adopter can focus on the remainder of what is an anything but simple task, the first step being to make the above approach to acquiring new roles the standard approach from that point on to any and every new role to be adopted. This requires no further comment. It is simply one of the tasks the adopter must tackle over the longer term: making sure all newly acquired roles are handled in a manner that aligns with transcendent rather than fixed self-view practices and perspectives and that regularly visiting and habitually identifying with empty consciousness continues.

The remainder of what is required falls under two headings. The first encompasses the knotty and very long-term problem of struggling to bring the older fixed self and its habits and perspectives under the control of the newly developing transcendent self-view. The second moves the adopter on from the switching aspect of the transcendent self-view covered in this section to an attempt to extend the embryonic transcendent self-view created as described above by adding both an all-encompassing response set repertoire and a bias-free response selection mechanism to the mix. Of necessity, these two processes must be tackled in a sequential fashion initially, but should probably be pursued in parallel once initiated.

Almost Acting: Tackling a Resident Fixed Self

Immersion With an Exit Facility

The key to bringing the older fixed self and its habits and perspectives under the control of the newly developing transcendent self-view is a variation on the immersion level control facility described in Chapter 14. This is a mental facility we all already have in place to some extent. Like an actor pulling out of an intensely felt role when a fire alarm goes off in the theatre, we all have the ability to pull out of a role we are already deeply immersed in when something happens to make that necessary. When a friend has an accident and needs our attention, say, or a milk pan boils over, or the smoke alarm beeps.

An adopter working to bring a fixed self under control can use this in two ways to help with the mental struggles involved.

Random Alarms And Stressful Incidents

The first is to have a friend set a smartphone alarm, with a preferred unique and easily identifiable associated alarm sound, to go off at random intervals several times during any day that the adopter is working on this. Whenever it goes off, the adopter should train the mind to move towards empty consciousness, then, after lingering there briefly, move to identify and analyse the area of the fixed self inhabited just before the alarm with a view to then working mentally to improve control in that area. This should entail mentally sitting outside of the role involved and seeing it as one self-world perspective among many, identifying alternatives to the role, and working both these and the original role into the embryonic new-roles area of transcendent self-view developed as described above. It might also entail taking the same approach to other such roles encompassed within the same basic area of the adopter's fixed self – those identified by a more methodical attempt to trawl aspects of the adopter's remembered self in and around the area identified by the alarm clock method.

The second is to associate the jump out to empty consciousness with any stressful or anxiety-inducing incident in life generally – most probably those associated with conflict between the fixed self and how the world actually is. This will entail selecting these by various means – remembering past examples, say, or identifying possibilities associated with self facets identified using the alarm clock method – then actively associating those identified with a mental note to move the mind towards empty consciousness to escape future stress or anxiety.

A Lengthy Struggle

The process of bringing the whole fixed self under control in this way will, of course, be a long-drawn-out struggle. It should, however, be one of a gradual and continual progression towards a fully instantiated transcendent self-view.

The final steps for the adopter are covered in Chapter 20.

20

Beyond the Core: Response Repertoire and Choice

Overview: Two Elements

As indicated above, the remainder of what the would-be adopter has to tackle entails working to extend the embryonic transcendent self-view created through the exercises described above under the switching mechanism by adding an all-encompassing response set repertoire and a bias-free response selection mechanism to the mix. Fortunately, some of the main work required under both headings – identifying habitually with empty consciousness and working to ensure that life experiences are not processed in ways that block responses and create bias – has already been done through the work on the switching mechanism (Chapter 19).

An All-Encompassing Response Repertoire
Nothing Blocked out

As far as the response repertoire is concerned, this earlier work should ensure that no possible response – not even an undiscovered one – is blocked out by the developing transcendent self-view. On the view taken here, habitually identifying with empty consciousness means ensuring that there is no limiting and dominant subset of possible responses in place to block out those not included, especially when there is an aide memoire in place reminding the adopter that even undiscovered perspectives are possible situational responses. Ensuring that life experiences are not processed in ways that block responses adds additional support to this; it is a second way of ensuring that no preference for a limited response set is in place to block out others. With these two elements in place, all the adopter need do in addition as regards work needed here is focus on the two areas below to improve things further on the response repertoire front.

Widening Access and Support for Self-World Relationships

This simply involves the adopter in an ongoing programme of reading books and websites, listening to lectures and podcasts, watching films and performances, taking educational courses, talking to others with differing views, and so on. The aim is to both acquire access to as wide a repertoire of self-world perspectives as possible and to develop expertise that will facilitate extending it further. This will expand the adopter's repertoire of known self-world perspectives and develop a skill set that will assist with the extraction, learning, and use of new known self-world perspectives from the world of knowledge.

Developing a Practised Ability for Seeing Things in Novel Ways

This involves the adopter in an ongoing programme of exploring imaginative fiction and philosophies, understanding the problems and possible solutions to scientific issues, acquiring associated thinking, analytical, and research skills, engaging in debate with others who have a different mindset, and so on. The aim is to acquire abilities that will make it more and more possible to discover and personally develop novel and imaginative perspectives on anything and everything in the world and so facilitate access to self-world perspectives that are not only unknown to the adopter but also to humans generally. On the view held here, identifying with empty consciousness as the core of the self ensures that there is an open path to the discovery of such responses, and the subordinate aide memoire reminds the adopter that even undiscovered perspectives are potential situational responses. Developing the ability to see and creatively discover such perspectives not only reinforces the message, it also facilitates access to such undiscovered potential responses.

Fully All-Encompassing

Taken together, the adopter's efforts in these two areas should widen the range of self-world perspectives available for switching to at need, even to the extent of potentially encompassing not only self-world perspectives unknown to particular individuals, but also those as yet undiscovered by humans generally.

A Bias-Free Response Selection Mechanism

Two Sources of Bias Removed

As indicated above, the key elements of work required in this area have also already been tackled under the work done with the switching mechanism. On the view taken here, making empty consciousness the core of the self and the place where response selection occurs means that the mind is not set in a way that will create bias when selection occurs – ensuring that there is no dominant idea-based focus there to bias selection for or against possible responses. Ensuring that life experiences are not processed in a way that will create bias related to individual responses removes a further potential source of bias for or against particular responses. With these two elements in place, all the adopter need do in addition, as regards work needed here, is to focus on the two areas below to improve things further on the bias-free response selection mechanism.

Practise Avoiding External Response Selection Bias

This exercise involves recognising that there are times when bias can be introduced by external factors and that these might sometimes confuse the issue and result in biased response selection despite an adopter's efforts to ensure bias is not introduced by internal factors like a fixed-self-style mental set. It involves training the mind to recognise and mitigate externally introduced response selection bias – learning to identify and deal with bias in the way something requiring a response is worded or presented by another individual who is biased, or just ill-informed or confused, for example. This is simply a matter of seeking out – perhaps with the help of friends and teachers – examples of such wording or presentation biases and developing an ability to see and master the sources of the biases.

Recognising the Value and Limitations of Individual Relationships

This exercise involves learning to be adept at seeing the potential value of all self-world perspectives in a wide range of situations and to recognise, in addition, that every perspective has its limits and does not necessarily offer the best response in every situation. It simply involves developing the habit of seeing both the value and the limitations of a wide range of self-world perspectives in a wide range of situations. This might begin with, then build on, the point made in earlier chapters to the effect that even the most wide-ranging scientific theory might not be the best answer to the requirements of an entertainer at a children's party. A silly-sounding idea like the world being made of blancmange might be of more value not only in that situation but in others. It might also, potentially, be of equal value to a teacher trying to illustrate some scientific point (to encourage students to consider how they might go about disproving the notion, for example) or to an actor playing the role of a court jester.

Taken together, the adopter's efforts in these two areas should work to ensure the bias-free selection of responses required as a key aspect of the transcendent self-view. They should help both to ensure the avoidance of bias in the selection mechanism itself and through developing an understanding of the fact that all self-world perspectives have value in a range of situations and that no one self-world perspective is always the best response in every situation.

Final Remarks: First-Pass Perspective and Beyond

An Ongoing Process

The key point to recognise when seeking to adopt the transcendent self-view is that there is no magic pill, clever mental trick, or mystical experience to make replacing the old self-view with the new an easy, simple, or instantaneous matter. Instantiating the transcendent self-view would be a relatively straightforward (though not necessarily easy) proposition for someone who is able to start the learning process from early childhood, but not for someone for whom this is now impossible. Although a point should be reached in attempting the above processes where the new self and the new habits will be stronger and more prevalent than the old, the effort required will not be minor or short-term. The new self and habits will become stronger and stronger, and the old self and habits weaker and weaker as the effort proceeds. However, slipping into old habits will be an ever-present possibility that must be guarded against and fought on an everyday basis. Identifying with and instantiating any self-view, fixed or transcendent, is a day-to-day – even a moment-to-moment – activity that arguably has no final endpoint.

Further Clarifications

Nor is a reasonable degree of success in adopting and instantiating the first-pass transcendent perspective itself the end of the matter. This first-pass perspective is a reasonably comprehensive view of this transcendent self-view for humans. However, as previously indicated, these adoption chapters and Chapters 21-28 of the book present a range of clarifications of the position and identify various pitfalls in understanding it that provide pointers towards a more complete view. Some of these, in particular those relating to empty consciousness and the transcendent perspective as experienced rather than as words on a page, are included above and offer a more developed perspective than the verbal first-pass view presented in Chapter 14. Others, as we shall see, arise from an examination of social and other educational situations, common scientific perspectives, and religious issues. All of them extend the position further in various ways and need to be taken on board by those seeking to understand, adopt, and instantiate the transcendent perspective in ways that will become clear as we proceed.

Other Pitfalls

Notice, moreover, that there may well be other things lurking in the human mind – other pitfalls that block full comprehension of the position and other issues that require clarification – than are considered in this book. Some of them may not even exist yet; some may not be an issue until some human somewhere comes up with a new idea or a new way of looking at things that somehow conflicts with the transcendent perspective as outlined in this book. For this reason, fully comprehending the transcendent perspective is an ongoing process, even beyond the end of this book. In fact, it is probably sensible to assume that it is a process that may never quite end, although obviously understanding should continuously improve as long as we all aim to be vigilant in respect of spotting new pitfalls and developing new clarifications.

21

Social and Educational Obstacles

The Impact of External Factors on the Personal Struggle

The Influence of our Social and Educational Environments

Although adoption of the transcendent self-view is largely a personal struggle as described in the last chapter, it would be a mistake to ignore the likely influence of external factors – those of the social and educational environment we all inhabit in particular. It is safe to say that the transcendent perspective on the self is neither a widely known nor a widely held and implemented view of the human self, and that this has been true in the past as well as the present. This being so, it is equally safe to say that the social and educational environments we all operate in will have been created by people with fixed selves and will continue to be influenced and developed by people with a fixed-self-based outlook on things.

A Struggle With the perspectives of Humanity in General

This covers anything and everything from everyday social interactions with friends, family, colleagues, and so on, to schools, colleges, universities, and professional and other learning and working interactions. Books, lectures, tutorials, everyday conversations, and the like will all be peppered with examples of language and ways of seeing and thinking inimical to the transcendent perspective on the self and the world that would-be adopters are aiming to implement. This will make their struggles with their own mental and emotional habits and perspectives harder to deal with.

Some of the ways these affect such would-be adopters will be obvious, others less so. Many may affect them by supporting or encouraging some of the unconscious or semi-unconscious habits of thought and perspective they are struggling to shrug off. Some may even introduce problems of perspective not covered in this book; problems would-be adopters will have to find their own intellectual solutions for if they are to integrate the problem perspectives with the transcendent position. In a way, it will be as if adopters are not just struggling with their own mental and emotional habits and perspectives but with those of the whole human race throughout history. Unless they can successfully blot out the noise this creates or, in those situations too close to their own life activities to allow this, deal with it in some other way, the task they face will become immeasurably harder.

Specific Barriers: The Scope of the Problem
Universal Adoption Likely to Take Centuries

Nor is this a problem likely to be readily or quickly resolved. As has been indicated from the first, the transcendent perspective is intended as a self-view for all humans; universal adoption is the underlying aim of the arguments made in this book.

The chances of achieving universal adoption overnight are as close to nil as makes no difference, however. The best that can be hoped for is that, over a number of centuries, it may begin to become the dominant self-view in socially and educationally developed societies and then gradually be encompassed in others.

The Problem of Books and Similar Materials

Acquisition, comprehension, acceptance, adoption, and implementation of the transcendent perspective by all human individuals is only part of the problem, however. Even if this could be magically managed all at once with the wave of a wand, the major issue of thereafter adapting a huge range of current educational and social environments would still exist. Most of them would encompass not just the impacts of involved humans from the present day but a range of books and other materials created in the past. These will themselves be a barrier to the instantiation of the transcendent perspective in all humans – something that, in turn, will slow the required environmental adjustments themselves, with non-transcendent humans continuing to spread their own contrary and conflicting view of the human self within these environments.

The Need for new Thinking and new Developments

Nor would dealing with existing environments always be a straightforward matter of simply working towards a re-alignment of the perspectives they encompass with those of the transcendent perspective. In some cases – perhaps many – new thinking and new developments will be required. An obvious example of this relates to adjusting school and preschool programmes of child education so as to steer developing children away from fixed-self habits and towards the transcendent perspective. This will likely involve whole new ways of working, talking, and thinking – how is it possible to even begin talking about such things in ways meaningful and helpful to a developing child's mind? And what about mind- and behaviour-related disciplines like psychology and psychiatry? Even if we assume a ready acceptance of the position within these disciplines – a dangerous assumption at best – aligning them with this new perspective would be a slow process. Adjusting how the disciplines talk, think, develop, and do research about issues in a whole range of subordinate areas of their fields will require programmes of complex thought, discussion, and argument likely to take many decades to complete.

Inhospitable Social and Educational Environments

In short, then, facilitating universal adoption of the transcendent perspective and the consequent changes needed to the social and educational environment is not a simple matter. It will, in all probability, take centuries to achieve. The upshot is that a range of social and educational factors in the wider human environment will probably be set up in a way likely to be inhospitable to the individual's efforts to adopt the transcendent perspective. In struggling to achieve personal adoption in the ways described in Chapters 18 to 20, they will be hampered by obstacles likely to be encountered in the social and educational environments they interact with as they proceed.

The aim of this chapter is to provide some assistance in dealing with these obstacles, primarily by raising awareness of problems likely to be encountered and suggesting ways of dealing with them.

Dealing With the Obstacles

Nonadopters and Related Environments

The obstacles fall under two interrelated headings. The first covers interacting with other humans who are themselves nonadopters. The second covers interaction with the wider environment – a social and educational environment that was created by nonadopters and that continues to be accepted, supported, developed, and (to a partial but significant extent) transmitted by them. Aside from books and the like, these nonadopters are the agency through which environmental factors impact those seeking to adopt the transcendent perspective. To a large extent, they *are* the social and educational environment encountered by those seeking to adopt the transcendent perspective.

The Transcendent Self-View: A View of all Humans

Explaining the problem as regards interacting with nonadopters requires a further clarification of the transcendent perspective – an implication of what has been written as regards universal adoption not drawn out as yet. To assert that the transcendent perspective is a full and accurate reflection of the true human behavioural and experiential relationship to the world is not simply to assert that it is an accurate way of seeing ourselves. It is also to assert that (potentially, at least) it is an accurate way of seeing all humans. It is to assert that, in circumstances where universal adoption has been achieved, the accurate and correct way of seeing others is not as *kinds* of humans like Scots, Buddhists, or Tories. Rather, it is to see them as variable-response humans, in terms of the same transcendent perspective that we have on ourselves. It is to see them from the inside in terms of the transcendent perspective on the human animal – as subjects like ourselves – rather than from the outside as objects.

Nor is this simply a matter of how we see others. It also has to do with a full and accurate instantiation of the transcendent perspective within ourselves. To see others habitually as *kinds* of humans is to instantiate a fixed relationship to the part of the world they represent. It is to abandon our own variable-response transcendent perspective on ourselves and the world in favour of a fixed relationship to what, after all, constitutes a large part of the world we inhabit. It is to fail to fully instantiate the transcendent mental and emotional landscape that a would-be adopter should be striving for.

A World Full of Nonadopters

This is a difficulty for would-be adopters in the meantime, which is to say, during the centuries we are supposing it would likely take to achieve universal adoption by the human population. Most of the other humans they encounter in such a world are likely to be nonadopters. As such, they will not tend to interact with adopters – act, think, and feel towards them – in ways that seeing them in terms of the transcendent perspective would suggest that they should. A full and correct instantiation of the transcendent perspective in themselves implies also seeing others in terms of this perspective, but such a perspective on other humans will only be factually correct once universal adoption has been realised. How they are to deal with this conundrum is a question that needs answered – a point we will return to presently.

Environments Created by Nonadopters

The second set of problems arises from the fact that the wider social and educational environments would-be adopters encounter as they struggle with their internal personal obstacles to adoption will have been created by nonadopters. This means that they will, in the short to medium term, continue to be strongly influenced – accepted, supported, developed, and transmitted – by nonadopters and will tend to throw up obstacles to successful personal adoption as a result.

Anything created, said, written, or even pictorially presented by the cadre of nonadopters, past and present, that imparts or even expresses information that impacts directly or indirectly on the transcendent perspective is a potential obstacle to the successful instantiation of the transcendent perspective by the would-be adopter. Books, live speeches, video tutorials, everyday comments, and perspectives on the world and on people, whether explicitly expressed or implicit in the language used, can potentially make personal adoption and instantiation harder if they encompass ways of seeing and thinking at variance with the transcendent perspective. They can add mental and emotional red herrings and banana skins to the mix of the personal struggle described in Chapters 18 to 20. Ways of seeing or thinking about ourselves and the world that either explicitly express views of the human self that encompass contrary or misleading perspectives or, worse, hide them or assume them in the language used or the positions taken. (Chapter 24 on the so-called hard problem of consciousness illustrates a particularly intractable example of this kind of issue.)

These are all potential problems for the individual adopter, which means that, to an extent, he is struggling to tame not just his own mind but the collective mind of humanity, past and present. A whole world and history of subject matter on scientific, religious, or other concerns entailing viewpoints or ways of thinking that have the potential to make the would-be adopter's internal struggles more difficult.

Being Aware of Obstacles and Possible Solutions

It is impossible to identify every possible specific problem that might be encountered by any and every would-be adopter and equally impossible to propose specific solutions for all of them; the possibilities in both the individual adopter and the world at large are simply too numerous. This being so, the best that can be managed in respect of covering these two sets of interrelated obstacles in this chapter is to suggest a general way forward. To indicate to the would-be adopter that dealing with them in practice is primarily a question of being aware in a general way of the obstacles themselves and of possible ways of dealing with them, and to suggest, in addition, ways in which this might best be managed.

The key to this has already been outlined in Chapters 18 to 20. In a sense, nothing in this present chapter is really new. The best strategy is still more or less the one proposed in these earlier chapters, or a minor extension of it. It is to focus on implementing the new transcendent-self-related habits, practise them till they become dominant, and identify and deal with fixed-self legacy problems 'on the fly' (after *and* while practicing the new habits). The same approach can be applied whether the problems come from inside the adopter's own mind or from the collective mind (so to speak) of all of humanity, past and present. All we really need to add to the approach proposed in previous chapters are programmes to ensure that any issues that might arise from these two sets of interrelated obstacles are identified and that a means of dealing with them is discovered and implemented.

Interacting With Nonadopters

Seeing Others as we see Ourselves...

The source of the problem as regards interacting with other humans who are nonadopters is a possible conflict between how the adopter should see the nonadopter and how the nonadopter may, at times, actually act, think, and feel during any interaction. How the adopter should see the nonadopter will determine how he expects the nonadopter to act, think, and feel during any interaction, and this may often be at odds with how the nonadopter actually acts, thinks, and feels.

The best way of dealing with the possibility is to assume, in the first instance, that the conflict does not exist, but be aware that events might prove such an assumption invalid. It is to see all humans in terms of basically the same inner transcendent perspective we have on ourselves, but be aware that some may not yet have worked through the process that makes that operationally true.

...But not as Identical to Ourselves

This does not mean seeing all humans as personality clones of ourselves. The transcendent perspective allows for the kinds of personal preferences that often make up fixed selves. To see other humans in terms of the transcendent perspective is not to ignore any preferences they may have for seeing themselves as Buddhists, Scots, or Socialists. It is merely to assume that any such preferences are under the overarching control of a variable response transcendent self – that they are not in place as the basis of a fixed self. The proposal, therefore, is not that adopters should ignore such differences, but rather that they should ignore the possibility that they are the basis of a fixed self rather than a transcendent self with individual differences in place (but also be aware that events might prove such an assumption invalid).

Seeing Others as we see Ourselves is the Best Approach

Taking this approach will mean that any predictions as regards how a nonadopter will act, think, and feel in the context of any interactions may sometimes turn out to be wrong, but is nevertheless the best approach overall. Even if it is likely in the present circumstances that most humans *are* nonadopters, taking the opposite view – seeing others as *kinds* of humans with fixed selves in place rather than as potential transcendent perspective humans – has negatives associated with it in two respects.

First, if the case argued in this book is sound, it is inaccurate to see the human relationship in terms of the fixed view and accurate to see it in terms of the transcendent perspective view. The fact that nonadopters have not yet seen this and instantiated the perspective themselves does not alter the fact of it being the correct view – the way we should see humans on the view expressed here.

Second, assuming that other humans are *kinds* of humans rather than fully-blown transcendent humans edges us in the direction of seeing and treating them as less than fully human and is the kind of thinking that encourages and supports prejudice and subhuman treatment generally. This will likely affect both parties negatively. It will affect the nonadopter negatively because he is thought of and treated as less than human, to his detriment. It will affect the adopter negatively on two counts. First, because he has abandoned his transcendent perspective in favour of an inaccurate view of the world, which will eventually lead him into conflict situations that may affect him negatively. Second, because always seeing a range of nonadopters as particular different *kinds* of human with some fixed relationship to the world is tantamount to adding a range of fixed-self facets to his own self-view and to undermining his own transcendent perspective in the process.

Advantages of the Approach

Seeing all humans in terms of basically the same inner transcendent perspective we have on ourselves but being aware that some may not yet have worked through the process that makes that operationally true, avoids these negatives. The view taken of nonadopters is the correct view of the actual human relationship to the world; the prejudicial potential of seeing them as *kinds* of humans is avoided; and the adopter's self-view does not take on fixed-self habits.

Moreover, seeing nonadopters in terms of a transcendent self-view that makes allowances for individual differences means the adopter will be right most of the time as regards how they are likely to act, think, and feel in the world. Problems will only arise when any fixed self in place in another human comes into conflict with the world at large and begins to have a negative impact on the nonadopter. This may make the person angry, overly emotional about something, or unreasonably uncooperative because the fixed self in place is blocking a mental or emotional move away from the perspective causing the conflict.

With the approach proposed, however, adopters will be ready for these situations if and when they arise. They will be aware that their assumption that the nonadopter is a transcendent human might be invalid, and – because they do see them as potential transcendents – they should be best set up to respond to behaviour arising from fixed-self-based conflict situations in a helpful way. They should be able to react in a way that is not based on the 'less than fully human' prejudice. They should be able to react in a way that will at least attempt to edge the nonadopter towards transcendence by seeking to get to the bottom of the conflict and point to ways out of it that involve a switch away from the fixed self causing the conflict.

Interacting With Environments Created by Nonadopters

Adjusting to the Challenges of Problem Environments

Moving on to the more general issue of the social and educational environments the adopter is likely to encounter – those created and supported by nonadopters, past and present – all that can be done is to adjust exercises covered in Chapters 18 to 20 to deal with them.

This should entail daily self-reminders of the need to be constantly aware of the possibility that social and educational environments encountered will throw up ways of thinking, seeing, and expressing thoughts that may cause difficulty to the would-be adopter because they undermine the transcendent perspective in some way.

It should entail regular attempts to reflect on environments engaged with every day, the identification of potentially or actually problematic examples of such ways of thinking, seeing, and expressing thoughts, and a search for ways of thinking, seeing, and expressing them that resolve the conflict with the transcendent perspective.

Finally, it should entail using these examples both to help identify the types of problematic ways of thinking, seeing, and expressing thoughts such environments throw up and to help identify a range of ways of resolving the kinds of conflict with the transcendent perspective they represent.

None of this will be easy, but the situation is such that there is no real alternative.

Challenging Detrimental Environments

It is unlikely that challenging these problematic ways of thinking, seeing, and expressing thoughts in the social and educational environments themselves is a sensible or worthwhile task for the would-be adopter of the transcendent perspective. Such attempts would be better made once the personal struggles outlined in Chapters 18 to 20 are close to being won and will, with nonadopters being in the vast majority in all such environments, represent a massive challenge even then.

Commonly Held Scientific and Religious Views

The kinds of issues raised and dealt with in the context of some further clarifications of the transcendent self-view covered in Chapters 22 onwards should also provide both general and specific help in identifying and resolving the kinds of problems that social and educational environments are likely to create. These deal with the integration of the transcendent self-view with commonly held scientific and religious views and cover: developing and maintaining a scientific, question everything, approach, being aware of the problem of fixed-self facets hidden in everyday assumptions, and dealing with some issues raised by religious beliefs.

22

The Transcendent Perspective and Science

No Weakening of the Status of Science in Human Affairs

Science and the Transcendent Self-View

The intention in the final seven chapters of the book is to further clarify the detail of the transcendent self-view by looking at its relationship to commonly held perspectives on the universe at large, the focus in this first chapter of the seven being science. It was noted in Chapter 11 that the question of the relationship between our scientific world-view and our alternative human self-view is a complex one best left for more detailed consideration in later chapters of the book. In the present chapter, a further clarification of the detail of the transcendent self-view is provided on two fronts. First, through a consideration of the position and role of science within it; second, by showing that the transcendent perspective on the self and the world in no way undermines the status and predominance of science in human affairs – that, to the contrary, it consolidates that position.

A Science-Based Fixed Self is Still Fixed

It was argued in Chapter 4 that the actual behavioural and experiential relationship of humans to the world is wholly-variable rather than fixed. It was argued that allowing a limited set of views of the human self-world relationship overarching control of the human self to the extent that it becomes the only view of self, world, or self in the world we ever use turns this on its head. It effectively takes that wholly-variable behavioural and experiential relationship to the world and makes it fixed. It was further argued (Chapter 11) that this applies even to the limited set of views of the human self-world relationship encompassed within a wholly complete, wholly correct, and wholly scientific world-view. Such a perspective would, of course, entail everything there is to know in terms of the nature of the things we encounter in the world: the sun, a flower, other people, a waterfall, an electricity pylon, and so on. What it would not do is encompass all of the possible behavioural and experiential relationships to these things available to us as humans. Instead, it would only encompass one – that of the scientist.

A person with only the set of scientific self-world perspectives in his repertoire, to the exclusion of all else, would only ever experience the world from a scientific viewpoint and feel and behave accordingly. Roles that allowed her to act, think, and feel in the world as a poet, a sunworshipper, or a silly comedian at a children's party claiming the world was made of blancmange would be outwith her repertoire. Assuming the relationship was truly fixed – or so ingrained as to be something very close to that – she would be something less than fully human. By allowing the scientific world-view to become her only world-view she would have effectively defined herself not as a fully developed human with a variable behavioural and experiential relationship to the world but as a scientist *kind* of human. She would, moreover, have made that misdefinition operationally true.

An Important Perspective but one Among Many

As a container for our knowledge of the world, a wholly complete, wholly scientific world-view can be assumed to be all-encompassing. But as a definition of who we are as humans, it represents only one of the many behavioural and experiential relationships we can bear to the world. Adopting it as our only self-view – not seeing and treating it as one of a range of relationships we can have to the world – would block out other ways of relating to the world. This would sometimes have negative effects, would block the open-ended response, and would misdefine us in the same ways as other fixed selves do.

If the transcendent perspective on the human self is an accurate reflection of our full behavioural and experiential relationship to the world – if the relationship is wholly-variable, as argued in this book – the scientific self-world perspective must be viewed in a way that recognises this. It must be viewed as a temporary behavioural and experiential perspective on the world – one of many that can define who and what we are and determine how we act, think, and feel. It must be recognised as one of a range of possibilities that can include anything from religious, philosophical, and political perspectives to fantasy and even nonsense perspectives.

Point 1: Fixing Conflicts With Variable Views

This may seem to imply that the transcendent perspective undermines the status and predominance of science in human affairs, but that is not the case for a variety of reasons. Four points are worth noting on this front, two of which – points 1 and 2 – were presented in Chapter 11. Point 1 is that if the actual human relationship is wholly-variable rather than fixed, then a wholly complete, wholly correct, scientific world-view will reflect that, which means that allowing the scientific world-view to fix our relationship to the world would conflict with the scientific view itself. We would be fixing our behavioural and experiential relationship to the world using a world-view that says that relationship is wholly-variable and making something we hold to be true false in the process.

Point 2: Fixing Breaks Scientific Principle

Fixing can Lead Science to an Erroneous Conclusion

Point 2 relates to an erroneous conclusion that might well be reached through the introduction of bias into a scientific study of the human self-world relationship prior to science reaching a conclusion on this. In a world where everyone took a scientist's perspective on things all of the time, scientists studying the human self-world relationship might well conclude that the relationship was fixed – that it was not wholly-variable – simply because everyone adopting the scientist's perspective all of the time would make it seem fixed.

This would be an issue for science on two fronts.

First, because – assuming the relationship is wholly-variable, as argued in this book – it would lead science to draw an erroneous conclusion that nevertheless appeared to be well supported by the observational evidence. Everyone would act, think, and feel as though the relationship was a fixed one.

Introducing a Form of Self Fulfilling Prophecy Bias

Second, because the reason for the erroneous conclusion would be the introduction of something we can think of as a form of self-fulfilling prophecy bias into the equation. In essence, the conclusion would appear to be true because the subjects studied took it to be true and made it true by adopting a self-view based on a fixed view of the human self-world relationship. Scientists do and must strive to avoid the introduction of bias into their attempts to discover the true nature of things, but this would be a case of erroneous results arising from the introduction of a bias whose source, ironically, would be science itself. It would be an erroneous result arising from the simple fact that the subjects studied had adopted and habitually used a perspective on the world espoused by the scientists observing them. Arguably, a slightly unusual form of self-fulfilling prophecy bias.

Permitting the scientific world-view to turn the human behavioural and experiential relationship to the world from wholly-variable to fixed could lead science to erroneous conclusions by introducing a bias whose source is the scientific view of things itself.

Clearly, any undermining of science would come not from a recognition of these things but from a failure to recognise them. To recognise them and incorporate them in the transcendent perspective is not to undermine the status of science in human affairs but to avoid doing so. To put it in its place as only one of an array of valid self-world perspectives is arguably in line with what science can observe about humans.

Point 3: Downgrading Neither Stated nor Implied
Still our Best View of how the World is and Works

Two further points – points 3 and 4 – can be added to the two above.

Point 3 is that there is no suggestion, explicit or implicit, in the transcendent perspective that the scientific view is on a par with the blancmange view of the world mentioned earlier in all circumstances or even in most. There is no suggestion that it is somehow downgraded by being seen as one among a range of possibilities that can include anything from religious, philosophical, and political perspectives to fantasy and even nonsense perspectives. The transcendent perspective neither states nor implies that the status and predominance of science in human affairs is undermined by seeing and treating it as one relational perspective among many in this fashion. It is easy to see why this might be assumed, but this is neither entailed nor implied in what has been stated so far.

Science is a human success story. There are no grounds for downgrading its importance in human affairs, and this is not what is being suggested by seeing and treating it as one relational perspective among many within the transcendent self-view. The claim is only that no one view should habitually be allowed sole dominance over all others as regards its role in the human self-view, not that science should lose the prominence in human affairs it has clearly earned over the centuries.

The Best Perspective on how the World is

What it amounts to, in essence, is this: science should still be seen as the most correct and accurate way of seeing the world at large and acting, thinking, and feeling in it in any situation where an accurate view of how the world is or works is a key consideration. It should still be seen as the best way of determining a response to any situation where an accurate view of how the world is or works is what matters.

Although any one of a limitless number of self-world perspectives can be an equally valid potential response to a given situation prior to the circumstances of a given situation being considered, all are not regarded as equally *good* responses to the specific circumstances of a particular situation. A view that saw the world as made of blancmange might be the best option in a circumstance where the aim was to raise a chuckle or two at a children's party or to teach the principles of scientific testing in a classroom. However, it would not be the best option where the protection of a plant crop from disease or getting an astronaut to and from the moon safely was the aim.

The view is that science and fantasy views should both be present in the initial mix, along with a whole range of others, as possible responses to any circumstance. However, it is not that they should be considered equal in specific situations, except as initial potential responses that may or may not be taken up as appropriate, necessary, or useful in the specific circumstances of a given situation. Clearly, if these specific circumstances were such that an accurate view of how the world is or works was a key consideration, a science-based self-world perspective would always be the best choice to make.

Calling it a Perspective Does not Downgrade it

One final point is worth making under this heading. Some might view calling the wholly correct, wholly complete scientific world-view a perspective on the world as opposed to a fully accurate reflection of *the* reality of the world as undermining the accepted status of science in human affairs, but it is no such thing. Calling it a perspective should not be taken to imply that it is not a completely accurate and wholly true reflection of the actual reality of the world, only that it is one, albeit wholly true, perspective on the world among a range of others.

Not only does this not diminish its status in any way, it is probably in line with the standard scientific approach to scientific world-views which never sees any particular view science has developed as necessarily final. Such ideas about how the world is are always seen as viewpoints that fit the facts as they are currently known rather than as final, fully accurate reflections of *the* reality of the aspect of the world that is their focus.

This is a sensible approach and is in line with Karl Popper's view that science should proceed not by looking for confirmatory evidence of existing theories but by making bold predictions about the nature of the world and discovering how resilient they are by seeking refutational evidence (Popper, 1963; see also Ebringer, 2011). If we start from the assumption that it is just obvious that all swans are white and look only for confirmatory evidence, confirmatory evidence is all we will likely find. If we start from a recognition that the notion that all swans are white is a perspective on reality that might be wrong and look for instances that disprove the theory, we will sooner or later find such instances, some swans being black. We will thereby learn something new: that the theory that all swans are white is not true.

The word 'perspective' implies something that might be wrong and that can be revisited and reworked in the light of new evidence, in a way that a view taken to represent *the* reality of some aspect of the world is not. Distinguishing between the two can be important;

consider some of the examples given earlier where assuming the world was flat made it hard to see beyond that assumption.

It can also be important in respect of illuminating scientific problems, as will hopefully become clear in Section 6 below when we come to consider the difficulties caused in respect of the so-called hard problem of consciousness. In this context, failing to distinguish between *the* reality of the human organism and a wholly true, wholly complete and accurate scientific perspective on it can seriously mislead us, suggesting that the problem of giving a scientific account of consciousness is impossible to solve by normal scientific methods. This provides a real-life instance where failure to recognise that even tried and tested scientific views of the world are ultimately perspectives that might be incorrect can block progress towards better alternatives. One of a number of reasons why the transcendent perspective is as important to science (see Chapter 25) as science is to the transcendent perspective (see point 4 below).

Point 4: Science's Status Strengthened
The Transcendent Perspective: A Strong Role for Science

Point 4 is that, if the transcendent perspective suggests anything as regards the status and predominance of science in human affairs, it is that science's role as an arbiter of how the world is should be strengthened rather than weakened or undermined. It suggests that science should be given a very significant role in the human self-view and be expected to impact on how other self-world perspectives are regarded. We can expect it to have an impact on which self-world perspectives are deemed appropriate to particular circumstances, the identification of alternative self-world perspectives in response to conflict situations, how nonscientific self-world perspectives are classified and treated within a fully variable self-view, and so on.

As our best way of arriving at a detailed and accurate understanding of the world, including ourselves, science is unmatched; it stands alone. If conflict with how the world actually is can have negative effects, as argued in Chapter 9, then science can play a key role within the transcendent perspective as a means of helping us avoid these negative effects. It can aid us in avoiding the conflicts in the first place by showing us how the world actually is. It can help us find a way out of any we might fail to avoid. It can even help us determine whether to use nonscientific self-world perspectives and what level of control they should be allowed when we allow them temporary control.

Avoiding Conflict With how the World is

As was shown in 1919 when Newton's view of gravity, accepted for centuries, was shown to be less accurate predictively than Einstein's (Dyson et al., 1920), established science can sometimes be wrong. That said, it is as good a guide to how the world is as we can have and is, after many centuries of development, a fairly sound basis for being correct about what the world is truly like. It is a sound basis for optimising the extent to which how we see the world is able to avoid conflict with how it actually is and how it can be expected to behave. It can therefore help strengthen the ability of the transcendent self-view adopter to avoid conflict with the world in the first place.

Moreover, whereas any one individual is unlikely to have the whole of science in his repertoire, a person with a developed scientific education will have a reasonable start. He will have a good chance of avoiding conflict in a fair range of areas by having a good idea of how the world actually is in those areas. He will also be in a good position to find self-world perspectives outwith his repertoire that can assist in avoiding the negative effects of any conflict with how the world actually is that does arise.

He will be aware of ways of finding established scientific perspectives on the world outside his own repertoire through books, websites, libraries, and the like. He will probably have the skills and knowledge to find new ways of avoiding the conflict through applying scientific methods to novel thinking and research. Failing that, he will likely be well-versed in what is sometimes referred to as the **abc** dictum, as applicable in science as it is in police work. Like a good detective, he will **a**ssume nothing, **b**elieve nobody, **c**heck or challenge everything (Cook & Tattersall, 2010) when deciding what is and is not a useful way of judging how the world is.

Not the Only Approach, but a Vital One

This is not to suggest, of course, that it should become the only approach to the world adopted within the transcendent perspective; that possibility has already been ruled out. Scientific perspectives on the world should be part of the range of all possible perspectives within the transcendent self-view – one part of a range that also includes everything from religious, philosophical, and political perspectives to fantasy and even nonsensical perspectives.

What is proposed, rather, is that scientific perspectives should be available as part of the whole range of choices whenever a new situation is encountered, so that they can play a key role in the transcendent human's approach to the world in two ways. First, by being available as actual choices if the situation turns out to demand a response that requires an accurate view of how the world is. Second, by informing the degree of wariness with which a particular nonscientific self-world perspective is adopted in circumstances that suggest a nonscientific approach is useful or necessary. (And so determine in part how much control it is given, the limitations that should be put on that control, and the conditions under which it should be revoked.)

This suggests a major role for such scientific perspectives – on four counts. The first being that they should play a key role in whether a scientific or nonscientific self-world perspective is adopted in a given situation. The second being that they should play a key role in determining how immersed in a nonscientific perspective and accompanying self-world relationship we should become. The third being that they should play a key role in determining how seriously we should take such a perspective as a way of interacting with the world.

The fourth being that they should also play a key role in determining how emotionally involved we should become with a given perspective and relationship and whether, and at what point, during the operation of a particular perspective and relationship, the immersion control mechanism should activate and take us back to the core self. On this last count, we should train our operational transcendent self to always be on the lookout for whether and how and when one or more of our range of self-world perspectives conflicts with what science tells us about the reality of the world. We should train it to take this into account when determining whether, and to what extent, and for how long, the perspective is permitted to control how we act, think, and feel in the world.

Again, as with points 1 and 2, the indication from points 3 and 4 is towards a strengthening of the position of science in human affairs rather than towards a weakening of its role.

Science as a Key Element of a Transcendent Self

For these four reasons, it is sensible to see a scientific outlook and education as a key element of the transcendent self. It is sensible to assume that adopting the transcendent perspective implies a strengthening of the role of science in human affairs, not a weakening of its role. To assume that a scientific education and approach to interacting with the world have a key role to play within the transcendent perspective – that a questioning, sceptical, scientific approach to everything should be part and parcel of the transcendent perspective. (Take nothing on trust, in other words. At minimum, always take an assume nothing, believe nobody, check or challenge everything approach to everything – including, needless to say, the thoughts presented in this book.)

In summary, it is not the case that the transcendent perspective undermines the status and predominance of science in human affairs. As the clarifications above indicate, the role of science in the transcendent perspective represents a strengthening of its status and predominance in human affairs, not a weakening of its role.

Nor is this quite the end of the matter. As Chapter 25 will show, there is more to be said and more to be clarified as regards the relationship between the scientific world-view and the transcendent perspective.

PART 6

The Hard Problem and Fixed-Self Facets

Part 6: Outline of the Case Presented

Fixed-self facets hidden in everyday assumptions can block a full instantiation of the transcendent self-view and act as a barrier to problem solving. The example tackled here – a fixed-self facet that assumes we are only ever outside observers of self and world – illustrates this point, shows us how to resolve the hard problem of consciousness, and further clarifies the transcendent perspective itself.

Assuming that the flesh, blood, and brain view of humans is *the* one reality of who and what we are can block the instantiation of the transcendent perspective. It can also make the problem of explaining conscious experience seem impossibly hard – a matter of bridging an explanatory gap between wholly unlike realities (firing neurons in the fleshy brain and experiences like redness, sweetness, and joy). Noting that the brain we know is a sensory construct will remove the block and lead to a resolution of the hard problem by allowing us to see it as entailing different perspectives on a single reality **(Chapter 23)**.

We are led to a position in which there is no hard problem but where our experiences are nonetheless an essential part of a scientific account. A perspective in which conscious experience is ontologically reducible to some aspect of brain functioning but epistemologically irreducible to the outside observer's knowledge of it **(Chapter 24)**.

In this view, a particular conscious experience is entirely subsumed within the reality underlying our experience of it as a brain state and can be explained in terms of brain function. However, it entails irreducible knowledge content (qualities like redness and sweetness) that cannot be ignored and must be mapped into the scientific account as a necessary element of any full description of the phenomenon being explained. This has implications for the relationship of the transcendent perspective to science (including a role as a reference point in disciplines like psychology) and leads to a further clarification of the transcendent self-view itself **(Chapter 25)**.

Habitually assuming our sensory constructs of things like the sun, a hill, or a brain to be something other than the real things can similarly create fixed-self facets we should avoid. **(Chapter 26)**.

23

Transcendence and the Brain as a Conscious Experience

Overview of Chapters 23-25

Chapters 23-25 argue that fixed-self facets hidden in everyday assumptions can block the full instantiation of the transcendent perspective and act as a barrier to problem solving, with the assumption that the flesh, blood, and brain view of humans is the one all-encompassing reality of who and what we are being a case in point. If the arguments presented in this and the two subsequent chapters are sound, an error in this assumption inevitably leads to the conclusion that the problem of explaining the relationship of consciousness to the brain is insolubly hard, whereas recognising and removing the error shows us a path to its solution. It opens a path to a view of conscious experience and the brain in which there is no hard problem, a position that, if true – as is argued and assumed here – further clarifies the transcendent perspective in various ways.

Flesh, Blood, and Brain: An Experiential Perspective

Everyday Assumptions and Fixed-Self Facets

Remnant fixed-self facets hidden in everyday assumptions can block a full instantiation of the transcendent self-view and act as a barrier to problem solving. The example tackled here is the notion that the flesh, blood, and brain view of humans is the one all-encompassing reality of who and what we are. This both illustrates the blocking issue and highlights a real-life instance of negative consequences arising from a mental environment dominated by a fixed self or a fixed-self facet. A small error in this assumption forces the erroneous conclusion that the problem of how conscious experience relates to the brain is so uniquely 'hard' as to appear unsolvable.

Over the last several centuries, science has been a major human success story. It has given us a massive degree of control over the physical world, allowing major advances to be made in a wide range of areas, from chemistry and astronomy to aeronautics and information technologies. Recognising the human organism as part of the physical world and focusing the methods of science on humans as creatures of flesh, blood, brain, and other physical things have taken these advances into areas like medicine and psychology – areas more directly concerned with human nature and well-being. This success encourages an assumption we are prone to make anyway on the basis of everyday experience – the assumption that the body of flesh, blood, and brain we experience from an external viewpoint is *the* reality of who and what we are and encompasses everything that we are.

The Body as Known not the Body as Such

The problem with this is that it is not quite true. What we have immediately before us whenever we are conscious of a body of flesh, blood, and brain is an actual body *as known*, as opposed to an actual body as such. As was touched on briefly in Chapters 11 and 12, this is the position implied in the transcendent perspective, although the point has not been much highlighted until now. All ways of viewing the world and interacting with it – all self-world perspectives – are explicitly recognised as perspectives in consciousness and thereby distinguished from whatever aspect of the world is their focus. Even those views of the world regarded as scientifically true are seen in this way in the transcendent perspective, and this clearly includes the flesh, blood, and brain view of the human body, with or without any scientifically researched detail.

The Logic of the Position

It is also the position shown to us by simple logic. Our bodies of flesh, blood, and brain are real enough – of course they are. However, what we have immediately before us when we encounter such bodies, whether it be in the form of the bodies of others or in the form of our own personal body, can only be those real bodies as known from the outside. It can only be those bodies known from the outside via outward looking senses like sight, smell, touch, taste, and smell and their extensions in our thoughts and images (cf. Russell, 1912, Chapter 5, p. 74 on our knowledge of a table as a physical object). Even if what we have before us in these instances is a fully researched and detailed scientifically enhanced version of what we encounter in everyday life, what it all amounts to, real as it seems, is a three- or four-dimensional multisensory representation of an underlying reality. A three- or four-dimensional multisensory representation mediated by our senses and our scientific knowledge rather than the actual physical reality as such. It cannot be otherwise.

Our senses and knowledge-enhanced thoughts are what give us access to reality. This is self-evident in respect of the bodies of others distinct from ourselves, where there is an actual physical separation that can only be bridged via our senses and other ways of knowing, but it is no less true of external access to our own bodies. When we look down at ourselves and see, touch, smell, taste, hear, or think about our hands, arms, legs, feet, torso, and even – with the aid of a mirror or a camera in the case of sight – our heads, we sense them as outside observers. Our access here too is via our external looking senses and their extensions in our thoughts and images (and does, in any case, look, feel, sound, taste, smell, and fit the same thought- and image-based extensions as do the bodies of others).

When we see and otherwise sense another human in front of us – or indeed, see and otherwise sense ourselves from the outside via a series of mirrors or something – there is, of course, a real physical human behind our seeing and sensing. That said, however, it cannot be the case that what we see and otherwise sense in these situations is the actual reality of the human being in question. It can only be a sensory construct such as a visual image that, while it may accurately reflect the nature of the real human behind or beyond it, can only really be a kind of three- or four-dimensional multisensory representation of the reality in question. It cannot be something that either is or somehow contains the reality itself.

Everything about it is made up, not of the substance of the thing itself, but of experiences induced in us by the reactions of our sensory and other systems to something outside of them. Even the feelings of solidity we get through touching a human organism from the outside and use to convince ourselves of its reality are sensory constructs or reflections in this sense. What we see and otherwise sense in such situations is not the actual reality of the human observed externally; it is an enhanced multisensory construct representing that reality.

It is not, in short, *the* reality of who and what we are that encompasses everything that we are, but an external observer's *perspective on*, *view of*, or *way of knowing* that reality. It is a *representation* of it made up of sensory and other information that is within our own panorama of conscious experience and is a subset of the totality of our conscious experience. As Gamez, D. (2018, p. 42) puts it, 'We cannot imagine the invisible physical world. So thought experiments and imagination cannot be used to study the relationship between invisible physical brains and conscious experiences. They can only be used to study the relationship between our conscious experiences of brains and other conscious experiences.'

Assuming This is a Problem: On two Fronts

Failing to see this – assuming instead that this outside observer's flesh, blood, and brain way of knowing is *the* reality of who and what we are and encompasses everything that we are – is a problem on two counts. On the one hand, it blocks the full instantiation of the transcendent perspective in a way that misdefines our true relationship to the world at large and makes that misdefinition operationally true; on the other, it acts as a barrier to resolving the so-called hard problem of consciousness.

Blocking the Adoption of the Transcendent Perspective

A Fixed-Self Facet and a Self-Fulfilling Prophecy

The first of these two problems is that habitually using this perspective as the one true way of seeing and relating to ourselves and others, even if only in some limited circumstances, entails two difficulties. One is that it effectively blocks the full adoption of the transcendent perspective by making our behavioural and experiential relationship to the world fixed rather than wholly-variable in the aforesaid limited circumstances. The other is that it does it in a way that not only assumes our one true relationship to ourselves and the generalised human organism to be that of an external observer but effectively makes that assumed relationship actual through habitual use in the circumstances in question.

If taken to extremes – always used and always assumed to be true in the circumstances in question – making this assumption about ourselves effectively blocks any attempt to successfully fully adopt and instantiate the transcendent perspective. We put a remnant fixed-self facet in place in particular circumstances that effectively makes our behavioural and experiential relationship the opposite of what it actually is, with all that this implies in terms of negative consequences and misdefinition. We block the full instantiation of the transcendent perspective by putting a fixed-self facet in place in particular circumstances that makes it as though our relationship to ourselves and the generalised human organism is fixed rather than wholly-variable.

An Illustration

Let us assume that a person has partially adopted the transcendent self-view but is still occasionally struggling with residual issues caused by older mental habits. He has had a very scientifically-oriented upbringing and is a trained working scientist whose focus is some aspect of the human organism. This has caused him to habitually assume that the flesh, blood, and brain perspective represents *the* reality of both individual humans, including himself, and the human organism generally. The assumption is so ingrained that he is entirely unaware of the argument presented above, which says it is more accurate to consider it to be a scientifically accurate external observer's *perspective* on the whole of the *substance* of that all-encompassing reality. More than that, he is also unaware that he is making an assumption about the reality of the human organism at all. As far as he is concerned, his view that the flesh, blood, and brain view is *the* reality of humans is a simple fact, uncritically accepted and assumed.

He has partially instantiated the transcendent self-view in other areas of his life but has a residual area he often slips into where, because of his mental habits, the only self-world perspective available to him is his erroneous assumption about the flesh, blood, and brain view of humans. He has taught himself to respond in transcendent terms to many situations but still has a habit, when certain types of circumstances are encountered and a scientific view of humans is called for, of slipping into a fixed-self facet based on his erroneous assumption. In those circumstances, he still slips into the assumption that the flesh, blood, and brain view represents *the* reality of the human animal, an assumption that is effectively hidden from him since he is wholly unaware that he is making it.

Sometimes but not Always a Problem

As long as the person in our example is a scientist whose professional work does not stray into the area of the problem with consciousness outlined below, the effect of this will be a limited one. As long as the success of his professional work is such that seeing humans in purely flesh, blood, and brain terms is entirely adequate to his activities as a scientist, the existence of this fixed-self facet will only be a problem in one limited sense. It will not in any way hamper his professional activities, but it will block his attempts to fully instantiate the transcendent perspective.

However successful he may have been as regards instantiating the transcendent self-view in other areas of his life, the dominance of this fixed-self facet in the kinds of circumstances he encounters professionally will block its full instantiation. It will ensure that, in those circumstances, his relationship to individual humans, including himself, as well as to the generalised human organism, will not be the transcendent perspective's wholly-variable relationship that reflects the full behavioural and experiential relationship of humans to the world at large. It will be a fixed relationship, one determined solely by our scientist's habit of assuming in the circumstances concerned that the flesh, blood, and brain view is *the* reality of humans. A view of the human self-world relationship that not only assumes the opposite of what is true – that our scientist's only true relationship to himself and the generalised human organism is that of an outside observer – but that also makes that assumed relationship operationally true.

We are not Solely External Observers of Humans but...

It is self-evidently not the case that the relationship of any given human to himself or to the generalised human organism is solely that of an outside observer. We also have an inside observer's view of ourselves and, by extension, of human organisms in general – one that we can also readily extrapolate to give us an inside observer's perspective of other individual humans. If, however, there are a range of circumstances in which we always and only see ourselves and humans in general via the assumption that the outside observer's flesh, blood, and brain view is *the* reality of the human organism, then we effectively assume otherwise. We effectively assume our relationship to ourselves, humans in general, and the generalised human organism is solely that of an outside observer, and we make this assumption operationally true by habitually blocking out other viewpoints.

In the circumstances in question, we make the outside observer's relationship the only relationship we ever adopt and, as long as we adhere to and remain unaware of our erroneous habit, the only relationship we can adopt. In these circumstances, we make the erroneous assumption that we are solely outside observers of ourselves, humans in general, and the generalised human organism true in practice, if not in fact. We also effectively make it so that our relationship to the world at large is always that of an outside observer in the circumstances concerned. We make it so that when the aspect of the world at large we relate to is that part of it represented by the human organism, our habits ensure that the relationship we always adopt is that of an outside observer. Although we are self-evidently part of the world, our habits ensure that we always adopt the relationship of an outside observer in the circumstances concerned.

A Misdefined Relationship Made Operationally True

The result is that we block the full instantiation of the transcendent perspective – we make it so that there are some residual circumstances in which the transcendent perspective does not operate or hold sway but is subverted by this particular fixed-self facet hidden in our erroneous assumption. In the circumstances where it holds sway, this blocks out all of the other relationships encompassed in the transcendent self-view in favour of the erroneous assumption that an outside observer of ourselves and the world is what we are and is all that we are. In those circumstances, it takes a particular misdefinition of who and what we are – the idea that we are only and always an external observer of ourselves, others, and the world that includes us – and makes it actual through habitual use. It takes one view of the human self-world relationship as the only view and, in the process, blocks out the remainder of the whole, limitless range of self-world perspectives that make up the transcendent self-view argued for in this book.

Making the Problem of Consciousness Uniquely Hard

Fixed-Self Facets can Have Negative Effects

As has been argued and illustrated in previous chapters, blockages of this kind can have a range of negative effects in terms of the options available to us in respect of interacting with the world and others in it. There can be negative effects if the self-world perspective in question conflicts with how the world actually is and if the habits or assumptions that underpin the fixing make it hard or impossible to switch to a perspective that will resolve the conflict and remove the negative effects.

One example might be a circumstance where acting, thinking, and feeling in an empathetic way towards others is required to successfully negotiate a particular problem situation, but where the approach is blocked by a fixed tendency to see and treat humans as biological robots made of flesh, blood, and brain.

A second example might be a circumstance where our scientist is so accustomed to seeing and treating humans in this way that there is a leakage beyond his scientific work. Leakage that causes him to see and treat the world at large as something to manipulate for particular human purposes rather than as something humans are part of and need to be in harmony with.

Blocking a Resolution of the Hard Problem

Many others could be readily added to the list, but there is one that is particularly worthy of note in that it deals with a scientific problem that appears to many thinkers to be so difficult as to be entirely unsolvable. Indeed, a scientist whose attempts to adopt the transcendent perspective were blocked by the kind of hidden fixed-self facet outlined above might well find it so. As was indicated above, the same assumption that blocks the full instantiation of the transcendent perspective causes a second difficulty, providing us with a real-life example of how negative effects can arise through strict adherence to a fixed viewpoint. The negative effect in this instance being the blocking of a route to the resolution of the so-called hard problem of consciousness.

Placing Consciousness Inside the Brain

The assumption that the external observer's perspective on the reality of who and what we are is *the* reality of who and what we are can also block our ability to deal with the problem of giving a scientific account of consciousness. It can make it seem that a key issue in the scientific study of the human organism – the question of how our conscious experience relates to the human brain – is a uniquely hard problem, impossibly difficult to solve, a phrase first coined by Chalmers (1995, p. 3; 1996, pp. xi-xii; p. 4; p. 114).

If we assume that the physical flesh, blood, and brain *perspective* on the reality of what we are is *the* physical reality of what we are and that everything of what we are is subsumed within it, we are led to conclude that consciousness is inside this physical reality. From here, we are led to conclude it is inside the brain – the part of this presumed reality it is found to be most closely associated with. We are forced to the conclusion that our conscious experience of our inner and outer worlds (everything we can sense, feel, and think regarding our internal and external environment) is inside this presumed physical reality we call the brain and is caused or brought about by its functioning. We are driven to conclude that consciousness must be something the brain we experience but presume to be the actual brain encompasses, creates, and causally interacts with.

This is a difficulty because it inevitably confronts us with the apparently unsolvable hard problem of consciousness.

Consciousness and the Brain: An Unbridgeable Gap?

If the brain we experience but presume to be real encompasses, creates, and causally interacts with our conscious experiences, we must somehow explain just how this is achieved. We must explain how things like tinkling sounds, orange flashes, or sad thoughts can causally interact with fleshy bundles of electrochemically active neurons. More, we must explain how the latter can somehow give rise to the former and answer such questions as 'why is seeing red like this?' and 'why is conscious experience like anything at all?' (cf. Chalmers, 2003, pp. 103-4).

Why is being human with a fleshy biochemical brain accompanied by experience? How does the transformation from firing fleshy neurons to tinkling sounds, orange flashes, or sad thoughts work? These are (demonstrably) difficult questions. They look impossible to solve. It seems impossible to imagine how one of these very unlike sets of things could ever create, or somehow transform itself into, the other – or even how they might causally interact. There is an apparently unbridgeable explanatory gap between them (Levine, 1983). To put it in terms used by McGinn (1989, p. 349), we cannot readily envisage how the 'technicolor phenomenology' of mental experiences can arise from the 'soggy grey matter' of the brain – it seems impossible that such a gap could ever be bridged.

Consciousness as the Hard Problem

In essence, at least, this is what Chalmers (1995, pp. 3-6; 1996, pp. 3-6; 2003, pp. 103-4) calls the hard problem of consciousness, and the need to tackle it in the terms just described is an inevitable consequence of assuming that the external observer's perspective on the reality of who and what we are is *the* reality of who and what we are. The assumption forces us to conclude that the presumed reality of conscious experience must be something that the presumed reality of the brain encompasses, creates, and causally interacts with, and this confronts us with the need to tackle the hard problem in the terms described above. It sets us the apparently impossible task of bridging the explanatory gap to explain how firing fleshy neurons can somehow work to fashion tinkling sounds, orange flashes, or sad thoughts.

Many thinkers have sought to tackle this conundrum, and there is an extensive literature on both the problem itself and the issues surrounding it. A flavour of the debate can be gleaned from the collections of papers gathered by Shear (1999) and Carruthers and Schier (2017), other sources such as Gray (2004) and Havlík et al. (2017), and peer reviewed overviews in online academic encyclopaedias (see Howell & Alter (2009) and Weisberg (n.d.)). The latter reference (Weisberg, n.d.) divides the kinds of positions held into 8 categories: eliminativism, strong and weak reductionism, mysterian, interactionist dualism, quantum theories of consciousness, epiphenomenalism, and 'Dual Aspect Theory/Neutral Monism/ Panpsychism' (although, there are variations of view even within these categories). Suffice it to say that there are almost as many views on the issue as there are thinkers who have a view, and it is clear from the references above that there is very little agreement across the field as to what the true position is.

A Path to Resolving the Hard Problem

With this in mind, it is interesting (and arguably instructive) to note that, whereas assuming the experienced brain to be the actual brain inevitably confronts us with the hard problem, as has just been argued above, recognising the error in this assumption shows us a path to its resolution. As we shall see over the next two chapters, it leads us to a new perspective on the question of conscious experience. One that resolves the so-called hard problem of consciousness by showing that it and the associated explanatory gap only arise because we confuse aspects of reality as known with reality as such – and that they cease to be an issue when we clarify our thinking in this regard.

Somewhere Between Chalmers and Dennett

The perspective in question allows us to retain both qualia and physicalism without undermining either of them. It leads us to a view on the relationship between conscious experience and the brain that sits somewhere between those of David Chalmers (1995, 1996, 1997, 2003) and Daniel Dennett (1988, 1991, 2005), who have famously taken opposing views on the topic.

Dennett has proposed in some of his work that inner states are so ephemeral that they will disappear entirely once science has solved all of the easy problems associated with the brain (1988, 1991, pp. 369-411, 2005). This reductionist view of conscious experience has some merit in that our fleshy, electrochemical brains can and do give rise to such brain states, and they can, presumably, causally interact with each other. It is, however, difficult to avoid the suspicion that all this claim really does is wish away the problems alluded to above, losing the unique aspects of conscious experience and the possibility of truly explaining them in the process.

Chalmers has suggested that the apparently unbridgeable gap between conscious experiences and brain states alluded to above makes the problem of consciousness (almost) uniquely hard in science – so hard that it cannot be explained purely in terms of brain functioning, as reductionists like Dennett suggest (see, e.g., Chalmers, 2003, pp. 102-124). He points to the difficulties entailed in explaining why blueness or redness is like it is or, indeed, why experience exists at all (why it is like anything rather than just unconscious) and suggests that such difficulties cannot be dealt with in the same way as science's 'easy' problems. This view also has its merits, affirming that the unique aspects of conscious experience are elements of the human organism that science must deal with, despite the difficulties. However, it also leads to at least one notion that most scientists would find hard to accept without a very good reason. The suggestion that these difficulties may require us to take experience itself as a fundamental property of the world alongside mass, charge, and space-time if we are to encompass it in our world-view (see, e.g., Chalmers, 1995, p. 14; 1996, pp. 126-7; 2003, pp. 123-4).

The Real Answer is Somewhere in Between

If what is argued in the next two chapters is true, the real answer lies somewhere in between these two opposing views. As we shall see, this becomes evident once we identify and correct the error in the assumption that the external observer's perspective on the reality of who and what we are is *the* reality of who and what we are. Chalmers may or may not have arrived at the notion of consciousness as the hard problem because of an assumption that the external observer's flesh, blood, and brain perspective is *the* reality of the human organism, but making that assumption leads us inevitably to the various issues outlined above.

Removing the Barrier and Resolving the Hard Problem

Not a Reality but a True Perspective on a Reality

Realising that this assumption is flawed – recognising that, in fact, the flesh, blood, and brain view of humans is a scientifically accurate external observer's *perspective* on the whole of the *substance* of the reality of the human organism allows us to take a different path. By identifying and removing the error in the assumption that it is *the* one all-encompassing reality of the human organism, we remove the block on the instantiation of the transcendent self-view and open up a path to the resolution of the hard problem.

No Barrier to Full Instantiation of the Transcendent Perspective

If the assumption is not there, it self-evidently cannot act as a barrier to the full instantiation of the transcendent perspective. The scientist in our example above cannot be thwarted in his already well-developed attempt to instantiate the transcendent perspective. He already sees the flesh, blood, and brain view of the human organism as a perspective; there is no fixed-self facet hidden in a false assumption in place to act as a barrier to its full adoption in certain circumstances.

If he encounters a situation where acting, thinking, and feeling in the world in an empathetic way towards other people is what is required to successfully negotiate the reality of a particular problem situation, he will not be blocked from doing so. There will be no barrier in place blocking a shift from a perspective that will tend to have him seeing and treating people as biological robots unworthy of such empathy. Nor will there be any leakage beyond his scientific work that causes him to see and treat the world at large as something to manipulate for particular human purposes rather than as something humans are part of and need to be in harmony with. With a well-developed transcendent perspective in place and no hidden fixed-self facet in place to block it, he will likely interact with the world in a way more appropriate to his true, wholly-variable relationship to it.

A Path to a Resolution of the Hard Problem

More important in the present context, he will be less likely to find the route to a solution of the so-called hard problem of consciousness blocked.

As was indicated above, the assumption that the experienced brain is the actual brain forces us to conclude that our conscious experiences are inside this experienced brain we presume to be the actual brain and are caused or brought about by its functioning. Answering the question of how conscious experience relates to what we have presumed to be the physical human brain then becomes a matter of explaining how its fleshy cells can somehow give rise to and encompass within themselves apparently nonphysical things like thoughts and sensations of colour.

Recognising the flaw in this assumption regarding the flesh, blood, and brain view of the human organism as drawn out above alters our perspective on this problem. It alters our perspective on the problem of how to explain conscious experience in scientific terms. Noting that the flesh, blood, and brain view is not quite *the* one all-encompassing reality of the human organism, but is rather a scientifically accurate external observer's *perspective* on the whole of the *substance* of that all-encompassing reality, opens up a path to a resolution of the problem.

A Perspective With no Hard Problem and no Explanatory Gap

It offers the first step in a line of reasoning that suggests a perspective on the brain and on conscious experience in which there is no explanatory gap and no hard problem. One that suggests we are dealing not with impossibly different realities, but with a single reality known from two irreconcilably different perspectives – that the problem is 'epistemic' rather than real (cf. Shand, 2021). One where the solution to the problem of explaining conscious experience in scientific terms lies somewhere between the perspectives offered by Chalmers and Dennett – an outcome that leads, in turn, to a further clarification of the detail of the transcendent perspective itself. It suggests the possibility that our conscious experiences can be ontologically reducible to brain states but have knowledge content that is epistemologically irreducible to an outside observer's knowledge of these brain states. A position in which Jackson's famous Mary (Jackson, 1982) can acquire new irreducible knowledge without this having ontological implications and in which there is no hard problem or explanatory gap unless we mistake a way of knowing a reality for the reality as such and epistemological irreducibility for ontological irreducibility. The argument for this is presented over the next two chapters, with the focus in the next (Chapter 24) being on the ontologically reducible but epistemologically irreducible claim.

24

The Hard Problem Made Easy

Ontologically Reducible but Epistemologically Irreducible

Recognising that the flesh, blood, and brain view is not quite the one all-encompassing reality of the human organism but is rather a scientifically accurate, external observer's perspective on the whole of the substance of that all-encompassing reality offers us a new take on the problem of consciousness. It allows us to begin to uncover a view of the relationship between the brain and conscious experience in which there is no explanatory gap and no hard problem.

The position in question has two facets. The first being that conscious experience is ontologically reducible to some aspect of brain functioning – nothing over and above it in terms of substance. The second being that it is also, for purely perspectival reasons, epistemologically irreducible to the outside observer's knowledge of that aspect of brain functioning, with this epistemologically irreducible knowledge content nevertheless being ontologically reducible to the aspect of brain functioning in question. The argument in support of this claim has the following steps:

1. The Human Body we Know is an Experiential Construct

The first step – the argument for claiming that the flesh, blood, and brain perspective on the human organism is the organism as *experienced* by an outside observer and encompasses the brain as experienced rather than the brain as such – has already been made above. What we see and otherwise sense when there is another human in front of us – or indeed, when we see and otherwise sense ourselves from the outside via a series of mirrors or cameras – cannot be the undoubtedly real physical human behind our seeing and sensing. Since it can only come to our awareness as information acquired via our outward-looking senses – information that comes to us from something that is, in reality, physically distinct from us – it can only be a (possibly scientifically enhanced) multisensory representation of that reality. What we see and otherwise sense in such situations is not the actual reality of the human (or brain) observed externally; it is a sensory representation of that reality. The brain it entails is – must be – the brain as experienced rather than the brain as such. It is a sensory construct that accurately reflects an underlying reality rather than the reality as such.

2. The Brain as an Experiential Construct Within Consciousness

The second step in the argument then follows as a clear implication of the conclusion that the human organism and its brain as we know them are sensory representations. Clearly, if this human organism and brain as we know them are sensory representations, then they are experiences within consciousness – the body and brain as we know them are the body and brain as experienced. They are inside consciousness as experienced in the sense of being a subset of the totality of our conscious experience. The externally observed human organism and its brain, as they are known to us, are experiential constructs within the panorama of conscious experience.

3. Consciousness in a Reality Underlying the Experienced Brain

Consciousness: Not Seen as Inside an Experiential Construct

This clearly has some impact on the notion that conscious experience is somehow inside the brain and is something the brain gives rise to or makes happen. Obviously, when we make such a claim, we do not mean to imply that conscious experience – an aspect of the reality of the human organism – is somehow inside a mental construct that is itself a subset of conscious experience. This is not what we usually intend to imply when we seek to place our conscious experiences inside the brain and ask how the brain can give rise to them, nor does it make any sense to think in these terms.

On the one hand, it makes no sense whatever to seek to place the totality of our conscious experience inside an experience – our sensory construct of the brain – that is a mere subset of the totality of conscious experience. On the other hand, it makes no sense to think of a mental construct as a container for anything other than more detailed aspects of itself – more detailed experiences of 'brainy stuff' in the context of a mental construct of the brain, for example.

If we think of our mental construct in mainly visual terms, a good analogy would be a video. We would not expect to find the real world inside the video, nor would we expect to find that the video was somehow responsible for creating or giving rise to some part of that real world, nor is it reasonable that we should expect these things. What we would expect to find inside a video if we explored inside it at deeper and deeper levels – or, indeed, inside a mental construct if we did a similar thing – would be more detail of the 'substance' of the video or the mental construct. We would not expect to find anything of the reality beyond either one – the reality that they are representations of.

Inside the Reality Underlying the Experienced Brain

Even if we do not necessarily say so explicitly because we tend not to recognise the brain we know as a mental construct, what we intend when we seek to place consciousness inside the brain is not that consciousness is inside our mental construct of the brain. What we intend – and the only thing that makes any sense given that the brain we know *is* a mental construct – is to place it inside the reality underlying our mental construct, the actual reality that is beyond our construct but is reflected within our construct.

If conscious experience is inside anything, it is inside that underlying reality. If anything contains, creates, and gives rise to conscious experience, it is not our mental construct of the brain part of the flesh, blood, and brain perspective on the organism; it is the reality that is reflected within that construct but is, in actuality, outwith and beyond it.

This is a minor qualification on the face of it, given that this is essentially what we usually mean to imply anyway, but it is an important one in respect of the clarity of our thinking about what is required to solve the problem of conscious experience.

4. Different Ways of Knowing the Same Underlying Thing

Experiences not Observed Inside This Underlying Reality

There is more to consider here, however. If our conscious experience is somehow inside the reality underlying the brain as the external observer knows it, it cannot be there in the simple sense of a chair being inside a house or a rock being inside a mountain.

It is safe to say that no one has ever observed anything like conscious experiences – things like tinkling sounds, orange flashes, or sad thoughts – inside this externally observed brain, nor is it possible to imagine how anyone ever could (cf., e.g., Kanai & Tsuchiya, 2012; Searle, 1998; Skokowski, 2022). The things that have been observed there to date – brain processes, fleshy bundles of electrochemically active neurons, ganglions, synapses, and so on (Scruton, 2020) – are clearly not anything remotely like the mental things like feelings, images, and ideas this perspective on things would have us place inside it. Indeed, these qualia of conscious experience seem, on the face of it, to be so very different from things like firing neuron cells that it is impossible to imagine we could ever observe these things of the mind inside these fleshy, electrochemical things we call brains.

But Science Demands They Must be Observed in Some Sense

This is a major problem for anyone seeking to adopt a scientific approach to the study of either the human organism or of conscious experience and consciousness. A scientist will not usually accept that something exists within some aspect of the world unless it can, in some form or fashion (cf. *Observation beyond our eyes*, 2022), be observed to exist there. If our conscious experiences are inside the reality underlying an outside observer's view of the brain – and it is reasonable to assume that they are there in some sense – they can only be there as things the outside observer knows or experiences differently. They can only be there in the sense of being things that the external observer *can* observe there but does not recognise as conscious experiences because they are known or experienced quite differently when they *are* known or experienced as conscious experiences.

Entirely Possible They are Observed as Direct Experiences

This represents a state of affairs not normally encountered in nature but is, of course, quite possible in the case of the human organism. It is entirely possible that our conscious experiences are not inside the reality of the human organism in the simple sense of a chair being inside a house or a rock being inside a mountain. We have an inner view of our own internal states in a way that mountains and houses do not – and that we ourselves do not have of mountains, houses, or anything else in nature. We have direct experience of our own thoughts, feelings, and other sensations in a way that is not found in most of nature. We know what it is like to feel pleasure, sense redness, think thoughts, experience solidity, and every other aspect of the panorama of our consciousness in a way that is only possible by knowing them directly from within and not by knowing them indirectly from without.

It is therefore possible that our conscious experiences are not inside the reality of the human organism in the simple sense of a chair being inside a house, a rock being inside a mountain, or a hypothalamus being inside a brain. It is possible that they are inside the reality underlying the brain we experience as outside observers in the special sense of being something inside that underlying reality that the outside observer knows and experiences in one way and the internal observer knows or experiences in another. It is possible that they are directly experienced aspects of some part or parts of the functioning brain that the outside observer only experiences in quite different indirect ways (cf., e.g., Jones, 2019 on Locke, Russell, and Strawson).

The Same Things Experienced in Very Different Ways

Indeed, given that our conscious experiences must surely be inside this underlying reality in some sense, this is the only possibility that fits the facts as we know them.

If our thoughts, feelings, and sensations are in the real brain underlying the outside observer's experience of that real brain but cannot be observed there, they can only be regarded by science as being in the brain if they *are* being observed there but are known differently. They can only be regarded by science as being in the brain if the outside observer *can* observe them there but observes – that is to say, experiences – them in a way that makes them seem quite different to the internal observer's experience of them. They can only be so regarded by science if some of the things the external observer observes when experiencing them indirectly are actually the same things that the internal observer observes when experiencing them directly – if they are really these same things experienced in a very different way.

If our thoughts, feelings, and sensations are in the brain but cannot be observed there by an outside observer and are so different from what can be observed there that we cannot even imagine them ever being observed there, this is the only possibility. They can only be there as things the external observer does observe there but in a very different form; they can only be aspects of the externally known or experienced brain that are also known – in a quite different internal and direct form – by an internal observer. Our conscious experiences *can be* some thing or things inside the reality underlying the brain we experience as external observers, but if they are, they must be the thing or things in question known directly as the inside observer knows them rather than indirectly as the outside observer knows them. Our conscious experiences and some kind of electrochemical activity inside the reality underlying the brain we know as external observers can be one thing or feature, but only if we take it that they are one thing known from entirely different viewpoints by the internal and external observers.

Not as Unlikely as it may at First Seem

This is not as unlikely as it may, at first, seem. It appears unlikely mainly because we often imagine the problem in a misleading way – a way that makes it seem impossible that something in the brain can be the same thing as a sensation or a thought. We think of the brain as something solid and fleshy with folds of matter and bundles of neurons and conclude that the idea that a thought or a sensation can be the same thing as such solid, fleshy stuff is more than a little far-fetched. But there are things in the brain that are not solid, fleshy stuff – electrical discharges being the obvious example.

If we think of an example where the inner experience is an orange flash of light that the external observer sees as an electrical discharge presented on a screen as a grey or white flash, the idea that the two might be different perspectives on the same thing seems more reasonable. The idea that there is a single electrical discharge that the internal observer experiences as an orange flash and the external observer experiences as a white flash is easier to accept than if we try to imagine a neuron cell and a sweet taste being the same thing. Especially when one considers that a little fiddling with the monitor showing the external observer a white flash might easily transform the white flash into a blue, a yellow, or an orange one.

The difference will seem more pronounced, of course, if we stick with a white flash on a screen for the external observer but choose a sound, a sensation of touch, or a thought as our inner experience. Again, though, it is not impossible to imagine changing the external observer's mode of observation so that an electrical discharge experienced as a sound or a thought by the internal observer is presented to the observer as a sound via a loudspeaker or as words on a screen. Or, indeed, transmitted to the external observer in a more direct way, so that it directly creates the sound or the thought in the observer's own consciousness. If we think of the one thing as an electrical discharge, the possibility that it can be known differently – perhaps even very differently – by different observers becomes entirely credible and much easier to accept. The assumption is that our internal observer knows the electrical discharge in a direct and unmediated way from the inside, and our external observer knows the same discharge from the outside in a way mediated by his senses and his observational instrumentation.

In these circumstances, it is surely unsurprising if the two observations of a single thing seem very different to the two observers. In the world at large, seeing the same thing from two different perspectives can make it look very different, even where both observations are made by an external observer – think of an upside-down pyramid observed from above and from the side, for example. So it is entirely possible for something in the reality that underlies the experienced brain to look very different to an internal observer experiencing it directly in an unmediated way from the inside and an external observer experiencing it indirectly in a mediated way from the outside.

The Same Things Experienced Differently

It is thus entirely possible that the panorama of our conscious experience is inside the reality that underlies the experienced brain in the special sense of being an inside observer's direct view of something that looks and feels quite different to the external observer. It is quite possible that it and some aspect or aspects of that underlying reality are the same physical thing, known in entirely different ways. If conscious experience is inside the reality underlying the experienced brain but cannot be observed there by an outside observer, then it can only be there in this special sense. It can only be there as something that is ontologically reducible to something the external observer *can* observe there but knows – or experiences – in a very different way. Conscious experiences must be the same thing as states in the brain in terms of substance, but known in very different ways – something that, as we have just seen, is entirely possible in the case of conscious experience. It is entirely possible that what an internal observer knows in a direct way as a conscious experience (by being it) is something an external observer knows in an indirect way via externally focused senses, as a state in the brain.

5. Inner View Epistemologically Irreducible to Outer View

The notion that conscious experiences are the same thing as states in the brain in terms of substance but known in very different ways by an outside observer dependent on indirect knowing and an inside observer capable of direct knowing suggests something else about them.

It suggests that, in addition to being entirely ontologically reducible to some aspect of brain functioning, our conscious experiences entail knowledge content that is epistemologically *irreducible* to an outside observer's knowledge of the aspect of brain functioning that these conscious experiences are entirely ontologically reducible to. If our thoughts, feelings, and sensations are in the brain but cannot be observed there by an outside observer and are so different from what can be observed there that we cannot even imagine them ever being observed there, this conclusion seems inescapable. It must be the case that our conscious experiences entail knowledge content that is epistemologically *irreducible* to an outside observer's knowledge of the aspect of brain functioning that these conscious experiences are entirely ontologically reducible to. Indeed, it is hard to argue the opposite case, for how could the external observer's outside view of fleshy brain matter, firing neurons, and electrochemical brain activity possibly encompass knowledge of pleasurable sensations, uncharitable thoughts, or direct experience of what blueness, sourness, or roughness is like? It seems clear that this is impossible, strongly suggesting that our conscious experiences are not only entirely ontologically reducible to some aspect of brain functioning but also entail knowledge content that is epistemologically *irreducible* to the outside observer's knowledge of that aspect of brain functioning. It seems clear that they are that aspect of brain functioning known in a more direct way and that, in consequence, they encompass knowledge content that is not knowable by an external observer who only knows them in a more indirect way.

6. Ontologically Reducible but Epistemologically Irreducible

An Unlikely Combination of Characteristics?

On first sight, this seems an unlikely combination of characteristics. If a conscious experience is the same thing as some aspect of brain functioning – if what is known by the internal and external observer is exactly the same thing, ontologically speaking – how can the internal observer know something of it not known to the external observer?

In fact, this not only can be true where conscious experiences are concerned; there is a case for claiming that it must be, and so is true. We shall see below that there are reasonable grounds for holding that conscious experiences are, in fact, both ontologically reducible to some aspect of brain functioning and epistemologically irreducible to the external observer's knowledge of that aspect of brain functioning.

This combination of characteristics appears problematic because the claim of ontological reducibility essentially asserts that there is no part of the inner view that is not encompassed within the same underlying reality as is known by the external observer. This appears to mean that, given an entirely complete and accurate external observer's view of the underlying reality in question, there should be no aspect of the reality that the inner view is entirely subsumed within that is not able to be known by the external observer. It seems to suggest that nothing can be known to the inside observer that is not also encompassed within the reality known to the external observer.

But how can the inner observer's view of a conscious experience be epistemologically irreducible to the external observer's view of it when the inner view that is the conscious experience is ontologically reducible to the reality that underlies it and is fully reflected within it? If every aspect of what is known by the inside observer is subsumed within the reality known to the external observer, then a complete external observer's knowledge of the reality must, on the face of it, encompass a knowledge of all of it. Surely this means that the directly experienced inner view cannot be epistemologically irreducible to the outer view?

An Irreconcilable Difference in Perspectives

The suggestion here is that the solution to this apparent difficulty lies in the possibility that, while a complete external observer's knowledge of the reality does encompass a knowledge of all of it, it does so in a different form. The inner view is epistemologically irreducible because something is lost in translation when switching from the internal observer's form to the external observer's form – something trivial in terms of information content but significant nonetheless. The suggestion, in short, is that the epistemological irreducibility is a function not of ontological differences but of an irreconcilable difference in perspectives.

Most of What we Know is Known Relationally

Seeing how this is possible requires a return to the idea of relational and nonrelational knowing explored in Chapter 12.

As was argued there, almost everything we know of ourselves and the world at large is relational in nature; the thing known is known indirectly in relation to other things.

This is true of the whole of our view of the world and of the human animal known externally. The sun we see and feel cannot be the sun as such; it can only be the sun known *in relation to* our sensory systems; we know it via the visual and other data transmitted from it and the images and feelings we construct from that data. Even the sun understood in more scientific terms – via verbally and mathematically expressed theories and models – is known relationally in this way. We know it not as itself but *via* those theories and models.

Indeed, since much of science is constructed by observing how things behave in particular physical circumstances – that is to say, by observing their behaviour in relation to other things in the physical world – this indirect and relational tag applies for a second reason. It applies not just because our theories and models sit between us and the sun itself, but because the detailed content of these theories and models is itself indirect and relational in nature. It tells us not what the sun is in itself but rather what it is in relation to planets, moons, photons, gravity, and so on. The same is true of everything else we know as external observers – of atoms, electrons, trees, brains and their various parts, and so on – they are all known indirectly and relationally.

Experiences Also Known Nonrelationally

As was also argued in Chapter 12, the situation as regards our inner experiences – the panorama of consciousness – is similar, but not the same. Most of what we know of conscious experience is also indirect and relational in nature, but some of it is direct and nonrelational. When we experience ourselves in particular ways – swimming in the sun, dreaming of a red balloon, feeling a pleasant sensation – there is a sense in which we know the inner experiential view, not directly *of itself* but indirectly *in relation to* these various experiential circumstances. We know it through its relationships with other things, which is to say, indirectly. We know it as sweetness when we taste sugar, blueness when we see a clear sky, and so on. As with our knowledge of the external world, there is relational knowledge content – it is sweet as opposed to orange, sharp, or sour.

What is different is the way in which we know this relational knowledge content. If the Chapter 12 arguments are sound, we must accept that our inner experiences are the one thing we can and must know, not just relationally and indirectly but also non-relationally and directly. We can and must know them directly, not just through their relationships to other things, but directly as themselves and in relation to nothing but themselves. Taking a contrary view leads us into a nonsensical infinite regress where one way of knowing must be known via another way of knowing, that way of knowing must be known via another, and so on ad infinitum. We know them 'as is' without any mediating factor to introduce a relational element.

If we ask ourselves the question, 'How do we know knowing?', there are only two possible answers. Either we know any given way of knowing via another, in which case we must ask how we know that way of knowing (and the one we know that through and the one we know that through), ad infinitum, or we know it directly by being it. Either we assume the knower and the known are in some sense separate and need to be linked by another (and another and another) way of knowing, in which case we are led into the infinite regress just described. Or we assume that the knower and the known in this case are one thing, and the knowing is known directly – which is to say, nonrelationally, as, or in terms of, itself. Our knowledge of our conscious experience is also largely relational in nature, but not wholly so. All of the relational content it entails is itself known directly and nonrelationally.

We do not just know the relationship as sweet or sour; we know what sweetness, sourness – and even what was labelled in Chapter 12 as empty consciousness itself – are *like* as direct, unmediated experiences. In a sense, we know the relationship by being it; it is a direct part of what we are, of how we experience ourselves. It is, in essence, our experience of ourselves – or, at any rate, one particular aspect of our experience of ourselves.

Ontologically Reducible and Epistemologically Irreducible

And this, of course, tells us how it is possible for our panorama of inner experiences to be very different from the external observer's view yet both ontologically reducible to the reality that underlies that external observer's view and epistemologically irreducible to the external view itself. The three elements of this position seem irreconcilable. It is hard to see how it can be true that the internal view is ontologically reducible to the reality that underlies the external observer's view if the internal view is also very different from the external observer's view itself. Ontological reducibility seems to imply epistemological reducibility, but epistemological reducibility seems to be impossible if the two ways of knowing are so very different – the two being very different implies epistemological irreducibility, but this, in turn, seems to imply ontological irreducibility. How can the inner way of knowing be very different to and epistemologically irreducible to the external way of knowing if it is entirely reducible to the same reality entirely known via the external way of knowing?

The Relational Cannot Encompass the Nonrelational

The answer is that the external observer knows the reality in question completely – as completely as an external observer knows anything studied by science – but only in the same relational terms as anything studied by science. The external observer knows the whole of the substance that is our conscious experience, but only in terms of a type of knowledge that cannot, by its very (relational) nature, encompass the nonrelational aspects of conscious experience. Everything of the inner view is subsumed within the reality underlying the external view and is therefore also known within the external observer's view, but it is known in a different way or in a different form. The inner view seems very different and is irreducible because it entails direct and nonrelational knowledge of the reality that subsumes it that is not and cannot be encompassed in the external observer's indirect and relational knowledge and experience of the same reality.

To put it more precisely, the same relationships are known, but they are known in a direct, nonrelational way. We know not just the relationships as such but also what it is like to experience them directly and nonrelationally. The external observer knows redness or the experience of sweetness as relationships between aspects of brain function; the internal observer knows the same relationships as direct experiences. He knows what it is like to have that aspect of brain functioning occur – what experiencing redness and sweetness is like.

Since these inner experiences are entirely subsumed within the substance of the aspect of brain functioning observed by the external observer, the external view encompasses everything about them in relational form. It encompasses everything about them that scientists would normally know about the things they study, including a *relational* knowledge of the nonrelational experiences of redness and sweetness. It is thus entirely possible for the inner view to be very different to the external view and entirely ontologically reducible to the reality underlying the external view because nothing is known in either view that is not known *in some form* in the other. But it is also entirely possible for the inner perspective to be epistemologically irreducible to the knowledge content of the external perspective.

Lost in Translation

It is entirely possible because, while both the substance and the nature of the nonrelational 'like something' qualities of conscious experience are encompassed within the external perspective, they can only be known relationally by an outside observer, so that the nonrelational aspect is essentially lost. The nonrelational 'like something' qualities of conscious experience are encompassed within the external perspective but not *as* the nonrelational 'like something' qualities of conscious experience – that aspect of their nature is lost, although it is encompassed in a different form. The external observer knows it from the outside in a purely relational way. It sits beyond his experience of the brain as a reality underlying his experience, a reality that the external observer can only know relationally – *via* and in relation to his external experience of it – but cannot know directly and nonrelationally while taking the external observer's perspective. The notion that our conscious experiences can be both ontologically reducible to some aspect of brain functioning and epistemologically *irreducible* to the external observer's view of that aspect of brain functioning is an entirely reasonable one because the epistemological irreducibility is purely perspectival and has no ontological implications.

A View of Conscious Experience That can and Must be True

We can take this argument a little further, however. As was asserted earlier, we can claim reasonable grounds for holding that this view of conscious experience not only can be true but must be and is true. There are two points here.

The first is that conscious experience must be inside the actual brain underlying the experienced brain – where else can it be? It cannot be observed there, however, and it is so different to what we can observe there that we cannot even imagine how it could be observed there. From a scientific perspective, this means it can only be accepted as being there if, at minimum, it is nothing over and above – entirely ontologically reducible to – something that can be observed there (ontological reducibility is a necessary condition but not, in itself, a sufficient one). If our conscious experiences are inside our brains, as most of us assume, they must be ontologically reducible to some aspect of brain functioning that an outside observer experiences in an entirely different way.

The second is that we can make a similar claim as regards epistemological irreducibility. If the case argued in Chapter 12 is sound, each of our conscious experiences is known directly and nonrelationally. If the case argued in the present chapter is sound, nonrelational knowledge cannot be encompassed *as nonrelational knowledge* within an external observer's knowledge of the human organism, since this is entirely relational.

On this basis, we can claim reasonable grounds for holding that it not only can be, but must be, and is true that our conscious experiences are both ontologically reducible to some functioning brain state and epistemologically *irreducible* to the external observer's view of that functioning brain state. It is reasonable to conclude that the view of conscious experience drawn out above – the view drawn out by recognising and correcting the flaw in the assumption that the flesh, blood, and brain view of humans is *the* reality of who and what we are – is correct in these two respects.

This, at any rate, is the view taken here and is the basis for the claims made in the next chapter as to the form a scientific account of conscious experience must take and the implications of this for both science and the transcendent perspective itself.

Summary: A Perspective With no Explanatory Gap

Recognising that the flesh, blood, and brain view is not the all-encompassing reality of the human organism but rather a scientifically accurate external observer's perspective on the substance of that reality suggests a view of conscious experience that has two facets. The first being that conscious experience is ontologically reducible to some aspect of brain functioning – nothing over and above it in terms of substance. The second being that it is also, for purely perspectival reasons, epistemologically irreducible to the outside observer's knowledge of that aspect of brain functioning, with this epistemologically irreducible knowledge content nevertheless being ontologically reducible to the aspect of brain functioning in question.

This is significant because it suggests a view of consciousness and conscious experience in which neither the position suggested by Chalmers nor the position suggested by Dennett is quite accurate. It suggests a perspective in which there is no explanatory gap and the problem of conscious experience is not so uniquely hard that we must add experience to our list of fundamental properties alongside mass, charge, and space-time, as Chalmers has suggested. But also one in which Dennett's notion – that conscious experience is so entirely reducible to states in the brain that it will essentially disappear entirely from our view of the nature of things once science has solved all of the 'easy' problems relating to the brain – is not true either. It suggests a view that lies somewhere between the positions taken by these thinkers. These points are explored further in the next chapter.

25

Implications for the Transcendent Perspective

Somewhere Between Chalmers and Dennett

The case offered in favour of the claim that the correct position as regards a scientific account of conscious experience lies somewhere between the views expressed by Chalmers and Dennett goes like this:

Mapping the Nonrelational and Relational Viewpoints

If conscious experience is both ontologically reducible to some aspect of brain functioning and epistemologically irreducible to the outside observer's knowledge of that aspect of brain functioning, as argued in Chapter 24, two things can be claimed to follow.

The first is that any conscious experience is entirely explicable by an account of the aspect of brain functioning it is ontologically reducible to. If all aspects of conscious experience are ontologically reducible to the reality underlying the brain as experienced, then even the inner qualities that occasion our 'why like this?' and 'why like anything?' questions about conscious experience are explicable in terms of a full account of that underlying reality. If these 'like something' qualities are wholly subsumed within this underlying reality – if they are that reality known in a more direct way – an external observer's relational account of the substance and functioning of that reality will be sufficient to account for these inner qualities it subsumes. They are, on this view, simply epistemologically irreducible ways of knowing the underlying reality in question that are nonetheless wholly ontologically reducible to – really nothing but – that underlying reality. They are part and parcel of that reality and can be fully explained in terms of a full account of its substance and functioning.

The second is that the irreducible nonrelational knowledge content of any given conscious experience is nonetheless an essential element of a scientific account of the conscious experience in question and must be mapped to the relational account. Its existence is a unique aspect of the reality in question and is part of what the relational account is explaining. Failure to include it in the account by mapping it in this way implies that the inner perspective on it does not exist and is not part of what is being explained. Mapping it to the relational account in this way adds no scientific or operationally useful information to the account; it merely recognises the fact and nature of the inner perspective. It tells us nothing additional over and above what is entailed in the relational scientific account in terms of hard scientific information. It simply recognises that the brain function being explained has an inner perspective that is 'like something' and tells us exactly what the inner view is like.

Nonrelational Explained but a Necessary Facet of our Account

Looking at this in terms of the whole of our conscious experience, we can say several things. First, that both the totality of conscious experience and the subset of that totality that is the brain as experienced are simply different perspectives on – different ways of knowing – the same underlying reality. Second, that there are aspects of our knowledge of conscious experience that are not reducible to our knowledge of its neural correlates, but that any conscious experience, including that irreducible knowledge content, is nevertheless ontologically reducible to the reality underlying its physical correlates. Third, that the solution to the problem of conscious experience lies in explaining how the brain gives rise to the neural correlates of the various experiences that make up the world of conscious experience and how these work to give us the externally observable characteristics of conscious experience. Fourth, that such an explanation of itself leaves some key information about conscious experience out. It is complete as far as our scientific account of it is concerned, but is incomplete as regards a full description of what it is we are explaining. Without the mapping of the nonrelational experiential perspective to the relational account, we fail to fully describe what we are explaining. We give the impression that there is no inner view and fail to include our knowledge of what it is like.

This suggests that a full account of how the brain functions to create and support the neural correlates of conscious experience will adequately explain both why our experiences are like what they are like and why they are like anything, but will be incomplete without a mapping to the experiences themselves. The full relational account will provide all of the explanatory details required but will, without the mapping suggested, omit the fact and nature of the inner perspective from our description of what it is we are explaining.

Part Dennett; Part Chalmers; no Explanatory gap

This produces a perspective on conscious experience that lies somewhere between the viewpoints espoused by Chalmers and Dennett – one in which neither the position suggested by Chalmers nor the position suggested by Dennett is quite accurate. In this perspective, the problem of conscious experience is not so uniquely hard that we must add experience to our list of fundamental properties alongside mass, charge, and space-time, as Chalmers would have it. Nor is it so reducible to states in the brain that it will essentially disappear entirely from our view of the nature of things once science has solved all of the 'easy' problems relating to the brain. On the one hand, the irreducible knowledge content of our inner experiences is an essential part of any scientific account of conscious experience and must be included in it. On the other hand, the whole of our panorama of inner experiences, including this irreducible knowledge content, is entirely ontologically reducible to states in the brain and can be solved in the same 'easy' way as any other problem encountered by science.

In brief, we are led to a view of the nature of conscious experience with two facets. The first being that we must regard the irreducible knowledge content of our 'like something' inner experiences as a key and essential part of our description of the scientific problem we are aiming to solve and of our knowledge about that problem. The second being that we need only deal with states in the brain and a mapping of these to the irreducible knowledge content of our inner experiences as far as finding and expressing the solution to the problem of our inner experiences is concerned. We are led to a position that echoes Dennett in so far as the ontological reducibility and 'easy' nature of explaining conscious experience is concerned, but echoes Chalmers as regards the need to retain conscious experience as a key part of the account that cannot simply be ignored. One in which conscious experience must be kept within the picture, not as a fundamental property but as a key element nonetheless. A position in which there is no explanatory gap – no hard problem – but no loss either of the unique 'like something' qualities of our inner experiences.

Conscious Experiences and Brain Functions

If all of our conscious experience – even its 'like something' qualities – is wholly ontologically reducible to the reality that underlies the external observer's view of the workings of the brain, there is no aspect of it that is not matched by a discoverable correlate in the brain. Thoughts, experiences like a red flash or a flush of pleasure or a solid feel, the fact that a person is experiencing consciousness, the fact that it is 'like something' and is like one thing rather than another, will all have externally observable correlates. All of these things and more regarding our inner experiences will be aspects of the reality that subsumes them and that underlies the perspective that is the external observer's view of the brain. All of them will therefore have discoverable and observable correlates in the brain and will be explicable in terms of those correlates and the environment they occur and exist in. At least they will be once we learn to identify the correlates and learn to draft our questions in terms appropriate to our external relational view of them.

If all of them are subsumed in the substance of the reality underlying the external observer's view of the brain, all of our questions about them will be expressible in external relational terms and will be answerable in the same terms. They will be answerable in terms of what function or functions of the brain they are identified with. We will not only be able to answer questions about why a particular experience – redness, sweetness, or what was referred to earlier as empty consciousness – is like it is; we will also be able to provide an answer to the question of why having a conscious experience is like anything.

The 'Why Like This?' Questions

The inner experiences of a red flash and a blue streak are known nonrelationally, but the differences between them are relational differences; both express slightly different relationships between light of particular wavelengths and aspects of our visual systems. These relational differences between a red flash and a blue streak inner experience will have relational correlates in the brain perspective, and it should be possible to explain the one in terms of the other. It should be possible to explain the differences in the inner experiences in terms of the differences in their external correlates, since these encompass the relational aspects of the red flash and the blue streak in a different form. The same should be true of the differences between one thought and another or between a thought and a solid feel or a tinkling sound – there will be relational differences in the associated brain functions that mirror those in the experiences. An account of the former will also provide us with an account of the latter.

The 'Why Like Anything?' Question

The same should also be true in respect of the question of why conscious experience is like anything and the related question of why empty consciousness – consciousness of consciousness itself – is like it is. There is a single answer to both of these questions; they are essentially the same question.

Almost all of our conscious experiences entail nonrelational knowledge of relational knowledge. Empty consciousness – the experience we have as a result of the sound of two hands clapping exercise – is a nonrelational experience with all of the relational knowledge of our conscious experiences removed. It is the one thing they all have in common – the one thing we have not explained when answering the (relational) question why is this or that experience like this as opposed to that – which means that it is the referent of the why is conscious experience like anything question.

It is also the one thing about every conscious experience that is not nonrelational knowledge of relational knowledge – the one thing that is simply the one aspect of every experience that is nonrelational. This means that it is nonrelational knowledge of nonrelational knowledge (the experience of nonrelational knowing itself with everything else removed), and hence also the referent of the empty consciousness 'why like this?' question.

In this case, the 'why is it like anything?' and the 'why is it like this?' questions are the same question; they both look to explain the why of the same thing – the fact and nature of nonrelational knowing itself. There is no relational knowledge content to explain in either of these questions, but it is still possible to give a relational account of them in terms of their external correlates. The differences between a person experiencing consciousness and being fully unconscious will also have correlates in the brain perspective, and it should also be possible to explain those differences in terms of the differences in the correlates. The question of why consciousness is like anything as opposed to being just an unconscious state of the brain should have a discoverable externally investigable correlate or correlates in the brain and should be similarly explicable once we can couch the question in terms of the correlates.

Being conscious – knowing something experientially – must be 'like something', even if what is known is only consciousness of consciousness itself. It must be different in some way from just having the information stored and not immediately known (in the sense of experienced); otherwise, how could it be known? How could it be other than unconscious?

If this view of the nature of consciousness is correct and all of our inner experience is subsumed in the reality underlying our view of the brain, then this difference that is 'like something' must and will have at least one external correlate, and it will be possible to explain how and why it occurs. It must be a function of the brain and be as explicable as any function of the brain.

Moreover, since in this instance the 'why is it like anything?' and the 'why is it like this?' questions are the same question, the 'why is it like this?' question will have the same answer. The 'why is it like this?' question will be associated with the same external correlate or correlates as the 'why is it like anything?' question and will be explained by an explanation of the associated aspect of brain functioning. The 'why is it like this?' question will also have a relational answer, even though it does not entail a relationship as such. It does not itself encompass relational knowledge, but it is still different to the unconscious state and can be explained in terms of its relationship to that unconscious state. We should eventually be able to say both why it is like it is and why it is like anything. We may even be able to say that if some small change were to exist in the reality underlying its external correlate or correlates, it would not be quite the same experience but a slightly different one. And we would certainly be able to account for it being like empty consciousness as opposed to experienced redness, sweetness, or hardness.

Answering, not Evading, Chalmers' Questions

Notice that it is not the case in this position that we are somehow explaining something other than the 'why is it like anything?' and the 'why is it like this?' questions by adopting the above approach to answering them. If our inner experiences are all subsumed in the reality underlying the brain perspective but are also that reality as known by an inside observer, then there is a single reality underlying all of our questions about our inner experiences – a single reality known in different ways.

There are not two questions here – only a single question expressed in two different ways. By identifying the correlates of the questions in the brain and answering the questions in terms of these correlates, we are answering the questions that Chalmers wants answered, not somehow denying or ducking them (1995, p. 9; 2003, pp. 109-10). We are identifying the external correlates of these internal 'like something' and like this' questions, posing the questions in terms of these correlates, and answering them in terms appropriate to these external views of them – the outside observer's environment where all scientific questions are identified, described, researched, and answered.

No Additional Question to Answer

Looking at this from the current perspective, where we do not yet have answers to such questions, it may seem to some that once we do, we will still want to ask why such and such a function creates the experiences of redness, softness, empty consciousness, or whatever. If so, there are two entirely reasonable responses we can make.

The first is to point out that such a question jumps the gun somewhat – to point out that we currently have very little notion of what answers we will find. We can suggest that there is every possibility that the functional explanations we find for such experiential qualities will illuminate the workings of experience to such an extent that the answers we find will satisfy us – that, at present, we just do not know whether they will or not. It may even be, who knows, that, once we have such explanations, we are able to apply our answers in other contexts and create consciousness and its associated experiences artificially, and that surely would stop any additional questions.

The second response is that asking why such and such a function creates the experiences of redness, softness, or empty consciousness is akin to asking why existence exists and why it is like it is. The only reasonable answer is that it just does exist and it just is like it is, and that the functions concerned just do create these experiences (cf. Papineau, 1998, pp. 5-6). After all, once we have an explanation of the ways in which the world and its constituents operate to produce lightning, we do not go on to ask why the world should be such that lightning is produced by the operations in question. We should not expect to take a different line as regards consciousness and experience. If these are ontologically identical to the functions that create them, there should be no additional question to answer.

Not Quite Chalmers, not Quite Dennett

The upshot is that we can explain all of these 'like something' and 'like this' questions that Chalmers says make the problem of consciousness uniquely hard entirely in terms of the brain and its functioning without making experience a fundamental property. If this perspective on consciousness is correct, Dennett is right – the problem of explaining consciousness is just another of the so-called 'easy' problems to be tackled by science. There is no explanatory gap, ontologically speaking, only the appearance of a gap created by a difference in viewpoints when we fail to regard them as viewpoints and see them as realities instead.

Dennett is only right up to a point, however. His claim that inner states are so ephemeral that they will disappear entirely once science has solved all of the easy problems associated with the brain does not hold in this view (although they do become trivial in scientific terms). We need the inner experiences to be part of our description of the problem we are answering in any account of conscious experience claimed to be complete. We need it to be part of what we know about the phenomena being described and explained – part of our scientific account of the phenomena in question.

If the nonrelational knowledge content of the inner perspective is also epistemologically irreducible to the relational knowledge content of the external perspective, then there is an aspect of the problem we are seeking to solve that a purely functional account omits. One that is only captured and made clear by including our inner experiences in our functional account through mapping them to their physical correlates and the associated explanation of how these physical correlates work.

All of the questions about conscious experience we want accounted for are relational in nature. A red experience is a relationship between light of a particular wavelength and our visual system; a blue experience is a different relationship between the two. One thought expresses a particular relationship between our language and imaging centres and the world or our memories of the world; another encompasses a different relationship. Being conscious entails a different relationship between parts of our brain than not being conscious, and so on. If the whole of our conscious experience is ontologically reducible to the reality that underlies the brain as experienced, then all of these relationships have correlates in the brain, and the relationships can be explained there. Our inner and outer perspectives are simply different ways of knowing the same reality, with the inner directly experienced nonrelational view subsumed within the substance of that reality and the outer indirect and relational view encompassing the whole of the same reality in its perspective. Nothing that is known via the inner perspective is not also known via the outer perspective *in some form*.

A Complete Account Maps the Nonrelational to the Relational

That does not mean, however, that nothing is lost if we simply adopt the external perspective and thereafter ignore the internal perspective entirely. The external perspective is a purely relational view; nothing known via our externally oriented senses and through relationships to other things in the world or ideas in our head can be anything other than purely relational. The inner direct and nonrelational aspect of conscious experience – the direct access that gives us the various experiences that are 'like something', whether it be redness, softness, or simply consciousness of consciousness itself – cannot be encompassed nonrelationally in the purely relational external observer's perspective. The fact of their existence as correlates and the fact and nature of their relationships to each other and to the non-conscious world can be encompassed, but the nonrelational knowledge of what they are like cannot. This is a nonverbal experience that cannot be expressed relationally.

We cannot know what red is like by reading about it in a book or seeing its correlates in the brain, only by actually experiencing it directly and nonrelationally (cf. Chalmers, 1996, p. 103 on Jackson's knowledge argument (Jackson, 1982, p. 130)). Accordingly, we cannot help but lose that direct and nonrelational aspect of our knowledge if we simply adopt the external perspective and thereafter ignore the internal perspective entirely. Only by including these direct nonrelational experiences *as* direct nonrelational experiences in our account through mapping them to their physical correlates and the associated explanation of how these physical correlates work can we avoid losing them in this way.

Nor is this a trivial matter. The direct, nonrelational experiences we would otherwise be discarding are a key characteristic of what we are seeking to explain. If we leave them out of our account and simply talk about conscious experience in terms of its external correlates, we give a misleading view of what it is we are aiming to explain. We essentially assume we are zombies lacking conscious experience (cf. Chalmers, 1996, p. 95) and that brain events and states exist with no associated inner experiences – that what we are explaining is not accompanied by these inner experiences. Because these are ontologically reducible to the reality underlying the brain and to their external correlates, our explanations of them in terms of their external correlates will be valid and complete. However, both our description of the problem we are solving and our scientific account of the encompassed ontological reality will be incomplete and misleading.

Only by including these experiences in our account through mapping them to their physical correlates and the associated explanation of how these correlates work can we avoid this situation. Our direct, nonrelational experiences must be part of our scientific account of conscious experience; we must keep them in the picture. Chalmers is right up to a point – we cannot simply have them disappear, as Dennett has suggested they might. If the perspective on conscious experience presented here is correct, the truth of things lies somewhere between the views of Chalmers and Dennett as expressed above (Chalmers 1995, 1996, 2003; Dennett 1988, 1991). There is no uniquely hard problem to solve, but neither is there a position where our inner experiences are discarded and left unexplained.

Nonrelational Knowledge is Physical Knowledge

Notice that this additional nonrelational knowledge is knowledge of something physical, is physical itself, and is physical knowledge in both senses – we are not adding something nonphysical to the equation. If these nonrelational experiences are entirely ontologically reducible to the reality underlying their external correlates, they are both knowledge of something physical and physical themselves. We are not adding something nonphysical to the equation by mapping them into the external observer's account. Nor are we adding something new to the physical reality already known to the external observer, as would presumably be the case if they were added as new 'fundamental properties'.

The position is that the nonrelational knowledge contained in these 'like something' and 'like this' experiences is entirely reducible to some ontological reality known to the external observer. Only direct experiential knowledge of the fact of these inner views and the accompanying details of what they are like to the inside observer are added, nothing else. Nothing of substance is added to the mix. All that is added are some additional nonrelational perspectives on relational things known. Perspectival knowledge that cannot be encompassed in the external observer's relational perspective 'as is' because, being nonrelational, it cannot be encompassed in relational form.

Nonrelational Knowledge: Trivial but Essential

Notice also, that this additional perspectival knowledge is trivial in respect of its information content. It does not add information that changes the science of it; it does not add operationally useful knowledge to the scientific account over and above encompassing the fact that there is an inner view and what it is like. It incorporates the recognition that our conscious experiences are 'like something' and that, in individual cases such as knowledge of redness, sweetness, or empty consciousness, they are 'like this' – like redness, sweetness, or empty consciousness. Our nonrelational knowledge is not knowledge that will somehow alter or add to the standard scientific account of the external correlates of these inner experiences and is trivial in that sense. It is, however, knowledge without which, as was indicated above, both our description of the problem we are solving and our scientific account of the encompassed ontological reality are incomplete and misleading – knowledge that is trivial in scientific terms but essential to a complete account nonetheless.

Scientifically Justifiable to Add Inner Experiences?

Is it scientifically justifiable to map (and so add) inner experiences such as redness, sweetness, or empty consciousness to a scientific account of the functioning of the brain? Can science ever justifiably accept the existence of such inner experiences as empirically established fact? Arguably, the answer is yes. When we set up a controlled experimental environment in the external world and find that every scientist who makes observations in that environment always reports the same results, we justifiably regard whatever is repeatedly observed in this way as empirical fact. Notice, however, that even in instances where several scientists are all observing a single instance of the experimental environment in question and all are reporting identical results, what each of them is really reporting is the effect of the external environment on his or her own experiential landscape. They are reporting, not on the external environment as such, but on how that environment impacts their inner experiences. If we conduct a particular scientific experiment that involves two white-coloured liquids that turn purple when mixed and all observers report the same purple colour change, we justifiably accept on that basis that the colour change in the chemicals in the circumstances in question is empirical fact. We accept this even though what each is actually reporting is the occurrence in their own experiential landscape of a purple effect - even though they are actually reporting the occurrence of a particular kind of inner experience.

What then is the difference between this situation and one in which the controlled experimental environment is a particular kind of electrical stimulation of some aspect of an individual observer's brain? If every human observer so stimulated reports the occurrence of blueness or sweetness or what we have labelled empty consciousness, can we not justifiably conclude that the occurrence of the experience in question in the experimental circumstances in question is empirical fact?

One might object that no one can actually ever jointly observe exactly the same experimental conditions, but only the conditions in question as set up in their own brain, but this is commonly the case in all scientific experimentation. If twenty scientists all set up identical experiments in entirely different labs across several continents and all report the same result, we do not quibble that each was observing a different instance of the experiment. Why, then, should we do so if the experimental conditions in question can only be set up and observed by individual scientists in different brains?

One might object that we cannot prove that what one scientist calls purple is the same as what another calls purple, but this also holds true for the mixing of chemicals experiment described above. We can only be sure that all of the observers are reporting the occurrence of an experience they have jointly agreed to call purple. We cannot be sure that the experience in question is exactly the same for everyone (although there are no grounds either for holding that it is not, especially if we can show that the same brain conditions occur in everyone whenever the experience is reported).

Arguably, therefore, we may in time be able to regard the occurrence of our various inner experiences in particular circumstances as empirical fact. There is no substantial difference between reporting on events in the external world and reporting on events in the internal world. All of our observations are observations of inner experiences. It may, in time, be scientifically justifiable to map (and so add) inner experiences such as redness, sweetness, or empty consciousness to a scientific account of the functioning of the brain as suggested above.

An Internal Scientific Account of Experience and Behaviour

We can say a number of things about the account of conscious experience we are left with on the basis of the above (at least, we can once it has been developed to the fullest scientific extent):

1. It is an account that can only be fully encompassed and completely understood from an internal observer's perspective – which is to say, from within the panorama of conscious experience.
2. It is a complete account of both experience and behaviour (since every possible experience will necessarily entail an associated behaviour and vice versa).
3. It is an account that offers us a full behavioural and experiential perspective on the human animal, one that includes both known and expected variations from a notional undamaged norm and known and expected variations caused by mental and physical damage.
4. It is an account where a fully correct external observer's flesh, blood, and brain view is the arbiter of scientifically arrived at truth, covering every aspect of the human organism and its variations knowable from both the inner and outer perspectives of the organism.
5. It is an account that encompasses and entails a relational, indirectly known, external observer's explanation of all of the ways of acting, thinking, and feeling possible within any and every possible human variation and developmental stage.
6. It is an account that covers every possible variation of fixed self and flavour of transcendent self-view (individual instantiations of which will vary as regards combinations of learned self facets and knowledge acquisition and creation skills).
7. It is an account that maps together the internal and external reflections of all of the possible ways of acting, thinking, and feeling required to produce a complete account of the human animal.
8. It is a complete account of the human organism that is itself recognised as a subset of the whole inner experience that the transcendent perspective encompasses.

Implications for the Transcendent Perspective | 411

9. It is a subset of the transcendent self-view that is recognised as one way of relating to and understanding both the nature of the universe at large and of the humans within it (albeit a very important one with the substance, detail, and experiential and analytical certainty of science behind it).

10. It is an account with significant explanatory power. An account that identifies and explains the functions that are the externally known correlates of every possible aspect and variation of the human inner world. One that maps these functions and explanations to the directly known, nonrelational inner observer's view of them – something that (self-evidently) is only possible from the internal observer's perspective. An account that thereby not only explains the single ontological reality that underlies both the functions and their inner correlates but clarifies the nature of what is being explained by mapping the externally known functions to the fact and the nature of the internally known experiences they are correlated with.

11. It is an account that sits comfortably within the transcendent self-view as a very important and significant self-world perspective. A perspective that is one among the many we are likely to find useful, but that, being scientifically correct, will always be key when humans encounter situations where the avoidance of conflict with the way the world actually is matters has an important bearing on appropriate response selection.

12. It is an account that allows us to understand why it is that conscious experiences have never been observed in the brain and do not seem to be things that could be observed there. An account in which the brain we know is the reality of the human organism as experienced by an outside observer. Where it is an experiential way of knowing that is itself a subset of that inner view and that cannot be reasonably held to contain anything other than more detailed aspects of the same outside observer's experienced way of knowing the reality of the human organism.

13. It is an account that allows us to explain experiences like redness, a solid feel, or simple empty consciousness in terms of externally known things and relationships. One that allows us to explain them in terms of differences between our visual or tactile systems and external world stimuli, say, or between some aspect of the sleeping but not dreaming organism and the awake organism, and a mapping of these to the inner experiences themselves.

14. It is an account characterised here as noneliminative physicalism. An account where the (noneliminated) inner view has to be mapped to the outer view because the nonrelational inner view is epistemologically irreducible to the outer relational view, but where this irreducibility is not a problem because the two are simply different ways of knowing the same thing. The inner view is entirely subsumed within the reality that underlies the outer view; all of it, including the irreducible nonrelational 'like something' directly known aspect, is ontologically reducible to that reality. Consciousness and why it is 'like something' is explained as a function in the brain: this or that is switched on, this or that threshold has been exceeded, or whatever. All that is left unaccounted for is what it is like for someone when these things happen in the reality underlying our experience of the brain – a problem readily solved by mapping the (noneliminated) epistemologically irreducible but ontologically reducible internal experience to our external view of it.

An Erroneous Assumption Revisited

It was noted in Chapter 9 that allowing a fixed view of the world to dominate our view of things could have negative consequences if and when a situation was encountered where that view was in conflict with how the world actually is. The problems associated with the erroneous assumption that our flesh, blood, and brain perspective is *the* reality of who and what we humans are and encompasses everything that we are arguably provide a real-life example of such negative consequences.

If what has been argued above is true, allowing the assumption to stand blocks the full instantiation of the transcendent perspective in a way that leads to the various difficulties described in Chapter 23 when we attempt to formulate a scientific account of conscious experience. It leads us to conclude that there is an unbridgeable gap between the experiential world of sensations, feelings, and thoughts and the 'fleshy grey matter' of the brain that makes the problem of explaining conscious experience look uniquely hard and impossible to resolve. Removing this erroneous assumption, on the other hand – recognising that this flesh, blood, and brain view is actually a scientifically accurate external observer's *perspective* on the whole of the *substance* of our human reality – seems to allow us to find a way to a solution. If what was argued above holds true, it opens up a path to a perspective on conscious experience and the flesh, blood, and brain perspective on the human organism where there is no explanatory gap and no hard problem of consciousness.

This, of course, is an important outcome in its own right, but it also helps highlight the first of three ways in which the transcendent perspective can be seen as important to science. If the case made on this front is sound, it shows how failing to distinguish between reality and our perspective on reality can block the path to solving a problem and how recognising the distinction – as someone with a fully instantiated transcendent perspective would – can remove the block. It shows us a situation where, on the face of it, having the transcendent self-view in place and recognising all world-views as perspectives might help someone solve a scientific problem.

The Transcendent Perspective and Science #1

Adopting and instantiating the transcendent self-view trains us to distinguish clearly between our views of the world and the world itself. It allows us to see even scientifically arrived at views of how the world is as perspectives on reality provisionally seen as true rather than as final, fully accurate reflections of *the* reality of the aspect of the world that is their focus.

This is a good attitude for scientists to adopt (cf. Chapter 22), in that it correctly reflects the preferred scientific view of scientifically arrived at knowledge. In theory at least, scientists never regard any particular view science has developed as necessarily final. Such ideas about how the world is are always seen as viewpoints that fit the facts as they are currently known rather than as final, fully accurate reflections of *the* reality of the aspect of the world that is their focus. This is a sensible approach, tried and tested more than once in the long history of scientific endeavour. Newton's view of gravity stood unchallenged for centuries before Einstein put forward an alternative view that matched the observed facts better (Siegel, 2019).

It is also in line with Karl Popper's widely accepted position that science does and should proceed, not by looking for confirmatory evidence of existing theories but by making bold predictions about the nature of the world and discovering how resilient they are by seeking refutational evidence (Popper, 1963). If we start from the assumption that it is just obvious that all swans are white and look only for confirmatory evidence, confirmatory evidence is all we will likely find. If we start from a recognition that the notion that all swans are white is a perspective on reality that might be wrong and look for instances that disprove the theory, we may eventually find that there are black swans in the world and thereby learn something new. We will likely discover that the theory that all swans are white is not true.

A perspective is something that might be wrong and that can be revisited and reworked in the light of new evidence in a way that a view taken to represent *the* reality of some aspect of the world is not. Distinguishing between the two can be important in respect of illuminating scientific problems and advancing scientific knowledge; the example of the allegedly hard problem of consciousness tackled above being a possible case in point. Adopting and instantiating the transcendent self-view of the world teaches us to see every view we can have as one view of the world among many rather than as some final and unchangeable view of how the world actually is. This is exactly the view on things we would expect a scientist to adopt, and it is arguably the case that adopting and instantiating the transcendent self-view should be both a key concern for the scientist and a key element of the education of any and every scientist.

The Transcendent Perspective and Science #2

There are two other ways in which the transcendent perspective can be seen as important to science. One relates to fully developed transcendent humans whose brains are nondivergent in the sense of being mentally and physically undamaged; the other relates to those outwith this category, either because they have nondivergent brains but fixed or underdeveloped but developing selves, or because they have brains that are in some sense damaged. The points made below under these headings also help further clarify the transcendent perspective itself.

1: Nondivergent Transcendent Humans

Given that the flesh, blood, and brain view of humans is itself an experience within consciousness as claimed, and assuming that the relationship of consciousness to the brain is as outlined above, we are left with a particular view of the relationship between the transcendent perspective and science. It is a view that looks like this:

The core of the transcendent perspective consists of empty consciousness as experienced and every possible descriptive and operational self-world perspective that it can contain, a panorama that encompasses the whole range of possible nondivergent transcendent human experiences and ways of acting and thinking in the world. This range includes the scientific view of the human organism and of the world at large. The scientific view of the human organism and of the world at large is an account that covers both divergent and nondivergent humans. However, the important point that we are focusing on here is that a subset of it identifies and explains the functions that are the externally known correlates of every possible aspect of our nondivergent transcendent inner world. It also maps these functions and explanations to the directly known, nonrelational inner observer's view of them.

In this way, the subset not only explains the single ontological reality that subsumes both the functions and their inner correlates but also clarifies the nature of what is being explained by mapping the externally known functions to the fact and the nature of their internally known correlates. It is an account that recognises our nondivergent transcendent inner experiences, including the 'like something' experience of consciousness itself, as having a key role in describing our knowledge of these brain functions and that therefore includes these experiences as an essential part of its account of these functions.

This means it is an account that must ultimately sit within our conscious experience to be fully understood, as well as having to be placed there because of its correct position within the transcendent perspective. It also means it is an account that requires a science that accepts the case made in this book about the transcendent self-view and the form of a scientific account of conscious experience to both recognise the existence of and encompass empty consciousness within the scientific view of the organism. This point is worth noting here, not only because it is important in its own right but also because it has a minor bearing on our consideration – in the final two chapters of the book – of the question of how the transcendent perspective impacts on our religious views.

2: Fixed-Self Nondivergent and Divergent Humans

The above is not, of course, all-encompassing. It deals only with what, in this book at least, is regarded as the standard nondivergent, fully developed human. It deals with how science relates to the transcendent perspective and nondivergent humans, but not with how science relates to humans in general.

As far as the transcendent perspective itself is concerned, it encompasses everything important about the relationship with science. As far as a science like psychology is concerned, however, it encompasses only the science of the nondivergent and fully developed human. It does not cover such things as the science of the wide variety of possible fixed-self nondivergent humans, the science of nondivergent humans developing towards either the fixed or the fully-developed transcendent state, or the science of humans who have brains damaged in some way.

These variations on the nondivergent and fully developed human are not especially important to a book on the transcendent perspective, except in one sense. We can assume that psychology and related sciences accepting the position taken in this book would regard a full scientific account of the nondivergent and fully developed transcendent human as a baseline. We can assume it would regard it as a baseline against which to describe, measure, and explain such fixed self, developmental, and damaged or divergent variants, as well as a basis for (where appropriate) planning action to resolve developmental issues or plan and implement remedial programmes. We can imagine a scientific psychology might categorise various kinds of experiential and behavioural 'conditions' as fixed-self type issues (some based on specific ideas, others on features like emotional attachment), developmental issues, or divergent or damaged brain issues according to how they varied from the fully-developed transcendental norm. We can also imagine it used as a basis for planning action to correct even the damaged brain through reprogramming or alternate programming based on transcendental principles.

Our Experienced World Also Maps to the World as Such

It is important to note in relation to the above that while it is valid in this view to see everything in the experienced world as a conscious experience we can map to brain events, it is equally valid to treat it as mapping to the world itself. These experiences map to brain events in terms of substance and the information content encompassed in that substance in the view presented, but their information content maps to the world at large. When we talk of conscious experience mapping to correlates in the brain, we are talking only in terms of substance – something taken here to encompass anything physical, including such 'non-solid' physical things as electrical discharges. In terms of information content, our experiential landscape maps to the world at large – something that is possible because information about the world at large is received via our senses, processed via our brain, and thereby encoded within the substance of these correlates in the brain.

Notice, moreover, that it is the panorama of all conscious experience that contains both the outside observer's view of the organism and its brain and the mapping of aspects of the brain as experienced to the wider panorama of conscious experience. The outside observer's experience of the human organism is a subset of the inside observer's experience of the human organism, not vice versa. To assume otherwise and to do so habitually, so that the inside observer's perspective is habitually made subordinate to the outside observer's perspective, is to assume that our true relationship to ourselves is that of an outside observer. This is a clearly erroneous position that, as we have just seen, can cause confusion when dealing with issues such as the question of the relationship of conscious experience to the brain. Particularly so if the erroneous perspective in question is allowed to become a fixed self or a fixed-self facet, a topic we will look at in more detail in Chapter 26, where we will look at the relationship between our sensory constructs and the world they reflect.

The Mental and the Physical in This Perspective

One final point worth noting here is that the mental is a particular aspect of the physical in this perspective; they are not two entirely different things with a mysterious gap between them. Some physical states are also experiences that contain, express, and present information; mental states are features of particular types of physical state. The mental is physical in this view, and the physical world entails a mental aspect (cf. Shand, 2021).

If we think in terms of an electronic discharge that is both experienced redness and the external observer's view of it as a brain event, we can see how it can be the same physical event known in different ways. We can see how the external observer can know it indirectly and relationally via its relationships to the senses and to other things in the world (and via a way of knowing that is physically distinct and separate from the reality known). We can see how the internal observer can know it directly and nonrelationally in circumstances where the way of knowing concerned is wholly subsumed within and entirely ontologically reducible to the reality of the electronic discharge itself. We can see how the external observer can know the whole of the reality that is the electronic discharge in relational terms and therefore be able to explain everything about it *in relational terms*, including the wholly subsumed inner experience that is the red experience. We can also see how the external observer would nonetheless be unable to encompass the nonrelational red experience itself within its relational account simply because it is a purely relational account.

We can see, in short, how the mental can be physical, despite the apparent gap between the two as we often envisage them. We can see that the gap can be purely perspectival in nature if the position regarding the ontological reducibility but epistemological irreducibility of conscious experiences to certain brain events is as proposed in this book.

Whether or not our experiences are electronic discharges is, of course, a matter requiring future research. It is simply easier to envisage experiences and brain events being one and the same thing if we think in terms of the possibility that we are talking about electronic discharges rather than some aspect of our brains we think of as more solid. It is easier to see how the mental can be physical and how the physical can have a mental aspect if we think in terms of electronic discharges. However, it is entirely possible to envisage that some other aspects of the working brain may be at the heart of this issue, especially when we consider that our notions of 'more solid' are themselves based on sensory experiences related to touch and the like.

Conscious Robots: An Aside

An interesting aside to this concerns whether or not a robot could ever be conscious. If mental experiences are wholly physical, then this must at least be a possibility. Especially if we take it that the empty consciousness experience (the referent of the 'why like anything?' question) is the core of the problem as regards making this feasible and that all other conscious experiences may well be merely variations on that core.

It might, of course, be that the only physical things that can also be mental are organic in nature, and that this might rule out conscious robots on either practical or moral grounds. It might, on the other hand, be that any organic elements required for such robots would be of a trivial nature and raise no difficult practical or moral difficulties, or that some non-organic elements of the physical world might have the right characteristics. (In this regard, it is worth noting that a range of neuroscientists 'seat minds in the electromagnetic (EM) fields generated by neural impulses' (Jones, 2019, p. 91)). Examples are John (2001); Jones (2019); McFadden (2020); and Pockett (2012). If such fields are the basis of consciousness, the development of a non-organic consciousness might become feasible. Some researchers certainly think it may be possible (see, for example, Fingelkurts et al., 2012).

This is all purely speculative, of course, but it is arguably worth a small aside here, not least because the possibility of conscious robots might have other implications related to several of the topics covered in this book. Would we aim to programme such robots so that they had a transcendent perspective on self and world in place? If so, how would we programme them to ensure they always acted in a moral and safe fashion? Would we prefer, rather, to give them fixed selves that would block out any harmful behaviour? If we did, how could we ensure they would not eventually arrive at the transcendent perspective on self and world by themselves? These, fortunately, are not questions we need tackle here but are, arguably, worth a mention in passing.

Summary

Recognising that the brain we know is an experience inside consciousness – a way of knowing the actual brain rather than the brain as such – involves a small shift in our perspective on things but arguably has significant consequences. These include removing a potential barrier to the instantiation of the transcendent perspective, leaving us with a perspective on conscious experience that resolves the hard problem of consciousness, and providing a practical illustration of the dangers of allowing a fixed view to dominate our view of how the world is. They also entail implications that further clarify the nature of the transcendent perspective and its relationship to the scientific worldview (and vice versa).

The next and final chapter of this section of the book adds some further clarification. It deals with the question of whether we should regard our images and other sensory constructs of such things as the sun, a mountain, or a brain as being something other than the real sun, the real mountain, or the real brain. This is a topic of interest in its own right. However, it is mainly of concern here because of its possible impact on the transcendent perspective, in that there is again the danger of creating a fixed self or fixed-self facet through an erroneous hidden assumption that we are always only outside observers of self and world.

26

Conscious Experience and the Real Thing

Fixed-Self Facets Hidden in Other Areas

We noted in Chapter 25 that, while it is valid to see everything in the experienced world as a conscious experience we can map to brain events, it is equally valid to treat our experienced world as the world as such. Our experiences map to brain events in terms of substance and the information content encompassed in that substance, but the information content itself maps to the world at large.

We further noted that we should be careful when considering these mappings to recognise that the outside observer's experience of the human organism is a subset of the inside observer's experience of the human organism, not vice versa. To assume the opposite of this and to do so habitually, so that the inside observer's perspective is habitually made subordinate to the outside observer's perspective, is to assume that our true relationship to ourselves is that of an outside observer.

This is a clearly erroneous position that gives rise to the difficulties addressed in Chapters 23-25 as regards the hard problem of consciousness and the blocking of the full implementation of the transcendent perspective.

The aim of the present chapter is to ensure that this same erroneous perspective is not permitted to creep into our ways of seeing things via another route.

A question that can sensibly arise from the perspective on conscious experience outlined above concerns whether we should regard our images and other sensory constructs of things like the sun, a mountain, or a brain as being something other than the real sun, mountain, or brain. This is interesting in its own right but is mainly of concern here because of its possible impact on the transcendent self-view. It carries the danger of creating a fixed self or fixed-self facet through the erroneous and hidden assumption that we are always only outside observers of self and world.

Not the Real Thing?

It is tempting to assume that, if what we have before us when we see the sun, a tree, or a brain is an image of the thing in question, we must or should regard this image as being something that is not the real thing. It is tempting to assume that we must or should regard the image in question as something that is somehow not the real sun, the real tree, or the real brain.

There is clearly a sense in which this is true – it is true in the sense that our image is something other than the sun, the tree, or the brain as such. Certainly we should and must regard it – and its equivalents in other sensory modes – as being the sun, the tree, or the brain *as known* and as being the thing in question as it relates to us and our senses and physicality.

There are, however, two reasons to be wary of adopting a view of the world in which our various sensory constructs of the sun, the mountain, the brain, and everything else are *habitually* seen as 'not the real thing'. The first is that it is a dubious position to take: there is a meaningful sense in which our sensory construct of a mountain, of the sun, or of the brain *is* the real thing for all intents and purposes. In a world where knowing is our only way of accessing real objects, it effectively is the real thing *as it is known to and relates to us*. The second is that to habitually assume otherwise is essentially the same as again blocking the successful instantiation of the transcendent perspective by always assuming we are always only outside observers of self and world.

The Real Thing as it is Known to and Relates to us

The claim that there is a meaningful sense in which our sensory construct of a mountain, the sun, or the brain is the real thing for all intents and purposes rests on four points.

The first is that it is a truism to say that our multi-modal sensory construct of a mountain, say, *is* the mountain *as it is known to and relates to us*. This is true even in an initial encounter where we see it for the first time and experience it by walking up it, exploring a cave on it, or studying its soil or its rock types and formations. Even in these initial circumstances, our multi-modal sensory construct entails a wealth of knowledge of how it relates to us via the various experiences it encompasses.

The second is that we can, in theory, build on the knowledge content of our initial experiential construct so that it ultimately encompasses a wholly complete knowledge of the object in question. We can, in theory, build on the initial knowledge content until it encompasses both a total experiential knowledge of it in all possible circumstances and (via scientific study) an associated knowledge of its various relationships to everything in the world, including ourselves. This enhanced multi-modal sensory construct can entail a full knowledge of all aspects of the reality of the mountain; it can entail knowledge and experience of every aspect of the real mountain. It is, so to speak, the real mountain expressed as information.

The third is that we can say that the externally observed physical system that creates consciousness of the mountain encompasses the whole externally observed sensed world and that, in this context, the part of it that gives us the sensory construct of the mountain is the actual mountain. Our conscious experience does not map to the whole world and the real mountain in terms of substance, but it does in terms of information content, and the information content that gives us the sensory construct of the mountain comes from the real mountain.

Moreover, if our enhanced multi-modal sensory construct can entail a full knowledge of all aspects of the reality of the mountain to the extent that it is the real mountain expressed as information, our sensory construct can potentially come from the whole of the reality of the real mountain. It can encompass the whole of the reality of the real mountain expressed as information. In the ever-changing ocean of information that is both our panorama of conscious experience and the real world to us – and that even encompasses the reality of ourselves to us – it is the part of that world that is the real mountain expressed as information. In a world in which every object and even the space between them is effectively an emitter of information, it is that aspect of the 'ocean' that is (or can be) the whole of the real mountain expressed as information transmitted to us by the real mountain.

The fourth is that it is safe to say that, without such knowledge and experience, there would effectively be no mountain as far as we are concerned – we either experience it and otherwise know it or it does not exist for us. Our access to reality is entirely dependent on our experiencing and otherwise knowing it. Our enhanced, multi-modal sensory construct may only be the mountain as experienced and otherwise known, but it is the closest to the reality of the mountain we can possibly come – the very best we can do. It is the reality of the mountain for all intents and purposes. It is the reality of the mountain as it is known to and relates both to us and (potentially) everything else – and the same applies to the sun, the brain, or anything else in our knowledge and experience. There is a meaningful sense in which they are the real thing for all intents and purposes.

Only Habitual Distinction a Problem
Mistake to Always see it in This way

Notice that none of this means that it is wrong to distinguish between our sensory constructs and the reality of the mountain, or the sun, or the brain as such. It is entirely valid to note that a sensory construct is the thing as known and as it relates to us and other things, rather than the thing as such. A problem with seeing our enhanced multi-modal sensory construct as not the real thing only arises if we *habitually* see our sensory world in this way; the problem is not distinguishing between it and the reality as such, but in doing so habitually in our everyday lives.

Adopting this perspective is not only unnecessary – as we have seen above, our ways of knowing the things in the world are the real things for all intents and purposes – but also, for a variety of reasons, unnecessarily unhelpful. Aside from anything else, always distinguishing between the things in the world we see and otherwise sense and some other 'thing itself' beyond them is certainly an awkward and possibly confusing approach to everyday life. But there are other, more serious, difficulties with the approach – it interferes with the successful instantiation of the transcendent perspective in two different, if linked, areas. It confuses the information we receive via our senses as regards the nature of any given situation we are in and creates a fixed self or a fixed-self facet that skews our behavioural and experiential relationship to the world in any such situation.

Interference With the Transcendent Perspective

The sun, mountain, or brain as we experience it at any given time is an encoding of information about the external aspect of the situation we are in at a given point in time. In a similar way, our experience of ourselves is an encoding of information about the internal aspect of the situation we are in at a given point in time. Left to themselves, these sources of information about our inner and outer environments act in the context of the transcendent self-view to select the best possible response choice from our wholly-variable repertoire as a reaction to the situation in question.

Overlaying our raw experiences of the sensed objects in our situation with the notion that they are something other than the real thing seems likely to confuse our response choice mechanism. It seems likely it will tend to skew the effect of the choosing mechanism in an unhelpful way, even if the remainder of the transcendent self-view is operating in a wholly-variable way. The remainder of the transcendent self-view is unlikely to be operating in a wholly-variable way in the circumstances described, however. In a mental landscape where sensed objects are habitually regarded as 'not the real thing', there will be a fixed self or a fixed-self facet in place, ensuring that the response repertoire will be something less than a wholly-variable one.

Always and Only Outside Observers?

Although it may not be immediately obvious on first consideration, habitually distinguishing between sensed or experienced objects and another real object beyond them entails the same difficulty we examined in Chapter 23. It is effectively the same as always assuming that the flesh, blood, and brain view of humans is *the* reality of humans and that our conscious experiences must therefore be encompassed within it.

If we habitually see the mountain *as known* as being not the real mountain, with the implication that there is a real mountain beyond it, we effectively assume we are always and only outside observers of ourselves and the world. We effectively take an outside observer's view of the sensing organism and the mountain, dividing them up on the grounds that they are separate things on the basis of substance and placing the images in the brain, and we make that perspective habitual. By envisaging a real mountain beyond the sensed mountain, we essentially envisage the sensed mountain as being inside the part of the physical world associated with ourselves and distinct from the part associated with the mountain. Doing this habitually is essentially the same as always adopting an outside observer's relationship to the world, creating either a fixed self or a fixed-self facet that blocks the successful operation of the transcendent self-view.

Another way of looking at this may make the point more clearly. Suppose we always treat the world we experience as the world as we know it without further qualification about experienced objects not being the real thing – an entirely reasonable approach given what we argued earlier. In this scenario, we experience a world in which the person we experience is the person we experience, the mountain we experience is the mountain we experience, and we are of or in the world we experience.

If we habitually think in terms of the person we experience, the mountain we experience, and the world as a whole we experience as being 'not the real thing', we adopt an entirely different perspective. We essentially take up a position where we habitually see both ourselves, the mountain, and the world they inhabit as being 'out there beyond us'. We habitually see ourselves as not being in or of the world but as being outside observers of it and everything it contains. This is true of ourselves, the mountain, and the world as a whole, but is particularly evident if we think of how we see ourselves in such a perspective. If our real self is somewhere beyond our experience of ourselves, we can only be standing outside of ourselves and viewing ourselves as an outside observer would.

Not the Real Thing?

In summary, we should avoid habitually seeing the mountain, the sun, or the brain we see and otherwise sense as being not the real thing but an image of the real thing with the real thing out there beyond it. To do so is confusing, unnecessary – it is the real thing for all intents and purposes – and a barrier to the successful instantiation and operation of the transcendent self-view. It creates either a fixed self or a fixed-self facet based on the mistaken assumption that we are always and only ever external observers of ourselves and the world.

PART 7
Being, Religion and Consciousness

Part 7: Outline of the Case Presented

Looking at the question of religious beliefs further clarifies the transcendent perspective. Adopting it as a self-view has various implications for how we should regard religious viewpoints – with a particular issue being the need to regard them as useful and meaningful fictions that reflect a real aspect of the human relationship to the universe:

In a fully instantiated transcendent self-view, a particular religious view has to be recognised as one among many religious and other viewpoints regarded as having a valid role in the total human relationship to the universe. This may not be wholly problematic for most believers, especially as their chosen religious position can be held, recognised, and used as the believer's preferred view, albeit only under the overarching control of the transcendent self. Another required adjustment may be problematic, however – this being the fact that religious views must be regarded as either partially or wholly fictional depending on the extent to which they do or do not align with the scientific view of how the world is **(Chapter 27)**.

For those who find the idea that their views on deities and creation are really just useful fictions unacceptable, there is an alternative that may be slightly more palatable. In this pantheistic position, the universe itself is viewed as the deity, and knowing empty consciousness can even be characterised as entailing direct knowledge of this 'deity'. Such a view would still be regarded as a useful fantasy in the context of the transcendent perspective but might be more acceptable to believers, given that both elements would arguably be accepted by science as having a real, observable existence. **(Chapter 28)**.

27

Creation, Being, Religion, Science, and Consciousness #1

On Being Transcendentally Religious
Self, World and Self-World Relationship

We noted in Chapter 2 that any given view of the self can equally well be held or expressed as a view of the world or of the self-world relationship. This, in essence, means that, in adopting a transcendent perspective on the self, we also effectively adopt a transcendent perspective on the world and on the self-world relationship. Adopting the transcendent perspective on the self effectively means adopting a transcendent perspective on everything. This has a particular bearing on the impact of the transcendent perspective on how we should see and relate to the kinds of questions addressed by the plethora of world religions – questions about creation, existence, being, and related issues.

The Transcendent Perspective and Religious Beliefs

There is, on the face of it, a conflict between the transcendent self-view (and, hence, the transcendent perspective on the world and on the self-world relationship) and religious beliefs. At least, we can assume so if the religious beliefs are seen as unarguably true, as coming from whatever deity is at their core, are seen as being the basis of an unquestioning faith, and are seen and treated as the dominant perspective of a fixed self (fundamentalist views of this kind are found in many religions; see, e.g., Pollack et al., 2023).

Religious beliefs this strongly held will clearly be at odds with a transcendent self-view that sees all human perspectives on self and world as temporary roles and sees none of them as the one dominant and unquestionably true perspective on either self or world. There will also likely be problems with the fact that it additionally encompasses a questioning, sceptical, scientific approach to everything as a key element (Chapter 22). Fortunately, a closer examination not only dispels the notion that there is necessarily a conflict – the position seems able to accommodate even faith-based religious beliefs to a significant degree (or arguably so) – it also helps further clarify the transcendent perspective itself.

Individual readers will obviously make up their own minds on whether or not the transcendent self-view (and, hence, the transcendent perspective on the world and on the self-world relationship) undermines religion-based views of the self and the world. The view taken here is that it does not – that the position seems able to accommodate religious beliefs to a significant degree. Except for those whose religious beliefs are very hard-line, the transcendent perspective does not appear to undermine religion any more than it does science, although it does require more flexibility from those espousing religious beliefs than may be palatable for some. The various facets of the issue are considered below and in the next chapter.

Religious Beliefs as Valid Subordinate Relationships [1]

Religious Beliefs: A Valid Role

There are four aspects to how the fully instantiated transcendent self-view sees and treats religious beliefs. The first of the four is that, since every possible self-world perspective is seen as part of the total human self-world relationship, religious perspectives are recognised as having a valid role in the human behavioural and experiential relationship to the world and are viewed and treated accordingly. This means they are in the total repertoire available within the transcendent self-view and that there is no barrier to, or bias against, using them if and when they are an appropriate response to an encountered circumstance.

This is as it should be. There are arguably things that religious perspectives on being and creation can help us deal with in terms of how we relate to existence that other ways of viewing the world – such as political positions or scientific perspectives – cannot normally offer. They can provide us with ways of recognising and responding to the various wonders of creation and celebrating an associated spiritual dimension to being, existence, and life in ways usually seen as beyond the scope of scientific or political perspectives. They can also offer ways in which we can share the experience of these things with others who share the same or a similar religious view of them.

This is not to say that either religious views in general or any particular example of such views are the only ways of allowing us to deal with these things. Nor is it to suggest that everyone will necessarily see them as the best ways of doing them. The point is simply that they are regarded as valid ways of doing such things, that they do offer the possibility, and that the transcendent perspective sees and treats them as possible responses to such situations.

Non-Religious Alternatives may Also Have a Valid Role

Of course, whether they are ever used or not by any given individual will depend on their circumstances. Such circumstances, as we have seen, are determined not just by conditions outwith the individual but by their own inner landscape of thoughts, needs, feelings, and past experiences. The inner landscape of some individuals may be such that they will respond to encountered situations via some particular religious belief system; the inner landscapes of others may respond to similar circumstances via other religious belief systems. Others may not feel the need to respond to 'the wonder of existence' at all, or they may find other ways – such as writing poetry or becoming humanists – more satisfying ways of doing so.

People's own inner landscapes of thoughts, needs, feelings, and past experiences are part of any circumstances they encounter. They may or may not have needs in these areas, and religious beliefs may or may not meet them. One particular set of beliefs may be found by an individual to be more satisfying in this regard than another, either because of its own inherent features or because it is preferred in the community the individual lives within. The point is that all ways of relating to the world, including all religious views, are available to the individual within the transcendent perspective and are regarded as valid ways of relating to the world should internal and external circumstances arise that make them an appropriate response.

Religious Beliefs: One Valid Aspect of our Total Relationship [2]

Not a Dominant, Habitually Preferred, Belief set

Second, since they *are* seen as sharing their valid role in the total human relationship with all other possible self-world perspectives, religious perspectives are not seen and treated as a dominant belief set habitually preferred over all other viewpoints. They are not seen and treated as they would be if used as the basis of a fixed self. In common with all other possible self-world perspectives, they are seen and treated as one among many equally valid ways of seeing and instantiating our relationship to the world at large – as one equally valid view among many.

A Valid Role of Temporary Value in Some Circumstances

In the operational and fully instantiated transcendent perspective, particular religious perspectives are seen and treated as having a valid role of possible temporary value in some circumstances. They share this position with all of the other possible self-world perspectives in the repertoire of the wholly-variable human – a repertoire that also encompasses all other religious views, non-religious alternative ways of responding to the wonder of existence, the scientific view of the universe, atheism, and so on. They do not dominate the mental and emotional landscape as they would if allowed to become the basis of a fixed self; they merely represent one possible, sometimes appropriate or optimal, temporary response among a myriad of other possible, sometimes appropriate or optimal, temporary responses.

Religious Beliefs: A Temporary True Believer [3]

Temporary Immersion a Permitted Possibility

Third, despite being under the overarching control of the transcendent self-view and seen and treated as no more (but no less) important than any other self-world perspective, they are also encompassed in an environment that permits immersion level control. One that leaves open the possibility of episodes where the perspective can be temporarily taken wholly seriously, temporarily emotionally engaged with, and temporarily regarded as true in the sense of being a valid human response to particular circumstances (a need to respond to the wonder of existence, for example). One that permits episodes where such immersion is possible and permitted under the auspices of the transcendent self-view but where there is always a return to the non-relational empty experience at the centre of the transcendent self-view at some point (see Chapter 16).

This means that, even if initial appearances suggest otherwise, there is nothing in the transcendent perspective that precludes someone from taking their religious beliefs seriously, being emotionally attached to them, or even regarding them as true. All that the transcendent self-view does is describe and instantiate a view that encompasses all possible ways of looking at and relating to the world and sees and treats every one of them as an equally valid possible response to any situation encountered. This does not preclude the inclusion of religious beliefs we take seriously, are emotionally attached to, and regard as a true or valid response to the world at large. It merely precludes taking these beliefs and that perspective on them and making them into the basis of a fixed self or a fixed-self facet that wholly or partially blocks out all other possible ways of relating to the world. It precludes ignoring the fact that there are other ways of looking at the world a person might apply when these are more appropriate to the circumstances they are in.

Rather like an actor who temporarily becomes so immersed in her role that she effectively becomes a character she is playing, we can, within the transcendent perspective, become temporarily so immersed (should we so desire it) in a particular religious perspective on things. We can temporarily take it wholly seriously, become emotionally engaged with its view of things, and even see it (temporarily) as true – unless and until the circumstances we are in change in such a way that the transcendent-self landscape reacts by pulling us out of our immersed state.

The Importance of an Immersion Control Facility

Whether we would be wise to become even temporarily immersed to this degree is another question, of course, but the transcendent perspective does not preclude it (assuming there is a reliably operational immersion control mechanism in place). We can, should we so desire it, be immersed in our religious viewpoint in these ways and to these extents on a temporary basis, knowing that the immersion level control mechanism of the transcendent self will pull us out of the immersion when the circumstances demand it. We can, for example, be so immersed that we believe our view of a deity who can save us from any threat with the magical wave of a hand is factually true. We can, with the transcendent self-view in place, do this knowing that if our world situation changes in a way that entails a need to avoid conflict with how the world actually is, we will immediately snap out of it thanks to our immersion level control facility.

This mechanism will pull us out of our religious take on things and have us adopt a more scientific or practical perspective on things that will (for example) have us running for the fire escape rather than praying to the deity for magically managed deliverance. At that point, while we will still see our religious view as a generally valid way of relating to the world at large, we will cease our emotional and other immersion in it and revert to a wider perspective on things. One where we only take it wholly seriously and regard it as factually true to the extent that it does not conflict with how science tells us the world actually is.

Science and Partially or Wholly Fictional Religious Beliefs [4]

The Deity as a Fictional Perspective

This latter point brings us to the fourth aspect of how religious beliefs are seen and treated in the fully instantiated transcendent self-view, one that may be the main problem for the religious believer. As was stated in Chapter 22, a key element of the transcendent self-view is the fact that a questioning, take-nothing-on-trust, scientific approach to everything is part and parcel of the position. This is arguably at variance with the not uncommon religious notion (see, e.g., Chao, A. D. &. T. X., 2004) of an all-powerful deity who brought the whole of creation into being, a notion that science finds no evidence of or need for in our scientific accounts of the universe (cf. Carroll, 2012; Jennings, 2011). In the context of a fully instantiated transcendent self and world-view, therefore, it is a claim that can only be regarded as a useful fiction. A wholly fictional perspective that happens to entail a real and valid way of experiencing and relating to being and existence, so long as it is not taken as true in the scientific sense. A fictional perspective on things that is useful in the sense that it provides one amongst a number of ways, religious and non-religious, of meeting a range of human needs in this area.

Immersion Only Goes so far

The transcendent position may permit immersion in the notion of an all-powerful deity who created everything, such that the believer may temporarily see this as a true view of things. However, the position adopted within the transcendent perspective before and after immersion is that the idea of a deity and an associated creation that any particular religion encompasses is a fictional viewpoint that does not align with a science-based view of the world. One that should not be used where alignment with how the world actually is matters in any circumstances encountered, even if it might be a personally preferred way of relating to the universe in other circumstances. A fictional viewpoint that encompasses a valid and potentially useful aspect of the actual total human relationship to the world at large, yes, but a fictional viewpoint nonetheless.

Transcendent Perspective Positives for the True Believer
One Among Many Valid Views Seen as Temporarily True

Individual believers will, of course, have their own views on how to regard these various elements of how the transcendent perspective sees and treats religious viewpoints, but only the last seems to represent a serious difficulty.

The first of the four is surely positive – it ensures that whatever religious beliefs an individual believer holds are seen and treated as having a valid and potentially useful role in the overall human relationship to the universe. This certainly supports the inclusion of a particular religious view in a person's repertoire of self-world perspectives.

The second of the four is, at worst, neutral. The religious position adopted is seen and treated as no more, but also no less, important than any other of the many self-world perspectives that make up the total human relationship. It is also a necessary element of the recognition that the human behavioural and experiential relationship to the world is wholly-variable – a necessary part of the truth of who we are and what we are like. A believer can take the view that this is how the deity made us and argue that said deity would therefore presumably approve of treating the associated religious perspective in this fashion. This may be more than a little convoluted, to say the least, but it still supports the contention that this second aspect of how the transcendent view sees and treats religious views is neutral, even edging into positive rather than negative for the believer.

The third of the four will surely be seen as positive – and perhaps also as edging the second further towards the positive. It offers religious believers the possibility of being able to temporarily treat their views as more important than other views of existence and being. They will be able to become temporarily so immersed in their own preferred religious beliefs that they can effectively become like true believers for a while. They will be able to mitigate the need to regard their religious viewpoint as no more important than any other viewpoint, with the possibility of temporarily seeing and treating it as a true believer might. They will be able to become wholly immersed in the role of the true believer whenever they so choose.

Transcendence as Part of the Plan?

This state will, of course, only be temporary in a transcendent mental and emotional landscape. Eventually, the circumstances they are in will change. They will revert to the rest state of the transcendent self-view, where all ways of seeing the world, including the set of religious beliefs they have just been immersed in, are seen and treated as equally valid alternative viewpoints. But this does not alter the fact that this aspect of how religious beliefs are seen and treated in the transcendent perspective can be seen as a positive in its own right as far as the true believer is concerned. Nor does it alter the fact that it can also be seen as one that offsets the fact that they are regarded as no more important than other ways of seeing things in the rest state of the transcendent perspective.

In the immersed state, they can effectively be true believers for a time, albeit under the overarching control of a state that sees and treats their beliefs as no more valid a way of relating to being and existence than any other. They can even, while in this immersed state, regard being under the overarching control of a transcendent perspective that sees and treats all views as equal as being in line with how humans were created by the deity associated with their religious beliefs. They can take the view that the deity planned things so that our overarching self-world relationship requires seeing and treating all views as equal, including their own religious views, but also so that temporary immersion in their particular preferred way of relating to the world was possible. They can take the view that these two perspectives on how their religious views are seen and treated are entirely in line with what their deity intended for them.

It is true that immersion level control implies treating immersion in their religious viewpoint as similar to how an actor treats a role, but recall that (see Chapter 14) it is more nuanced than that. The religious element of their self is seen as a role rather than their real self, not in the sense that it is wholly imaginary but in the sense that it is a limited aspect of their real or total self rather than the totality of that real self.

The fourth of the four aspects of how religious views are seen and treated in the context of the instantiated transcendent self-view is arguably the most serious source of potential conflict between the transcendent perspective and religious beliefs. More will be said on this in Chapter 28 below.

28

Creation, Being, Religion, Science, and Consciousness #2

Religious Beliefs as Useful Fictions: A Problem or not?

The Limits of Immersion

As was indicated in the last chapter, the transcendent perspective permits immersion in a religious position where the notion of an all-powerful deity who created everything is seen temporarily as an acceptable view of things. However, the view taken before and after immersion is that the idea of a deity and an associated creation that a particular religion encompasses is a fictional viewpoint in the sense that it does not align with what science regards as a defensible view of how the world is. It should not be used where alignment with a scientifically defensible view of how the world actually is matters. It may be a fictional viewpoint that encompasses a real and valid way of experiencing and relating to existence and can be regarded as a potentially useful aspect of the actual total human relationship to the world at large, but it is a fictional viewpoint nonetheless.

Acceptable to Some Believers, but Perhaps not all

This may not be a problem for all believers. Some may be able to accept that some aspects of their religions are fantasies with a kernel of truth – tales that express something true even if they are fictions. Some believers may be comfortable with the notion that their own preferred deity and creation story are something less than scientifically factual (see, e.g., Pepinster, 2017 on believers and creation myths).

It may, however, be a problem for those whose religious beliefs are very hard-line. Arguably, the transcendent perspective does not undermine religion any more than it does science, although it does require more flexibility from those espousing religious beliefs than may be palatable for some.

The Transcendent Perspective and the Universe as Deity

Pantheism of Possible Value

For those who feel a need for something more concrete at the heart of their religious beliefs, there is one particular viewpoint regarding a deity and an associated creation story that is worth a brief mention. One that must still be seen as ultimately fictional in nature, but that may feel more satisfactory to anyone persuaded to adopt the transcendent perspective but unhappy at the thought of a religion in which the deity is a fantasy and the associated story of creation a myth. A religiously-oriented outlook on questions about creation, being, and the notion of a deity that arguably aligns better than others do with the transcendent perspective on the self, the world, and the self-world relationship presented in this book.

This is not to suggest that the position in question is any more corrrect in religious terms than any other religious belief system, nor to argue that we should favour it over any other such belief system. It is simply worth a mention here for three reasons. First, because, as indicated above, it may be seen by some believers as preferable to a religion in which the deity is a fantasy and the associated story of creation a myth. Second, because it illustrates both the extent and the limits of what is possible as regards harmonising the transcendent perspective with religious viewpoints. Third, because it not only aligns better with the transcendent perspective than other religious belief systems do but also potentially provides a vehicle for its transmission.

The position in question is a form of pantheism (see, e.g., Mander, 2023; Reese, 2023). Specifically, it is a perspective that identifies the universe itself as the deity, assumes that this deity has always existed in some form and always will, and sees it as encompassing the whole of what is, including humans generally and the individual believer in particular.

Resolving the Creation Conundrum

Such a position has various useful features. The notion of an all-powerful deity that brought the universe into being by some magical means is not a helpful one. If what we are aiming to explain is how the world we know (and we ourselves) came into being out of nothingness, it is a fairly useless answer. It simply moves the problem on to the question of where the deity in question came from (and then on again presumably to what came before that and before that, and so on ad infinitum – as Close (2009, p. 42) puts it, 'you still have the question of what was the situation immediately before creation').

Identifying the universe itself as the deity and assuming this deity has always existed in some form and always will resolves this conundrum. There is no deity that brought the universe into being, only a deity that is the universe and everything in it. We are left with a deity that has always been here and always will be. A deity that exists everywhere and everywhen and encompasses everything, including ourselves and our consciousness of existence. A deity that can be seen as something amazing and unimaginable that we are all part of, that is both creator and destroyer, that brings us into being and accepts us back into its bosom when we go. A deity that is both alive and not alive, male and female and somewhere in between, timeless, omnipresent (and so on). Part of the problem we face in imagining what a creator of the universe could possibly be like is that existence itself is so strange, amazing, and wonderful that it seems we must envisage a creator even greater and more amazing – something we inevitably find hard to do. But the problem falls away if we associate our deity with creation itself.

Accepted by Science as a Known Fact?

Another positive feature is that a deity that is equated with the universe itself also has the value of being something whose existence science regards as an observed fact and something, moreover, whose nature is also increasingly known to science. As long as this religion held to the scientific view of it, it would have a deity whose existence and nature are both a matter of scientific fact, albeit one coloured by the nonscientific notion of it as a deity. Adherents need not treat the deity as a fantasy as such; its existence is a scientific and generally observable fact. Treating it as a deity may be a fanciful or somewhat poetic view of the associated scientific facts, but it does have one point in its favour. A deity whose existence and nature are within the realms of scientific fact is not one that is at variance with how the world actually is in any significant sense. Especially if any fanciful or poetic aspects that are added are recognised as such and that aspect of the religious view is recognised as useful fantasy.

No Need to Explain Creation

Nor need they regard an associated creation story as a fantasy. There is no need, in this view, to explain how either creation or the deity came into being out of a preceding nothingness; simply a need to accept that the question of how substance and energy could come out of a preceding nothingness has no good answer. We need only accept that something cannot come out of nothing and that the something (the deity in this perspective) must always have been there in some form or other – that there never was a nothingness and never will be ever.

Stephen Hawking (Hawking & Mlodinow, 2011, p. 227) has famously claimed, 'Because there is a law such as gravity, the universe can and will create itself from nothing.' But where was the law of gravity when there was only nothing? Where and how did it operate? As Meyer was quoted as commenting in a counter to Hawking's view, 'The laws of nature describe how stuff behaves once it exists. They do not explain where that stuff came from.' (Evolution News, 2023, May 18). It is also worth noting the claim of theoretical physicist Sean Carroll (2012, p. 187) that an assumption that the universe began with the big bang may yet turn out to be false. It may be that it merely marks a phase in the history of a universe that may stretch infinitely far into the past – that what it really marks at present is 'an end to our theoretical comprehension'.

Transcendence: Pantheism, Consciousness, and Knowing God

Empty Consciousness: Directly Knowing God?

There is, moreover, a further feature of interest worth mentioning here. Another attractive aspect of a religion based on creation itself as deity is that it opens up the interesting possibility that adherents can learn to know or experience the deity of the religion concerned directly and nonrelationally 'as is' by knowing nonrelational empty consciousness directly 'as is'.

The whole of creation encompasses everything that is, including us and our consciousness. It was argued in Chapter 12 that empty consciousness – the core of our transcendent self-view – was the essence of our experience, known directly and nonrelationally as itself. This means it is an aspect of creation that we can know or experience directly as itself – in a religion where creation itself is the deity, a way of knowing or experiencing an aspect of the deity directly as itself.

This is arguably an attractive feature for believers because it allows the possibility that they and any future converts can be taught how they can 'know God' or have 'direct experience of God' within the religion in question. It allows this possibility, not just in some fanciful sense but in the very real sense of directly knowing nonrelational empty consciousness – something whose existence must ultimately be accepted by science if the arguments presented in this book are sound. After all, if the points argued in chapters 12 and 25 of this book are true, then empty consciousness can arguably be held to exist on both logical and (potentially – see under the subheading '*Scientifically Justifiable to Add Inner Experiences?*' in Chapter 25) empirical grounds and has a place in a scientific view of the human organism. It is the inner observer's referent of the 'why is conscious experience like anything?' question and the central core of the transcendent self-view.

A Religion That Transmits the Transcendent Perspective?

This, in turn, suggests the possibility that a religion based on these ideas – or a religion that has adapted its notion of the deity and of creation to encompass them – might well have the teaching and transmission of the transcendent perspective as a central goal. It suggests that religion itself – or some religions at least – might offer one mechanism for moving us towards the goal of universal adoption and instantiation of the one perspective that accurately reflects our full behavioural and experiential nature.

There would, of course, be other schools and transmission vehicles with no basis in religion; every member of the human race does not have religious tendencies and would not be attracted to the religious route. Both types, of course – religious and non-religious – would, of necessity, teach the same thing. They would teach adopters a transcendent perspective that recognises religious ways of relating to the world at large as valid aspects of the total human relationship to the world at large and sees them in the ways described in this chapter. They would represent religious ways of relating to the world as views that encompass real aspects of the total human relationship to the universe but that are either partially or wholly fictional. The distinction between the two being dependent on the extent to which their view of the world aligns with what science regards as the way the world is.

There would, moreover, be a need for standards and accreditation to ensure that the teaching of the transcendent perspective did not become corrupted. All organisations – religious ones included – can have their goals and practices skewed over time, and standards and accreditation would be necessary to help prevent this. It might even be that joint religious and non-religious work on the kind of transcendence described in this book will help answer the question raised in Chapter 1 as to whether this was the same transcendence often mentioned by writers and thinkers of a religious or mystical inclination.

Useful Fictions: Pantheism, Consciousness, and Knowing God

It is, of course, important to recognise the limitations of the notion of seeing creation itself as the deity. There is, as has been noted above, no suggestion in any of this that the idea of creation as the deity is true – that it is not a fictional view of creation. As seen from within the transcendent perspective, religious belief systems are always useful fantasies that encompass real ways in which humans can relate to the universe – ways that may well have a valid role in particular circumstances – and this particular notion is no exception. Science undoubtedly accepts the existence of 'creation' – everything that is and is the focus of scientific study – but it sees no need in its explanations for the notion that creation is a deity.

The idea of seeing creation itself as the deity is still just a useful fantasy in this perspective; it is simply that it is a useful fantasy that is not in serious conflict with the world as shown to us by science. One that does not postulate the existence of something that science sees no evidence of and sees no need to invent to explain what it does find evidence of. This, in turn, means that it is less likely to be the source of negative effects caused by conflict with how the world actually is. It also means that those who wish to have something science regards as real as their deity have something more satisfactory to pay their religious respects to and wonder at than something that can otherwise only be wholly imaginary.

Mumbo Jumbo and a Mystical Spin

This can – perhaps should – still be described as 'mumbo jumbo', to use a term used early in the book. However, it is mumbo jumbo that would be specifically recognised and treated as such within the context of the transcendent perspective. A view of things that, within the overarching control of the transcendent perspective, would be seen and used as a temporary way of relating to the world that is useful and valuable in some circumstances.

This is what was meant when it was said in Chapter 1 that it was possible to put a 'mystical spin' on transcendence and its aspects as described in this book. Notions like creation as a deity, empty consciousness as direct knowledge of the deity, and the idea of transcendence as the goal of the fully developed human and part of a deity's plan for us are all examples of the kind of 'mumbo jumbo' meant. Fictions useful in certain contexts that have a valid role in our total relationship as long as they are not taken wholly seriously but, rather, recognised at some level as the fictions they are.

No Irresolvable Conflict With Religious Beliefs

In conclusion then, based on this clarification of the relationship between religious beliefs and the transcendent perspective, there is no irresolvable conflict between the two. The transcendent self-view will allow – indeed, insist on – the inclusion of religious ways of seeing and relating to the world as being of possible value in certain situations. It recognises that they can have value if we are seeking to remind ourselves of the wonder, or strangeness, or inexplicability of our existence and find ways of responding to it in line with these notions. It will even allow immersion in such viewpoints under the overarching control of the transcendent perspective itself.

The one area of difficulty is with the notion of an all-powerful deity that created the universe and ourselves. This will only align with the transcendent perspective in two sets of circumstances. The first is if the whole notion is regarded as a useful fantasy or fiction. The second is if creation itself is seen as the deity and empty consciousness as a knowable aspect of it. In this latter scenario, the deity itself and the knowable aspect of it arguably align with science and can be held to have an actual, real existence. However, other more peripheral aspects of the religious mythology surrounding creation and the creator must nonetheless be regarded as fanciful, poetic, or fictional. They cannot be regarded as immutable pronouncements from a deity so unshakeably true that we might justifiably take them as always being so unquestionable as to the basis of a fixed self.

Summary

In summary, religious beliefs do not emerge unscathed from an encounter with the transcendent perspective, but they are not necessarily irrevocably in conflict with it. Adopters of the transcendent perspective can retain religious beliefs in some form. Despite seeing all self-world perspectives as initially equivalent and equal temporary perspectives to be used and relinquished as expedient and also placing a high value on the scientific view of how the world is, the transcendent self-view can potentially accommodate faith-based religious beliefs to a significant degree. There is a case for claiming that the transcendent perspective does not undermine religion in any fatal way any more than it does science. However, it does imply and require a move away from a hard and unwavering view of religious beliefs towards a position that essentially sees and treats them as useful and meaningful fictions that reflect a real aspect of the human relationship to the universe.

Appendices

APPENDIX A

The Transcendent Perspective and Free Will

Free Will in a Deterministic Universe?

An interesting adjunct to this work concerns the transcendent self-view and the notion of free will. There is a case for saying that free will is impossible in a nondeterministic universe. How can we exercise free will unless the universe is an orderly place where cause follows effect in a predictable way so that we can make it do our bidding? But a deterministic universe would seem to preclude the possibility of free will in any true sense, for surely whatever decisions and actions we take are inevitably predetermined in such a universe?

The Transcendent Perspective and Freedom of Response Choice

The transcendent perspective cannot and does not alter this equation. What it arguably can and does do, however, is allow us to optimise the extent to which we can have freedom of response choice within a deterministic universe. The end result is not exactly what is usually meant by free will; both the path towards such optimisation and the actual response choice in any and every given situation will have been predetermined by our own nature and self-view and the nature of the universe at large. However, it will, in all probability, be sufficient to satisfy most humans who are interested enough to concern themselves with such issues.

We do Have a Level of Response Choice

There are times when there are alternative paths available, and a concerted effort will allow us to push in one direction rather than take the easy path. Most of us can learn to overcome inertia or laziness; to add that new skill and apply it – in certain instances at least. No doubt, the question of whether or not we can do this and the extent to which we can be successful is predetermined by our nature and our circumstances. But there is no question that most of us can learn to do it – it is a level of freedom of response choice possible within our deterministic universe.

Most of us can also learn to adopt a particular way of seeing ourselves and to change our way of seeing ourselves. We can learn to see ourselves as Buddhists rather than Christians or Socialists or change from seeing ourselves as Christians to seeing ourselves as Atheists (or vice versa). Again, the question of whether or not we can do this and the extent to which we can be successful will be predetermined by our nature and our circumstances, but there is no doubt that most of us can learn to do it. It too is a level of freedom of response choice possible within our deterministic universe.

Our Level of Response Choice can be Optimised

This tells us that a level of response choice is possible within our deterministic universe, which means that it is at least possible to optimise the extent to which we can have freedom of response choice within such a universe. It also tells us that most of us can choose to see ourselves in a particular way, which is to say, we can learn to adopt and instantiate the transcendent self-view as opposed to some version of a fixed self-view. If the transcendent self-view allows us to optimise the extent to which we can have freedom of response choice within our deterministic universe – and it does appear to, as we shall see – we should be able to take advantage of that. Which means our actions in respect of choosing a self-view can predetermine the extent to which we have freedom of choice in all future situations.

This is not quite free will – our future choices and actions are not unconstrained, nor are our actions in respect of choosing to adopt the self-view. On the one hand, whether or not we are able to successfully adopt the transcendent self-view will be determined by our own nature and that of the universe at large. On the other hand, the actual choices we make in any given future situation will be similarly determined. It is, however, something sufficiently like free will to satisfy most of us, especially considering the fact that free will in a nondeterministic universe is impossible. It is the best we can do in a deterministic universe, and it is arguably enough.

Our actions in respect of whether or not we adopt the transcendent self-view now will determine the extent to which our brain has an optimal ability to choose between response choices in the future. Any actual future choice made will still be determined at the point of response by our own nature and that of the universe at large, but the ability to choose the best option will have been improved by our decision to adopt the transcendent self-view in our past. We will have taken the small amount of ability to choose within our deterministic universe as seen in the overcoming inertia and choice of self-view examples touched on above and – through our own choices and actions – optimised our ability to leverage it to its optimum extent. We will have optimised the extent to which we have freedom of response choice within our deterministic universe.

The Transcendent Perspective and Optimising Response Choice

The only question then is whether or not the claim as regards the transcendent perspective optimising the extent to which we can have freedom of response choice within a deterministic universe is true, and the reasons why it is may already be obvious. Having free will arguably presupposes both having a choice between all possible alternative courses of action – anything less than all possibilities is a constraint on the level of freedom enjoyed – and also having the ability to then adopt whichever response is preferred. The habits and practices that underpin the fixed self impose an artificial limit on the range of possible situational responses available to the organism and bias the basis of any choice made between those that are available. They block out responses that might have been preferred were they available as possibilities and introduce emotional and other biases to the process of determining a preferred response from even this limited set.

If the view developed in this book is true, the transcendent perspective removes these habits and practices and replaces them with alternatives that actively work against the accidental adoption of the fixed-self habits and practices. It effectively removes any barrier to all possible response options being available as possible response choices and removes any bias from the process of determining which is then preferred as a response.

A Real Advantage

That this is a real advantage – a real movement in the direction of something approaching the notion of free will – is best seen by looking at an example.

Imagine two fishermen, Frank Flatish and Rodney Roundish, faced with failing fish stocks close to shore. Although both have heard of the theory that the world is round and not flat, both believe it is flat and that you can fall off the edge to your doom if you sail too far out to sea. Roundish, who happens to have been brought up to see himself in terms of the transcendent perspective, believes it is flat because the evidence of his senses seems to confirm this. Flatish believes it partly for the same reason but also because his religion has indoctrinated him to such an extent that he believes it implicitly in any case. It has indoctrinated him with the view that it is indeed flat and that God made it that way to keep the faithful safe and destroy unbelievers who would not heed his word. He has been taught that any unbeliever who sailed too far out to sea would fall over the edge of the world to his doom and anyone who even thought about doubting that this was the case would burn in hell more or less immediately for thinking it.

Faced with starvation because of the fish stocks, Roundish appears to have three options, none of which are appealing. He can starve, he can go up into the cannibal-infested mountains to hunt rabbits, or he can risk sailing out beyond the horizon. His brain extrapolates negative outcomes arising from all three options; none is really preferred. It is, however, open to new possibilities, if any can be found. Eventually, it comes up with the notion of secretly visiting a nearby island and eavesdropping on the inhabitants of the village there, who are reputed to be great sailors. He tries this and learns enough to convince himself that the world may well be round and that trying his luck further out to sea, may just be worth the risk.

Flatish is faced with the same three options initially faced by Roundish. In his circumstances, though, there can be only one preferred option. He cannot starve, and sailing further out is something he dare not even think about for fear of the wrath of his God (as is the notion that the world ius round). His only option is to risk the cannibal-infested mountains. His religion-created fixed self blocks out the possibility of considering the wider range of options considered by Roundish. Even when he hears a rumour that Roundish, who is now reputedly thriving, owes his good fortune to an eavesdropping trip to another island (which Flatish has not heard the outcome of), he cannot countenance a similar trip. He believes, among other things, that he will immediately burn in hell if he even entertains the notion that what he has been taught about god and unbelievers and the world being flat is untrue and will, in any case, tumble over the edge of the world if he sails too far out to sea to fish.

He cannot adopt the preferred response of Roundish both because the range of options available that his brain will consider does not include the possibility of considering options beyond the initial three and because, in any case, his ability to choose the route to the final preference of Roundish is blocked by what he believes about the world and his god. His only option is – or seems to him to be – to risk the cannibal-infested mountains.

The final choices made by both fishermen are equally determined; how can it be otherwise in a deterministic universe? However, Roundish's decision to adopt the transcendent self-view has given his brain response options not available to Flatish; it has optimised the extent to which he later enjoyed freedom of response choice with positive results. Both the initial decision and the final response are determined, but it is nonetheless true that his brain's choice to adopt the transcendent perspective has optimised his later freedom of choice.

Results of the Optimisation not Necessarily Conscious

Notice that, while both the decision to adopt the transcendent perspective and the work involved in its instantiation as an operational self-view are conscious, the same does not necessarily apply to the final response in a given situation. The instantiation work will have programmed his brain in such a way as to open up neural pathways and offer decision-making algorithms and response options blocked in the fixed-self brain. These will work more or less automatically to offer a preferred response choice from the wider range available in a way that will only come to consciousness if that becomes a requirement in the decision-making process. If there are alternative options that can only be chosen between at a conscious level, the problem will come to consciousness; if not, it will not. If the brain determines only one preferred option at the end of the decision-making process, the response option itself may come to consciousness before or during the response process, but the decision itself will occur without the involvement of consciousness.

Not Quite Free Will, but a Positive Outcome

Instantiating the transcendent self-view optimises the extent to which we can enjoy improved freedom of response choice in all later situations encountered – the best we can do in terms of free will in a deterministic universe – at both a conscious and an unconscious level. This is a positive outcome, even if it is not how we usually envisage free will, which is usually assumed to be a facility we can only exercise consciously.

Overcoming an Otherwise Indicated Response Choice

One final point is worth considering as regards the ability that instantiation of the transcendent self-view gives us in respect of optimising freedom of response choice. Instantiating it at all optimises freedom of response choice in a general way, as we have just seen. However, the mental and emotional environment we create as a result also provides the additional possibility of overcoming what might otherwise be a preferred response choice as determined by the circumstances in place. A practised ability to lend an additional impetus to a particular course of action or type of action by temporarily associating a positive emotion with it opens up the possibility of overcoming a tendency to act in one particular way in our deterministic universe. It opens up the possibility of using such a ploy to change what would otherwise be the determined outcome and add impetus to an alternative action.

Imagine a person who has an operational transcendent self-view in place to the extent that she has become adept at applying the immersion level control facility. She has mastered the trick of mentally jumping into a particular view of things and of acting, thinking, feeling, and actively associating a positive emotion with it, while retaining overall control via her overarching transcendent self-view. Such a person could actively learn over a period of time to respond to situations where her own self-interest would tend to determine one particular self-interested response and learn to see a more altruistic and moral approach as a more positive thing. This might not ensure an altruistic and moral response in every situation, but it could at least improve the chances of such an outcome more often than would otherwise have been the case.

She could develop a fixed-self facet under the overall control of her overarching transcendent self that temporarily caused her to invoke, consciously or unconsciously, a personally preferred self-view of herself as an altruistic and moral being. One that boosted her chances of adopting the moral course and thereby overcoming what would otherwise have been the determined preferred outcome. This, again, would not change the fact that her actions would be fully determined in a deterministic universe. It would simply change the factors operating to determine the outcome, adding an additional possibility that might also alter the outcome as far as the determined preferred choice was concerned.

Optimising Response Choice: The Best we can do

The transcendent self-view does not change the fact that a deterministic universe makes free will impossible in the usual sense, but it does provide additional possibilities in regard to optimising freedom of response choice. The end result, as was noted above, is not quite free will. It is, however, something sufficiently like free will to satisfy most of us, especially considering the fact that free will in a nondeterministic universe is impossible. It is the best we can do in a deterministic universe, and it is arguably enough.

APPENDIX B

What if the Self is an Illusion?

Even Illusions Can Affect how we act, Think, and Feel

As was noted in Chapter 1, many psychologists and philosophers argue that our experience of a unified self is an illusion created by the brain (see, e.g., Hood, 2012; Hume, 1888, pp. 251-252). This may appear to suggest that considering and discussing the best design for the human self is not a worthwhile exercise, but that is to misconstrue what is being asserted when the unified self is argued to be an illusion created by the brain. The claim is not that the subjective experience of a unified self does not exist, but that it is no more real than a dream or a fantasy is and could not and would not persist once the brain that gives rise to it ceased to function.

This does not mean that it does not have a real existence in the human mind – while it persists, even a dream or a fantasy has a real existence in the human mind. It does not mean either that this subjective experience of self does not exist in a physical sense – that it does not have physical correlates and there is somehow no physical difference between experiencing the self as a unity and not doing so. While it persists, even a dream or a fantasy must have such physical correlates. Nor does it mean – how could it – that the unity we experience is itself an illusion. The unity we experience reflects an actual unity in the organism itself; each of us is a single unified entity and operates as such, and the 'illusion' of a unified self almost certainly plays a role in this. Finally, and this is the key point in the present context, it does not mean that, illusion or not, the unified self we experience and how we see and construct it does not have an impact on how we act, think, and feel in the world.

Even the Design of an Illusory Self has Consequences

Since even the dreams and fantasies we sometimes entertain can have behavioural and experiential consequences, it is reasonable to suppose that the unified self we experience and how we see and construct it can also have such consequences – and that its design is therefore worth discussing. No position is taken on whether or not the self is an illusion in this work. It is, however, assumed that, illusion or not, how we envisage and construct our subjective experience of self nevertheless has behavioural and experiential consequences, and hence that the question of how we should construct it is worth consideration. As it turns out, the view of the human self arrived at in the book neither conflicts with the claim that the self is an illusion nor with the claim that it is not. In fact, it allows us to see it in both ways in different circumstances and for different purposes. However, it does tend towards a more disaggregated view of the self that is possibly more in line with the view of it as an 'illusory' construct of the brain than not.

References

The biggest questions in science. (2018, May 10). Nature. https://www.nature.com/collections/mnwshvsswk

Observation beyond our eyes. (2022, September 10). Understanding Science. UCMP. https://undsci.berkeley.edu/understanding-science-101/how-science-works/observation-beyond-our-eyes/

Transcendence: Definition, Meaning & Synonyms. (n.d.). In *Vocabulary.com.* https://www.vocabulary.com/dictionary/transcendence#

Abdissa, D., Hamba, N., & Gerbi, A. (2020). Review Article on adult neurogenesis in humans. *Translational Research in Anatomy, 20,* 100074. https://doi.org/10.1016/j.tria.2020.100074

Ackerman, C. E., (2023). What is neuroplasticity? a psychologist explains [+14 tools]. *PositivePsychology.com.* https://positivepsychology.com/neuroplasticity/

Albert, P. R. (2019). Adult neuroplasticity: A new "cure" for major depression?*Journal of Psychiatry & Neuroscience,44*(3), 147–150. https://doi.org/10.1503/jpn.190072

Alquist, J. L., Ainsworth, S. E., & Baumeister, R. F. (2013). Determined to conform: Disbelief in free will increases conformity. *Journal of Experimental Social Psychology, 49*(1), 80–86. https://doi.org/10.1016/j.jesp.2012.08.015

Arias, F. D., Navarro, M., Elfanagely, Y., & Elfanagely, O. (2023). Biases in research studies. In *Elsevier eBooks* (pp. 191–194). *https://doi.org/10.1016/b978-0-323-90300-4.00082-3*

Askenasy, J. M., & Lehmann, J. (2013). Consciousness, brain, neuroplasticity. *Frontiers in Psychology, 4*. *https://pubmed.ncbi.nlm.nih.gov/23847580/*

Baumeister, R. F. (1990). Suicide as escape from self. *Psychological Review, 97*(1), 90–113. *https://doi.org/10.1037/0033-295x.97.1.90*

Blanke, O., & Metzinger, T. (2009). Full-body illusions and minimal phenomenal selfhood. *Trends in Cognitive Sciences, 13*(1), 7–13. *https://doi.org/10.1016/j.tics.2008.10.003*

Botin, M. (2023). Russellian Physicalists get our phenomenal concepts wrong. *Philosophical Studies, 180*(7), 1829–1848. *https://doi.org/10.1007/s11098-023-01955-1*

Brandt, S. (2021). Ryle on knowing how: Some clarifications and corrections. *European Journal of Philosophy, 29*(1), 152–167. *https://doi.org/10.1111/ejop.12574*

Brown, H. I. (2008). The case for indirect realism. In *The MIT Press eBooks* (pp. 45–58). *https://doi.org/10.7551/mitpress/9780262232661.003.0002*

Brunoni, A. R., Lopes, M., & Fregni, F. (2008). A systematic review and meta-analysis of clinical studies on major depression and BDNF levels: implications for the role of neuroplasticity in depression. *The International Journal of Neuropsychopharmacology, 11*(8), 1169–1180. *https://doi.org/10.1017/s1461145708009309*

Cameron, R. (2022). Infinite Regress Arguments. In E. N. Zalta & U. Nodelman(Eds.), *The Stanford Encyclopedia of Philosophy* (Fall 2022 Edition). Metaphysics Research Lab, Stanford University. *https://plato.stanford.edu/archives/fall2022/entries/infinite-regress/*

Carroll, S. (2012). Does the Universe Need God? In J.B. Stump & A.G. Padgett (Eds.), *The Blackwell Companion to Science and Christianity* (pp. 185-197). Blackwell Publishing.*https://doi.org/10.1002/9781118241455.ch17*

Carruthers, G. & Schier, E. (2017). Introduction: The Hard Problem of Consciousness. *Topoi* 36, 1–195. https://doi.org/10.1007/s11245-017-9459-7

Chalmers, D. J. (1995). Facing up to the problem of consciousness. *Journal of Consciousness Studies*, 2 (3), 200–219. https://consc.net/papers/facing.pdf

Chalmers, D. J. (1996). *The Conscious Mind*. New York and Oxford: Oxford University Press.

Chalmers, David (1997). Moving forward on the problem of consciousness. *Journal of Consciousness Studies* 4 (1): 3-46. http://cogprints.org/317/

Chalmers, D.J. (2003). Consciousness and its Place in Nature. In S. Stich & F. Warfield (Eds), *Blackwell Guide to the Philosophy of Mind* (102–42). Oxford: Blackwell. https://doi.org/10.1002/9780470998762.ch5

Chao, A. D. &. T. X. (2004, December 19). The top 10 intelligent designs (or creation myths). livescience.com. https://www.livescience.com/11316-top-10-intelligent-designs-creation-myths.html

Chen, Q., Yang, W., Li, W., Wei, D., Li, H., Qiao, L., Zhang, Q., & Qiu, J. (2014). Association of creative achievement with cognitive flexibility by a combined voxel-based morphometry and resting-state functional connectivity study. *NeuroImage*, 102, 474–483. https://doi.org/10.1016/j.neuroimage.2014.08.008

Close, F. (2009). *Nothing: a very short introduction*. OUP Oxford.

Cohen, J. D. (2004). Color Properties and Color Ascriptions: A Relationalist Manifesto. *The Philosophical Review*, 113(4), 451–506. https://doi.org/10.1215/00318108-113-4-451

Conee, E. (1994). Phenomenal Knowledge. *Australasian Journal of Philosophy*, 72 (2), 136–150. https://doi.org/10.1080/00048409412345971

Cook, T., & Tattersall, A. (2010). *Blackstone's Senior Investigating Officers' Handbook*. Oxford University Press, USA.

Dajani, D. R., & Uddin, L. Q. (2015). Demystifying cognitive flexibility: Implications for clinical and developmental neuroscience. *Trends in Neurosciences*, *38*(9), 571–578. https://doi.org/10.1016/j.tins.2015.07.003

Damisch, L., Stoberock, B., & Mussweiler, T. (2010). Keep your fingers crossed! *Psychological Science*, *21*(7), 1014–1020. https://doi.org/10.1177/0956797610372631

Deffenbacher, J. L., Lynch, R. S., Oetting, E. R., & Kemper, C. C. (1996). Anger reduction in early adolescents. *Journal of Counseling Psychology*, *43*(2), 149–157. https://doi.org/10.1037/0022-0167.43.2.149

De Gelder, B. E. (2010). The grand challenge for frontiers in emotion science. *Frontiers in Psychology*, *1*. https://doi.org/10.3389/fpsyg.2010.00187

Dennett, D. C. (1988). Quining Qualia. In A. J. Marcel & E. Bisiach (eds.), *Consciousness in Contemporary Science*. Oxford University Press. https://doi.org/10.1093/acprof:oso/9780198522379.003.0003,

Dennett, D. C. (1991).*Consciousness explained*. New York: Back Bay Books/Little, Brown and Company. https://freethoughts.dorshon.com/wp-content/uploads/Consciousness-Explained.pdf

Dennett, D.C. (2005). *Sweet Dreams: Philosophical Obstacles To A Science Of Consciousness*. Cambridge, MA: MIT Press

Desbordes, G., Gard, T., Hoge, E. A., Hölzel, B. K., Kerr, C. E., Lazar, S. W., Olendzki, A., & Vago, D. R. (2014). Moving Beyond Mindfulness: Defining Equanimity as an Outcome Measure in Meditation and Contemplative Research. *Mindfulness*, *6*(2), 356–372. https://doi.org/10.1007/s12671-013-0269-8

Ditto, P. H., & Lopez, D. F. (1992). Motivated skepticism: Use of differential decision criteria for preferred and nonpreferred conclusions. *Journal of Personality and Social Psychology*, *63*(4), 568–584. https://doi.org/10.1037/0022-3514.63.4.568

Doidge, N. (2008). *The brain that changes itself: Stories of Personal Triumph from the Frontiers of Brain Science*. Penguin UK.

Drigas, A., Karyotaki, M., & Skianis, C. (2018). An integrated approach to neuro-development, neuroplasticity and cognitive improvement. *International Journal of Recent Contributions From Engineering, Science & IT, 6*(3), 4. https://doi.org/10.3991/ijes.v6i3.9034

De Aldecoa, P. I., De Wit, S., & Tebbich, S. (2021). Can habits impede creativity by inducing fixation? *Frontiers in Psychology, 12.* https://doi.org/10.3389/fpsyg.2021.683024

Dweck, C. S. (2013). Self-theories. In *Psychology Press eBooks.* https://doi.org/10.4324/9781315783048

Duncan, M. (2021). Acquaintance. *Philosophy Compass, 16*(3). https://doi.org/10.1111/phc3.12727

Dyson, F. W., Eddington, A. S., & Davidson, C. (1920). A Determination of the Deflection of Light by the Sun's Gravitational Field, from Observations Made at the Total Eclipse of May 29, 1919. https://doi.org/10.1098/rsta.1920.0009

Ebringer, A. (2011). The scientific method of Sir Karl Popper. In *Springer eBooks* (pp. 191–200). https://doi.org/10.1007/978-0-85729-950-5_18

Editors of Encyclopaedia Britannica. (2017, April 24). koan. Encyclopedia Britannica. https://www.britannica.com/topic/koan

Evolution News. (2023, May 18). "Spontaneous Creation": Meyer on Stephen Hawking's category error. *Evolution News*, 2023, May 18 https://evolutionnews.org/2018/03/spontaneous-creation-meyer-on-stephen-hawkings-category-error/

Eidelson, R. J., & Eidelson, J. I. (2003). Dangerous ideas: Five beliefs that propel groups toward conflict. *American Psychologist, 58*(3), 182–192. https://doi.org/10.1037/0003-066x.58.3.182

Fein, S., & Spencer, S. J. (1997). Prejudice as self-image maintenance: Affirming the self through derogating others. *Journal of Personality and Social Psychology, 73*(1), 31–44. https://doi.org/10.1037/0022-3514.73.1.31

Fingelkurts, A. A., Fingelkurts, A. A., & Neves, C. F. (2012). "Machine" consciousness and "artificial" thought: An operational architectonics model guided approach. *Brain Research*, *1428*, 80–92. https://doi.org/10.1016/j.brainres.2010.11.079

Freeman, A., Santini, Z. I., Tyrovolas, S., Rummel-Kluge, C., Haro, J. M., & Koyanagi, A. (2016). Negative perceptions of ageing predict the onset and persistence of depression and anxiety: Findings from a prospective analysis of the Irish Longitudinal Study on Ageing (TILDA). *Journal of Affective Disorders*, *199*, 132–138. https://doi.org/10.1016/j.jad.2016.03.042

Frijda, N. H., Manstead, A. S. R., & Bem, S. (2000). The influence of emotions on beliefs. In *Cambridge University Press eBooks* (pp. 1–9). https://doi.org/10.1017/cbo9780511659904.001

Fuchs, E., & Flügge, G. (2014). Adult Neuroplasticity: More than 40 years of research. *Neural Plasticity*, *2014*, 1–10. https://doi.org/10.1155/2014/541870

Gál, É., Tóth-Király, I., & Orosz, G. (2022). Fixed Intelligence Mindset, Self-Esteem, and Failure-Related Negative Emotions: a Cross-Cultural Mediation Model. *Frontiers in Psychology*, *13*. https://doi.org/10.3389/fpsyg.2022.852638

Gamez, D. (2018). The Philosophy and Science of Consciousness. In Gamez, D., *Human and Machine Consciousness* (pp. 33-43). https://www.openbookpublishers.com/books/10.11647/obp.0107

Gamma, A., & Metzinger, T. (2021). The Minimal Phenomenal Experience questionnaire (MPE-92M): Towards a phenomenological profile of "pure awareness" experiences in meditators. *PLOS ONE*, *16*(7), e0253694. https://doi.org/10.1371/journal.pone.0253694

Genet, J. J., & Siemer, M. (2011). Flexible control in processing affective and non-affective material predicts individual differences in trait resilience. *Cognition & Emotion*, *25*(2), 380–388. https://doi.org/10.1080/02699931.2010.491647

Gibbs, J. J., & Goldbach, J. T. (2015). Religious Conflict, Sexual Identity, and Suicidal Behaviors among LGBT Young Adults. *Archives of Suicide Research, 19*(4), 472–488. *https://doi.org/10.1080/13811118.2015.1004476*

Giustina, A. (2022). Introspective knowledge by acquaintance. *Synthese, 200*(2). *https://doi.org/10.1007/s11229-022-03578-1*

Gray, J. A. (2004). *Consciousness: Creeping Up on the Hard Problem.* Oxford University Press, USA.

Griffiths, P. (2021). Against Direct Realism. *Philosophy Now.* Issue 146. *https://philosophynow.org/issues/146/Against_Direct_Realism*

Guerra, N. G., & Slaby, R. G. (1990). Cognitive mediators of aggression in adolescent offenders: II. Intervention. *Developmental Psychology, 26*(2), 269–277. *https://doi.org/10.1037/0012-1649.26.2.269*

Guggisberg, A. G., & Mottaz, A. (2013). Timing and awareness of movement decisions: does consciousness really come too late? *Frontiers in Human Neuroscience, 7. https://doi.org/10.3389/fnhum.2013.00385*

Gunn, R., & Bortolotti, L. (2018). Can delusions play a protective role? *Phenomenology and the Cognitive Sciences, 17*(4), 813–833. *https://doi.org/10.1007/s11097-017-9555-6*

Hasan, A. and Fumerton, R. (2020). Knowledge by Acquaintance vs. Description. In E. N. Zalta(Ed.), *The Stanford Encyclopedia of Philosophy (Spring 2020 Edition).* Metaphysics Research Lab, Stanford University. *https://plato.stanford.edu/archives/spr2020/entries/knowledge-acquaindescrip/*

Havlík, M., Kozáková, E., & Horáček, J. (2017). Why and How. The Future of the Central Questions of Consciousness. *Frontiers in Psychology,* 8. *https://doi.org/10.3389/fpsyg.2017.01797*

Hawking, S., & Mlodinow, L. (2011). *The grand design.* Random House.

Hill, A. E. (1999). Phantom Limb Pain. *Journal of Pain and Symptom Management, 17*(2), 125–142. *https://doi.org/10.1016/s0885-3924(98)00136-5*

Hongo, T., Yakou, T., Yoshinaga, K., Kano, T., Miyazaki, M., & Hanakawa, T. (2022). Structural neuroplasticity in computer programming beginners.*Cerebral Cortex*. *https://doi.org/10.1093/cercor/bhac425*

Hood, B. (2012). The self illusion: How the social brain creates identity. Oxford University Press.

Howell, R. R., & Alter, T. (2009). Hard problem of consciousness. Scholarpedia, 4(6), 4948. *https://doi.org/10.4249/scholarpedia.4948*

Huemer, M. (2016). Approaching Infinity. In *Palgrave Macmillan UK eBooks*. *https://link.springer.com/content/pdf/10.1057/9781137560872.pdf*

Huemer, M. (2018). The Virtues Of Direct Realism. In Smythies, J. R., & French, R. E. (Eds). (2018). *Direct versus Indirect Realism: A Neurophilosophical Debate on Consciousness*. (95-112). *https://doi.org/10.1016/b978-0-12-812141-2.00007-6*

Hume, D. (1888). *A Treatise Of Human Nature* (L. A. Selby-Bigge, Ed.). Clarendon Press. Internet Archive, *https://archive.org/details/treatiseofhumann002393mbp/page/n5/mode/2up*

Jackson, F. (1982). Epiphenomenal Qualia. *The Philosophical Quarterly*, 32 (April), 127-136. *https://doi.org/10.2307/2960077*

Jennings, B. (2011). There is No Need for God as a Hypothesis. *Quantum diaries*, 2011, September 16. *https://www.quantumdiaries.org/2011/09/16/there-is-no-need-for-god-as-a-hypothesis/*

John, E. R. (2001). A field theory of consciousness. *Consciousness and Cognition*, 10(2), 184–213. *https://doi.org/10.1006/ccog.2001.0508*

Jones, M. W. (2019). Growing Evidence that Perceptual Qualia are Neuroelectrical Not Computational. *Journal of Consciousness Studies*, 26 (5-6): 89-116. *https://philarchive.org/rec/JONGET*

Josipovic, Z., & Miskovic, V. (2020). Nondual Awareness and Minimal Phenomenal Experience. *Frontiers in Psychology*, 11. *https://doi.org/10.3389/fpsyg.2020.02087*

Kaanders, P., Sepulveda, P., Folke, T., Ortoleva, P., & De Martino, B. (2022). Humans actively sample evidence to support prior beliefs. *Elife*, 11. https://doi.org/10.7554/elife.71768

Kanai, R., & Tsuchiya, N. (2012). Qualia. *Current Biology*, 22(10), R392–R396. https://doi.org/10.1016/j.cub.2012.03.033

Kärgel, C., Massau, C., Weiß, S., Walter, M., Borchardt, V., Krueger, T. H., Tenbergen, G., Kneer, J., Wittfoth, M., Pohl, A., Gerwinn, H., Ponseti, J., Amelung, T., Beier, K. M., Mohnke, S., Walter, H., & Schiffer, B. (2016). Evidence for superior neurobiological and behavioral inhibitory control abilities in non-offending as compared to offending pedophiles. *Human Brain Mapping*, 38(2), 1092–1104. https://doi.org/10.1002/hbm.23443

Kashdan, T. B., & Rottenberg, J. (2010). Psychological flexibility as a fundamental aspect of health. *Clinical Psychology Review*,30(7), 865–878. https://doi.org/10.1016/j.cpr.2010.03.001

Kent, E. W. (2018). Is Direct Realism Falsifiable? In Smythies, J. R., & French, R. E. (Eds). (2018). *Direct versus Indirect Realism: A Neurophilosophical Debate on Consciousness*. (33-59) Academic Press. https://doi.org/10.1016/b978-0-12-812141-2.00004-0

King, R. B. (2017). A fixed mindset leads to negative affect: The relations between implicit theories of intelligence and subjective well-being. *Zeitschrift für Psychologie*, 225(2), 137–145. https://doi.org/10.1027/2151-2604/a000290

Kitson, A., Chirico, A., Gaggioli, A., & Riecke, B. E. (2020). A review on research and Evaluation Methods for Investigating Self-Transcendence.*Frontiers in Psychology*, 11. https://doi.org/10.3389/fpsyg.2020.547687

Koenig, H. G. (2012). Religion, Spirituality, and Health: the research and Clinical Implications. *ISRN Psychiatry (Online)*, 2012, 1–33. https://doi.org/10.5402/2012/278730

Koltko-Rivera, M. E. (2004). The psychology of worldviews. *Review of General Psychology*, 8(1), 3–58. https://doi.org/10.1037/1089-2680.8.1.3

Krueger, F., & Grafman, J. (Eds.). (2012). The Neural Basis of Human Belief Systems (1st ed.). Psychology Press. https://doi.org/10.4324/9780203101407

Kuldas, S., Ismail, H. N., Hashim, S., & Bakar, Z. A. (2013). Unconscious learning processes: mental integration of verbal and pictorial instructional materials. *SpringerPlus*, 2(1). https://doi.org/10.1186/2193-1801-2-105

Lao, J. R., & Young, J. (2019). *Resistance to belief change: Limits of Learning.* Routledge.

Larsen, R.J., & Fredrickson, B.L. (1999). Measurement Issues in Emotion Research. In Kahneman, D., Diener, E., & Schwarz, N. (Eds), *Well-being Foundations of Hedonic Psychology* (pp. 40-60). New York: Russel Sage. https://peplab.web.unc.edu/wp-content/uploads/sites/18901/2018/11/larsenfredrickson1999.pdf

Lee, B., Park, J. Y., Jung, W. H., Kim, H. S., Oh, J. S., Choi, C. H., Jang, J. H., Kang, D. H., & Kwon, J. S. (2010). White matter neuroplastic changes in long-term trained players of the game of "Baduk" (GO): A voxel-based diffusion-tensor imaging study. *NeuroImage*, (1), 9–19. https://doi.org/10.1016/j.neuroimage.2010.04.014

Lehar, S. (2018). The Epistemology Of Visual Experience. In Smythies, J. R., & French, R. E. (Eds). (2018). *Direct versus Indirect Realism: A Neurophilosophical Debate on Consciousness*. (73-92) Academic Press. https://www.sciencedirect.com/science/article/pii/B9780128121412000064

Le Morvan, Pierre (2004). Arguments against direct realism and how to counter them. *American Philosophical Quarterly* 41 (3):221-234. https://owd.tcnj.edu/~lemorvan/DR_web.pdf

Levine, J. (1983). Materialism and Qualia: The Explanatory Gap. *Pacific Philosophical Quarterly*, 64(4), 354–361 https://doi.org/10.1111/j.1468-0114.1983.tb00207.x

Levy, S.R., Ramírez, L. Rosenthal, L., & Karafantis, D.M. (2013). The Study of Lay Theories: A Piece of the Puzzle for Understanding Prejudice. In Banaji, M.R. & Gelman, S.A. (Eds), *Navigating the Social World: What Infants, Children, and Other Species Can Teach Us* (pp. 318-322). Social Cognition and Social Neuroscience (New York, 2013; online edn, Oxford Academic, 23 May 2013), *https://doi.org/10.1093/acprof:oso/9780199890712.003.0058*

Lewis, D. (1983). Extrinsic properties. *Philosophical Studies, 44*(2), 197-200. *https://doi.org/10.1007/BF00354100*

Lieberman, J. D., Arndt, J., Personius, J., & Cook, A. (2001). Vicarious annihilation: The effect of mortality salience on perceptions of hate crimes. *Law And Human Behavior, 25*(6), 547–566. *https://doi.org/10.1023/a:1012738706166*

Li, P., Legault, J., & Litcofsky, K. A. (2014). Neuroplasticity as a function of second language learning: Anatomical changes in the human brain. *Cortex, 58*, 301–324. *https://doi.org/10.1016/j.cortex.2014.05.001*

Libet, B., Gleason, C.A., Wright, E., & Pearl, D.K. (1983). Time of conscious intention to act in relation to onset of cerebral activity (readiness-potential). The unconscious initiation of a freely voluntary act. *Brain*, 106 (Pt 3), 623-42. *https://doi.org/10.1093/brain/106.3.623*

Lipina, S. J., & Posner, M. I. (2012). The impact of poverty on the development of brain networks. *Frontiers in Human Neuroscience, 6*. *https://doi.org/10.3389/fnhum.2012.00238*

Malik, J., Stemplewski, R., & Maciaszek, J. (2022). The Effect of juggling as Dual-Task activity on Human Neuroplasticity: A Systematic review. *International Journal of Environmental Research and Public Health, 19*(12), 7102. *https://doi.org/10.3390/ijerph19127102*

Mander, W. (2023). Pantheism. In E. N. Zalta & U. Nodelman (Eds.), *The Stanford Encyclopedia of Philosophy* (Spring 2023 Edition). Metaphysics Research Lab, Stanford University. *https://plato.stanford.edu/archives/spr2023/entries/pantheism/*

Mauss, I.B. & Robinson, M.D. (2009) Measures of emotion: A review. *Cogn Emot.* 2009 Feb 1;23(2):209-237. https://www.ncbi.nlm.nih.gov/pmc/articles/PMC2756702/pdf/nihms134765.pdf

McFadden, J. (2020). Integrating information in the brain's EM field: the cemi field theory of consciousness. *Neuroscience of Consciousness, 2020*(1). https://doi.org/10.1093/nc/niaa016

McGinn, Colin (1989). Can We Solve the Mind-Body Problem? *Mind*, Vol xcviii, no. 891, 349–366. https://doi.org/10.1093/mind/xcviii.391.349 Reprinted in McGinn, Colin 1991: *The Problem of Consciousness*. Oxford: Basil Blackwell, pp. 1-22.

Medow, H. (2011). Neuroplasticity-Biology of psychotherapy. *ResearchGate*. https://www.researchgate.net/publication/280926585_Neuroplasticity-Biology_of_Psychotherapy

Meier, S. T. (2023). Editorial: Persistence of measurement problems in psychological research.*Frontiers in Psychology,14*. https://doi.org/10.3389/fpsyg.2023.1132185

Mele, A. R. (2009). The power of conscious will. In *Oxford University Press eBooks* (pp. 131–144). https://doi.org/10.1093/acprof:oso/9780195384260.003.0007

Memon, Z. A., & Treur, J. (2010). On the reciprocal interaction between believing and feeling: an adaptive agent modelling perspective. *Cognitive Neurodynamics, 4*(4), 377–394. https://doi.org/10.1007/s11571-010-9136-7

Mercer, J. (2010). Emotional beliefs. *International Organization, 64*(1), 1–31. https://doi.org/10.1017/s0020818309990221

Merzenich, M. M. (2013). *Soft-Wired: How the New Science of Brain Plasticity Can Change Your Life*. San Francisco, CA: Parnassus Publishing.

Metzinger, T. (2010). The self-model theory of subjectivity: A brief summary with examples. *Humana Mente, 4*(14).

Metzinger, T. (2020). Minimal phenomenal experience. *Philosophy and the Mind Sciences, 1* (I),1-44. *https://doi.org/10.33735/phimisci.2020.i.46*

Mitrovic, I., De Peña, L. F., Frassetto, L., & Mellin, L. (2011). Rewiring the stress response: A new paradigm for health care.*Hypothesis,9*(1). *https://doi.org/10.5779/hypothesis.v9i1.198*

Mueller, C., & Dweck, C. S. (1998). Praise for intelligence can undermine children's motivation and performance. *Journal of Personality and Social Psychology,75*(1), 33–52. *https://doi.org/10.1037/0022-3514.75.1.33*

Münte, T. F., Altenmüller, E., & Jäncke, L. (2002). The musician's brain as a model of neuroplasticity.*Nature Reviews Neuroscience, 3*(6), 473–478. *https://doi.org/10.1038/nrn843*

Nagel, T. (1974). What is it like to be a bat? *The Philosophical Review, 83*(4), 435. *https://www.sas.upenn.edu/~cavitch/pdf-library/Nagel_Bat.pdf*

Noble, K. G., Hart, E. R., & Sperber, J. F. (2021). Socioeconomic disparities and neuroplasticity: Moving toward adaptation, intersectionality, and inclusion. *American Psychologist, 76*(9), 1486–1495. *https://doi.org/10.1037/amp0000934*

O'Brien, D. (n.d.). Perception, Objects of. In *Internet Encyclopedia of Philosophy. https://iep.utm.edu/perc-obj/#H2*

Öllinger, M., Jones, G. A., & Knoblich, G. (2008). Investigating the effect of mental set on insight problem solving. *Experimental Psychology, 55*(4), 269–282. *https://doi.org/10.1027/1618-3169.55.4.269*

Papineau, D. (1998). Mind the gap. *Philosophical Perspectives* 12:373-89. *http://www.davidpapineau.co.uk/uploads/1/8/5/5/18551740/mind_the_gap.pdf*

Pauwels, L., Chalavi, S., & Swinnen, S. P. (2018). Aging and brain plasticity. *Aging,10*(8), 1789–1790. *https://doi.org/10.18632/aging.101514*

Pepinster, C. (2017, December 2). Would you Adam and Eve it? Why creation story is at heart of a new spiritual divide. *The Guardian*. *https:// www.theguardian.com/world/2017/sep/16/would-you-adam- and-eve-it-why-creation-story-is-at-heart-of-a-new-spiritual-divide*

Peterson, J. C. (2012). The Adaptive Neuroplasticity hypothesis of Behavioral Maintenance.*Neural Plasticity, 2012*, 1–12. *https://doi. org/10.1155/2012/516364*

Pockett, S. (2012). The Electromagnetic Field Theory of Consciousness. *Journal of Consciousness Studies* 19 (11-12):191-223. *https://cdn.auckland. ac.nz/assets/psych/about/our-people/documents/sue-pockett/Pockett_2012.pdf*

Pollack, D., Demmrich, S. & Müller, O. L. (2023). Editorial—Religious fundamentalism: new theoretical and empirical challenges across religions and cultures. *Zeitschrift FüR Religion, Gesellschaft Und Politik*, 7(1), 1–11. *https://doi.org/10.1007/s41682-023-00159-y*

Popper, K. R. (1963). *Conjectures and refutations. The growth of scientific knowledge*. New York: Routledge & Kegan Paul.

Porot, N., & Mandelbaum, E. (2020). The science of belief: A progress report. *Wiley Interdisciplinary Reviews: Cognitive Science, 12*(2). *https:// doi.org/10.1002/wcs.1539*

Reese, W. L. (2023, July 16). Pantheism | Definition, Beliefs, History, & Facts. *Encyclopedia Britannica*. *https://www.britannica.com/topic/ pantheism*

Ren, H. (2012). The Distinction between Knowledge-That and Knowledge-How. *Philosophia*, 40 (4), 857–875. *https://doi.org/10.1007/ s11406-012-9361-x*

Rosenthal, N.E. (2011) Transcendence: Healing And Transformation Through Transcendental Meditation. P. 38. New York: Penguin Group (US) Inc.

Russell, B. (1912). *The Problems Of Philosophy*. London: William & Norgate. *https://archive.org/details/problemsofphilo00russuoft/page/72/ mode/2up*

Russell, B. (1914). Our Knowledge of the External World as a Field for Scientific Method in Philosophy. [The Lowell Lectures, 1914]. London: The Open Court Publishing Company. *https://archive.org/ details/ourknowledgeofth005200mbp/page/n63/mode/2up*

Russell, Bertrand (1927). The Analysis of Matter. London: Kegan Paul. *https://archive.org/details/in.ernet.dli.2015.221533/page/n3/mode/2up*

Sale, A., Berardi, N., & Maffei, L. (2014). Environment and brain plasticity: towards an endogenous pharmacotherapy.*physiological Reviews*,*94*(1), 189–234. *https://doi.org/10.1152/physrev.00036.2012*

Sari, C. K., Tondok, M. S., & Muttaqin, D. (2020). The Role of Sexual Self-Control as Moderator between Sexual Desire and Premarital Sexual Behaviors. *Jurnal Psikologi, 47*(1), 43. *https://doi.org/10.22146/ jpsi.41159*

Sauer, S., Walach, H., Schmidt, S., Hinterberger, T., Lynch, S., Büssing, A., & Kohls, N. (2012). Assessment of Mindfulness: Review on state of the art. *Mindfulness, 4*(1), 3–17. *https://doi.org/10.1007/ s12671-012-0122-5*

Scheffer, M., Borsboom, D., Nieuwenhuis, S., & Westley, F. (2022). Belief traps: Tackling the inertia of harmful beliefs. *Proceedings of the National Academy of Sciences of the United States of America, 119*(32). *https://doi.org/10.1073/pnas.2203149119*

Schmidt-Wilcke, T., Rosengarth, K., Luerding, R., Bogdahn, U., & Greenlee, M. W. (2010). Distinct patterns of functional and structural neuroplasticity associated with learning Morse code. *NeuroImage, 51*(3), 1234–1241. *https://doi.org/10.1016/j.neuroimage.2010.03.042*

Scholtz, Salome & Klerk, Werner & de Beer, Leon. (2020). The Use of Research Methods in Psychological Research: A Systematised Review. Frontiers in Research Metrics and Analytics. 5. 1. *https://www. frontiersin.org/articles/10.3389/frma.2020.00001/full*

Scholtz, S. E., De Klerk, W., & De Beer, L. T. (2020). The Use of Research Methods in Psychological Research: A Systematised review. *Frontiers in Research Metrics and Analytics, 5*. *https://doi.org/10.3389/ frma.2020.00001*

Schroder, H. S. (2021). Mindsets in the clinic: Applying mindset theory to clinical psychology. *Clinical Psychology Review, 83*, 101957. https://doi.org/10.1016/j.cpr.2020.101957

Scribbr. (n.d.). *Types of Bias in Research | Definition & Examples.* https://www.scribbr.co.uk/category/bias-in-research/

Scruton, R. (2020, April 2). The Unobservable Mind. *MIT Technology Review.* https://www.technologyreview.com/2005/02/01/231672/the-unobservable-mind/

Searle, J. R. (1998). How to study consciousness scientifically. *Philosophical Transactions of the Royal Society B, 353*(1377), 1935–1942. https://doi.org/10.1098/rstb.1998.0346

Sebastianelli, L., Saltuari, L., & Nardone, R. (2017). How the brain can rewire itself after an injury: the lesson from hemispherectomy. *Neural Regeneration Research, 12*(9), 1426. https://doi.org/10.4103/1673-5374.215247

Shaffer, J. (2016). Neuroplasticity and Clinical Practice: Building Brain Power for health. *Frontiers in Psychology, 7.* https://doi.org/10.3389/fpsyg.2016.01118

Shand, John (2021).Consciousness: Removing the Hardness and Solving the Problem. *Revista Portuguesa de Filosofia,* 77(4) pp. 1279–1296. DOI: https://doi.org/10.17990/rpf/2021_77_4_1279

Shear, J. (1999). *Explaining Consciousness: The Hard Problem.* MIT Press.

Sider, T. (1996). Intrinsic properties. *Philosophical Studies, 83*(1), 1–27. https://doi.org/10.1007/BF00372433

Siegel, E. (2019, May 29). This Is How, 100 Years Ago, A Solar Eclipse Proved Einstein Right And Newton Wrong. *Forbes.* https://www.forbes.com/sites/startswithabang/2019/05/29/this-is-how-100-years-ago-a-solar-eclipse-proved-einstein-right-and-newton-wrong/

Skokowski, P. (2022). Sensing qualia. *Frontiers in Systems Neuroscience,* 16:795405. https://doi.org/10.3389/fnsys.2022.795405

Skottnik, L., & Linden, D. (2019). Mental Imagery and Brain Regulation—New links between Psychotherapy and Neuroscience. *Frontiers in Psychiatry,10*. https://doi.org/10.3389/fpsyt.2019.00779

Slors, M. (2013). Conscious intending as self-programming. *Philosophical Psychology,28*(1), 94–113. https://doi.org/10.1080/09515089.2013.803922

Smiley, P. A., Buttitta, K. V., Chung, S. Y., Dubon, V., & Chang, L. (2016). Mediation models of implicit theories and achievement goals predict planning and withdrawal after failure. *Motivation and Emotion, 40*(6), 878–894. https://doi.org/10.1007/s11031-016-9575-5

Smythies, J. R., & French, R. E. (Eds). (2018). *Direct versus Indirect Realism: A Neurophilosophical Debate on Consciousness*. Academic Press. https://www.sciencedirect.com/book/9780128121412/direct-versus-indirect-realism

Soon, C., Brass, M., Heinze, H. & Haynes, J. (2008). Unconscious determinants of free decisions in the human brain. *Nature Neuroscience*, 11(5), 543–545. https://doi.org/10.1038/nn.2112

Srinivasan N. (2020). Consciousness Without Content: A Look at Evidence and Prospects. *Frontiers in Psychology, 11*. https://doi.org/10.3389/fpsyg.2020.01992

Stanley, J., & Williamson, T. (2001). Knowing how. *The Journal of Philosophy, 98*(8), 411–444. https://doi.org/10.2307/2678403

Stukas, A. A., & Snyder, M. (2016). Self-Fulfilling prophecies. In *Elsevier eBooks* (pp. 92–100). https://doi.org/10.1016/b978-0-12-397045-9.00220-2

Subhi, N., & Geelan, D. (2012). When Christianity and homosexuality collide: Understanding the potential intrapersonal conflict.*Journal of Homosexuality, 59*(10), 1382–1402. https://doi.org/10.1080/00918369.2012.724638

Svensson, I., & Nilsson, D. (2017). Disputes over the Divine. *Journal of Conflict Resolution, 62*(5), 1127–1148. https://doi.org/10.1177/0022002717737057

Taschereau-Dumouchel, V., Cortese, A., Chiba, T., Knotts, J. D., Kawato, M., & Lau, H. (2018). Towards an unconscious neural reinforcement intervention for common fears.*Proceedings of the National Academy of Sciences of the United States of America, 115*(13), 3470–3475. https://doi.org/10.1073/pnas.1721572115

Travis, F., & Pearson, C. J. (2000). Pure Consciousness: Distinct Phenomenological and Physiological Correlates of "Consciousness Itself." *International Journal of Neuroscience, 100*(1–4), 77–89. https://doi.org/10.3109/00207450008999678

Tye, M. (2020). Qualia. In E. N. Zalta(Ed.), *The Stanford Encyclopedia of Philosophy* (Spring 2020 Edition). Metaphysics Research Lab, Stanford University. https://plato.stanford.edu/archives/fall2021/entries/qualia/

Van Roeyen, I., Riem, M. M. E., Tončić, M., & Vingerhoets, A. (2020). The damaging effects of perceived crocodile tears for a crier's image. *Frontiers in Psychology, 11.* https://doi.org/10.3389/fpsyg.2020.00172

Wegner, D. M. (2002). The illusion of conscious will. In *The MIT Press ebooks.* https://doi.org/10.7551/mitpress/3650.001.0001

Wenzel, K., Schindler, S., & Reinhard, M. (2017). General Belief in a Just World Is Positively Associated with Dishonest Behavior. *Frontiers in Psychology, 8.* https://doi.org/10.3389/fpsyg.2017.01770

Weisberg, J. (n.d.). Hard Problem of Consciousness | *Internet Encyclopedia of Philosophy.* https://iep.utm.edu/hard-problem-of-conciousness/

Wright, J. D., & Khoo, Y. (2019). Empirical perspectives on religion and violence. *Contemporary Voices, 1*(3), 75. https://doi.org/10.15664/jtr.1482

Yaden, D. B., Iwry, J., & Newberg, A. (2016). Neuroscience and Religion: Surveying the Field. 17, 227–299. In N.K. Clements (ed.), *Religion: Mental Religion.* Macmillan Reference. (chapter available online: http://behavioralhealth2000.com/wp-content/uploads/2017/12/Neuroscience-and-Religion-Surveying-the-Field.pdf)

Also Consulted

Shah-Kazemi, R. (2006). Paths to transcendence according to Shankara, Ibn Arabi, and Meister Eckhart. Bloomington, Indiana: World Wisdom.

Watts, A. (1957). The way of Zen. New York: Vintage Books.

Watts, A. (1977). The book on the taboo against knowing who you are. London: Abacus.

Index

ABC dictum, role of science 353
acting but not playacting 6, 22, 223-229, 238, 319, 321
additional skill sets 22, 241-250
all ideas reference human experience 51, 52-56
all ideas self-world perspectives 50-62
any idea about anything a self-world perspective 6, 16, 18, 32, 50-62, 66, 96, 97, 102, 110, 127, 128, 209, 213, 221, 223, 305
any self or world view a self-world view 13, 16, 44-49, 51, 56-65
artificial fixing 32-33, 67, 68, 71, 72, 74, 75-95, 96-107, 108-118, 162, 272, 457
artificial fixing, notion of self 7, 17, 33, 108-118
baseline transcendent self-view 206, 208-242, 249-250, 259-60, 261, 310, 315
behavioural and experiential consequences 8, 264

behavioural and experiential nature reflected 2, 4, 5, 7-8, 9, 10, 12, 13, 15, 17, 18, 21, 23-24, 32, 33, 49, 51, 52, 60, 61-62, 66-71, 74, 75-76, 106-107, 113, 118, 120, 122-123, 131-132, 154, 155, 172, 174, 199, 200, 211, 253, 264, 286, 287, 292-3, 295, 297, 311, 449
behavioural and experiential self-world relationship, human 2, 4-5, 7-10, 12-13, 15-17, 18-20, 23, 24, 32-9, 46, 47, 49, 51-62, 66-74, 75, 76, 77, 80, 82, 91, 110, 112, 113, 116, 118, 120, 122, 123, 124, 125, 128, 130-132, 154, 155, 164-172, 207, 209, 211, 213, 221, 286-299
best design for a human self *see* fully human self-view, criteria; fully human self-view, design requirements
biased unless disaggregated 133-134
block on transcendent self-view in everyday assumption 25, 343, 358, 360-376, 421-429

brain as a sensory construct
 358, 359, 361-364, 378-394,
 395, 396, 404, 411, 417, 418,
 422-429
brain programming,
 neuroplasticity and 64, 76-82,
 85, 88, 89, 90, 91, 92, 93, 94,
 97, 103, 109, 111-112, 129, 130-
 131, 157, 160, 211, 218, 222,
 223, 224, 225, 231, 232, 233,
 234, 235, 236, 237, 239, 316,
 417, 459
caveats 14-15, 209-212, 239-240,
 297-299
Chalmers, D. 11, 26, 180, 200,
 369, 370, 372, 373, 375,
 394, 395, 397, 398, 402-403,
 405-406
 answering not evading
 Chalmers' questions
 402-403
conflict and the fixed self 135-153,
 164-172, 264-285, 339, 340,
 341, 342, 351-352, 368, 412
conscious experience
 see conscious experiences
 explicable as brain
 functions; consciously
 experienced world: the real
 thing?; consciousness within
 the reality underlying the
 experienced brain; empty
 consciousness; hard problem
 of consciousness resolved;
 qualia; why like this, why
 like anything questions

conscious experiences explicable as
 brain functions 26-27, 358, 372,
 377, 385-387, 391-394, 395-412
consciously experienced world: the
 real thing? 421, 422-429
consciousness within the reality
 underlying the experienced
 brain 379-380
core and interactive role-playing
 elements 4-6, 10, 21, 206, 208-
 240, 241-257, 260, 304-331
creative and imaginative thinking
 7, 18, 22, 23, 84, 87, 89, 99,
 111, 128, 129, 130, 133, 155,
 157, 214, 215, 224, 236, 247-
 248, 261, 268, 271, 275, 276,
 278, 288, 292, 327-328, 352
Dennett, D. 27, 372, 375, 394,
 395, 397, 398, 403, 406
design requirements met 258-299
empty consciousness
 core, dominant focus, resting
 state 2, 4-6, 9-10, 11, 21-22,
 23, 24, 28, 173-174, 175,
 177, 187-188, 191-195, 200,
 206, 208, 212, 213, 214,
 216-218, 219, 220, 221,
 222-223, 224, 225-226, 228,
 232, 233, 234, 235, 236,
 237, 238, 246, 251, 252,
 255, 260, 266, 267, 270,
 280, 283, 291, 293, 304,
 305-306, 307, 310, 311-312,
 313-317, 318-321, 322, 323,
 328, 354, 415, 442, 448, 449

definition and characteristics
4-5, 8, 9, 10, 11, 20-21, 24,
173-203, 214, 216, 224, 233,
235, 236, 237, 270, 314,
328-329
everyday transcendence and
4-10, 304-331
identifying with 21, 175, 188,
192, 194-5, 311, 323, 327, 328
infinite regress and 20-21, 176-
177, 184, 185, 186, 187, 188,
190, 389-390,
instantiation and 8-10, 208-
240, 304-331
key role in the transcendent
self-view 2, 4-5, 8-10, 19-20,
23-24, 174, 188-189, 199,
201-203, 302
mental exercises and 24, 193-
194, 216-218, 220-222, 224,
226, 305, 306, 307, 310-316,
318-325
mental set, absence of 193, 214,
216, 224, 233, 235, 236,
237, 270, 314, 328-329
need not be known in isolation
4-5, 195
nonrelational nature of 9, 10-11,
20, 21, 23, 26, 120-121, 173,
174, 175-7, 182-91, 197-203,
206, 208, 216, 217-218, 224,
226, 232, 236, 251, 272, 280,
291, 292, 293. 302, 310, 311,
312, 313, 388, 389, 390, 391,
392, 400-402, 407, 438,
448-449

not a basis for a fixed self 9-10,
19-20, 23-24, 173, 175-177,
187-189, 191, 199, 200
not known via another
perspective 8, 9-10, 20, 24,
173, 176, 183-184, 187-191,
198-199
transcendence and 2, 4-6, 8, 9,
10, 12, 13, 21, 24, 29
uniquely nonrelational 10, 23,
174, 185-187, 199, 201-203,
292-293, 311
see also fully human self-view,
design requirements;
nonrelational and relational;
qualia; religion and the
transcendent perspective;
why like this, why like
anything questions
endpoint of human personal
development and education 2,
9, 12, 295, 330
see also fully human self-view,
criteria; fully human self-
view, design requirements
epistemologically irreducible but
ontologically reducible
see under hard problem of
consciousness resolved
everyday transcendence 4-14,
304-331
see also transcendent perspective
on self and world
explanatory gap
see under hard problem of
consciousness resolved

facets and roles
  see repertoire of facets or roles
fantastic, nonsensical, meaningless notions as useful self-world perspectives 6, 52-54, 57-59, 125-126, 170, 213, 221, 255, 303, 346, 348-349, 353
first-pass transcendent perspective 206, 209, 210, 212, 215, 241-257, 258-261, 263, 264, 265, 271, 273, 284, 286, 294, 296, 297, 298-299, 302, 308, 310, 330-331
fixed in practice, wholly-variable in theory 66-107, 127-128, 288-289, 296
fixed self 6, 7, 8, 9, 10, 11, 15, 16, 17, 18, 19, 20, 22, 23, 32-33, 62, 66-118, 120, 121, 122-124, 132, 135-172, 173, 175, 177, 187, 189, 191, 200, 206-207, 208, 209, 211, 213, 214, 217, 219-220, 223, 226, 227, 229-233, 234-236, 237, 238, 239, 241, 242, 243, 244, 245, 246, 248, 249, 251, 252-253, 255-256, 257, 258-299
fixed-self-facet barrier to full transcendence 25-26, 360-376, 412-413
fixed-self facets 25, 116, 159, 299, 340, 343, 358, 359, 360-361, 364, 365, 366, 367, 368, 369, 374, 418, 421, 422, 423, 426, 427, 428, 429, 438, 461
fixed self not beliefs effect 137-149

fixed-self-type blocks or barriers 18, 19, 20, 22-26, 48, 66, 67, 68, 73, 81-93, 142-143, 154-163, 167, 168, 171-172, 200, 206, 208, 214, 218, 219, 230-231, 233, 234-237, 238, 239, 243-244, 252, 258, 260-261, 262-263, 265-266, 267-268, 269-270, 271-273, 275, 276, 277, 278, 287, 288, 291, 294, 302, 311, 318, 326-327, 341, 346, 351, 358, 360, 361, 364-365, 366, 367-369, 370, 374, 413, 421, 423, 424, 428, 438, 457, 458, 459
fixing happens to all proof 296
flesh, blood, and brain view of humans 11, 25-26, 358, 360-362, 364, 365-367, 368, 369, 373-374, 375, 377, 378, 380, 393, 394, 410, 412, 413, 415-416, 427
free will and the transcendent perspective 278, 454-462
fully developed human 2, 8, 10, 17-18, 21, 33, 117-118, 166, 207, 253, 283, 286, 295-296, 299, 345, 415, 416, 417, 451
fully human self-view, criteria
  a relationship that varies with our views of it 34-49
  a self-world perspective in every idea 50-65
  wholly-variable in theory, fixed in practice 66-107, 127-128, 288-289, 296

fully human self-view, design requirements
  (1) misdefinition avoidance 108-118
  (2) open-ended 122-134
  (3) negatives, positives, individual preferences 135-153
  (4) no fixed self blocks 154-163
  (5) scientific world-view insufficient 164-172
  (6) empty consciousness core 173-203
fully human self-view, design requirements met 258-299
further clarifications (transcendent self-view) 23-29, 209, 250, 298, 304-452
generic human self-view 4, 23
habitual identification with self-views 10, 13, 17, 20, 33, 81-82, 86-87, 89, 90, 91, 93, 103, 114-115, 118, 121, 127-8, 132, 153, 173-175, 177, 187-188, 191, 192, 194, 200, 207, 217, 234-236, 253, 286, 289, 290, 291, 293, 295, 304, 306, 311, 313,-314, 316-317, 320-323, 326, 327, 328
hard problem of consciousness resolved
  all 10-11, 24-28, 358-421
  answering not evading Chalmers' questions 402-403
  brain a sensory construct 11, 25, 358, 360-364, 378-379

Chalmers and 11, 26, 180, 200, 369, 370, 372, 373, 375, 394, 395, 397, 398, 402-403, 405-406
consciousness in actual brain not brain as experienced 379-380
Dennett and 27, 372, 375, 394, 395, 397, 398, 403, 406
epistemic rather than real 11-12, 26-27, 375
epistemologically irreducible but ontologically reducible 11-12, 26, 358, 375-376, 377-421
explanatory gap 11-12, 25-26, 358, 370-372, 375-376, 377, 394, 395-421
fixed self facet barrier to full transcendence 25-26, 360-376, 412-413
functional scientific account and 26-28, 358-359, 370, 372, 377-421
infinite regress 389-390
mapping experiences to functions 26-27, 358-359, 395-421
mistaken assumption and 11-12, 25-26, 358-376, 393, 412-413
outside observer's perspective and 25, 26, 171, 358, 363, 364, 366, 367, 368, 375, 377, 378, 381, 382-383, 385-386, 392, 393, 394, 395, 402, 411, 418, 421, 422-423, 424, 427-428

physicalism 27-28, 181, 372-412
relational knowledge cannot
encompass nonrelational
knowledge 26, 387-388,
391-413
see also consciously experienced
world: the real thing?;
qualia; why like this, why
like anything questions
idea-based subsidiary self-world
perspectives 6-7, 8, 9, 10, 11,
16, 17, 18, 19, 20-21, 22, 23, 32,
51-52, 59-62, 66-74, 80-81, 83,
84, 86, 87, 88, 92, 93, 96, 97,
98, 99, 100, 101, 102, 103, 105,
106, 108, 109, 111, 112, 113,
114, 115, 116, 117, 118, 120,
121, 122, 123, 124, 125, 126,
127, 128, 129, 130, 131, 133,
139, 142, 144, 146, 147, 148,
149, 150, 151, 152, 154, 155,
157, 158, 159, 160, 161, 162,
165, 166, 168, 171, 172, 175,
187, 212, 213, 214, 215, 217,
218, 220, 226, 230, 242, 243,
246, 247, 248, 250, 251, 252,
253, 254, 255, 257, 262-263,
264-285, 287-299, 318, 319, 320
illusion, self as 13-14, 296, 463-464
immersion level control 22, 28,
152, 215, 221, 227, 228, 229,
242, 244-246, 251, 260-261,
266, 279-282, 324, 353, 354,
437-442, 444, 452, 461
incidentally acquired self-views 6,
8, 9, 10, 17, 118

including everything by excluding
nothing 128-129, 237, 239, 262,
267, 327
individually unique personal and
collective selves
see personally unique facets of
the self
infinity of views issue 18-19, 69,
102, 127-128, 131, 172, 253,
287-294
instantiation (personal) 8-9, 10, 18,
21, 23, 24, 25, 33, 304-331
instantiation (transcendent self-
view) 8-9, 10, 18, 21, 23, 24,
25, 33, 208-257
kinds of humans 17-18, 33, 116,
117, 132, 166, 253, 295, 299,
302, 336, 340, 341, 345
knowing that and knowing how
62-65
knowledge and knowing
see under nonrelational and
relational
koan 194, 312, 314
long-term responses 133, 257,
275-277
McGinn, C. 370
meaningless, fantastic, nonsensical
notions as useful self-world
perspectives 6, 52-54, 57-59,
125-126, 170, 213, 221, 255,
303, 346, 348-349, 353
misdefinition of self 8, 10-11, 15,
17-18, 20, 23, 33, 74-76, 107,
108-118, 121, 132, 139, 166,

200, 207, 208, 252-253, 284, 286-299, 345, 346, 364-368
mystical or spiritual slant 12, 13, 28-29, 433-452
negative effects 10-11, 15-16, 19, 23, 24, 139-153, 164, 165-167, 170, 207, 208, 248, 252, 263, 264-285, 295, 340-341, 346, 352, 361, 365, 368-369, 412-413
neuroplasticity and brain programming 64, 76-82, 85, 88, 89, 90, 91, 92, 93, 94, 97, 103, 109, 111-112, 129, 130-131, 157, 160, 211, 218, 222, 223, 224, 225, 231, 232, 233, 234, 235, 236, 237, 239, 316, 417, 459
noneliminative physicalism 27-28, 181, 412
nonrelational and relational aspects of self and 9-10, 11, 20, 21, 23, 57, 120-121, 173, 174, 206, 208, 216, 217, 218, 224, 226, 232, 236, 237, 251, 252, 270, 272, 280, 291, 292, 293, 298, 302, 310, 311-312, 313
   empty consciousness and 9-10, 11, 20, 21, 23, 120-121, 173-203, 206, 208, 216, 217, 218, 224, 226, 232, 236, 237, 251, 252, 270, 272, 280, 291, 292, 293, 298, 302, 310, 311-312, 313, 399, 400-403, 407, 408, 409, 412, 415, 416, 438, 448-449, 451, 452
   hard problem of consciousness and 26, 175-177, 178-182, 183-188, 189-191, 198-199, 200-201, 388-393, 395-421
   knowledge and knowing 9, 10, 20, 120-121, 173-203, 388-393
   religion and 432, 438, 448-449, 451, 452
   transcendent perspective and 9, 10, 11, 20, 21, 23, 120-121, 173-203, 206, 208, 216, 217, 218, 224, 226, 232, 236, 237, 251, 252, 270, 272, 280, 291, 292, 293, 298, 302, 310, 311-312, 313, 395-421
nonsensical, fantastic, meaningless notions as useful self-world perspectives 6, 52-54, 57-59, 125-126, 170, 213, 221, 255, 303, 346, 348-349, 353
not fully developed as humans without transcendence 2, 10, 21, 166, 207, 253, 286, 295-286, 299, 345, 415-417
open-ended, wholly-variable self 11, 15, 17, 18, 19-20, 22, 23, 32-33, 62, 66-74, 75, 78, 106, 115, 117, 118, 120, 122-134, 135-153, 154-163, 208-299
optimal responses 136, 151-153, 252, 263, 264-285, 437, 454-462

ontologically reducible but epistemologically irreducible 11-12, 26, 358, 375-376, 377-421

others, transcendent view of 24, 332-343

overarching relationship a self-view 7, 15, 17, 33, 35, 49, 51-52, 61-62, 69, 71, 74, 110, 112-114, 117-118

overarching self-world perspectives defined 6-7, 49, 51-52, 60-62, 66-74

perceptions determine how we act, think, and feel 35-49, 50-51, 57-9, 61, 63, 65

personally unique facets of the self 4, 19, 23, 120, 136, 152-153, 207, 215, 252, 263, 279- 264, 279-284, 296

Popper, K. 15, 165, 210, 350, 414

positive effects 19, 23, 120, 132, 135-140, 151-153, 264, 279-281, 283, 284, 295

qualia 27, 174, 200-201, 372, 381, *see also* hard problem of consciousness resolved; why like this, why like anything questions

range of views effect 32, 35, 40-49, 50-51, 60-61

realism, direct and indirect 174, 177, 201-203

relational and nonrelational *see* nonrelational and relational

relational perspectives that can become actual 57-58

relationship varies with our view of it 15-16, 34-49, 50-65, 66-74

religion and the transcendent perspective 12, 13, 28-29, 433-452

repertoire of facets or roles 7, 19-20, 22, 32, 47, 50, 52, 54-55, 56, 60, 84-85, 87, 88, 91, 97-99, 100, 101, 102, 106, 111, 117, 130-131, 132, 136, 143-144, 149-150, 155, 157-160, 163, 166, 172, 214, 218-219, 220, 221, 222, 223, 225, 231, 234-237, 239, 242, 243, 247-248, 253, 259, 260, 261, 262, 267-268, 269, 271, 274, 275, 276, 278, 295, 310, 320, 324, 326-328, 345, 352, 427, 435, 437, 441

requirements of a fully human self-view 108-203

resting state, core, dominant focus and *see under* empty consciousness: core, dominant focus and resting state,

robots, conscious 420-421

science, role of 2, 19, 24-25, 27-28, 29, 164-172, 299, 344-355

scientific account of conscious experience 26-28, 358-359, 370, 372, 377-421

scientific testing and the transcendent self-view 2, 15, 135, 210-211, 239-240, 297-298

scientific world-view insufficient 19-20, 120, 164-172, 252, 294 selection of facets or roles mechanism 22, 67-69, 70, 71, 72, 93, 133, 160, 163, 213-214, 219, 223, 225, 231, 237-238, 239, 241-242, 248-249, 253-255, 256, 257, 259, 260, 261, 262, 267, 269-270, 271, 310, 324, 326, 328-330, 411

self as illusion 13-14, 296, 463-464

self-fulfilling prophecy bias 169-70, 347-348, 364-365

self-world perspectives, subsidiary *see* idea-based subsidiary self-world perspectives

spiritual slant, mystical or 12, 13, 28-29, 433-452

switching of facets or roles 5-6, 22, 142, 149, 150, 151-152, 163, 206, 212, 213, 214, 215, 219, 221, 222-223, 224, 225, 230-236, 238-239, 242-244, 246, 247, 248, 250, 251, 259, 260-261, 262, 265-267, 271, 272, 274, 310, 318-325, 326, 328, 341, 368

transcendence, everyday 4-14, 304-331

see also transcendent perspective on self and world

transcendent perspective on self and world

behavioural and experiential nature reflected 2, 4, 5, 7-8, 9, 10, 12, 13, 15, 17, 18, 21, 23-24, 32, 33, 49, 51, 52, 60, 61-62, 66-71, 74, 75-76, 106-107, 113, 118, 120, 122-123, 131-132, 154, 155, 172, 174, 199, 200, 211, 253, 264, 286, 287, 292-293, 295, 297, 311, 449

caveats 14-15, 239-40, 297-9

requirements met uniquely 2, 23-24, 286-293, 295, 296

social and educational obstacles 332-343

transcendent self-view, baseline 206, 208-242, 249-250, 259-260, 261, 310, 315

transcendent self-view, first-pass 206, 209, 210, 212, 215, 241-257, 258-261, 263, 264, 265, 271, 273, 284, 286, 294, 296, 297, 298-299, 302, 308, 310, 330-331

transcendent self-view, meets requirements 258-299

transcendent self-view, personal instantiation 4, 8, 19, 21, 23, 24, 120, 136, 152-153, 207, 215, 252, 253, 263, 264, 279-285, 286, 295-296, 302, 304-331

transcendent self-view, perspective on others 24, 332-343

transcendent self-view, prioritising science 24-25, 344-355

transcendent self-view, resolving the hard problem, 2, 10-12, 25-28, 133, 200, 299, 338, 351, 360-421

transcendent self-view,
spirituality and religion 12,
13, 28-29, 433-452
see also empty consciousness;
free will and the
transcendent perspective;
fully human self-view,
design requirements; hard
problem of consciousness
resolved; instantiation
(transcendent self- view)
transcendent view of everything
13, 433-452
transcendent view of others 24,
332-343
unconscious elements of self 110,
112, 113, 114
uniquely able to meet requirements
2, 23, 286-299
universal adoption 2, 10, 12, 13,
253, 296, 333, 334, 335, 336,
337

unknown and undiscovered
responses 7, 18, 19, 20, 21, 23,
69, 128-130, 131, 133, 155, 157,
162, 172, 206, 209, 213, 214,
215 , 221, 222, 223, 224, 236-
237, 238, 239, 247, 248, 261,
262, 268, 271, 272, 273, 275,
287, 288, 289, 290, 291, 293,
306, 315, 326, 327, 328
wholly-variable in theory, fixed
in practice 6-7, 17-18, 32, 62,
70-71, 75-107, 286-299
wholly-variable, open-ended self
11, 15, 17, 18, 19-20, 22, 23,
32-33, 62, 66-74, 75, 78, 106,
115, 117, 118, 120, 122-134,
135-153, 154-163, 208-299
why like this, why like anything
questions 26-27, 200-201, 395-
396, 392, 396, 398-403, 405,
407, 412, 416, 420
see also qualia; hard problem of
consciousness resolved
zen koan 194, 312, 314

Note on the Author

Dennis Nicholson dates his interest in developing a transcendent perspective on the self to philosophy of science and psychology classes taken at Edinburgh University prior to graduating in 1973. Employed at Strathclyde University in Glasgow in the decades that followed, most recently in a joint role as Director of Research in Information Services and research group leader (CDLR) in the Computer and Information Sciences Department, he continued to explore the question of the best design for the human self in parallel with his formal work. Ultimately deciding to devote himself full-time to what had become his primary research interest, he left his post to set out the compelling logical and observational case for the transcendent self-view presented in this book. Dennis comes from Dundee on the east coast of Scotland and now lives in Edinburgh.

www.ingramcontent.com/pod-product-compliance
Lightning Source LLC
Chambersburg PA
CBHW070406100426
42812CB00005B/1647